edited by Stella E. Stiegeler BSc

A Dictionary
of Earth Sciences

Pan Books in association with The Macmillan Press

First published 1976 by The Macmillan Press Ltd
This edition published 1978 by Pan Books Ltd, Cavaye Place, London SW10 9PG
© Laurence Urdang Associates Limited 1976
ISBN 0 330 25434 0

Prepared for Automatic typesetting by Laurence Urdang Associates Ltd
Typesetting by
Oriel Computer Services Ltd, Shipston-on-Stour
Printed in Great Britain by
Richard Clay (The Chaucer Press) Ltd, Bungay, Suffolk

Key to Symbols

Asterisks before words in the text denote
cross-references to entries that will provide additional
information. Entries are defined under the most
commonly used term, with synonyms shown in brackets.

aa. A *lava with an extremely rough spinose surface. *Compare* block lava, pahoehoe.

abandoned cliff. *See* cliff.

ablation. The disappearance of snow and ice by melting and evaporation. This can refer to ice crystals or snow flakes in the atmosphere but is most commonly used for glacier ice and surface snow cover, when it can also include avalanching. The rate of ablation is primarily controlled by air temperature but sunshine, rainfall, humidity, and wind speed also affect the process.

ablation till. *Till material formerly present on the ice surface and subsequently deposited as a result of the melting of the ice beneath. These deposits tend to contain relatively little fine material since this may be removed by meltwater prior to deposition. *Compare* lodgement till.

Abney level. A simple surveying instrument for measuring slope angles. The level is held by hand, objects being viewed through a sighting tube. The observer may stand at the top or bottom of a slope, but must sight onto a point at a height equivalent to his eye-level. Once an object is sighted, adjustment is made to a tilting spirit level, an image of the bubble being visible in the sighting tube. When the bubble image coincides with the object sight the angle of slope can be read off an attached scale, which is provided with a vernier to permit reading down to ten minutes of arc. The instrument is not very accurate, but is small and quick to use.

abnormal (accelerated) erosion. Erosion acting faster than normal as a result of the removal of the vegetation cover by human agencies. It is abnormal in the sense that it is superimposed upon natural processes. *See also* human influence on geomorphology, blowout.

abrasion. The wearing away of rocks by an agent of transportation charged with a load of already eroded material, which acts as a tool for cutting, grinding, scratching, and polishing. All the major transportation agents (running water, wind, moving ice, and sea waves and currents) can abrade so long as they carry debris. Abrasion by water and ice characteristically produces rounded forms, and abrasion by ice also produces striations, whilst the sand-blasting effect of wind abrasion is most effective in a narrow zone just above ground level, resulting in undercut features. As abrasion takes place, the corresponding reduction in size of the initial load debris is known as *attrition. A distinction is sometimes made between abrasion and *corrasion*, which refers to the erosional processes that result in abraded rock surfaces.

absolute temperature. A temperature scale based on the coldest temperature that is physically possible. This absolute zero of temperature is $-273.15\,°C$, but for meteorological purposes the absolute temperature is taken as the Celsius temperature plus $273°$, so that the freezing point of water is $273°$ and boiling point $373°$. Formerly measured in degrees absolute ($°A$), it is now measured in *kelvins.

absorption (in meterology). The conversion of short- or long-wave radiation to a different form of energy by gases in the atmosphere. Absorption is highly selective in terms of wavelength; some wavelengths are entirely absorbed and others are totally unaffected. The main atmospheric gases, oxygen and nitrogen, are not very important as absorbers of radiation, but minor gases such as carbon dioxide, water vapour, ozone, and nitrous oxide have a significant effect. *See also* atmospheric window.

abyssal plain. An extremely smooth portion of the deep-sea floor. The gradients across abyssal plains fall within the range of 1:1000 to 1:10 000, which means that variations in depth amount to only a few metres. This remarkable degree of flatness has come to light because of deep-sea photographs and high-precision sounding techniques. In the Atlantic Ocean, abyssal plains range between 200 and 400 kilometres in width, but they can be several hundred kilometres wide. They tail upwards into the continental rise and frequently, in a seaward direction, merge into abyssal hills. Their sediments are varied; while most are thinly veneered with pelagic sediment, perhaps globigerina ooze and red clay, they also display sediments and plant and animal remains that normally characterize shallow-water environments. The reason for this may be the operation of *turbidity currents.

abyssal rocks. Intrusive igneous rocks formed deep within the earth's crust.

abyssal zone. A zone of greatest ocean depth, lying seaward of and deeper than the *bathyal zone of the continental slope, that is below a depth of some 1000 m, and including the deeper parts of the oceans and the deep-sea trenches. Lying between the abyssal and bathyal zones is the *continental rise, which is often bordered on its seaward flank by abyssal plains and abyssal hills. The *pelagic-abyssal environment, which is not reached for at least several hundred kilometres from the coast, globally represents an area of 250×10^6 sq. km, i.e. roughly half the area of the earth. Few organisms live in these depths, where pressure is high and light does not reach, and deposition of sediment is very slow.

accelerated erosion. See abnormal erosion.

acceleration of free fall (acceleration due to gravity). The acceleration (g) of a body falling freely in a vacuum in the earth's gravitational field. The standard value is $9.806\ 65$ m s^{-2}, although actual values depend on the distance from the earth's centre of mass.

accessory mineral. A mineral that is present in small quantities in a rock and does not affect the overall character of that rock for classification purposes.

acclimatization. The process by which man becomes adapted to living in a markedly unfamiliar climatic regime. This normally refers to a change to hot and humid or especially cold climatic conditions. If acclimatization has not taken place, severe physiological stress may result. The full process may take up to ten years.

accordant (conformable). Denoting a drainage pattern that is controlled by the structures over which it flows. Actual patterns vary greatly, depending on the nature of the structures or lithologies. Compare discordant (def. 2).

accordian folding. A type of folding in rocks, in which the beds of the hinge area are markedly thickened and sharply folded, whilst on the limbs the beds are straight and of uniform thickness.

accretion. 1. The process of ice crystal growth by collision with water droplets in clouds. This is one of the mechanisms by which minute cloud droplets achieve sufficient size to give rainfall. **2.** See nucleation.

accumulated temperature. A method of indicating the excess or deficit of temperature with reference to a specified value for a specified period. Two temperature bases that have been frequently used are 6°C for the commencement of plant growth and 16°C for heating requirements. The accumulated temperature is calculated by taking the number of hours in a specific period the temperature was above or below the set value and multiplying by the mean temperature during this time to give the number of degree hours. More commonly, daily or monthly values of accumulated temperature are obtained from daily or mean values rather than hourly ones.

achondrite. A stony meteorite that does not contain *chondrules. Compare chondrite.

acicular. Denoting a crystal having a needle-like habit. See crystal habit.

acid brown soils. Soils found in the *brown earth zone on base-deficient parent materials. They are strongly acid, with a moder humus, and although the B horizon is more clearly differentiated by colour than in the true brown earth there is no appreciable eluviation of clay or iron oxides. They are typically found on the hard sediments in N and W Britain. With time it seems likely that these soils would become podzolic brown earths.

acid rocks. The dominant chemical constituent of igneous rocks is SiO_2, which typically ranges from 35-75% (by weight). Arbitrary divisions are made as follows: acid—SiO_2 >66%, intermediate—SiO_2 55-66%, basic—SiO_2 45-55%, and ultrabasic—SiO_2<45%. These strict divisions have been largely abandoned but the general descriptive terms acid, basic, etc., remain. In current usage, an acid rock contains in excess of about 10% free quartz, e.g.: granite, granodiorite, rhyolite.

acid soil. Soil acidity is measured on the pH scale, which is related to the concentration of hydrogen ions in the soil. A neutral soil is given a pH value of 7.0; if the value is less than this it is termed an acid soil and if greater an alkaline soil. Thus there is an inverse relationship between pH value and the concentration of hydrogen ions. Acid soils develop where, for some reason, there is a lack of the exchangeable bases in the soil, such as calcium and sodium. The bases have been largely replaced by the two cations hydrogen and aluminium, which control soil acidity. Possible acid-forming factors are leaching, organic matter containing few bases, and an acid parent material. Acid soils are therefore particularly common in the humid tropics and the humid temperate lands. Examples of typical acid soils are podzols, brown earths, and latosols. From the agricultural viewpoint most cultivated crops will thrive on mildly acid soils.

acmite (aegirine). See pyroxene.

actinolite. A monoclinic *amphibole.

actinomycetes. Aerobic microorganisms that have a filamentous habit as do fungi. They are next in abundance to bacteria in the soil. Optimum conditions are a moist well-aerated soil with a pH between 6.0 and 7.5. They are more prolific than bacteria and fungi in drier areas and are important also in that they can decompose the more resistant soil organic matter.

Actinopterygii. Ray-finned bony fish in which the paired fins are not fleshy (compare Crossopterygii) but have narrow bases and are supported by thin fin rays. The Actinopterygii also have a single dorsal fin. The group includes the modern *Teleostei. See also Osteichthyes.

active layer. See permafrost.

actualism. See uniformitarianism.

actuopalaeontology. The branch of palaeontology in which investigations into modern organisms, including their effects and remains in modern environments, are directed toward the understanding of fossil analogues. Based upon uniformitarian principles (see uniformitarianism), actuopalaeontology provides a means of relating various *trace fossils to the particular animals from which they are derived and of understanding the changes that an organism undergoes between death and fossilization (see taphonomy, thanatocoenosis). *Biostratonomy is one aspect of actuopalaeontology.

adamellite. A variety of granite consisting of about equal proportions of potassium feldspar and sodic plagioclase feldspar together with one or more ferromagnesian minerals.

adiabatic. Denoting an atmospheric process in which there is no exchange of heat between the system and its environment. In the more rapid exchanges, such as thermals rising from the ground surface, this is a reasonable approximation. In these circumstances, the change of temperature of rising air is determined by the physical properties of the air and the external pressure. As air pressure decreases with height above the ground surface, rising air expands, and exerts mechanical work on its environment. This necessitates a loss of heat energy from the rising air and its temperature falls. The rate of fall of temperature in an adiabatic process is constant for our atmospheric composition, being 0.98°C/100 metres, and is known as the *dry adiabatic lapse rate.

adjacent seas. Marginal seas and inland seas. They lie adjacent to the oceans but generally they are much smaller. Because many adjacent seas are largely encircled by land, the characteristics of the water and sediments they contain, and to a certain extent their topography, are strongly influenced by the landmass, for example in the amounts and nature of terrigenous sediments transported down rivers to the coast and the climatic effects associated with the land-sea margin.

adularia. A variety of alkali *feldspar.

advection. The horizontal component in the transfer of air properties. For example, the heat and water vapour content of the air at the earth's surface varies appreciably and by the wind systems these properties are transferred to other areas. With winds from tropical latitudes there is advection of warm air, and from polar latitudes, advection of cold air.

advection fog. Fog formed by the horizontal transfer of moist air over a cold surface, which sufficiently cools the lower layers of the atmosphere to give saturation and condensation. In summer it occurs over cool seas, such as the North Sea, the Labrador area, and off the coast of California, frequently affecting the adjacent coasts. In winter the advection of warm moist air over a cold snow-covered ground can also produce this type of fog.

aegirine (acmite). A sodic clino-pyroxene. See pyroxene.

aegirine-augite. See pyroxene.

aeolian erosion. The direct erosive action of wind. This is the least important aspect of wind action, generally of little consequence in landscape formation when compared with the role of wind transport and deposition. Sand blast, from the impact of saltating grains, is limited to below one metre or so from the ground surface; it can undercut rocks leaving pedestals, although in some instances increased weathering at the foot of the rock weakens it beforehand.

More significant than aeolian erosion by abrasion is the production of *deflation hollows. These can reach 100 km across, and although partly due in some cases to faulting or rock solution, they are mainly due to wind removal of preweathered material down to the water table, which halts further removal and produces oases.

aeolian forms. Landforms produced by material transported by wind. Large-scale features include dunes, sand shadows, and sand sheets, while small-scale features include sand ripples and ridges. Sand shadows, unlike true dunes, are deposited in the shelter of an obstacle, while sand sheets or seas are amorphous sheets with gentle swellings reaching 3-6 metres. Ripples are the products of irregularities in the surface over which the sand is passing: these initiate local concentrations of sand grain impacts on the slopes facing the wind, which become built up as ripples. Further, each ripple acts as a take-off point for grains in *saltation, and since the average length of travel per jump is related to wind speed, an even repetition of areas of concentrated grain impacts occurs downwind, leading to regular ripple patterns.

aeolian transport. The movement of sediment by wind. Below a threshold of 16 km per hour wind is incapable of moving sand, but thereafter sand movement rises as a cubic function of wind speed. Short periods of high-velocity winds are therefore very much more effective than longer periods of gentle winds.

Aeolian transport takes place concurrently in three forms: suspension, *saltation, and surface creep. A small proportion of grains of less than 0.2 mm in diameter can be carried wholly in suspension; the particle is totally buoyed up by the rising eddies in the air and carried along parallel to the air stream. Surface creep accounts for about 25% of actual sand movement, and involves the movement of grains of coarse sand along the surface by the impact of the saltating grains. Saltation accounts for about 75% of sand flow and involves the bouncing of grains along the surface at heights of less than 1 metre, and mostly within 200 mm of the ground surface.

aerodynamic roughness. An index of the nature of airflow near the ground surface. A surface is aerodynamically smooth if there is a layer of air immediately above it that has laminar flow. However, in meteorological terms, nearly all surfaces are aerodynamically rough, producing turbulent flow down to the ground surface, even for the lightest winds.

aeronautical chart. A form of map produced essentially for air navigation or pilotage. In addition to showing the relevant topographical features, such as contours, vegetation, roads, and cultural detail, the map shows supplementary information for specialized use, such as detailed vertical obstruction information, flight areas, air corridors, etc.

aeronomy. The science of the upper atmosphere, where dissociation and ionization of gas molecules takes place. The lower limit for these processes to occur is about 30 km. As the relationships between the upper and lower atmosphere are as yet little understood, there has been considerable research

recently into the possible effects of these upper levels in tropospheric weather.

aerosol. A particle of matter that is larger than a molecule but small enough to remain suspended in the atmosphere. Aerosols may be solid or liquid and play an important part in many atmospheric processes, such as precipitation formation, atmospheric electrification, radiation balances, and visibility. The origins of aerosols are diverse. Over sea areas, sea spray provides large salt nuclei and over land, weathering dusts of clay particles are probably the major source.

aftershocks. A series of minor shocks or vibrations that follow the main series of earthquake shocks. In general they originate at or near the focus of the main earthquake as a result of the readjustment of rocks that have overreacted during the main period of movement. Depending upon the size of the earthquake they can continue for a few days or months.

agate. A banded or concentrically zoned *cryptocrystalline form of silica. See silica minerals.

age. An interval of geological time in the Chronomeric Standard scale of chronostratigraphic classification (see chronostratigraphy). The equivalent Stratomeric Standard term, indicating the body of rock formed during this time, is the *stage. Ages may be grouped together to form *epochs and may themselves be comprised of several *chrons.

ageostrophic wind. The vector difference between the actual and the geostrophic wind. Without an ageostrophic component there would be no changes in pressure systems and atmospheric circulation would be a perfect balance between the pressure gradient and the *Coriolis force.

agglomerate. A mixture of coarse angular fragments of rock and finer-grained material formed during a volcanic explosion. See pyroclastic rocks.

long profile of stream

height of spillway = new base level

SEA (ultimate base level)

aggradation in this stretch

erosion downstream

Aggradation in a dammed stream

aggradation. The raising of the level of the land surface, especially by rivers. The cause of aggradation is incompetence (*see* competence) or incapacity (*see* capacity) of the river to transport its load, leading to deposition. This may arise through an increase in the volume of load supplied to the river, a loss of speed or volume of flow, or most commonly a rise in base level. In S England, the rise in sea level since the end of the Pleistocene has resulted in aggradation in many rivers, producing buried channels; for example, the River Arun in Sussex has aggraded deposits over 30 metres deep in places. Another common cause of aggradation is the damming of a stream, artificially creating a new base level for the upper reaches of a river. Originally graded to sea level, the upper reaches will aggrade to the new base level, the height of the dam's spillway. *See also* degradation.

agmatite. A migmatite in which melanocratic material occurs as angular inclusions in a leucocratic granitic host, giving an overall appearance resembling a breccia.

Agnatha. Primitive jawless fish, from which all more advanced vertebrate types have presumably evolved. Modern species are few and represent groups unknown as fossils. The diverse extinct forms can be grouped together as the *Ostracodermi, which were abundant in the Silurian and Devonian and are used in stratigraphic *correlation. *Compare* Gnathostomata.

air. The mixture of gases in the atmosphere. Its composition is almost uniform throughout the troposphere and is shown in the table below. Only water vapour and carbon dioxide vary appreciably, the former in relation to evaporation and precipitation and the latter through plant photosynthesis.

Composition of Air ($\%$ by volume)

nitrogen (N_2) 78.08	krypton (Kr)
oxygen (O_2) 20.95	1.14×10^{-4}
carbon dioxide	xenon (Xe)
(CO_2) 0.03	8.7×10^{-5}
argon (Ar) 0.93	ozone (O_3)
neon (Ne)	1×10^{-5}
1.82×10^{-3}	nitrous oxide
helium (He)	(N_2O) 3×10^{-5}
5.24×10^{-4}	water (H_2O) variable, up to 1.00
methane (CH_4)	
1.5×10^{-4}	hydrogen (H_2)
	5×10^{-5}

air mass. An area of the lower atmosphere with similar properties of temperature and moisture in the horizontal field. At the margins of the air mass, temperature gradients become steep at a transition zone known as a *front. The uniformity of properties is achieved by prolonged contact with the underlying surface and little horizontal or vertical mixing. These requirements are experienced in areas of high pressure or anticyclones, which are the main source areas for air masses. Away from their source areas, air masses undergo modification by coming in contact with different surfaces with the result that in a short period of time they can become indistinguishable. As most parts of the world represent modification zones rather than source areas, air mass terminology is less frequently used than formerly. There have been many attempts to classify air masses, but the most frequently quoted is that by Bergeron. Two basic air masses are identified on thermal properties—polar (P) and tropical (T), and two by moisture categories—maritime (m) and continental (c). The temperature of the air mass relative to the surface over which it is passing is included as warm (w) or cold (k) to give a wide range of combinations—mPw, cTk, etc. Willett modified this system slightly to add stable (s) or unstable (u) to indicate the likelihood of precipitation in the system. Other classifications distinguish equatorial, monsoon, and Arctic (or Antarctic) but difficulties can arise in identification.

air stream. A flow of air that is not necessarily homogeneous but has a distinctive origin. Air streams are therefore distinguished by their direction of approach rather than assuming any specific thermal or stability properties. The mid-latitude westerlies can be regarded as being a mixture of slightly baroclinic air streams bounded by sharp frontal zones.

Airy's hypothesis of isostasy. George Bedell Airy proposed that in order for isostatic equilibrium to exist, mountain ranges must have roots proportional to their height, i.e. the highest mountains have the deepest roots. These roots are composed of sialic material and displace an equivalent volume of sima, thereby causing the gravity anomalies present near mountain chains.

Aitken nucleus. See nucleus.

Aitoff's equal-area projection. A cylindrical map projection of a hemisphere. The major axis, the equator, is twice the length of the minor, central meridian, axis. The projection is bounded by an ellipse. The main characteristics of this projection are that it is an equal-area projection and landmasses near the centre of the area covered are of quite good shape, though the distortion increases towards the east and west limits of the projection.

albedo. An index of reflection comprising the ratio of reflected radiation to the total incident radiation. Usually this value is expressed in a percentage form for visible wavelengths. Typical values for surface albedo are: forest 5-10%, wet soil 10%, sand 20-30%, grass 25%, old snow 55%, concrete 17-27%, fresh snow 80%. Water surfaces vary from about 5% with high sun and calm seas to 70% at low elevation and rough seas. The planetary albedo of the earth measured from artificial satellites is approximately 34%, which means that over one third of the sun's radiation is returned to space without a change of wavelength.

albite. A sodic plagioclase *feldspar.

Aleutian Low. The mean low pressure centre in the N Pacific Ocean. It represents a statistical average of pressure value and location, which in turn are determined by the tracks of the depressions and the point at which they reach their lowest pressure. It is most marked in the winter.

alfisol. One of the ten soil orders of the *Seventh Approximation, covering pedalfers that are equivalent to the grey-brown podzolic, grey-wooded, grey-forest, sol lessivé, degraded chernozem, and planosol soils of the old American classification. They are found in the humid regions of the world under deciduous woodland or grassland vegetation. The dominant soil-forming process is leaching, which is more intense in these soils than in the inceptisols but less than in the spodosols. They are productive soils and favour the more common agricultural crops.

Algae. A group of primitive and largely aquatic plants that have no flowers, leaves, or vascular system. The group includes both microscopic plants, such as the *diatoms, as well as the multicellular seaweeds, which may grow to a large size. Algae are often subdivided into different categories; for example, single-celled forms are sometimes considered as belonging to a separate kingdom, the Protista.
The only geologically significant algae are those having hard parts, which may form bioherms, either by trapping sediment or by secreting massive laminated structures of calcium carbonate. Such structures commonly constitute lower Palaeozoic *reefs. Precambrian struc-

tures called *stromatolites may also be of algal origin.

Compared with bacteria, fungi, and actinomycetes, algae are relatively unimportant in soils but certain blue-green algae do fix atmospheric nitrogen. They are often pioneers in colonizing new ground and may number up to 100 000 per gram of dry surface soil.

alidade. A surveying instrument used for sighting onto objects of detail and for defining the rays to be drawn to them in *plane table surveying. The alidade is basically a ruler of metal or wood with a vertical slit sight at the observer's end and a vertical stretched wire sight at the other. (A telescope is fixed parallel to the ruler in more sophisticated types of alidade.) The ruler edge is placed against the point marked on the table over which the apparatus is standing, and detail to be fixed is sighted onto. A ray is then drawn on the plane table sheet along the ruler edge. Though either side of the ruler may be used initially, once one ray has been drawn, only that side may be used until that sheet is completed.

alkali (alkaline) (in petrology and mineralogy). Denoting igneous rocks and minerals that have high contents of the alkali metal oxides, Na_2O and K_2O. For a given silica content such rocks are relatively richer in sodium and potassium and poorer in calcium compared with calc-alkaline rocks. See alkali basalt, alkali gabbro, nephelinite, ijolite, granite.

alkali basalt. A basic undersaturated volcanic rock that is the fine-grained equivalent of *alkali gabbro. The essential minerals of all basalts are plagioclase feldspar of labradorite-bytownite composition and pyroxene. In alkali basalts the pyroxene is augite or titanaugite and olivine is present in abundance. Olivine is frequently rimmed or pseudomorphed by the alteration products iddingsite and/or serpentine. Small amounts of alkali feldspar and/or feldspathoid (nepheline or analcite) may be present. Alkali basalts are typically porphyritic. Basalts containing large plagioclase phenocrysts are referred to as *feldsparphyric* or *big feldspar* basalts. Those rich in olivine and augite are termed picrite basalts. Oceanite and ankaramite are varieties in which olivine and augite respectively have become concentrated.

Alkali basalts are usually holocrystalline and have ophitic or intergranular textures. Nodules of gabbro and peridotite are often found in alkali basalt lavas.

With an increase in the amount of nepheline to greater than 10%, alkali basalts pass into basanites (olivine-bearing) and tephrites (olivine-free). In some rocks, the place of nepheline is taken by analcite or leucite and such terms as analcite-basanite and leucite-tephrite are appropriate. See also basalt.

alkali feldspars. A series of minerals with composition varying between the two end-members albite ($NaAlSi_3O_8$) and orthoclase ($KAlSi_3O_8$). See feldspar.

alkali gabbro. Alkali gabbros and syenogabbros are basic plutonic rocks containing, in addition to the normal gabbro mineralogy, alkali feldspar and/or feldspathoids. Syenogabbros contain approximately equal amounts of alkali and plagioclase feldspar with *titanaugite, *analcite, and/or *nepheline plus or minus olivine. Having more sodium and potassium than gabbros, syenogabbros are, as the name implies, related to *syenites.

Essexite consists of labradorite, titanaugite, and olivine plus small amounts of nepheline and/or analcime. Alkali feldspar, apatite, and ilmenite may also be present. *Teschenite* and *crinanite* are analcime-bearing varieties from which nepheline is excluded. *Theralite* is a nepheline-bearing gabbro containing no analcime.

Kentallenite is a saturated rock containing augite, olivine, biotite, labradorite, and orthoclase and is equivalent to olivine-monzonite.

The names of the plutonic rocks are

applied to the medium-grained varieties of doleritic aspect but with the prefix *micro-*. The volcanic equivalents include basanites, tephrites, and trachybasalts.

Teschenite and theralite are found in differentiated sills and dykes.

alkaline soil. *See* acid soil.

allanite (orthite). *See* epidote.

Alleröd. A phase of warming of about 1000 years during the period of deglaciation after the Würm/Weichsel/Wisconsin ice age. In many parts of NW Europe this was followed by a sudden cooling from 8800 to 8300 B.C. The type-site from which the period takes its name is in Denmark.

allivalite. A gabbro consisting of olivine and plagioclase feldspar of bytownite-anorthite composition.

allochems. Discrete calcareous particles that have usually been transported at some stage, including *fossils, ooliths (see oolite), *intraclasts, and *pellets, found in *limestones; the terminology used in the petrographic description and classification of limestones is based upon these constituents and the matrix in which they are set (*see* micrite, sparite). Thus a limestone composed of fossil fragments set in a micrite matrix is a biomicrite; a pellet limestone with a sparite matrix is a pelsparite.

allochthonous. Denoting an isolated mass of rock displaced over a considerable distance from its original source by low-angle thrusting. *Compare* autochthonous.

allogenic (allothigenous). Denoting rock constituents that were formed at some distance from their present location, particularly minerals or rock fragments derived from existing rocks. *Compare* authigenic.

allotriomorphic. Denoting a rock in which the majority of crystals are euhedral. *Compare* idiomorphic, hypidiomorphic.

Alluvial fan

alluvial fan. A fan or cone of material deposited by a stream where it debouches from a mountain front onto a plain, with the apex of the fan at the point of emergence from the mountains. In its mountain tract, the stream will have been confined into a single flow in a rock-cut gorge, but on reaching the plain this control is lost, and it breaks up into a number of distributaries. This increases the wetted perimeter, or area of contact between water and land, and hence friction increases; with more of its energy used in overcoming friction, less is available for sediment transport, so deposition occurs, in the form of a fan. This is the direct landborne analogy to *delta formation, and is a landform characteristic of arid and semiarid environments.

alluvium. The products of *sedimentation by rivers, sometimes including deposits in estuaries, lakes, and other bodies of fresh water. It covers material of a wide range of *particle sizes, though in the British Standard classification it is restricted to the silt size fraction of 0.006–0.02 mm.

There is a marked decrease in the size of alluvial material down-valley, with finer material in the lower reaches. This may be due to *sorting, which leaves coarse material behind and carries finer material down-valley, or it may be due to progressive wear of the material as it travels downstream. Another cause may be that smaller valley-side slopes downstream supply a finer calibre of material to the stream.

Within the *floodplain alluvium (in the looser sense) varies in size from the finest clay and silt-sized material through sands to coarse angular gravels. The gravels form the basal portions of alluvial valleys, and may have originated at the end of the *Pleistocene period under *periglacial conditions; in some rivers they are attributed to deposition within the channel in conditions in which severe scour removed the fine material. Silts, sands, and gravels are more important, constituting 75% of the Mississippi alluvium. Sands constitute the point bars formed on the inside of meander bends, and are an important constituent of levées. Silts and clays are deposited in the lee of point bars or as overbank deposits in times of flood, covering the far reaches of the flood-plains with backswamp deposits.

almandine. *See* garnet.

alnoite. A basic or ultrabasic dyke rock composed largely of melilite and biotite with subordinate pyroxene, calcite, and olivine. Alnoite is found in ijolite-carbonatite complexes.

Alpine-Himalayan chain. A predominantly east-west trending orogenic belt, extending from Spain through Europe to S Asia. It was formed mainly in the Tertiary by the closure of the former Tethyan Ocean, mainly as a result of the northerly drift of the African continent. It consists of a series of igneous, metamorphic, and deformed sedimentary rocks, which now form the Alps and Himalayan Mountains.

altiplanation. A process associated with a *periglacial environment in which terraces or benches are cut in solid rock in hillside or summit locations. The weathering and erosion of the rocks is achieved by a combination of *frost shattering, *solifluction, and *congeliturbation. Terrace formation is probably initiated by the production of a *nivation hollow in hard rock, the backwall of which then retreats, causing an enlargement of the flat or gently sloping terrace in front. Altiplanation terraces may have a cover of debris, which can exhibit *patterned ground.

altocumulus cloud. A type of cloud indicating some form of vertical motion at medium levels in the atmosphere. It includes a wide range of cloud origins from genuine convection to billow and orographic clouds where the atmosphere is essentially stable, but the uplift is forced by mountains. Altocumulus clouds generally occur as globular masses in bands across the sky.

altostratus cloud. A greyish cloud sheet normally composed of a mixture of ice crystals and water drops. It is distinguished from cirrostratus by lying at lower levels, being somewhat thicker, and not exhibiting halo phenomena. The sun may be seen through the thinner parts of the cloud. It is frequently followed by rain as the approach of a warm front is heralded by this cloud type.

aluminium silicates. There are three aluminium silicates with the composition Al_2SiO_5, the polymorphs andalusite, kyanite, and sillimanite. They are found in metamorphic rocks mostly of argillaceous composition. Each has a different yet closely related crystal structure and is stable over a different range of pressures and temperatures.
Andalusite is *orthorhombic and usually pink or white in colour. The variety *chiastolite* shows a regular arrangement of impurities in the form of a cross. Andalusite is characteristic of the low-pressure and high-temperature conditions associated with contact metamorphism around igneous intrusions.
Kyanite is triclinic and often blue-green to white in colour. It is stable at higher pressures than andalusite and is found in intermediate- to high-grade regionally metamorphosed rocks.
Sillimanite is orthorhombic, usually white in colour, and commonly occurs as acicular crystals, hence the alternative name *fibrolite*. It is stable at higher temperatures than kyanite or andalusite and is found in the highest grades of thermally and regionally metamorphosed rocks.
The orthorhombic aluminium silicate *mullite* has a composition $Al_6Si_2O_{13}$. It

is found in argillaceous xenoliths *(buchites)* in basic igneous rocks.

amber. Yellow translucent resin exuded by trees and often enclosing insects that have been trapped on the sticky surface prior to hardening.

amethyst. A purple variety of quartz. The colour is due to impurities of iron oxide. *See* silica minerals.

ammonite. One of the more advanced molluscs of the subclass *Ammonoidea, whose shells had extremely convoluted crinkled suture lines. They are known from the Permian, are valuable as Mesozoic zone fossils, and became extinct at the end of the Cretaceous Period.

Ammonoidea. An extinct subclass of marine molluscs of the class *Cephalopoda. Ammonoids had external shells, usually coiled in a plane spiral and divided by septa into chambers. The shells ranged from about 25 mm in diameter to over 2 metres in some species. The animal inhabited the terminal, and most recently formed, of these. The chambers were connected by a sometimes discontinuous calcareous tube known as a *siphuncle.* The septa met the inner wall of the shell at intersections called *suture lines,* and the character of these in fossil shells is used in taxonomic classification. The Ammonoidea had relatively complex suture lines compared with those of the *Nautiloidea; early ammonoids had angular folded suture lines (*see* goniatite) but in the later *ammonites the suture lines were highly convoluted and crinkled. Ammonoids probably evolved from the nautiloids and the earliest are known from rocks of Silurian age. They reached their peak of development in the Mesozoic, for which they are important *zone fossils, and became extinct at the end of this era.

amorphous. Having no regular atomic structure.

Amphibia. The first class of vertebrates to colonize land, evolving from crossopterygian fishes in the late Devonian. These fish had a bony skeleton that could provide support out of water; they also had lungs and their fleshy paired fins evolved into the more substantial limbs of the Amphibia. Amphibian eggs remain unprotected and must be laid in water, where the animals, too, spend their early life as tadpole larvae before undergoing metamorphosis into the terrestrial adults. The Amphibia were abundant in Carboniferous swamps, some reaching the size of modern crocodiles, but the class was in decline by the end of the Palaeozoic. Modern representatives include newts, salamanders, and frogs. Amphibians were the ancestors of the reptiles.

amphiboles. A group of rock-forming minerals that have $(Si,Al)O_4$ tetrahedra linked to form a double chain. *Pyroxenes are a similar group but with a single chain structure. The general amphibole formula is $X_{2\,3}$ $Y_5Z_8O_{22}(OH)_2$, where X = Ca, Na, K, Mg, or Fe^{2+}, Y = Mg, Fe^{2+}, Fe^{3+}, Al, Ti, or Mn, and Z = Si or Al. The hydroxyl ions may be replaced by F, Cl, or O.

Most amphiboles are monoclinic but anthophyllite and gedrite are *orthorhombic. Sub-groups are based on the dominant cation occupying the X position.

1. *anthophyllite-cummingtonite subgroup:*
anthophyllite
$(Mg,Fe^{2+})_7(Si_8O_{22})(OH,F)_2$
gedrite
$(Mg,Fe^{2+})_6Al((Si,Al)_8O_{22})(OH,F)_2$
cummingtonite $(Mg,Fe^{2+})_7(Si_8O_{22})(OH)_2$
grunerite
$(Fe^{2+})_4(Fe^{2+},Mg)_3(Si_8O_{22})(OH)_2$
2. *hornblende sub-group:*
tremolite $Ca_2Mg_5(Si_8O_{22})(OH,F)_2$
actinolite $Ca_2(Mg,Fe^{2+})_5(Si_8O_{22})(OH,F)_2$
hornblende
$NaCa_2(Mg,Fe^{2+},Fe^{3+},Al)_5((Si,Al)_8O_{22})-$
$(OH,F)_2$

edenite $NaCa_2(Mg,Fe^{2+})_5(Si_7AlO_{22})(OH,F)_2$

hastingsite $NaCa_2(Fe^{2+},Mg,Al,Fe^{3+})_5(Si_6Al_2O_{22})(OH,F)_2$

kaersutite $Ca_2(Na,K)(Mg,Fe^{2+},Fe^{3+})_4Ti(Si_6Al_2O_{22})(O,OH,F)_2$

3. *alkali amphibole sub-group:*

glaucophane $Na_2,Mg_3,Al_2(Si_8O_{22})(OH,F)_2$

riebeckite $Na_2,Fe_3^{2+}Fe_2^{3+}(Si_8O_{22})(OH,F)_2$

richterite $Na_2Ca(Mg,Fe^{2+},Mn,Fe^{3+},Al)_5(Si_8O_{22})(OH,F)_2$

katophorite $Na_2CaFe_4^{2+}(Fe^{3+},Al)(Si_7AlO_{22})(OH,F)_2$

The angle between the prismatic cleavages of amphiboles is 124°, the corresponding angle for pyroxenes being 87°. Some amphiboles occur in fibrous forms; asbestos is a fibrous form of actinolite.

Members of the anthophyllite-cummingtonite sub-group together with tremolite, actinolite, :and hornblende occur in metamorphic rocks. Hornblende is also common in igneous rocks. The alkali amphiboles occur in alkali igneous rocks with the exception of glaucophane, which is an index mineral of the glaucophane schist facies.

amphibolite. A metamorphic rock consisting predominantly of amphibole. *See also* metamorphic facies.

amphidromic system. A type of tide or tidal system in which the high water rotates around a central point (the *amphidromic point*). It is one consequence of the modifying influence that the earth's rotation has on a standing oscillation. The range of the tide is nil, or very small, at the amphidromic point itself but increases outwards from the point. The times of low and high water progress in an anticlockwise or clockwise direction around the amphidromic point. In the N hemisphere, high water rotates anticlockwise round the central point.

amygdale. A spheroidal or ellipsoidal *vesicle within a lava, filled with deuteric or secondary minerals often in a zonal arrangement. Typical amygdaloidal minerals include calcite, zeolites, and quartz.

anabatic wind. An upslope breeze often developing when mountain slopes are heated by the sun during calm conditions. As turbulence is greater during the day it is more often suppressed than the night-time equivalent, the *katabatic wind.

anafront. Any frontal surface at which the warm air is rising. As air cools on rising, condensation and precipitation are more extensive with this type of front than on a *katafront, where air is descending.

analcime (analcite). *See* feldspathoids.

analogues. Similar patterns of the surface atmospheric pressure field that occur at different times or different places. The basic assumption in analogue forecasting is that if two pressure situations are identical then the weather sequences that followed the first occasion will also follow the second. However, since analogues are never identical in all important features, only general trends can be deduced.

anatase. A brown to black tetragonal polymorph of TiO_2 found in vein deposits and pegmatites. *See* brookite, rutile.

andalusite. *See* aluminium silicates.

andesine. A variety of plagioclase *feldspar.

Andesite Line. A line that delimits those parts of the earth's surface that are of true oceanic structure as compared with true continental structure. The line can be drawn throughout the Pacific Ocean: on the ocean side of it are volcanic rocks that are entirely basic in character, but no in-situ volcanic rocks of the continental type. In the case of the W coast of North and South America, the Andesite Line runs parallel to and comparatively close to the coast.

andesites. The fine-grained volcanic equivalents of *diorites, oversaturated or saturated in composition (*see* silica saturation). They are characterized by the presence of plagioclase in the range oligoclase-andesine, often occurring as strongly zoned phenocrysts. The mafic minerals, augite, hypersthene, hornblende, biotite, and olivine, occur both as phenocrysts and in the groundmass. Small amounts of quartz and alkali feldspar may also be present. With an increase in the amount of quartz, andesites pass into *dacites and with an increase in the proportions of alkali feldspar, into *latites (trachyandesites). Most andesites are porphyritic and have pilotaxitic or trachytic textures. Andesites are the intermediate members of the calc-alkaline volcanic suite and are associated with basalts and rhyolites in island arcs and orogenic regions.

Members of the alkaline basalt-trachyte suite containing dominant oligoclase and andesine are called *mugearite* and *hawaiite* respectively. These rocks may be distinguished from andesites by their basic generally undersaturated compositions, higher olivine contents, and differing field associations. Classification of volcanic rocks is often very difficult in petrographic terms owing to the fine grain size, and divisions are made on a chemical basis.

andosols. Soils that have developed recently on base-rich volcanic materials. The upper A horizon of these soils is dark owing to the presence of organic matter that is well mixed by earthworm activity. This is a low-density friable layer and it overlies a more compact B horizon in which there has been little appreciable change in the content of clay. With increased duration of soil formation these soils become deeper and profile differentiation becomes more apparent. In humid temperate regions they may alter to form podzols and in the humid tropics they may form grumusols. *See also* inceptisol.

andradite. *See* garnet.

anemometer. An instrument for measuring wind speed and often direction. The most common type has three cups mounted symmetrically about a vertical rotating axis, so that the rate of rotation is proportional to the wind speed. Wind can also be measured by the pressure it exerts on a plate or in a tube, or by the degree of cooling of a hot wire.

aneroid barometer. The most commonly used instrument for measuring air pressure. In its simplest form it consists of a corrugated metal box from which the air is evacuated. The top and bottom of the box are separated by a spring and changes of atmospheric pressure produce movements in the distance apart of the faces. The changes are then amplified by a series of levers and can be recorded on a chart.

Angiospermae. The flowering plants. They differ from the *Gymnospermae in that their seeds are protected by an outer casing known as a *carpel.* Angiosperms are thought to have arisen in the Triassic; they became common during the Cretaceous and by the end of this period had replaced the gymnosperms as the dominant land plants, a position they still hold today. They occupy a great variety of terrestrial and freshwater environments and range in size from small shrubs to giant trees. Angiosperms form an important source of food and habitats for both birds and mammals, reflected in the fact that these groups, too, began their main evolutionary radiation during the Cretaceous. The evolution and spread of the grasses, probably during the Miocene, had a particularly important effect on the environment, and therefore on animal life.

There are two main divisions, the Monocotyledoneae and the Dicotyledoneae.

angle of declination. The angle between geographical north and the direction of the magnetic meridian.

angle of incidence. The angle between a ray arriving at a surface and the normal to that surface at that point.

angle of reflection. The angle between a ray reflected from a surface and the normal to that surface at the point of reflection.

angle of refraction. The angle between a refracted ray and the normal from the surface at which the ray is refracted at the point of refraction.

talus slope
(constant slope,
colluvial slope)

rock wall

angle of rest   scree or alluvium

Angle of rest

angle of rest. The characteristic maximum angle of slope at which a pile of unconsolidated material is stable, the angle depending on the size of the material. Above that angle, the slope will be unstable and subject to slides and flow, which will reduce the angle of slope until it is again stable.

At rest, the particles interdigitate with each other, so that the weight of each one is balanced against the one below. As the angle becomes too steep, the particles upslope tend to lack support at the base and slide over the particles in front, moving downslope until the debris pile is again balanced. Larger material has a higher angle of rest than fine material; in most rocks and sands the angle is 30-35°. Where the material forming a slope is unconsolidated, its angle of rest determines the angle of slope; such slopes are called *talus slopes, constant slopes,* or *colluvial slopes* (*see* colluvium).

angular momentum. The product of the linear velocity of a point on the earth's surface, as it moves from west to east owing to the earth's rotation, and the perpendicular distance of that point from the earth's axis of rotation, a line through the north and south poles. Its value is greatest at the equator, where the perpendicular distance is at a maximum, and zero at the poles.

angular unconformity. A plane of erosion, generally related to earth movements, marking the boundary between two rock units of different age. The beds above and below the plane of erosion have different angles of dip, the lower beds generally dipping more steeply.

angular velocity. The rate of turning of a rotating body, expressed in degrees, radians, or revolutions per unit of time. In meteorology, it can be used to indicate the horizontal rate of rotation around an area of low pressure or, on a large scale, the rotation of the earth. As the earth makes one complete rotation in a day, its angular velocity is 15° longitude per hour, or 7.29×10^{-5} radians per second.

angulate drainage. A drainage pattern in which streams are developed equally in two directions, like the *rectangular drainage pattern, but in this case the streams meet at an acute angle rather than right angles. The pattern results from structural guidance by two sets of joints or faults in an area with homogeneous strata.

anhedral. Denoting crystals having irregular boundaries, and having no crystal faces. *Compare* euhedral, subhedral.

anhydrite. An orthorhombic mineral of composition $CaSO_4$. It is usually white or colourless, occurring in massive or fibrous forms in evaporite deposits. *See also* gypsum.

anisotropic. Having different physical properties when measured in different directions. Crystals belonging to systems other than cubic are optically anisotropic and light is transmitted at differing velocities along different directions within each crystal. When a ray of light enters an anisotropic crystal it is split into two rays, the ordinary and extraordinary rays, which travel in different directions and are polarized in perpendicular planes. Such crystals are said to exhibit double refraction or *birefringence.

ankaramite. A basaltic rock containing a high proportion of augite phenocrysts. *Compare* oceanite.

ankerite. *See* carbonate minerals.

Annelida. The phylum of animals consisting of worms, such as the common earthworm, whose bodies are divided into a number of segments. Annelids of one group secrete calcareous tubes, and fossil specimens of these exist, but most annelids are soft bodied and not often preserved after death. Certain small siliceous or chitinous remains known as *scolecodonts*, occurring in rocks of Ordovician age onwards, are thought to be annelid jaw parts. The effects of worms are often seen in rocks as *trace fossils, trails, burrows, or other characteristic disturbances of the sediment, features present even in some Precambrian rocks.

anomaly. 1. (In climatology). The departure of any climatic element from the long-period average for that location. The spatial distribution of an anomaly is an interesting feature as it helps to provide a greater understanding of the interaction between the atmosphere and the surface. A good example of a temperature anomaly is the area of NW Europe where mean annual temperatures are much higher than the latitudinal average by as much as 12°C in parts of coastal Norway.
2. (In geophysics). The difference between observed and computed geophysical values, especially with regard

to the thermal, gravitational, and magnetic properties of the earth. *See* gravity anomaly.

anorthite. A calcic plagioclase *feldspar.

anorthoclase. A variety of alkali *feldspar.

anorthosites. Coarse-grained leucocratic igneous rocks that occur as vast intrusive bodies or as members of layered basic complexes. Plagioclase feldspar constitutes over 90% of anorthosite and is generally of labradorite composition but anorthosites composed of plagioclase ranging from andesine to anorthite are known. Minor mafic minerals include augite and hypersthene and with an increase in the amount of mafic minerals, anorthosites pass into gabbros.

antecedence. A type of *discordant drainage, originating when a pre-existing drainage pattern cuts down into a rising fold, or a series of rising folds, in its path. The cause of the folding will be tectonic, and in the best developed examples, the rate of uplift of the folds is equalled by the rate of downcutting of the streams, eventually leaving them in deep *canyons. As an explanation of discordance, it is less commonly used than *superimposition, but is often used to explain the origin of streams cutting through mountain ranges in deep gorges, e.g. the streams that cut through the Himalayas.

anthophyllite. An orthorhombic mineral of the *amphibole group.

Anthozoa. A class of the phylum *Coelenterata that includes the sea anemones and *corals. The corals are geologically the most important anthozoans as many of them possess hard parts that may be fossilized. Their evolution may be used in *biostratigraphy and the colonial forms are important reef-builders. Typically, corals secrete a cup (*corallum*), from whose wall (*theca*) supporting platelike septa project radially towards the centre. The Tabulata (tabulate corals) are known from the Ordovician Period to the Jurassic, though the group had greatly declined by the end of the Palaeozoic. They were colonial forms having only rudimentary septa or none at all. The walls were reinforced by *tabulae*, calcareous plates extending across each coralite. The Rugosa, or Tetracoralla, (rugose corals) are first known from the Ordovician and are confined to the Palaeozoic. Their septa occur in multiples of four and are strengthened by many small plates known as *dissepiments*. The group included both solitary and colonial species. The Scleractinia, or Hexacoralla, includes the modern reef-building corals, whose septa are in multiples of six. They range from the Triassic Period onwards.

anthracite. Coal that has a very high fixed carbon content and a low amount of volatiles.

anthropomorphic soils. Intrazonal soils that have been formed as a direct result of man's activities. Farming practices through the ages have, in some cases, produced distinctive soils or distinctive surface horizons. An important anthropomorphic soil is the paddy soil. This is similar to a gley and its features have been formed by the process of alternate wetting and drying, which has been controlled by man. Many soils have anthropic *epipedons (surface horizons) or plaggen epipedons. The former have a high phosphate content and the latter a high organic matter content.

anticline. An arch-shaped fold into which rock strata have been compressed, the oldest rocks occurring in the core. See *fold*.

anticlinorium. A large-scale regional feature, many kilometres in diameter, consisting of an anticlinal structure with several minor folds on its limbs.

anticyclone (high). An area in the air of higher pressure than the surrounding air, with a closed isobar of approximately circular form at its centre. Winds circulate in a clockwise manner around the high pressure centre in the N hemisphere, and anticlockwise in the S hemisphere, but are generally light. Once established, the anticyclone moves only slowly and normally is a significant feature of surface pressure charts for a much longer period than cyclones. Anticyclones can be subdivided into two categories, cold and warm. Cold anticyclones are shallow features produced by strong radiational cooling at the surface or in the cold air behind a depression. The tropopause tends to be low above a cold anticyclone. Far more important are the warm anticyclones, which are characterized by warmer temperatures throughout a deep troposphere, with a cold stratosphere above. Their most frequent locations are in the subtropical high-pressure belts, but they do move polewards and block the normal westerly circulation producing temperature and precipitation anomalies in these areas. Descending motion is characteristic of anticyclones. They represent the parts of the atmosphere in which air slowly subsides from higher levels, warming and drying as it does so. This has the effect of stabilizing the atmosphere within an anticyclone so that rain is infrequent. In the surface layers, divergence of airflow takes place to maintain the continuity of subsidence. *Compare* cyclone.

anticyclonic gloom. Under anticyclonic conditions, the layer of air near the ground undergoes little descent and if moist can easily become saturated to give a uniform layer of cloud. This is a stable situation with the cloud slowly gaining in thickness through radiational cooling of the layer aloft. Above this level the air is much warmer due to descent; a temperature *inversion and stability are maintained. At the surface, little light penetrates the cloud and pollution can be trapped to give poor illumination. If prolonged, these circumstances can give high pollution concentrations, which may reach dangerous levels, as happened in London in

1952 and 1962, Donora and Liège in 1948.

antiform. An upward-closing structure, the precise stratigraphic relationships of whose strata are not known, i.e. the core need not be the oldest rocks. It results from complex folding in orogenic areas. See fold.

antigorite. See serpentine.

antiperthite. An intergrowth of orthoclase and albite feldspar in which the orthoclase occurs as patches in the albite host. See also perthite, exsolution.

antithetic faults. Minor normal faults associated with a major fault but whose planes dip into the main fault plane.

antitrades. Originally considered to be the returning flow in the upper atmosphere for the surface *trade winds, antitrades now more generally indicate the airflow above the NE or SE trade winds, blowing in a general westerly direction at heights of about 1800 metres.

antitriptic wind. A wind in which the forces controlling air movement are the pressure gradient force and friction. The *Coriolis force and centripetal acceleration are neglected either because of the small scale of the system, such as a sea breeze, or because the Coriolis force is negligible, as it is near the equator.

anvil. If the top of a cumulonimbus cloud reaches the tropopause, a temperature inversion, or strong wind shear, the main cloud updraughts are deflected horizontally causing the ice crystals at that level to spread out. From the ground, the whole cloud has the appearance of a blacksmith's anvil.

apatite. A hexagonal mineral of composition $Ca_5(PO_4)_3(OH,F,Cl)$, the commonest phosphorus mineral. It may be formed as an accessory mineral in igneous rocks of most compositions. Apatite also occurs as a detrital mineral in sedimentary rocks and in metamorphic rocks.

aphanitic. Denoting an igneous rock that is so fine-grained that individual crystals cannot be resolved with the naked eye. Compare phanerocrystalline.

aphelion. The point on the orbit of a planet that is farthest from the central axis of rotation. Compare perihelion.

aphotic zone. Ocean depths below the maximum depth at which photosynthesis takes place because of lack of light, stretching from 200 metres to the sea floor. See also disphotic zone, euphotic zone.

aphyric. Denoting an igneous rock that is not *porphyritic.

aplites. Leucocratic acid igneous rocks of medium to fine grain size occurring as thin veins and dykes around granite intrusions. Aplites consist largely of quartz and alkali feldspar and have micrographic or *saccharoidal textures. They are thought to have crystallized from residual liquids lower in volatiles than pegmatites.

apophyllite. A rare mineral of composition $KFCa_4(Si_8O_{20}).8H_2O$ found in *amygdales in basalts.

apparent dip. The angle between a structural surface, i.e. a bedding plane, and the horizontal, measured vertically in any direction except that which is at 90° to the strike of the surface. This results in a value of dip that is less than that of true *dip.

appinite. A melanocratic variety of *diorite.

APT. Automatic Picture Transmission from satellites to receiving stations. Instead of storing picture information and then transmitting to a central unit, the satellite constantly transmits data, which can be received at any suitably equipped station within the line of sight, a distance of about 1500 kilometres. This enables up-to-date forecasts of cloud and weather conditions to be given.

aquamarine. A blue-green gem variety of *beryl.

aquifer. Any water-saturated rock horizon that has sufficient porosity and permeability to yield economic supplies of groundwater, either as springs or in wells.

aragonite. *See* carbonate minerals.

Archaean. A division of the *Precambrian on the basis of its igneous and metamorphic rocks. Originally the Archaean in all parts of the world was thought to be earlier than the time represented by unmetamorphosed Precambrian rocks (*see* Proterozoic), but it is unlikely that this time division is consistent in all parts of the world and the term has little significance.

Archaeopteryx. The earliest known bird, whose fossils come from late Jurassic strata. Good fossil preservation reveals that Archaeopteryx had feathers but in its skeletal structure it resembled the archosaur reptiles from which it had evolved. The wings were primitive and the three separate fingers had claws. Other reptilian features included teeth, a long tail, and solid bones (*compare* Aves). Its flying ability was probably poor.

Archaeozoic. An era of *Precambrian time following the *Eozoic and preceding the *Proterozoic. The term is now little used.

archipelagic apron. The moatlike rock filling that may surround a group of volcanic islands or seamounts. The moat filling is usually gently sloping and smooth, the upper surface being called an *archipelagic plain*. These groups of islands or seamounts probably depress the earth's crust to the extent that a moat or depression is developed, but the depression may be concealed by a sedimentary overlay. Part of the Hawaiian Islands display a moatlike form surrounding them.

archipelago. A group of islands in fairly close proximity. The term is sometimes used to describe sea areas that contain numerous scattered islands.

Archosauria. A subclass of the Reptilia consisting principally of the extinct *dinosaurs and *Pterosauria and the modern crocodiles. Primarily carnivorous, with simple pointed teeth, they show a tendency to bipedalism involving development of the hind limbs, a corresponding reduction of the fore limbs, and a well-developed tail for balancing the body. Archosaurs became the dominant form of terrestrial life during the Jurassic and Cretaceous periods; some became secondarily quadrupedal and vegetarian.

Arctic sea smoke. A type of fog formed by evaporation from a relatively warm sea surface into cold air aloft. Condensation takes place in the cold air, but unless an inversion develops, further mixing prevents the extensive development of fog. In the Aleutian Islands, fog depths up to 1500 metres may occur under suitable conditions.

Arctic warming. The marked warming of the Arctic area that took place between the 1920s and 1950s. The ice-free period increased and mean annual temperatures rose by about 4-10°C. It was primarily the result of the more northerly tracks of the Atlantic and Pacific depressions carrying moist warm air towards the poles. Although the amount of warming has decreased considerably, Arctic temperatures are still higher than pre-1920.

arcuate delta. A *delta with a rounded convex margin.

arenaceous. Denoting a *clastic sedimentary deposit or rock in which the constituent fragments are of *sand grade in size. This includes particles from 1/16 mm to 2 mm in diameter. Arenaceous rocks are also referred to as *sandstones. The grains are often fragments of crystals, although lithic sandstones are known (*see* greywacke).

arête. A sharp ridge bounded by steep slopes and found in glaciated or formerly glaciated areas. These forms seldom develop in isolation and headwall erosion of two adjacent cirques causes the formation of an arête. Continued headwall recession will result in the destruction of the arête and the cirques will merge.

argillaceous. Denoting a *clastic sedimentary deposit or rock in which the constituent fragments are of *silt or *clay grade in size. This includes particles smaller than 1/16 mm in diameter. These consist of finely ground rock as well as the various clay minerals that have been produced in the course of weathering of the parent rock. Siltstones and *mudstones are rocks formed of sediment in this size range.

argon. An inert gas comprising about 1% of the atmosphere by volume. It has no meteorological significance.

arid climate. A climate that experiences a moisture deficiency sufficient to inhibit but not prevent natural vegetative growth and a mean annual rainfall usually taken as below 250 mm. Attempts to produce a precise definition of aridity involve an assessment of the efficiency of precipitation. Arid climates are found in areas of semipermanent anticyclones, where cold ocean currents stabilize the lower atmosphere, within extensive mountain ranges, and in locations at enormous distances from the sea. See also desert.

aridity index. An assessment of the degree of dryness of a climate. There are a variety of such indices, the best known being devised by Thornthwaite in 1948. Most involve the relationships between temperature, total rainfall, and humidity.

aridosol. One of the ten soil orders of the *Seventh Approximation classification, including saline and alkaline mineral soils of desert areas. They are characterized by low organic matter contents and a horizon of calcium or sodium accumulation within 1 metre of the surface. They are infertile owing to lack of moisture, coarse particle size, and their susceptibility to erosion due to lack of vegetation. In some profiles, groundwater may concentrate sodium to toxic proportions, forming a salic horizon in which sodium salts exceed 2% of the mineral matter. The aridosols include true desert soils, sierozem, solonchak, and solonetz.

arkose. An *arenaceous sedimentary rock that includes more than 25% *feldspar in its composition.

Armorican orogeny. A period of mountain-building during the Upper Palaeozoic affecting Western Europe, named after Armorica (Brittany). It is part of the more complex *Variscan orogeny but characterized by a roughly northwest-southeast trend.

arroyo. An ephemeral stream of the semiarid U.S. and Latin America. Arroyos originate as discontinuous gullies on a hillside where the vegetation has been locally weakened by trampling, grazing, or fire. Headward erosion during periods when the gullies contain water leads to coalescence, and the formation of a continuous gully, or arroyo. See also gully erosion, abnormal erosion.

arsenopyrite. An orthorhombic arsenic mineral of composition FeAsS, found in hydrothermal veins.

Arthropoda. The phylum of animals having jointed limbs and a segmented body protected by a chitinous exoskeleton. The Arthropoda is the largest phylum in the animal kingdom and its six most important classes are the *Crustacea, Arachnida (spiders and scorpions), Myriapoda (centipedes and millipedes), Merostomata (king crabs and the extinct eurypterids), *Insecta, and the extinct *Trilobita. Fossils of arthropods represent mainly aquatic benthonic forms, which lived in the most favourable environments for preservation; such arthropods are thought to have been recognized in the Cambrian, perhaps even the Precambrian.

Artiodactyla. The order of herbivorous hoofed mammals comprising those with an even number of toes, such as antelopes, cattle, deer, and pigs. Originating in the Eocene and at first outnumbered by early perissodactyls, they are now the more successful group. The most primitive members are the pigs, which still possess four toes. In the ruminants the limbs are developed for fast running with the loss of all but two of the digits, and the teeth are modified to deal with a coarse vegetable diet. *Compare* Perissodactyla.

asbestos. A fibrous variety of *amphibole, usually tremolite or actinolite. The *serpentine mineral chrysotile is used in the manufacture of commercial asbestos.

aseismic plates. Large areas of the earth's crust above the asthenosphere, within which there are relatively few earthquakes.

ash. *See* pyroclastic rocks.

assimilation. During intrusion, magma forces its way along joints and cracks in the country or wall rock so that large blocks (*xenoliths) may become detached and sink into the magma. This process, known as *stoping*, may occur on a large scale when large volumes of magma are emplaced.
The complex interactions taking place between the magma and solid rock are known by the term *syntexis*. Melting of the rock and chemical reaction with the magma may result in the complete digestion or assimilation of the incorporated material. Xenoliths only survive when assimilation is incomplete. Contaminated magma that has assimilated large quantities of country rock is said to be hybrid. Hybridization also occurs when two different magmas are mixed. That such a process has taken place may be indicated by the occurrence of

corroded *xenocrysts within an igneous rock.

asthenosphere. A zone within the earth's upper *mantle in which the velocity of seismic waves is considerably reduced. Movement between the earth's outer lithosphere and inner mesosphere is thought to take place along this zone, which is capable of prolonged plastic deformation. It is thought to be composed of partially molten peridotite, with a liquid fraction having the composition of basalt. It is developed between 50 and 240 km beneath the earth's surface.

astrobleme. An ancient crater on the earth's surface resulting from the impact of an extraterrestrial body.

asymmetric fold. A fold in which the axial plane is not vertical, with the result that the two limbs have different angles of dip. See diagram at *fold.

Atlantic period. The period from 5000 to 3000 B.C., within the present interglacial, when the climate of much of NW Europe was warm and moist, achieving the highest mean annual temperatures since the last glaciation. It is also known as the *climatic optimum*.

atmophile. *See* lithophile.

atmosphere. The mixture of gases surrounding the earth, which we breathe and which provides our weather. The atmosphere can be divided into a number of layers on thermal and lapse-rate properties. The troposphere is the lowest, extending up to approximately 10 to 15 km. Throughout this layer, there is a decrease of temperature with height, and it is the source of all precipitation and most of our weather phenomena. Above this layer, temperatures gradually increase through the stratosphere to about 50 km, decrease through the mesosphere reaching values of about -90°C between 80 and 90 km, and finally there is the thermosphere or ionosphere where absorption of ultraviolet radiation of shorter wavelengths than that absorbed by ozone

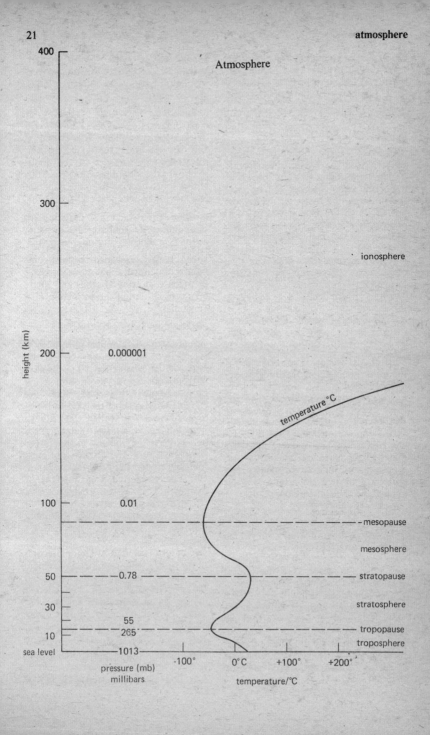

Atmosphere

causes a rise of temperature to values of 1500 to 2000°C at between 300 and 400 km. Gases become ionized at these high levels, which is of vital importance in radio communication.

The distribution of water vapour in the atmosphere is very variable. It depends upon the amount of evaporation from the surface and the amount of moisture advected from elsewhere. In continental interiors the value is very low. It is important as an absorber of long-wave radiation, so that moist air reduces the rate at which the ground surface cools at night by increasing counter-radiation. Moisture is also required in the atmosphere for precipitation, though the absolute amount is less important than other factors favouring precipitation formation.

The atmosphere acts as a protection to the ground surface by burning up most cosmic particles, which can be seen as meteors in the night sky. *See also* air, general circulation of the atmosphere.

atmospheric window. The region in the radiation spectrum containing wavelengths between 8.5 and 11 micrometres, which are not absorbed to any great extent by atmospheric gases. In the absence of cloud, terrestrial radiation of this wavelength is lost to space, enabling the cooling of the earth to take place. Other narrower wavebands also do not absorb long-wave radiation, but these are of less importance in this context. *See also* absorption.

atoll. A ring-shaped reef, island, or islands that surround or nearly surround a lagoonal area of water, in which detrital material may collect. The surrounding rim may itself lie in shallow water, in which case the central area of water is rather deeper, sometimes very deep (the average depth according to one authority is 45 metres). Not all oceanic atolls are formed entirely of coral, since certain calcareous algae may constitute the bulk of the reef material. Atolls are based on some kind of platform, often an eroded platform that subsided at some stage and on

which coral growth or other organic growth later occurred. An *atollon* is a small atoll lying on the flank of a larger atoll. *See also* reef.

attenuation. The loss of energy of electromagnetic waves as they pass through the atmosphere. It is caused by *absorption and *scattering by the molecules and particles of the atmosphere. In the ionosphere, free electrons absorb kinetic energy from the radiation and lose it in subsequent collisions.

attrition. The reduction in particle sizes of sediment by rubbing and grinding action (*see* abrasion) during transport.

augen. Large eye-shaped crystals, commonly of feldspar, that have survived the intense shearing of schist and gneiss taking place during the formation of a *mylonite.

augite. A monoclinic *pyroxene.

aurora. A transient optical phenomenon usually seen in the polar skies at the time of solar flare activity. The displays of the aurora can vary from shimmering rays to coloured corona efects occupying large parts of the sky. In the N hemisphere it is called the *aurora borealis* (or *northern lights*) and in the S hemisphere the *aurora australis* (or *southern lights*). The displays are most frequent around the geomagnetic poles, with a daily occurrence maximum about midnight. There is some evidence of a seasonal maximum about the time of the equinoxes, but the major maximum follows the 11.2 year solar activity cycle.

The aurora is caused by the interaction of the earth's tenuous upper atmosphere and charged particles streaming from the sun. The solar particles are deflected by the geomagnetic field and so only occur in limited parts of the upper atmosphere, at a height of around 100 km.

authigenic (authigenous). Denoting rock constituents that were formed in situ, coming into existence during or after the formation of the rock in which they lie. *Compare* allogenic.

autochthonous. Denoting rocks that are still in their place of formation and have not been displaced by thrusting, e.g. a folded sequence of rocks whose roots are still connected. *Compare* allochthonous.

avalanche. A rapid movement of snow en masse down steep slopes, which must usually have an angle greater than 22°. It may consist of fresh powdery snow, sliding over the contact surface of compacted older snow, of slabs of consolidated snow, which roll down the slope, or of the whole ice and snow cover of a slope, in which case much rock material is carried with the fall. If avalanches are a frequent occurrence in any one location, they can be important from the geomorphological point of view, as they maintain an exposed bedrock surface, which is therefore susceptible to continued weathering.

Aves. The birds: a class of vertebrates distinguished from the *Reptilia by the presence of feathers. They probably arose from primitive archosaur reptiles (*see* Archaeopteryx) and most of their evolution is connected with adaptation for flight. The wings are formed from the whole forearm and three fused fingers (*compare* Pterosauria). They are warm-blooded and have short tails, a large breast bone for the attachment of flight muscles, and light hollow bones. All modern birds are toothless but teeth were present in their Mesozoic ancestors. Because of the fragile nature of the skeleton, fossils are few. There have been a number of secondarily flightless forms—the ostrich, emu, etc.—often of large size.

axial modulus (in geophysics). The ratio of stress to strain, when in the presence of laterally confining forces.

axial plane. A plane that passes through the successive hinge lines of the beds in a *fold. Different types of fold are

characterized by different angles of inclination from this plane.

axial plane cleavage. Cleavage planes that are parallel to the axial plane of a *fold. Generally the cleavage is related to minor fold axes, but occasionally it may be more closely related to the region's fold trend.

axial rift zone. *See* median valley.

axial trace. The intersection of a *fold axis with the earth's surface, reflecting the trend of the fold. (See diagram at *fold*.)

axinite. A lilac-brown triclinic mineral of composition $Ca_2(Mn,Fe^{2+})Al_2$ $BO_3(Si_4O_{12})OH$, produced during the boron metasomatism of calcium-rich sediments and igneous rocks.

azimuth. 1. (In surveying). A horizontal angle measured clockwise from true north (true azimuth) or magnetic north (magnetic azimuth) to another point.
2. (In astronomy). The angle between the plane of the meridian of the observer and the vertical plane passing through a heavenly body.

azimuthal equal-area projection. A map projection differing from the other azimuthal projections in that the spacing of the parallels decreases with increasing distance from the centre of the projection, producing the equal-area property.

azimuthal equidistant projection. A map projection that is the same as the azimuthal projection in that the straight lines radiating from the centre of the projection all have their true bearings, but it has the additional property that the distances along these lines are true to scale. It is not an equal-area projection, nor is it conformal.

azimuthal (zenithal) projection. A map projection constructed as though a plane were placed at a tangent to the earth's surface and the portion of the earth covered by it were projected onto the plane. The result is that all points have their true compass bearings. The tangent plane is not always drawn at the pole; it can be constructed anywhere on the surface of the globe, the point where the tangent touches the earth being the centre of the map.

Azoic. Designating *Precambrian rocks that were deposited before the origin of life. In practice, however, it is difficult to distinguish such rocks and the term is little used. It is never used for unfossiliferous *Phanerozoic strata.

azonal soil. Soil lacking a B horizon owing to insufficient time for complete pedogenesis. Profiles of azonal soils therefore mainly reflect the influence of parent material and show an A horizon slightly darker than the C horizon because of additions of organic matter. The three main groups are lithosols, regosols, and alluvial soils. In the *Seventh Approximation azonal soils are classified as entisols.

Azores anticyclone. The semipermanent anticyclone centred in the Atlantic near the Azores Islands. It is part of the subtropical high-pressure systems of the N hemisphere. Its mean latitudinal position oscillates, being further south in winter and further north in summer, with high-pressure cells occasionally drifting northeastwards from the main centre to form blocking anticyclones within the westerly circulation.

azurite. See carbonate minerals.

B

backshore. The part of a beach that lies above the level of normal high spring tides. Only when exceptionally high spring tides occur, or severe storms take place, does this zone come under the influence of wave action. Cliffs or sand dunes behind beaches are usually included as part of the backshore.

backsight. See levelling.

backwash. The return of water down a beach, under the influence of gravity, following the breaking of a wave and

the associated *swash. The difference in load-carrying capacity between the swash and backwash of prevalent waves determines whether a beach will aggrade or degrade. Whilst flat waves tend to produce a strong swash, steep waves, which break vertically onto the beach, result in a powerful backwash and cause a net seaward movement of beach materials.

bacteria. Single-celled microorganisms that are fundamental to soil productivity. Where oxygen is lacking they account for most of the biochemical changes in the soil. Environmental controls such as moisture, aeration, temperature, acidity, and organic matter result in a constantly fluctuating bacterial population in the soil. It has been estimated there may be as many as 4000 million per gram of soil. They are commonly classified into two broad groups in relation to energy supply: 1) *autotrophic bacteria*, which obtain their energy from the oxidation of mineral substances and their carbon mostly from carbon dioxide; 2) *heterotrophic bacteria*, which obtain their energy and carbon directly from the soil organic matter. Certain enzymic transformations in the soil are dominated by bacteria. Autotrophic bacteria are much less abundant than heterotrophic but as they include the bacteria responsible for nitrification and sulphur oxidation they are of paramount importance. See nitrification, nitrogen fixation, sulphur oxidation.
Bacteria are uncommon as fossils, but by their action of breaking down organic matter they are probably instrumental in the formation of oil. They are also involved in inorganic reactions, such as those leading to the origin of iron ore deposits. There is evidence to suggest that bacteria were present as long ago as the *Precambrian. They are sometimes included in a separate kingdom of organisms, the *Protista, along with the Protozoa and single-celled plants.

bahada. *See* bajada.

Bai-u season. A period in early June when the summer circulation of China and Japan commences, bringing with it a marked rainfall maximum. The rains are the result of weak nonfrontal disturbances within the southwesterly flow, which rapidly moves northwards at this time as the upper westerlies move to the north of the Himalayas.

bajada (bahada). The gently sloping surface leading from a mountain range down to an *inland basin in arid and semiarid areas. The term has been used both for coalesced alluvial fans occurring on the rock-cut *pediment at the foot of the mountain front and also for a gently sloping concave surface (composed of increasingly fine-grained particles) leading down from the pediment to the flat basin or playa. When the term is applied to the former case, this sloping surface, which still exists, is known as a *peripediment*. In either case, the composing material is derived from the mountains and is brought down by surface runoff, which follows the infrequent but heavy downpours.

bald-headed. Denoting an anticlinal fold whose upper beds have been eroded away, exposing the older rocks of its core.

balled-up structure. An isolated patch of silty sediment contorted into spherical nodules and enclosed within mud-sized sediments, resulting from slump movements whilst in a poorly consolidated state. The term was proposed by O. T. Jones in 1937.

ball lightning. A rare form of lightning that is not, as yet, adequately understood. Its very existence has been debated as most reported cases follow brilliant lightning flashes and so could be physiological in origin, an after-image being produced in the eye. Reports of the lightning suggest a brilliant sphere with a diameter of 1 cm to 1 m, which can drift almost randomly at a few metres per second.

ballstone (crogball). A quarryman's term for the unbedded elliptical bodies present within the Wenlock Limestone. Their rich fauna of corals and stromatoporoids led Lyell in 1841 to describe them as coral reefs. Their lack of a rigid framework suggests that they should be thought of as carbonate mud banks.

bank. 1. Either side of a river channel, best marked where the river has considerable powers of vertical erosion. At *bankfull no banks are exposed. 2. A mass of sand, mud, shells, etc., usually below the water surface, and often elliptical in shape. Banks of unbedded limestone are distinguished from reefs by their lack of rigid framework formed by corals or other calcareous organisms.

bankfull. The state of flow of a river immediately prior to flooding when the river's channel is full with water to its brim. In streams of very different sizes, and in different environments, it has a fairly constant recurrence interval of about once every 1.5 years.

banner cloud. A stationary cloud that appears to be attached to an isolated mountain peak. It extends downwind from the peak for some distance and so resembles a flag or banner. The Matterhorn is probably the best known summit with a frequent occurrence of this type of cloud. The origin of the cloud is due to the lifting of air in the eddy of the leeward side of the peak, though an aerodynamic pressure reduction may play some part in its formation.

bar. 1. An elongated body of sediment, such as sand or shingle, occurring in the sea more or less parallel with the coastline and sometimes attached to it. It may be permanently submerged (*see* submarine bar) or be submerged for part of the tide, for instance at the mouth of a river or near the entrance to a harbour. Some such bars are much exposed at low tide. *See also* offshore bar, longshore bar, barrier beach, bay bar, spit, tombolo. 2. A unit of pressure. *See* millibar.

Barbed drainage

barbed drainage. A drainage pattern in which a stream suddenly bends back on itself and flows in an almost reverse direction, often due to glacial blocking, river capture, or local tectonic movement in its path.

Barchan

barchan. A crescentic dune characterized by an oval shape upwind, with a slip face and two wings spreading out downwind. Barchans occur in desert areas with a uni-directional wind regime. The slip face is formed by erosion of material from the upwind side, and its transport to the summit where it builds up until unstable, at which point it slumps forward to its angle of rest. The wings develop because the rate of advance of the dune is inversely proportional to its height, so the lower sides extend downwind faster than the centre; at their tips they end in a dwindling of the sand pile to nil, which is reached at the point where the slip face upwind ceases to shelter the wings, and they become subject to wind erosion. Barchans typically occur in belts up to 300 km long and over 12 km wide.

baroclinic. Denoting a state of the atmosphere where the surfaces of constant pressure (isobars) intersect into surfaces of constant density (isopycnics). This state is the result of large horizontal temperature gradients and is believed to be responsible in part for the formation of mid-latitude depressions.

barometer. An instrument for measuring pressure, invented in 1643 by Torricelli. The standard instrument (Kew pattern or Fortin barometer) measures the height to which a column of pure mercury can be supported by the atmospheric pressure exerted upon it. Corrections have to be made to this value to allow for variations in gravity, the purity of the mercury, and the ambient temperature.

barotropic. Denoting the state of the atmosphere when the surfaces of constant pressure are parallel to the surfaces of constant density. Although this is a useful concept in theoretical studies, such an ideal state rarely, if ever, occurs.

barrier beach. An elongated accumulation of sand, shingle, or in-situ rock lying roughly parallel to the coast but separated from it by a channel, lagoon, or other water area. The distance offshore may vary from a few metres to several kilometres. Some lie across bay mouths or estuaries. Off low coasts, barriers are often in the form of *barrier islands*, the lagoonal areas behind being of the mangrove type in warm sea regions and of the salt-marsh type or even devoid of vegetation in the case of temperate or cold sea regions. Many barriers, such as those off the E coast of the U.S. and the Gulf of Mexico coast, carry dunes. Most sand and shingle barriers are destined to overwash, even breaching on occasions during severe storms. The more common sandy barriers are formed by the continued activity of *constructive waves, which can progressively build up material above water level. Shingle barriers are formed by storm waves, the main input of material resulting from longshore movements.

barrier island. See barrier beach.

barrier reef. An elongate accumulation of coral, extending upwards from the sea floor to about low-tide level, parallel with the coast but separated from it .by a lagoon. A reef may lie between several metres and several kilometres offshore. They are believed to have been formed as a result of the submergence of a flat surface as the post-glacial sea level rose. The growth of coral organisms kept pace with the rising water so that great thicknesses could develop. The finest example is the *Great Barrier Reef.

Barrow zone. See zone (def. 1).

barysphere. All. of the earth's interior beneath the lithosphere, i.e. the asthenosphere, most of the upper mantle, and the outer and inner core.

barytes (barite). An orthorhombic mineral of composition $BaSO_4$. It is usually white but impure varieties are coloured. Barytes has a high density, which distinguishes it from calcite. A continuous chemical series exists between barytes and celestite ($SrSO_4$). Both minerals are found in hydrothermal veins with galena, sphalerite, fluorite, and calcite as well as in cavities in limestone.

basal sapping. Any of a range of processes that act to remove debris from the foot of a slope. Basal sapping is important in the creation and maintenance of *free faces, leading to near vertical or steep slopes that are often unstable, hence causing *mass move-

ments. For this reason it constitutes the major explanation of *parallel retreat of slopes, since the debris at the foot is constantly removed and the steepness of the slope is maintained, thus preventing slope decline.

Types of basal sapping include wave action at the foot of a sea cliff, lateral erosion by a river at the foot of a bluff, headward erosion of streams issuing at the foot of a slope, and mass movements produced by heterogeneity of rock strata. As an example of the latter, it is common in the scarpland areas of S and E England to find sandstone or limestone overlying clay; the sandstone and limestone allow water to permeate, but the clay stores it. Retention of water lowers the *shear strength of the clay and the weight of the overlying sandstone or limestone forces the clay to bulge out, leaving the front of the chalk or sandstone unsupported: this is an unstable situation leading to a mass movement, which moves the whole slope back but keeps it near vertical.

basalt. A basic volcanic rock, the fine-grained equivalent of *gabbro. Its essential constituents are calcic plagioclase, generally in the range labradorite-by-townite, and pyroxene. Olivine may not always be present but magnetite and apatite are invariable accessories. Basalts range from undersaturated to oversaturated compositions (see silica saturation) but two extremes are recognized, named *alkali basalt and tholeiite.

Alkali basalts are undersaturated and contain abundant olivine both as phenocrysts and in the groundmass. The pyroxenes of alkali basalt are calcium-rich augite or titanaugite. Tholeiites are saturated or slightly oversaturated in composition. They contain sufficient silica to partially or completely convert olivine to orthopyroxene and are characterized by this reaction relationship, which is indicated by the mantling of olivine by calcium-poor pyroxene (hypersthene or pigeonite). When present, olivine occurs only as phenocrysts and is absent from the ground-mass. Tholeiites typically have inter-sertal textures and contain silica minerals in the groundmass.

A third type of basalt is now widely recognized, namely high-alumina basalt (or calc-alkali basalt) but mineralogical criteria alone are insufficient to dis-tinguish the different basalt types and chemical criteria are applied. Even so, the three basalt types, alkali basalt, high-alumina basalt, and tholeiite, are gradational in composition. High-alumina basalt is distinguished by an Al_2O_3 content in excess of 17% in aphyric rocks. The $Na_2O + K_2O$ con-tent lies between those of the other two types but mineralogically, high-alumina basalt has a strong affinity with tholeiite.

Three volcanic associations correspond-ing to the three basalt types may be considered.
1. alkali olivine-basalt—mugearite —trachyte/phonolite
2. high-alumina basalt—andesite—daci-te—rhyolite (calc-alkaline suite)
3. tholeiite—tholeiitic andesite—rhyo-lite
Members of the alkali basalt association are found on oceanic islands and con-tinents. Calc-alkaline volcanic rocks are characteristic of island arcs and oro-genic belts. Tholeiites occur on the continents, especially along continental margins. Most of the plateau or flood basalts of the world are of tholeiitic composition. The basalts of the ocean floor generated at the *mid-ocean ridges are tholeiites with extremely low K_2O and TiO_2 contents. See also alkali basalts.

basanite. See alkali basalt.

base construction line. The line drawn at right angles to the *central meridian of a map projection, from which the other meridians of the map are established.

base level. An imaginary line running from *sea level under the landmass, rising slightly above the horizontal. It constitutes the controlling level down to which, but not below which, a river can cut its valley.

Local base levels may replace sea level as the controlling lower limit of erosion for certain parts of streams, or in certain regions; for example, a dam across a stream, a hard rock band, or a lake will constitute the local base levels for the upstream section of a river. In inland drainage basins, the base level will be the lake to which the streams flow; the Lake Eyre basin in Australia has a local level 14 metres below sea level. No river ever actually reaches base level, except at its mouth, as it must retain some gradient in order to flow.

Sea level change, tectonic movement, or the removal of ice pressure from a formerly glaciated area can all change the position of sea level (the ultimate base level) relative to the land. Base level, along with climate and geology, is one of the independent variables that control the processes in a particular cycle of erosion. Changes in base level therefore produce fundamental changes in the geomorphological system, to the extent that a major base level change initiates a new cycle of erosion.

If the land is raised relative to the sea, base level movement is negative; if vice versa, it is positive. The former tends to increase erosional activity, the latter to initiate deposition. See also eustasy, rejuvenation.

base line. A line that is measured very accurately as part of a *triangulation scheme. Great accuracy is required since the location of all the points within the triangulation area is based upon this one measured line, though the largest schemes may use two or three base lines. They are usually measured using long tapes or wires, supported above the ground. Several corrections must be applied to the taped lengths to allow for such factors as slope, thermal conditions, and sag. More recent developments in surveying allow the measurements of long base lines without the need for tapes: both the *geodimeter

bay bar. A barrier of sand or shingle that extends across the entrance to a bay, effectively straightening the coastline. The most likely causes of a bay bar are an enlargement of a single *spit in one direction or the independent growth, and subsequent coalescence, of two spits that increase their lengths towards each other. Once closed off by a bay bar, the bay will gradually fill up with sediment.

beach. An accumulation of unconsolidated materials found in the zone of intersection between land and sea. For most practical purposes the beach can be considered to extend from the highest point of severe storm-wave activity (see storm beach) down to the point at which waves approaching the coast first start to cause extensive movement of sea-bed materials. Beach materials are located on a foundation of eroded solid rock (see wave-cut platform); they usually form a smooth profile that is gently convex and is sometimes interrupted by *beach ridges. The response of a beach to the activity of waves and other agents of erosion and deposition largely depends upon the nature and thickness of the deposits, sand and shingle behaving very differently.

beach cusp. See cusp.

beach ridge. An upstanding linear accumulation found on shingle beaches (those developed in sand are known as *berms). Whenever *constructive waves are active on a shingle beach, a small ridge will be produced at the limit of *swash for each high tide. As maximum tide level falls from spring to neap level, a series of ridges will be produced; these will be destroyed again on tidal rise to spring level, when just one ridge remains at high-water spring level. Much larger shingle ridges can be produced in connection with severe storms. These develop far above the swash limits of normal waves (see storm beach).

beach rock. Consolidated and erosion-resistant sand-forms, often reeflike, that develop along some inter-tidal shores in tropical and subtropical regions. Beach rock has also been found in Portugal, Hawaii, Morocco, and certain temperate regions. Its origin has provoked a great deal of argument and speculation. In general, it appears to develop on account of cementation or lithification processes, the cement being of a calcareous type (often calcite or aragonite). Hence, geologists classify beach rock as a calcarenite. Its rapid consolidation may be aided by the presence of microorganisms such as bacteria and unicellular algae, and certainly by high temperatures. Beach rock, which tends to form as small outcrops, is not always found on all beaches in the same locality. Once formed, however, it tends to resist the action of waves and may act as a barrier to sediment movement.

beaded esker. An *esker comprising alternate wide and narrow segments, which reflect differential input rates of fluvioglacial sediments. The narrow sections were formed during colder periods, when there was less meltwater and hence less sediment, whilst the wider parts were deposited in warmer periods. These segments may mark successive winter and summer accumulations as an ice front (or glacier snout) retreated. Beaded eskers are comparatively rare.

bearing. A horizontal angle measured clockwise from a known direction, usually north, to another point. If the initial direction is true north then the angles are true bearings. Angles measured with reference to magnetic north, such as those obtained with a prismatic compass, are known as magnetic or compass bearings.

Beaufort Scale. A scale of wind speed based on easily observable indications such as tree movement and smoke. The scale ranges from 0 to 12 with the numbers and indicators as shown opposite.

Beaufort Scale   *Speed (knots)*
0	Calm	Smoke rises vertically	<1
1	Light air	Smoke or leaves indicates movement, otherwise almost calm	1–3
2	Light breeze	Wind felt on face, leaves rustle, etc.	4–6
3	Gentle breeze	Flag extended; leaves and twigs in constant motion	7–10
4	Mod. breeze	Small branches moved; dust and litter raised	11–16
5	Fresh breeze	Small trees begin to sway	17–21
6	Strong breeze	Large branches in motion; whistling in telephone wires	22–27
7	Near gale	Whole trees in motion; inconvenience experienced in walking	28–33
8	Gale	Twigs broken off; walking impeded	34–40
9	Strong gale	Slight structural damage experienced	41–47
10	Storm	Widespread damage to trees and buildings	48–55
11	Violent storm	Very rarely experienced inland, severe damage results	56–63
12	Hurricane	Very rarely experienced inland, severe damage results	>64

bedding-plane slip. The displacement of one bed of rock over another, taking place along the bedding plane between adjacent beds. It is usually associated with folding, where in extreme cases it can lead to *décollement.

bed (stratum). The smallest division of stratified sedimentary rocks, consisting of a single distinct sheetlike layer of sedimentary material, separated from the beds above and below by relatively well-defined planar surfaces called *bedding planes*, which mark a break in sedimentation. A bed may be part of a *member (see also marker bed). See stratigraphy, lithostratigraphy.

beef. Thin beds and veins of fibrous calcite. See carbonate minerals.

belemnite. Any mollusc of the extinct subclass *Belemnoidea. Belemnites are important fossils from rocks of the Mesozoic Era.

Belemnoidea. An extinct subclass of marine molluscs of the class *Cephalopoda. With squids and octopuses, they are classified as Coleoidea (or Dibranchiata). They had an internal bullet-shaped shell with simple septa dividing it into chambers; this shell is usually the only part of the animal to be fossilized. Belemnites are known from Lower Carboniferous rocks and extend to the beginning of the Tertiary, but they reached their maximum development in the Jurassic and Cretaceous Periods.

bench mark. A mark indicating a point of known position and height, which has been surveyed extremely accurately by the national surveying body of the country concerned. In Britain the Ordnance Survey bench marks consist of a broad upward-pointing arrow with a horizontal bar across the apex, which are usually chiselled into the wall of some permanent feature. If the position is below sea level, the mark is inverted. The published height of that point is indicated by the centre line of the horizontal bar. Bench marks are indicated on British Ordnance Survey maps by the letters B.M., alongside which the height is given.

Benguela current. A sea current that flows northwards off the coast of southwest Africa. Part of the region in which it flows is important because of the existence of an *upwelling of cold water and a zone of marked divergence. The upwelling water comes from subsurface water perhaps only two or three hundred metres deep. The most marked flow in the Benguela current, which can be up to about 16 million cubic metres per second, occurs between the Cape of Good Hope and latitude 18°S.

Benioff zone. The inclined seismic zone within the earth's lithosphere extending down at an angle of usually around 45° from the base of an ocean trench to the asthenosphere. It is typical of destructive plate margins where one plate overrides another as a result of sea-floor spreading. These are zones where ocean floor is consumed. The shallowest earthquake foci along the zone occur near the base of the trench, the foci becoming progressively deeper with distance along the Benioff zone from the trench.

benmoreite. See trachybasalt.

benthos. Plant and animal marine life, both small and large, living within the waters of the sea or on the sea bed (see also pelagic (def. 2)). They are a fundamental part of the complex food chains that operate within marine environments. Benthos exist in numerous forms, the greatest variety occurring within the shallow-water environments associated with continental shelves. In the *photic zone, the benthos feed on both phytoplankton and zooplankton; they are especially well developed in plankton-rich areas and often poorly developed in less fertile areas. The benthos help to make available to larger marine creatures the tiny food particles that they consume or produce. Vagrant benthos are capable of active movement on or within the sediment; sessile benthos remain attached to the sea floor.

bentonite. Clay formed by the alteration and weathering of tuffs and volcanic ash. See clay minerals.

Bergeron-Findeisen theory. A theory of precipitation formation proposed by Bergeron in 1933 and subsequently modified by Findeisen. It suggested that ice crystals and supercooled water droplets could exist together at certain levels in the clouds where the temperature was between -15° and -30°C. Because the saturation vapour pressure for ice is lower than that for a water surface, there would be preferential deposition of moisture on the ice crystals, causing them to grow sufficiently for snowflakes or raindrops to result.

bergschrund. A deep narrow chasm frequently found in *cirques in which the upper part of the *cirque glacier has become separated from the rock headwall. They were formerly believed to be the most favourable sites for *freeze-thaw activity, which causes headwall retreat. However, recent work has shown that fluctuations of temperature within bergschrunds are infrequently of sufficient magnitude or rapidity to cause any rock breakdown. Only in the upper parts of open bergschrunds, where cold air can circulate freely, will there be any appreciable attack on the rock of the headwall.

berm. An accumulation of material found a little way above the mean high-water mark on sand beaches. The berm is usually flat (although it may slope gently landwards), is of variable width, and is characterized by a marked break of slope at the seaward edge. Berms are created by the action of *constructive waves but their growth is not a very rapid process. A beach of coarse sand, having a steeper gradient than one of finer material, will develop a berm more rapidly, since wave action is restricted to a narrower width of beach. See also beach ridge.

beryl. A hexagonal mineral of composition $Be_3Al_2Si_6O_{18}$ found in granitic rocks and *pegmatites. Beryl is white to pale green in colour. The gem variety aquamarine is bluish green. The bright green variety is emerald, found mainly in metamorphic rocks.

bifurcation ratio. The quantitative relationship between *stream orders, expressed as the number of streams of one order divided by the number of streams of the next highest order. Values are commonly between 2.5 and 3.5, but are higher in long thin drainage basins dominated by one master stream.

billow clouds. Clouds found in a series of regular bands with clear areas between, usually of similar width to that of the cloud. They occur most frequently about 6-8 km, and appear to be due to a strong increase of wind speed with height when the airflow is stable, but the precise mechanism is still in doubt.

bimineralic. Denoting a rock consisting of only two kinds of minerals, e.g. websterite.

biocoenosis (life assemblage). An assemblage of fossil organisms associated and occurring in the same position as they occupied in life. Some bioherms and reefs approximate to this condition but such assemblages are usually rare, as most organisms suffer damage and transport after death. *Compare* thanatocoenosis. *See also* taphonomy.

bioherm. A *reef of unstratified limestone, e.g. a ballstone, formed by organic processes and usually having the shape of a dome rather than a linear feature. Most recent bioherms are produced by *corals, but in the past important reef-building organisms have included *sponges and certain algae. A bioherm may include a hard skeletal structure secreted by the organism itself, the remains of animals that live in the environment it produces, and also trapped sediment. They are mainly marine.

biostratigraphy. The branch of stratigraphy that utilizes information from fossils in the *calibration of stratigraphic sequences of rock in which they occur. The evolution of organisms is believed to be a continuous unidirectional process and it therefore provides an important means of correlating and comparing separate rock sections. The fundamental biostratigraphic division is the *zone. Some geologists make no distinction between biostratigraphy and *chronostratigraphy and include the biostratigraphic zone within the chronostratigraphic hierarchy of terms. Others consider biostratigraphy to be simply one method of calibrating the essentially separate chronostratigraphic scale (*see* chronozone).

biostratonomy. The branch of palaeontology concerned with the processes by which the remains of organisms become embedded in rock. This is important in interpreting the significance of fossil assemblages, many of which are *thanatocoenoses. *See* actuopalaeontology, taphonomy.

biostrome. A structure similar to a *bioherm but not swelling into a mound or lenslike body. It more closely resembles a broad sheet of sediment consisting of a large quantity of organic remains.

biotite. *See* mica.

bioturbation. The reworking and further degradation of sediment by the action of organisms moving through it and feeding on it.

birds. *See* Aves.

bird's foot delta. An elongated form of *delta, with sediment deposited in a finger-like pattern following the courses of the various distributary streams.

birefringence. The double refraction of light entering an anisotropic crystal, when it is split into two plane polarized rays, the ordinary and extraordinary rays. The two rays vibrate in mutually perpendicular planes and travel through the crystal in different directions and with different velocities (there is a fast ray and a slow ray) and thus have different refractive indices. This may be illustrated by the well-known experiment of viewing a single spot on a piece of paper through a piece of Iceland spar. Two images of the spot are seen representing the ordinary and extraordinary rays.
When an anisotropic crystal is viewed under a petrological (polarizing) microscope, bright polarization colours are seen and the crystal is said to exhibit birefringence. The two rays produced by the mineral are recombined in the microscope and their optical interference produces the polarization colours. These colours are of great use in the identification of minerals.

Bivalvia (Lamellibranchia, Pelecypoda). A class of the phylum *Mollusca whose members are characterized by a two-valved shell protecting the body. The valves are secreted by the mantle and meet at a hinge line, where they are joined by an elastic ligament. The hinge is aligned and strengthened by a system of interlocking teeth and sockets, which are used in the taxonomic classification of the group. The shell has growth lines and often ornamentation. The animals are bilaterally symmetrical, with the plane of symmetry passing between the valves, unlike the *Brachiopoda, which are symmetrical across the valves. Some bivalves have secondarily lost this symmetry and the valves are unequal.

Bivalves are aquatic (mostly marine), occupying a great variety of habitats, and include free-swimming, sessile, and burrowing forms. They range from the Cambrian Period to the present day and have been used biostratigraphically as *zone fossils, particularly in the Upper Carboniferous and Tertiary.

black alkali soil. *See* solonetz.

black-body radiation. A perfect black body is one that absorbs all radiation falling upon it and emits, for any temperature, the maximum amount of radiant energy. No real substance achieves this degree of physical perfection, but the inside of a sphere coated with carbon black approaches it. Some substances can act as black bodies for certain wavelengths only. An extreme example of this is snow, which has a high albedo for visible light, but effectively acts as a black body for wavelengths greater than 1.5 μm.

black earth. *See* chernozem.

black ice (glazed frost). A smooth transparent thin coating of ice formed on asphalted road or other surfaces, having a black almost invisible appearance. It is formed when drizzle or light rain falls onto a surface that is at a temperature below 0°C.

blanket bog. *See* organic soils.

blizzard. Heavy snow falling or drifting during strong winds.

block-faulting. A series of normal faults that separate an area into a series of horsts and grabens. (*See* fault.)

blocking. The situation arising when anomalous pressure patterns develop in the zone of the mid-latitude westerlies. It more commonly refers to anticyclone formations that act as a block to the normal depression tracks, which then move towards the northeast and southeast around the anticyclone to give spells of quiet and dry weather near the blocking high. The two favoured sites for the location of blocking highs are over NW Europe and the NW Pacific. The precise reasons for these positions are not understood but they are believed to be due to the interaction between the westerly circulation and the north-south oriented mountain ranges such as the Rockies.

block lava. A *lava the surface of which is broken into large retangular blocks. *Compare* aa, pahoehoe.

Blowout formation

blowout. A break in the crest of a sand dune, caused by vegetation destruction or gullying. It leads to increased sand mobility and wind speed at the break point, with the sand being blown down-

35

Boreal climate

wind as a parabolic dune bowing out from the transverse line.

By the time stage 3 is reached, unless practical measures are taken to break wind speed and reinstate the vegetation, the blowout becomes progressively enlarged by advancing downwind and widens itself through undercutting of the vegetation on either side.

blue ground. *See* kimberlite.

blue john. *See* fluorite.

body waves. Seismic waves, generated either by an earthquake or explosion, which reach a recording station after having travelled through the earth's interior. Body waves include primary (P or longitudinal) and secondary (S or shear) waves.

bog soils. *See* organic soils.

bole. Thin red weathered horizons formed between basalt lava flows. The presence of bole indicates subaerial extrusion and a tropical climate. *See* laterite.

bolson. *See* inland basin.

bomb (volcanic bomb). *See* pyroclastic rocks.

Bonne's projection

Bonne's projection. A type of *conical map projection, with the central meridian straight and truly divided, the parallels all concentric circles, and the

other meridians composite curves joining divisions on the correctly divided parallels. The scale along the parallels is kept true. The shapes of landmasses are distorted with distance from the central meridian but the projection is equal-area.

bora. A cold, dry, and gusty northeasterly wind that sweeps through the mountain gaps of Yugoslavia to the Adriatic coast. It is strongest in winter, with mean speeds of about 50 km/hr., and is the result of high pressure over central Europe and a deep depression to the southwest. The presence of the mountains helps the funnelling of the wind and its rapid descent prevents adiabatic warming. *See also* mistral.

bore. A tidal phenomenon that occurs in certain rivers or estuaries. The tidal range is usually fairly large and may lead to a tidal flood wave with a high sharply developed front. The frontal area is often characterized by subsidiary waves or furrows. With the initial flooding of the tide, a surging inflow may develop and travel rapidly some kilometres upstream. Well-known bores occur in the Amazon, the Tsing Kiang River in China, the River Hugli in India, and the Bay of Fundy. The better known ones in England include those of the Severn, Trent, and Ouse. The large bore that travels up the Tsing Kiang River has a fast-moving abrupt front up to 4 metres in height, necessitating the prior removal of boats from the river.

Boreal climate. A climatic type in Köppen's classification system characterized by cold snowy winters and warm summers, giving a large annual range of temperature. Precipitation totals are small. It is found over the American, European, and Asian continents between latitudes 40°N an 65°N with the S boundary being further north on the warmer W coasts and trending WNW–ESE towards the colder continental interiors.

Boreal period. The period from 7500 BC to 5000 BC, which was characterized by an improving climate following the deglaciation of the last Ice Age. It was named Boreal as the vegetation at this time in NW Europe, where the first investigations were conducted, was predominantly coniferous as in the Boreal areas at present.

borer. A marine borer is an organism that is capable of performing marine erosion, usually by a boring process. Such erosion may be limited to fairly local areas but is significant not only because of the way in which rocks become riddled with holes but also because many boulders, smaller stones, shells, and flakes of rock may be affected in this way. Particularly susceptible are soft limestones and sandstones. Borers abound in the sea and are particularly active in the shallow littoral zone. Boring algae are effective, and certain sponges attack rocks; some worms, chiefly the annelids, together with a variety of molluscs, excavate pits and tubes in rocks. Crustaceans and fish such as the eel often enlarge the cavities they tend to occupy. Serious damage may even be caused to timber and concrete structures, for example groynes.

bornhardt. See inselberg.

bornite. A red-brown copper mineral, Cu_5FeS_4, found in basic igneous rocks and vein deposits.

borolonite. See syenite.

boss. A roughly circular igneous intrusion that has a diameter of less than 25 km. Compare stock.

botryoidal. Denoting a mineral consisting of spheroidal aggregates resembling a bunch of grapes. Compare reniform.

bottom current. A current that flows close to the sea floor or within the lowermost layers of water in deep-sea areas. The term has also been used to describe the currents over shelf areas

that arise owing to density-driven flow, tidal flow, or wave-induced flow. In the case of deep-water bottom currents, flow velocities have been calculated theoretically, others have been measured using current meters or special floats. Bottom flow in part of the Antarctic bottom current can attain 3 cm/sec but is usually much less. The speed of the bottom current on the W flank of the Atlantic Ocean is, theoretically at least, between 0.5 to 2 cm/sec. Bottom topography may significantly hinder the flow of bottom water, for example the transverse ridges in the South Atlantic, which the Antarctic bottom current has to negotiate. Deep gashes or gaps through such features are important in channelling bottom flow. Some sub-Arctic bottom water has its progress southwards off the Labrador coast partially blocked by the Labrador submarine rise.

bottomset beds. See delta deposits.

bottom water. The lowermost layer of water in the sea, particularly the water masses that move slowly in deep ocean areas. Bottom water is relatively cold and dense. Most of the North Atlantic bottom water has a temperature around 1°-2° C. The Polar Antarctic bottom water originates in the surface layers of the Antarctic and later flows as a deep-water layer. During the autumn and early winter, the very cold shelf water sinks owing to convection, and slides down the continental slope to the abyssal depths. This happens especially in the Weddell Sea area. The deep water then spreads outwards, especially eastwards into the Southern Indian Ocean, though influenced by bottom topography. In contrast, the bulk of North Atlantic bottom water originates outside the Arctic.

boudinage. When a competent bed of rock is enclosed by incompetent material and is then stretched or squeezed, the competent bed breaks in a series of short sections, as it cannot deform plastically to the same extent as the incompetent material. As the competent layer deforms, it thins locally and *pinch and swell structures develop. On further stretching this thinning continues until necks are formed; finally the layer breaks. They were originally described as boudins by French geologists, to whom they resembled black sausages.

Bouguer anomaly. A gravity anomaly that takes into account the effect of topography but not isostatic compensation, first observed by P. Bouguer in 1735.

boulder clay. See till.

boundary current. A fairly fast-moving current that flows near the edge of an ocean, usually along its W flank. Theoretical models of oceanic flow, particularly that of Stommel, reveal that there should be a fairly localized current flowing at depth, in a southward direction, along the W flank of the Atlantic. The necessity for such currents arises from a consideration of pressure gradients within the oceans and the forces associated with earth rotation. Stommel's theory suggests that there should also be a current along the W flank of the Pacific Ocean, though not in this case everywhere directed southwards. Field measurements have demonstrated that in the case of the Atlantic, there is a south-flowing current underneath the Gulf Stream.

boundary layer. The layer of the atmosphere in which movement is closely determined by the presence of the ground surface. In practice, this layer is subdivided into the surface boundary layer, extending to approximately 100 m, and the planetary boundary layer, with an upper limit of about 600 m above the ground. In the former, the influence of the surface is paramount, whilst in the latter layer, it remains significant but not dominant.

boundary waves. See internal waves.

Bowen ratio. The ratio of the transfer of sensible heat from the ground surface to that of latent heat effected by the processes of turbulence and conduction. Over oceans, the value of this ratio can be as low as 0.1 indicating that 90% of the heat flux from the surface is in the form of latent heat. Desert areas represent the converse, with no latent heat component as all heat transfer is in the form of sensible heat.

Brachiopoda. A phylum of invertebrate animals having a body enclosed by two valves of a chitinous or calcareous material. Brachiopods are bilaterally symmetrical, but unlike the *Bivalvia the plane of symmetry passes across the valves, not between them. The valves are thus dissimilar but each is symmetrical about its left and right halves. The phylum is divided into two classes, the Inarticulata and the Articulata. In the latter the shells are connected by teeth and sockets along a hinge line. The shells of the Inarticulata are held together only by muscles. Brachiopods are marine benthonic animals attached to the substrate by a pedicle, which commonly protrudes through an opening in the larger valve (the pedicle valve). The other valve is called the brachial valve. It has an internal brachidium, which supports the structure responsible for maintaining a current of water for respiratory and feeding purposes. Brachiopods show variations in shell morphology and ornamentation that are valuable in taxonomic classification.

The earliest fossil brachiopods are known from Lower Cambrian rocks; they flourished throughout the Palaeozoic Era and were especially abundant and diverse in the Silurian and Devonian Periods. Many became extinct at the end of the Palaeozoic. There was a revival of a few groups in the Mesozoic but brachiopods are relatively insignificant today. They have been used in the stratigraphic classification of the rocks in which they occur.

brackish water. Water that is partly fresh and partly saline. Areas of such water occur, for instance, behind coastal barriers that partially inhibit tidal penetration, hence the incursion of saline water, but still allow the incursion of fresh water from streams and rivers. Such an area exists in the Fleet, a shallow lagoonal stretch of water behind Chesil Bank on the Dorset coast.

braiding. The division of a stream into a complex pattern of several small channels divided by mid-channel bars. After straight and meandering channels, braiding is the third major channel pattern a river can have. It is often due to lack of *competence or *capacity of the river to carry the load supplied to it. As a result the excess load is dumped in mid-channel to form the characteristic mid-channel bars that divide the channel into many separate sub-channels. In this form, it is often seen in the periglacial environment (*see* river terrace). Easily erodible banks and variable discharge are also said to favour braiding. Meandering patterns may change to braided patterns if the stream gradient or discharge is increased.

breaker. A mass of turbulent water moving landwards, as a result of the breaking of a wave on approaching the coast and reaching shallower water. The decrease in water depth causes a reduction in velocity of the wave, an increase in height, and a decrease in length. The orbital paths of water particles within the wave form also change, from open circles to open ellipses, until the water under the crest is moving faster than the wave form, at which point the wave breaks. Whether a breaker results in net accumulation or erosion of beach materials depends largely upon the nature of the breaking. The crest of a *plunging breaker* falls vertically into the trough, producing little *swash, but considerable *backwash. *Spilling breakers*, however, break forwards and the associated stronger swash aids con-

structive activity. *See also* constructive wave, destructive wave.

breaker (surf) zone. The strip of water along the shore in which breaking waves are actively dissipating their energy. They do this by a process that involves surface turbulence at a time when the waves or swell have become unstable and break. Usually this is because of their encountering very shallow water, but it may also be due to their meeting with opposing currents or wind. This complete breakdown of waves or swell must not be confused with breaking seas or so-called white horses, in which there is only partial collapse, at sea, of wave crests. The breaker zone is characteristically wide off gently sloping coasts and relatively narrow off steeply shelving coasts. The existence of banks and channels close to the coast further complicates this simple zonation.

breccia. A *rudaceous sedimentary rock in which the constituent clasts or fragments are angular. *Compare* conglomerate.

brickearth. Fine-grained unconsolidated deposits (sand, silt, and clay) associated with periglacial conditions in the Pleistocene. There are two types of brickearth. Aeolian loess consists of very well sorted material of predominantly silt size, picked up from glacial outwash, frost-shattered debris, or the floodplains of rivers, and transported by cold dry winds in steppelike conditions. The deposit is largely quartz, but with a mineralogy reflecting the rocks of origin, and forms a sheet over the pre-existing landscape when deposited in a wedge that thins away from the source. It is commonest in E Europe, but thin veneers reach SE England and East Anglia.

Overbank material deposited on floodplains by Pleistocene rivers is also termed brickearth. This type has a lower silt content than the wind-lain type, and is less well sorted.

brittle failure. The breaking of a rock whilst still within the elastic range.

brittle strength. The stress applied to a rock at the point at which it breaks within the elastic range.

bronzite. An orthorhombic *pyroxene.

bronzitite. A monomineralic ultramafic rock consisting wholly of bronzite.

brookite. A brown to black orthorhombic polymorph of TiO_2 found in hydrothermal vein deposits. *See also* anatase, rutile.

brown calcareous soils. Calcimorphic soils, typically found in the humid temperate regions of Europe and America under base-rich vegetation. Soil development is more advanced than in a rendzina, producing a soil with an A (B) C system of horizons. The soil is deeper, though rarely more than 70 cm, owing to its development over a parent material with a greater insoluble residue. An example of such a parent material in Great Britain is the Jurassic limestones of the Cotswolds. The upper part of the soil has a mull humus and is dark red/brown in colour with a neutral or slightly acid reaction. It has a crumb structure and is rich in organic matter. With depth the A horizon merges into an ill-defined B horizon, which is often lighter in colour and contains many fragments of parent material. They are good agricultural soils and fall into the *mollisol order of the Seventh Approximation.

brown clay. *See* red clay.

brown earth (brown forest soil). A type of soil ranging from a true brown earth, which exhibits only mild leaching, to a podzol, which exhibits extreme leaching. Brown earths are found to the south of the pozdol zone where precipitation is in excess of evaporation. True brown earths lack the distinctive horizonation of a podzol. Organic matter is rapidly formed owing to the deciduous forest vegetation being decomposed by the more abundant soil fauna. There is a thorough mixing of the mull humus into the A horizon. Carbonates are completely leached from the soil but there is no movement of the sesquioxides, as is shown by the constant silica : sesquioxide ratio down the profile. Consequently there is a weakly developed B horizon. These soils cover large areas of the middle latitudes, often forming on deposits of the Pleistocene glaciations. With their good crumb structure, mild acidity, and free drainage they are important agriculturally. *See also* acid brown soil, brown podzolic soil, sol lessivé.

brown podzolic soil. A soil that is transitional in location and properties between brown earths and podzols. They can be found in N and central Wales on well-drained middle slopes above lowland acid brown earths and below upland peaty podzols. An Ea (eluvial) horizon is still lacking but they are more acid in nature and have a lower base status than a brown earth. An increase in free iron oxide results in a loose crumb structured B horizon. These soils are also typical of the northeastern U.S. where they are found to the south of the true podzol zone. They fall into the *spodosol order of the Seventh Approximation.

brucite. A white or greenish mineral with a layered structure and composition $Mg(OH)_2$. It commonly occurs as a hydration product of periclase in thermally metamorphosed dolomites.

Brückner Cycle. A climatic cycle of about 35 years, which was deduced by Brückner in 1890 on the basis of non-instrumental data, such as harvests. He distinguished alternating warm and dry spells and cold and wet spells, but the cycle is not well defined and has too small an amplitude to have any forecasting value.

Bryozoa (Polyzoa). A phylum of small aquatic colonial invertebrate animals. A bryozoan colony, known as a *zooarium*, is made up of numerous polyps, each of which inhabits a small tube of calcareous or chitinous material. The colonies show great diversity in shape: many resemble seaweeds and are attached to the sea floor; others are encrusted on the hard parts of other animals or rocks. The two subphyla, the Entoprocta and Ectoprocta, are considered by many zoologists to be separate and distinct phyla. Fossils of the Ectoprocta are known from rocks of the Cambrian Period onwards and the group is still flourishing today. Ectoprocts have a potential use in micropalaeontological stratigraphy and correlation.

Buchan spells. Periods of the year when temperatures were anomalously cool or warm as deduced by Buchan working on 50 years of records prior to 1867 for SE Scotland. The periods of below-average temperature were 7-14 Feb., 11-14 April, 9-14 May, 29 June-4 July, 6-11Aug., and 6-13 Nov., and of above-average temperatures 12-15 July, 12-15 Aug., and 3-14 Dec. Whilst there is some evidence of such periodicities from year to year they are not sufficiently persistent or clearly defined to specific dates and so Buchan's spells are largely of climatological curiosity only.

Buchan zone. *See* zone (def.1).

bulk modulus. The ratio of compressive stress in rocks to the resulting change in volume.

buoyancy (in meteorology). The temperature difference between parcels of warm air and the surrounding cooler environment. Because air density is inversely proportional to air temperature, parcels or thermals of warm air have an upward acceleration through the cooler surroundings just as a cork rises through water because of its lower density. Where parts of the earth's surface are heated differentially, the warmer parts will heat the air in contact, which will then possess buoyancy relative to its surroundings. This is the basis of natural convection within the atmosphere.

buried topography. A pre-existing landscape that has been subsequently buried by younger strata.

butte. A small upstanding mass of rock, usually consisting of resistant capping material overlying some softer though protected rock type. It has steep sides and is produced as a result of long-continued back-wearing of a *mesa.

Buys Ballot's Law. A law stating that if an observer stands with his back to the wind, then pressure will be lower on his left hand side than to his right in the N hemisphere. For the S hemisphere the converse is true. This means that winds will blow in an anticlockwise manner around a depression in the N hemisphere, and vice versa in the S hemisphere.

bysmalith. A steep-sided vertical igneous body, roughly cylindrical in form and following a steeply inclined fault. It arches up the overlying country rock or becomes exposed at the surface.

bytownite. A calcic plagioclase *feldspar.

C

cadastral map. Usually a large-scale map, showing the boundaries of subdivisions of land. It is used for recording ownership of land.

Cainozoic. *See* Cenozoic.

calc-alkaline. Denoting igneous rocks that have relatively lower sodium and potassium contents and higher calcium contents for a given silica percentage than do *alkaline rocks. The calc-alkaline volcanic suite is represented by the association of basalt, andesite, and rhyolite in orogenic regions and island arcs.

calcarenite. A clastic *limestone of average grain size between that of *calcisiltite and *calcirudite. It is composed of particles between 0.06 mm and 2.0 mm in diameter. Calcarenites are subdivided into: very fine, between 0.06

and 0.12 mm; fine, from 0.12 mm to 0.25 mm; medium, from 0.25 mm to 0.5 mm; coarse, from 0.5 mm to 1.0 mm; very coarse, having diameters from 1.0 to 2.0 mm.

calcilutite. A clastic limestone of average grain size less than that of *calcisiltites, i.e. less than 0.004 mm in diameter.

calcimorphic soils. Alkaline soils occurring within broad climatic zones where parent material is the dominant factor in soil formation. The parent material is calcareous and its extreme nature resists any development towards acidity. Such soils are usually dark, organic-rich, and abundant in soil fauna. Two main soil types can be recognized belonging to this group: the rendzina and the brown calcareous soil.

calcirudite. A clastic limestone of average grain size larger than that of *calcarenites, i.e. greater than 2 mm in diameter.

calcisiltite. A clastic limestone of a grain size intermediate between that of *calcilutites and *calcarenites. It is formed of particles between 0.004 mm and 0.06 mm in diameter. Those of grades up to 0.03 mm are fine calcisiltites; those above this are coarse calcisiltites.

calcite. See carbonate minerals.

calcium carbonate (lime) (in oceanography). Calcium carbonate is present in seawater in a dissolved state and is also locked up in the skeletons and shells of marine organisms. The factors that determine the amount of lime dissolved in seawater are numerous and quite complex, and the theories relating to lime solution have not as yet been altogether satisfactorily explained. Much of the lime in seawater originates from river discharge. An analysis of marine deposits shows that, in general, neritic sediments tend to have a far lower lime content than pelagic deposits. Also, in general, lime present in surface waters of the sea is of low concentra-

tion, perhaps because of its consumption by minute plankton, while average lime concentrations near the sea floor increase markedly. For example, sediments in the Atlantic Ocean that lie below 3000 m are very lime-rich. However, while the low lime content at the sea surface is very marked at low latitudes, it is far less so at high latitudes.

caldera. A volcanic crater whose diameter exceeds one kilometre and can reach up to 20 km, generally resulting from the collapse or explosive removal of the top of a volcano.

Caledonian orogeny. The Lower Palaeozoic orogeny in which the Caledonian mountains, extending from Ireland via Scotland to Scandinavia, were formed. It resulted from the closure of the Proto-Atlantic Ocean, between the Baltic and Canadian Shields.

calibration (in stratigraphy). The determination of a rock sequence in relation to an independent time scale. This scale may be determined radiometrically or by correlation with another continuously operating undirectional non-reversible process such as *evolution, using the fossils contained in the rocks.

caliper log. A subsurface logging technique, which records the variations with depth in the diameter of an uncased bore hole.

calorie. A unit of heat now superseded by the joule. It was based on the amount of heat required to raise the temperature of 1 gram of water by 1°C. As this amount depended on the initial water temperature, the standard calorie was taken as that at 15°C, raising the water temperature from 14.5°C to 15.5°C. 1 cal (15°C) = 4.1855 joules.

cambering. An apparently increased dip towards valley bottoms found within horizontally bedded solid rocks located above weaker unconsolidated rocks, such as clays. This phenomenon, for which no clear explanation has yet been discovered, is characteristically seen in the iron-rich Jurassic sands of Northamptonshire.

Cambrian. The earliest period of *Phanerozoic time and of the *Palaeozoic Era. Rocks laid down during this period are the first to show an abundance of fossils, which consist of primitive representatives of most of the invertebrate animal phyla known today. The Cambrian began about 590 million yers ago, following the *Precambrian, and was succeeded after a period of some 75 million years by the *Ordovician. The Cambrian System is divided into Lower, Middle, and Upper. In Britain Cambrian rocks seem to represent a marine transgression across the underlying Precambrian strata, on which they rest unconformably. They consist of marine sandstones and silts, some of which, through metamorphism, have later become slates. The Cambrian of NW Scotland appears to be of relatively shallow water facies throughout the period.

Cambrian fossils represent the animals that lived in the seas of this period. Trilobites were especially abundant and are used in the stratigraphic subdivision of the system. Other important groups include the brachiopods (inarticulate species being dominant), gastropods, primitive echinoderms, and ostracods and there is evidence from *trace fossils of a variety of worms. Bivalves and graptolites had appeared by the end of the period.

Campbell-Stokes recorder. *See* sunshine recorder.

camptonite. *See* lamprophyre.

cancrinite. *See* feldspathoids.

canyon. A deep steep-sided section of a river valley, the depth of which considerably exceeds its width, normally found in arid or semiarid regions. They are usually produced where rivers have been deeply incised owing to *antecedence, or as a result of down-cutting by rivers whose sources are located in areas of greater precipitation than those in which the canyons are formed. This continuous external source of water enables efficient downward erosion to proceed, whilst the local lack of precipitation hinders weathering of the sides and hence their degradation. Many canyons are formed by erosion of horizontally bedded rock alternations, which produce a stepped valley crossprofile, owing to their differential resistances to erosion. Others are said to have been formed by cavern collapse or by the frozen ground and blocked valley phenomena of the Pleistocene. *See also* submarine canyon.

capacity. The maximum amount of sediment of a certain size that a stream can carry as bedload. This decreases as the grain size of the sediment becomes larger, but increases as stream gradient becomes steeper or discharge becomes greater. Since the transporting surface is the stream bed, the wider it is the more it can transport; to cancel this out capacity is usually expressed as a weight of sediment per unit width of bed. Even so, capacity is still very much a function of bed width, since for a given slope and discharge, the velocity at the bed is greater in a wide shallow stream than a narrow deep one. If the grain sizes being transported are a fair mixture of large and small, capacity varies with the third power of the velocity, with a lower power if the material is mostly coarse, and with a higher power if it is mostly fine.

capillarity (in soil science). The mechanism whereby capillary water moves vertically up the soil profile from the groundwater table or moist subsoil; it is a process typical of arid and semiarid zones where evaporation of water exceeds precipitation. It is more effective on clayey than sandy soils, with a maximum height of rise of 2.5 metres in clays, 0.7 m in sands. As the water rises it brings with it dissolved salts and these are precipitated at the point where the capillary "current" finally dries out, which may be at the soil surface or within the profile, forming a salt accumulation, e.g. in *solonetz and *solonchak soils. In arid zones subject to irrigation, excessive watering artificially accelerates the capillary currents, and formerly fertile areas can be ruined by the vast salt deposits that result.

capillary water (in soil science). Water held in the small pores within the soil, existing as a film around soil particles. It is this water that is mostly taken up by plant roots for plant growth, as opposed to the gravitational water that rapidly flows through the soil and removes plant nutrients during wet periods, and hygroscopic water, which is the water that remains in the soil even after air drying and is not available to plants.

capillary wave. A water wave whose length is less than one inch. Its speed of propagation is largely determined by the measure of surface tension that exists in the water, a force that tends to restore the water surface to a horizontal position. As with all sea waves, the generation of capillary waves requires the transference of energy from wind flow to the surface water in the sea. Capillary waves may develop, for instance, from the action of dropping a tiny stone into a pond.

carbonate minerals. The anion $(CO_3)^{2-}$ is the fundamental unit in the structure of the carbonates. The common rock-forming carbonate minerals fall into three sub-groups as follows:
1. *calcite*—$CaCO_3$, *magnesite*—$MgCO_3$, *siderite*—$FeCO_3$, *rhodocrosite*—$MnCO_3$.
2. *dolomite*—$CaMg(CO_3)_2$, *ankerite*—$CaFe(CO_3)_2$.
3. *aragonite*—$CaCO_3$, *strontianite*—$SrCO_3$, *witherite*—$BaCO_3$.
The calcite and dolomite minerals have trigonal symmetry. Dolomite results from the substitution of calcium ions in calcite by the divalent cations Mg^{2+} and Fe^{2+}, and there is continuous replacement of Mg^{2+} by Fe^{2+} between dolomite

and ankerite. Calcite and aragonite are polymorphs of calcium carbonate, the latter being orthorhombic and the higher-pressure form.

Calcite is usually colourless or white with a *hardness 3 and cleaves into perfect rhombs. Its extreme double refraction (see birefringence) is apparent in crystals of the transparent variety, Iceland spar. Calcite effervesces strongly in cold dilute HCl, other carbonates reacting weakly unless the acid is warmed.

Most limestones consist largely of calcite, which may be a primary precipitate or in the form of fossil shells. Calcite also occurs as a secondary cementing material in sediments. Veins and beds of fibrous calcite are called *beef*. During metamorphism, a pure limestone recrystallizes to form *marble* but if impure calcite reacts to produce such minerals as *diopside, wollastonite,* and *grossular garnet.* Calcite occurs in hydrothermal veins, in amygdales, and as a primary magmatic mineral in carbonatites.

Magnesite is white or colourless and occurs as an alteration product of magnesium-rich rocks under conditions in which carbon dioxide is available. Rhodocrosite is pink and is found in metasomatic veins and pegmatites. Siderite is usually brown and is a major constituent of bedded ironstones, an important iron ore. It is also found in hydrothermal veins.

Dolomite is colourless, white, or grey and may form as a primary precipitate. Dolomitization of calcite and aragonite takes place by reaction with magnesium-bearing sea water or by the permeation of magnesium-rich solutions along cracks and joints in limestones. During metamorphism, dolomite breaks down to produce periclase and brucite. Yellow brown ankerite is found with dolomite in hydrothermal veins and carbonatites.

Aragonite is colourless or white and is metastable at normal temperatures and pressures. Many shells are formed of aragonite, which in time undergoes recrystallization to calcite. Aragonite occurs as a primary precipitate and in amygdales. Strontianite and witherite are usually colourless, white, or yellow, occurring in hydrothermal veins and carbonatites.

The hydrated copper carbonates, *malachite* ($Cu_2(OH)_2CO_3$) and *azurite* ($Cu_3(CO_3)_2(OH)_2$), are bright green and bright blue respectively. Malachite has a banded botryoidal form and occurs with crystals of azurite in the oxidized zones of copper deposits.

carbonation. A process of chemical weathering that involves the dissolving of soluble rocks and minerals by weak carbonic acid, formed by the combination of water with carbon dioxide derived from the atmosphere or from soils. Carbonation is most effective on limestones, in which calcium carbonate is converted to calcium bicarbonate and is removed in solution.

carbonatite. An igneous rock composed chiefly of the carbonate minerals calcite, dolomite, and ankerite. Apatite and magnetite are common accessories together with the silicate minerals, alkali feldspar, nepheline, melilite, biotite, melanite, and sodic pyroxene. Certain elements, particularly niobium, barium, strontium, and the rare earths, are concentrated in carbonatites, which are often of economic importance. Carbonatites occur as central intrusive masses, dykes, and cone sheets in ijolite complexes and are often surrounded by zones of *fenitization. Such alkaline complexes are confined to stable continental regions, particularly those that have been subject to rifting.

carbon dioxide. A gas occupying only a small proportion of the atmosphere (0.05% by weight) but having very important consequences. It has the property of absorbing radiation in wavelengths similar to those emitted by the earth, thus it prevents the loss of much terrestrial radiation and maintains, together with water vapour, a higher temperature for the earth than would otherwise occur. It is vitally important in plant growth for the process of photosynthesis. The combustion of fossil fuel, such as coal and oil, releases carbon dioxide and so the amount in the atmosphere has been increasing since the Industrial Revolution. It is believed that this could have the effect of increasing radiation absorption and so raise the earth's mean temperature. However, the oceans are a great store of carbon dioxide and absorb much of the increase.

Carboniferous. The period of the *Palaeozoic Era that follows the *Devonian and precedes the *Permian. It began about 370 million years ago and lasted for some 90 million years. North American geologists divide this unit of time into two periods, the *Mississippian and *Pennsylvanian, corresponding approximately to the time represented by the Lower and Upper Carboniferous respectively. The lower part of the Carboniferous System, sometimes referred to as the Dinantian, is formed of two divisions, the Tournasian and Viséan Stages. The upper part, the Silesian, consists of the Namurian, Westphalian, and Stephanian Stages. Following a marine transgression, Lower Carboniferous environments in Britain appear to have been shallow seas. They supported a diverse fauna of Foraminifera, corals, Bryozoa, brachiopods, crinoids, blastoids, and other invertebrates, some of which contributed to reef-building. Limestone is so characteristic of this division that it is often called the Carboniferous Limestone, although deeper-water facies of shales and sandstones were also formed. Similarly the Upper Carboniferous may be divided into two major units, the Millstone Grit and the Coal Measures. They mark a return to more terrestrial and freshwater conditions, being composed of cyclothems of deltaic sandstones and shales with coal seams. The coal is especially prominent in the upper part of the division, being formed from vast forests of primitive land plants, such as the Pteridophyta. The

Upper Carboniferous contains fossils of freshwater bivalves, which are used stratigraphically. Fish remained abundant and amphibians became more common, some of them evolving into reptiles at the end of the period. The Variscan episode of orogenic movements began towards the end of the period.

Carboniferous Limestone. The lowest lithological division of the *Carboniferous System in Britain. It corresponds to the Lower Carboniferous (or Dinantian).

cardinal points. The four main points or directions of the compass: north, south, east, and west.

carnegieite. See feldspathoids.

carnelian. See silica minerals.

Carnivora. The order of the class *Mammalia that includes cats, dogs, bears, weasels, etc. Carnivores have teeth modified for eating flesh and a skeletal structure suited to rapid locomotion and the capture of prey. They evolved from the *Insectivora during the Palaeocene Epoch. Early Tertiary forms, classified as the Creodonta and now extinct, included the largest carnivores known, some having skulls up to one metre in length. Modern carnivore groups evolved during the late Eocene and Oligocene.

cartography. The technique of preparing maps and charts. This includes working from original surveys, photography, and other *compiled maps, covering every aspect of map production from carrying out surveys to final printing of the completed copies, including such problems as *map projections and research into all available information.

cartometric testing. A technique enabling a cartographer to assess the accuracy value of a map provided the map concerned is gridded. Accepted mathematical formulae are used to test the horizontal and vertical accuracy of the map against a control. The resultant answer gives the average deviation of the distances or elevations on the map from the true position or elevation on the ground.

cartouche. A panel on a map giving its title, scale, etc. The cartographers of the Dutch Renaissance and the Elizabethans specialized in highly decorative cartouches.

cascade fold. One of a series of minor folds developed on the limb of a major fold, as a result of gravity collapse.

cassiterite. A brown to black tin mineral, SnO_2, found in hydrothermal veins and metasomatic deposits associated with acid igneous rocks and in alluvial deposits.

cast. A type of fossil consisting of a *pseudomorph in which the skeletal parts of the organism have been dissolved and the resulting space replaced by a secondary material, producing a replica of the original form. In some cases a cast may preserve features of only the outer or inner surfaces of a structure such as a shell. These are known respectively as *external* and *internal casts*. Compare mould.

castle kopje. A type of *inselberg developed by *deep weathering and *exhumation in a rock divided by evenly spaced vertical and horizontal joints. Stacks of these fairly regular blocks give a castle-like stepped appearance. The term has also been applied to heaps of joint-blocks in haphazard arrangements, which have resulted from the collapse of other landforms or from the exhumation of isolated *corestones. Inselberg domes may degenerate into similar features following undercutting and collapse.

cataclasis. The deformation of rocks by the mechanical process of shearing and granulation. Such cataclastic rocks are said to have undergone dislocation metamorphism and range from coarsely broken breccias to intensely deformed mylonites.

catastrophism. The theory, now generally thought to be false, that past geological changes have occurred as a result of a number of sudden catastrophes (*compare* uniformitarianism). A succession of catastrophes was also invoked to explain the extinction of organisms, linked to special creations to account for the appearance of new forms.

catena. The regular repetition of a characteristic sequence of soil profiles associated with a particular topography in the tropics. Relief and drainage are the dominant controlling factors of formation. Milne first used the term when mapping the soils of East Africa. There has been confusion as to whether it refers to soils on a uniform lithology or whether it can be used where another soil-forming factor besides relief and drainage varies (the term *toposequence* is used in the latter instance).

cation exchange (in soil science). An internal chemical phenomenon in soils whereby a positively charged ion (cation) held on the surface of a colloid (either a clay or humus particle) can be exchanged for another cation present in the surrounding electrolyte. Cations include the soil bases, notably calcium, potassium, sodium, magnesium, and the acidity-inducing cations, notably hydrogen and aluminium. A typical example is for a calcium ion, held by its positive charge to the negatively charged surface of the colloid, to be replaced by hydrogen from the surrounding fluid. This makes the colloid more acid, the displaced calcium possibly being leached away. The cation exchange capacity of the soil is expressed in milli-equivalents per 100 grams of clay. This varies with different colloids: in the simplest most highly weathered clays (kaolin) it is lowest, perhaps 3-15 m.e./100 grams, reaching 80-100 in the 2:1 lattice clays (e.g. montmorillonite), and then highest of all, perhaps 200 + m.e./100g, in humus colloids.

cauldron. Any collapse structure of volcanic origin, as where a block of country rock sinks into the underlying magma. There are no limitations as to the size of the structure or the extent of subsequent erosion.

cavitation. One of the processes of fluvial erosion that characterizes the high-velocity parts of streams, such as waterfalls and rapids. It is relatively rare compared with the common processes of *corrosion and *abrasion, but very effective in terms of erosive power where it does occur, being largely responsible for the rapid destruction of waterfalls and rapids. Constriction of flow raises the velocity and kinetic energy of a stream, which is compensated by a decrease in the pressure of the water. This may lead to the formation of bubbles in the stream, which subsequently collapse, giving off severe shock waves when velocity decreases as the channel widens again and water pressure can rise. The stress produced by the collapsing bubbles exerts a severe stress on the channel walls, speeding up erosion.

cay (key). A fairly small sea island. It is generally low-lying, possibly displaying a little vegetation, and usually formed in sand or coral. The term as applied for example to tiny islands or islets off the South Florida coast refers to quite small coral shoals.

celestite (celestine). A strontium mineral, $SrSO_4$, that often occurs with gypsum. It is the principal source of strontium. *See also* barytes.

celsian. A barium feldspar mineral, $BaAl_2Si_2O_8$.

Celsius scale. A scale of temperature named after a Swedish astronomer who was the first to divide the interval between the freezing point and boiling point of water into 100 parts. Although it is more commonly known as the centigrade scale, an international agreement on units favoured the term Celsius.

Cenozoic (Cainozoic, Kainozoic). The era of geological time following the *Mesozoic and beginning about 65 million years ago. It includes the *Tertiary and *Quaternary Periods, although it is sometimes incorrectly referred to as being synonymous with the Tertiary. Following the extinction of most of the reptiles, the dominant animals of the Mesozoic, the previously insignificant mammals underwent evolutionary radiation into an abundant, diverse, and dominant group. For this reason the Cenozoic is often known as the age of mammals. Birds and flowering plants also flourished and the invertebrate types characteristic of the Mesozoic were replaced by essentially modern forms. The Alpine episode of orogenic activity extends into this era. See also chronostratigraphy (for table of the major divisions of geological time).

centigrade scale. See Celsius scale.

central meridian. The line of longitude that forms the axis of a map projection. Usually the central meridian is in the middle of the projection, as in the *Sanson-Flamsteed projection.

central-vent volcano. A volcano that has one central vent, around which there is a tendency for volcanic debris to accumulate into a roughly symmetrical cone.

centrifugal force. The apparent force acting outwards from the axis of rotation in a rotating system. Its magnitude is v^2/r where v is the linear velocity and r is the radius of curvature of the body's path, or $\omega^2 r$ where ω is the angular velocity of the body. This force is equal and opposite to the centripetal force, which tends to maintain the body in its curved path. In the atmosphere, these two forces operate when air is moving in a curved path relative to the ground surface (i.e. around a depression). It is also a part of the observed force of gravity, which is the resultant of the true gravitational attraction towards the earth's axis and the centrifugal force resulting from the earth's rotation.

However, the centrifugal acceleration is less than 1% of the acceleration of free fall.

centripetal acceleration. The acceleration of a body travelling in a curved path. It is equal and opposite to the *centrifugal force per unit mass.

centroclinal. Denoting a basin in which the rock strata all dip towards a central low point, characteristic of cratonic areas. See also pericline.

Cephalopoda. A class of the phylum *Mollusca whose members usually have an internal or external shell divided into chambers and a foot modified into a set of tentacles surrounding the mouth. All cephalopods are marine. They are usually subdivided into three groups: the *Nautiloidea, the extinct *Ammonoidea, and the Coleoidea (or Dibranchiata), which includes the modern squid and octopus and the extinct *Belemnoidea. Fossils of cephalopods are known from the Cambrian onwards and have been used as zone fossils.

chabazite. See zeolites.

chain. The main equipment used in chain surveying (see chaining), consisting of links of thick steel wire each connected to the next by three rings. Most chains now in use have an overall length of 20 metres, each individual link being 200 mm long from its centre to the centre of the middle connecting ring. Markers designate each whole metre, whilst those at five-metre intervals have a different colour.

chaining. A surveying method used for areas containing concentrated detail, such as urban areas, where high accuracy is required. The *chain is run out along a convenient line, the direction of which is obtained using a prismatic compass or theodolite. Points of detail are then fixed by measuring the perpendicular distance from the chain to the feature using a tape, these measurements being known as offsets. The distance along the chain and the length of the offset, for every detail point, are noted on the booking sheet. As an alternative to offsets, a point may be fixed by measuring two lines, known as *ties*, from different parts of the chain, thereby forming a triangle.

chalcedony. A uniformly coloured cryptocrystalline silica mineral.

chalcophile. *See* lithophile.

chalcopyrite. A brass-yellow copper mineral, $CuFeS_2$, found in hydrothermal and metasomatic veins and associated with the upper portions of acid igneous intrusions.

chalk. A very fine-grained pure white *limestone formed predominantly from *coccoliths, but including other invertebrate skeletal fragments. It is the characteristic rock of much of the upper *Cretaceous system in Western Europe.

chamosite. *See* chlorite.

Chandler wobble. The small measurable wobble of the earth with respect to its axis of rotation, discovered in 1891 and found to have a period of 14 months and an amplitude of $0°5'$. Its origin is unknown but it is assumed to be connected with earthquake activity.

charnockite. A rock that is mineralogically similar to leucocratic *granulites and contains hypersthene, quartz, and feldspar with or without garnet. Unlike granulites, the quartz does not occur in a platy flattened form. Basic varieties rich in plagioclase feldspar may be termed *enderbite*. The formation of charnockites is controversial but it is likely that they originate either by the crystallization of granite magma under high-grade metamorphic conditions or by the high-grade metamorphism of pre-existing igneous rocks.

chart. A specialized form of map used for navigation and other specific purposes, e.g. synoptic (weather) charts, star charts. The most common chart is the hydrographic chart.

chatter marks. 1. Crescentic fractures seen in hard rocks subjected to some time to the passage of *glacier ice. Although the convexity of these marks can point in either direction, a study of the fracture plane from which rock material has been removed will indicate the actual direction of former ice movement. The marks are believed to be created by the impact and rolling of boulders held loosely within the base of the glacier. **2.** The impact marks frequently seen on beach cobbles.

chelation (in soil science). The combination of sesquioxides with organic acids. Water passing through leaf litter acquires an extract from the organic material that is capable of combining with the metallic cations in the soil, notably iron and aluminium, to form a *chelate* of organic and metal constituents. Experiments suggest that leaf litter is a more powerful chelating agent than peat or humus, and that the process involved is one of reduction and solution that renders the metal more mobile. The chelating agent in the litter is easily extracted by water passing over it, but its strength varies between different types of litter, pine needles being amongst the most powerful. This is generally thought to be an important process in podzolization.

cheluviation. The combination of *chelation and *eluviation. Water with organic extracts forms a chelate with sesquioxides in the soil and then moves down through the profile carrying the sesquioxides in solution. It is most effective in moving iron and aluminium.

chemical weathering. The breakdown of solid rock through a number of chemical reactions, which may cause the removal of cements, resulting in weakness, or the formation of secondary minerals less resistant to erosion than those of the fresh rock. The different types of chemical action important in weathering are *carbonation, *hydration, *hydrolysis, *limestone solution, *oxidation, *reduction.

chernozem (black earth). A pedocal similar to a prairie soil. It is typically found in continental interiors, such as the Russian steppes, where there is an annual precipitation of approximately 500 mm with a slight rainfall maximum in summer. The process of calcification is dominant resulting in a soil with an A Cca C system of horizons (a B horizon is absent from true chernozems). The dark base-rich A horizon has mull humus resulting from the decomposition of the natural vegetation of grassland, incorporated to a considerable depth by rich faunal activity. This horizon may extend down to 100 cm before passing into the Cca horizon of calcium carbonate concretions. The parent material often resembles loess. These soils with their neutral to slightly acid reaction and their excellent crumb structure are agriculturally some of the most important in the world. They fall into the *mollisol order of the Seventh Approximation.

chert. *See* silica minerals.

chestnut soil. A pedocal typical in the Ukraine and the Great Plains of North America. Conditions here are more arid than in the chernozem belt and consequently the natural vegetation consists of a tussocky grass cover. These soils are much shallower than chernozems and horizonation is not so distinct. The A horizon is chestnut brown in colour and has a platy or prismatic rather than a crumb structure. This merges at about 25 cm into the B horizon, which is lighter in colour owing to the presence of calcium carbonate and often gypsum. The calcium carbonate may form a distinct concretionary horizon (Cca) at only 50 cm depth. This lies above the parent material, which is often loess. These soils in the American West are subject to severe wind erosion and are used mainly for grazing. They fall into the *mollisol order of the Seventh Approximation.

chevron fold. An accordian fold whose limbs are of equal length.

chiastolite. A variety of andalusite in which impurities are arranged in the form of a cross. *See* aluminium silicates.

china clay. Deposits of kaolinite produced by the weathering and hydrothermal alteration of feldspars in granitic rocks. *See* clay minerals.

chinook. A type of föhn wind found on the E slopes of the Rocky Mountains. It is named after an Indian tribe that lived near the mouth of the Columbia River and originally referred to a warm moist SW wind that blew across this area. Later it was used for a warm dry wind on the E slopes blowing from the Chinook region. It is now only used for the dry wind bringing sudden increases of temperature and very low humidities with rapid thaw conditions when snow is on the ground.

chlorite. The group of minerals having a general composition $(Mg,Al,Fe)_{12}$ $(Si,Al)_8O_{20}(OH)_{16}$. They are structurally similar to the micas and are composed of alternating layers of talc, $Y_6Z_8O_{20}(OH)_4$, and brucite, $Y_6(OH)_{12}$, where $Y = Mg, Al, Fe$ and $Z = Si, Al$. Chlorites are monoclinic and typically green or white in colour, They are common in low-grade metamorphic rocks, particularly those of the greenschist facies. Chlorites also occur as secondary minerals in igneous rocks owing to the hydrothermal alteration of ferromagnesian minerals such as pyriboles. Oxidized chlorites such as *chamosite*, which have a high content of iron, are found in argillaceous sediments as authigenic and detrital grains.

chloritoids. A group of dark green minerals with composition $(Fe^{2+},Mg)_2$ $Al(OH)_4Al_3O_2(SiO_4)_2$, having a structure made up of layers $(Fe^{2+},Mg)_4Al_2$ $O_4(OH)_8$ and Al_6O_{16} linked by SiO_4 tetrahedra. Chloritoid minerals are found in aluminium- and iron-rich low-grade metamorphosed argillaceous sediments.

Chondrichthyes. Cartilaginous jawed fish, including modern sharks and rays.

Because of the absence of bone good fossils are rare, although teeth are often preserved. The Chondrichthyes probably evolved from the *Placodermi and are almost exclusively marine. They first appeared in the late Devonian and continued to be important through the Mesozoic and Cenozoic to the present day. *Compare* Osteichthyes.

chondrite. A stony meteorite that contains chondrules. *Compare* achondrite.

chondrules. Small rounded bodies usually of olivine or enstatite found in stony meteorites.

chop. The sea surface under the influence of a fairly moderate breeze, with waves having pointed crests and steep slopes, quickly developing as the breeze mounts.

Chordata. The phylum of animals possessing, at least primitively, an internal skeletal rod, the *notochord*, running the length of the body. Members of this phylum include the *Vertebrata, which contribute significantly to the fossil record. Other subphyla consist predominantly of small soft-bodied sessile marine creatures, which are rarely preserved as fossils. Some of these have an active larval stage, and the evolution of vertebrates may have begun with the retention of the characteristics of the larvae into the adult state. The extinct *Graptolithina are also thought to have belonged to this phylum.

chorochromatic map. A map in which nonquantitative spatial distributions are shown by colour tinting (e.g. of coal-fields in an area).

chorographic map. A map on which regions are delineated, usually large regions, e.g. countries or continents. Atlases and small-scale wall maps, particularly those showing political divisions, come into this category.

choropleth map. A map showing quantitative spatial distributions (e.g. of population) calculated from average values per unit area.

chromite. *See* spinel.

chron. The smallest interval of geological time in the hierarchy of the Chronomeric Standard terms used in *chronostratigraphy. The equivalent Stratomeric Standard term, indicating the body of rock formed during this time, is the *chronozone. Chrons may be grouped together to form an *age.

chronomere (in chronostratigraphy). Any interval of geological time. Chronomeres are not of standard uniform duration.

chronostratigraphy. The branch of *stratigraphy linked to the concept of time, rather than being limited only to considerations of lithology and spatial distribution (*see* lithostratigraphy). There are two parallel hierarchies of formal terms. The *Chronomeric Standard* terms are applied to intervals of geological time; the *Stratomeric Standard* terms are applied to the bodies of rock laid down during these time intervals. The Chronomeric Standard hierarchy is as follows: eon, era, period, epoch, age, and chron; the major divisions of geological time are shown in the table. The Stratomeric Standard hierarchy of terms has no equivalents to the eon and era; it consists of the system, series, stage, and chronozone. The individual time intervals are not of standard duration and, similarly, the rock divisions are not of uniform magnitude. Some geologists regard chronostratigraphy as essentially identical to *biostratigraphy, while others insist on a formal separation of the concepts involved, regarding biostratigraphy as simply one method of calibrating chronostratigraphic scales.

chronotaxis. The occurrence of units of rocks of equivalent age in separate successions. These rock units are described as *chronotaxial*. Chronotaxis can rarely be demonstrated with cer-

Table of Major Divisions of Geological Time

Era	Period	Epoch	millions of years
		HOLOCENE	0·01
	QUATERNARY	PLEISTOCENE	1·8
		PLIOCENE	5·5
		MIOCENE	22·5
		OLIGOCENE	36
		EOCENE	53·5
CENOZOIC	TERTIARY	PALAEOCENE	65
	CRETACEOUS		135
	JURASSIC		200
MESOZOIC	TRIASSIC		240
	PERMIAN		280
(UPPER)	CARBONIFEROUS		370
	DEVONIAN		415
	SILURIAN		445
(LOWER)	ORDOVICIAN		515
PALAEOZOIC	CAMBRIAN		590
	PRECAMBRIAN Origin of Earth's crust		about 4500

tainty. *Compare* homotaxis. *See also* correlation.

chronozone. The smallest division of rock in the Standard Stratomeric scheme of stratigraphic classification (*see* chronostratigraphy). It indicates the body of rock that has formed during one *chron. Chronozones are defined at a particular *type section and should be named after geographical localities. At the *type locality a chronozone may correspond to a biostratigraphical *zone but other criteria are often used in calibration and in correlation with other areas.

chrysotile. *See* serpentine.

cinnabar. A bright red mercury ore mineral, HgS, found in veins and impregnations associated with volcanic rocks.

C.I.P.W. classification. *See* norm.

circulation index. A measure of the strength of the atmospheric circulation: used for any wind system, it commonly refers to the zonal component of the westerlies or the trade winds. *See also* general circulation of the atmosphere.

Circum-Pacific Belt. A narrow belt bordering the Pacific Ocean, in which 75% of the present earthquakes occur. It consists of igneous, metamorphic, and tectonically deformed sedimentary rocks.

Cirque (cross section)

cirque (corrie). A rounded rock basin, often containing a lake or *cirque

glacier, enclosed by high headwalls and sidewalls, which are steep and frequently frost-shattered. The floor is usually of smoothed striated rock and frequently has a deepened basin form, with an associated convex rock lip, which may be moraine-covered. Though varying considerably in size, many cirques possess roughly the same proportions having a length to height ratio of about 3:1.

It is believed that cirques can develop from any hollow in which snow can accumulate, but in many cases they have developed from pre-existing water-eroded features. The processes responsible for their creation include: *freeze-thaw action on the headwall, which enlarges the cirque overall; abrasion by rotationally slipping ice, which deepens the rock basin; joint block removal, which can act over the whole surface area. Cirques constitute some of the most characteristic features of glacial erosion.

cirque glacier. A small glacier found in a valley head or depression on a mountain slope. Being small, they can form quickly (within 100 years) and are usually the first glaciers to form and the last to disappear during a period of glaciation. The ice occurs in distinct bands reflecting successive years' accumulation of *firn. The ice tends to move downwards in the upper part (firn zone), parallel with the glacier surface in the central area, and upwards in the lowest zone, i.e. a rotational movement. This is because most accumulation occurs in the upper zone, beneath the headwall, whilst most melting is from the lower part. This results in over-steepening of the glacier surface, and in order to return to a more balanced shape, rotation occurs when the imbalance is sufficient to overcome friction between the ice and the bedrock. *See also* cirque.

cirrocumulus cloud. A cloud type indicating convection in the upper levels of the troposphere. Composed of ice crystals, the cloud has a mottled appearance consisting of small convective elements, often regularly arranged, with clear spaces between.

cirrostratus cloud. A thin high-level layer cloud composed of ice crystals. It is transparent and gives the impression of a veil spreading across the sky. During the day, cirrostratus clouds produce a halo effect, which can be seen quite clearly around the sun. They are usually the precursor of precipitation, heralding the approach of depressions.

cirrus cloud. A detached cloud in the form of a wispy streamer or filament of ice crystals. They occur at the higher levels of the troposphere, above 6000 metres, and with temperatures below $-25°C$. When they have a hooked appearance, they are known as *mare's tails* and signify rain.

citrine. See silica minerals.

clapotis. A *standing wave that is generally formed when the incident waves meet waves being reflected from a vertical barrier and where the depth of water in front of the barrier exceeds the wavelength of the incident waves. An interference pattern is set up, in which there is no horizontal travel of the standing wave crests. The incident waves generally approach the barrier, perhaps a seawall, breakwater, or vertical cliff-face, more or less head on, i.e. their crests are roughly parallel to the barrier. Occasionally, the same phenomenon occurs when waves approach a very steep beach, though in this case the amount of reflection is less.

class. A group in the taxonomic classification of organisms. Several related classes form a *phylum, and a class itself is composed of one or more *orders grouped together. For example, the Mammalia and Reptilia are two classes of the phylum Chordata. See taxonomy.

clastic sediments. Sediments consisting of fragments of broken rock (*clasts*) eroded and transported generally to a different site to be deposited. They include a wide range of sediment particle sizes from large boulders to fine-grained sediments such as silt. Such sediments are characteristic of coastal and shelf areas, and especially the littoral zone. The particle sizes may display wide and abrupt variations, for rarely are littoral or shelf sediments neatly sorted and graded, at least over large distances. Detrital sediments are often described as having a clastic structure. Clastic rocks (consolidated clastic sediments) include *sandstone and *shale.

clay. Particles of a size less than $1/256$ mm in diameter. They are usually small flaky *clay minerals formed during the weathering of other roks. The grade of particles immediately larger than clay is *silt. Together they form the *argillaceous division of clastic sediments.

clay minerals. Hydrous silicates, mainly of aluminium and magnesium, occurring as platy or fibrous crystals that have a layered structure and the ability to take up and lose water. They are the main constituents of argillaceous rocks and are responsible for the plastic properties of clay. Four main groups may be considered:
1. *Kaolinite group:* kaolinite, $Al_4(Si_4|O_{10})(OH)_8$, is produced during the weathering and hydrothermal alteration of feldspars and feldspathoids under acid conditions. The large-scale production of kaolinite by the alteration of granite gives rise to china clay deposits.
2. *Illite group:* illite and hydromicas are the dominant clay minerals in shales and mudstones and are derived from the alteration of micas and feldspars under alkaline conditions.
3. *Montmorillonite-smectite group:* these minerals are produced during the alteration of basic rocks under alkaline conditions and are the principal components of bentonite and fuller's earth.
4. *Vermiculite:* this mineral is produced during the hydrothermal alteration of biotite and also occurs at contacts where acid magma has intruded basic rock.

clay-with-flints. A common deposit of SE England, which varies in thickness from a few centimetres to several metres. It is found on chalk and is often overlain by plateau drift. Common characteristics are a rich reddish brown colour, a sticky texture, and the presence of numerous rounded and nodular flints. Two alternative theories of formation have been proposed, firstly that it is the residue left by chalk solution, and secondly that the clay from overlying pervious Eocene deposits has been leached down and redeposited around the flints of the dissolved chalk below. The first theory is doubtful as chalk is so pure that it would take more time than can be accounted for to form such a thickness. The second theory is upheld as the mineralogical assemblage of the clay-with-flints has been found to be identical to that of the Eocene Reading beds. It seems likely, therefore, that the widespread clay-with-flints were formed in Tertiary or interglacial times when humid conditions prevailed. See sol lessivé.

clear air turbulence (CAT). Sudden severe turbulence occasionally encountered by planes flying at high levels of the atmosphere, which is unconnected with the vertical turbulence of convection clouds. It appears to be the result of large vertical wind shears associated with high static stability. These conditions produce the effect of two unmixed layers and on the boundary between them this wavelike motion develops, producing billowing. Clear air turbulence can be seen by high-powered radar. See also Kelvin-Helmholtz instability.

cleat. A joint or system of joints developed within a coal seam. Generally two sets occur at right angles to each other, along which the coal fractures preferentially.

cleavage. The tendency of a rock to break into closely spaced planar structures or fractures as a result of deformation or metamorphism. See also fracture cleavage, flow cleavage, slaty cleavage, fan cleavage.
Cleavage in minerals refers to the tendency to split along planes of weakness in the molecular framework.

cleavage plane. The plane of fracture or a series of planar structures developed in a deformed or metamorphosed rock, along which it splits preferentially. Cleavage planes also occur in mineral cleavage.

cliff. A high steep rock face. Coastal cliffs are attacked at their base by wave action and above by subaerial weathering and erosional processes. The steepest cliffs are those formed in resistant massive rock types, such as granite, whereas softer rocks, being more susceptible to erosion by both waves and subaerial processes, retreat and degrade comparatively rapidly. As cliffs retreat a *wave-cut platform is frequently left projecting out to sea.
Abandoned cliffs were eroded at their base by waves at a time when sea level was some way above that of the present, as on the melting of the Pleistocene ice sheets, so that they now stand some distance from the sea.

climate. The synthesis of day-to-day *weather variations in a locality. The "normal" climatic conditions prevailing can be summarized, but since it is impossible to include the wide range of values in a single number and climate is not an unchanging feature, this method on its own is not a very satisfactory indicator of actual conditions.
Climate is usually taken to include the following weather elements: temperature, precipitation, humidity, sunshine, and wind velocity. Minor aspects include cloud amount, fog, snow, thunder, and gale frequencies. The major factors are summarized in terms of arithmetic averages for specific periods, usually based on at least 30 years of records. To indicate the range of values within the instrumental records, extremes are often quoted. More recently, greater emphasis

has been made on the factors determining climate.

On a large scale, the climate is determined by latitude, by altitude, and by location relative to the continental margins and the main circulation belts of the earth. On a smaller scale, more local factors can be important, such as aspect and degree of exposure to prevailing winds.

climatic changes. Climate is not static but constantly changes in response to variations in the factors that control it, primarily the nature of the main circulation belts. If records of temperature had been maintained for the past million years, it would be evident that throughout this period there were oscillations between warmer periods and cooler periods on a wide range of time scales. On a large scale there would be the swings between the *ice ages and the warmer *interglacial periods, continuing through the whole time spectrum to individual years. Most of the evidence for these changes comes from the nature of sediments deposited and the fauna and flora they contain, as it is obviously only relatively recently that documentary evidence and finally meteorological instruments give us more precise indicators of the prevailing climate. The diagram illustrates known changes of temperature in NW Europe in this period. During this period much smaller changes became apparent, which would not have been preserved by geological or biological evidence, so the curve is not based on consistent evidence.

The causes of climatic changes are not well understood and likely to prove very complex. The shorter-period fluctuations will probably have a different origin from the factors producing an ice age, but whilst mathematical models can show changes that could be produced by varying climatic controls, it is almost impossible to prove that any cause or combination of causes was the real reason for past climatic changes. Amongst probable factors influencing

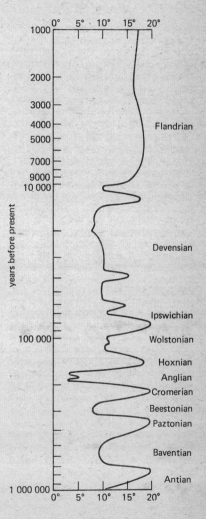

Changes in July mean temperature in
lowland England

the major changes are variations in solar output, the movement of continental positions to affect the oceanic circulation, mountain building, volcanic eruptions, and the increase in the carbon dioxide content of the atmosphere.

climatic classification. The climate of any individual site on the earth's surface is unique, but there are great similarities between many records. To rationalize the large amount of data from observing points, many attempts have been made to classify climates into a small number of categories based on specific factors of similarity. There are two main bases for classification, empirical and genetic, the former being based on analysis of the observations and the latter on the atmospheric circulations from which the climate results. Most systems have used the empirical approach, with the earlier ones linking this with vegetation boundaries.

The most popular classification, which is still used in a modified form, was proposed by Köppen in 1918. He adopted $50°F$ ($10°C$) and $64°F$ ($18°C$) as critical values to produce five major climatic categories incorporating precipitation regions too. These are (A) tropical rainy climates with an average temperature for every month above $18°C$, no cool season, and abundant precipitation that exceeds evaporation; (B) dry climates, where evaporation exceeds precipitation on average throughout the year; (C) humid mesothermal climates, where the coldest month has an average temperature less than $18°C$ but above $-3°C$, with at least one month having an average temperature above $10°C$; (D) humid microthermal, where the warmest month is above $10°C$ but the coldest below $-3°C$; (E) ice climates where the mean temperature of the warmest month is less than $10°C$. These are further subdivided into a large number of climatic types based upon seasonal temperature differences and variations in amount and distribution of precipitation. The simplicity of the system and its relationships with vegetation types have made this classification very popular although it does have limitations due to its arbitrary temperature boundaries.

A more detailed classification (see Thornthwaite classification) system was devised initially in 1933 and modified in 1948. This was based on two climatic factors, a moisture index and a thermal efficiency index, which are independent of any other geographical factor. However, the values were more difficult to calculate and, whilst frequently quoted as an example, the system is rarely used in practice. Individual aspects of the system, such as potential evapotranspiration, have been more fully developed.

Other empirical classifications have been proposed, some being based on man's physiological responses to climate in terms of wind speed, temperature, and humidity combinations, others on the relationship between the actual climate of a site and a stated ideal climate.

Genetic classifications are based on the atmospheric circulations that determine climate. Whilst being meteorologically sound, in terms of the resulting temperature and precipitation, quite varied weather conditions can be found within the same circulation belt and so such classifications have received little popular appeal.

climatic geomorphology. The branch of geomorphology concerning the role of climate in landscape evolution. Landscapes are a product of processes that are conditioned by climate, geology, and base level: of these three, climate is said to be the most important, such that by its control, areas of differing climate tend also to have different landforms. The concept is particularly popular amongst Continental geomorphologists: Tricart and Cailleux have elaborated it as an alternative to the Davisian *cycle of erosion concept, the difference being that the latter states that stage of evolution is the major factor determining the appearance of a landscape, while climatic geomorphology emphasizes that it is the processes operating, as conditioned by climate, that dictate the form of an area. The role of past climatic fluctuations in influencing the appearance of current landscapes is also involved.

climatic optimum. The period during which temperatures reached their highest levels within an interglacial stage of the Pleistocene period. The climatic optimum of the present interglacial occurred about 5000 years ago and is known as the *Atlantic period.

climatic region. An area of the earth's surface having relatively uniform climatic properties and usually determined through a climatic classification system.

climatic zone. The present distribution of climates on the earth's surface exhibits a measure of zonal symmetry with the boundaries running approximately along lines of latitude. Because of this, eight principal climatic zones have been distinguished within which there is a certain amount of homogeneity. These zones are the tropical rainy climate near the equator, the two steppe and desert areas north and south of the equator, the humid temperate zones, a Boreal climate in the N hemisphere, and the two polar zones.

climatograph. A circular diagram showing the seasonal temperature variations of an area in graphical form. (See diagram.)

climatology. The study of *climate. The emphasis on particular aspects of climatology has produced many subdivisions, such as applied, regional, physical, and synoptic climatology. *See also* meteorology.

climograph (climogram). A diagram in the form of a graph in which climatic features at any one place are plotted against each other, for example wet-bulb temperatures against relative humidities.

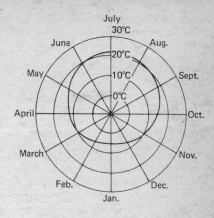

Mean monthly maximum temperatures at Kew (London)

Climatograph

clinopyroxene. *See* pyroxene.

clinozoisite. *See* epidote.

clint. *See* limestone pavement.

clintonite. *See* mica.

closed fold. A fold that has been compressed so much that both limbs are parallel.

closure. The distance between the highest point of a structure of folded rocks or structural traps and the lowest contour that totally encloses the structure. The closure determines the maximum area in which the structure can contain a fluid, e.g. oil.

cloud. A mixture of minute water droplets and ice crystals, or a combination of both, produced by condensation in the atmosphere. They remain suspended within the cloud because of their small size and only grow when conditions are favourable for precipitation. Lower clouds are usually composed almost entirely of supercooled water droplets, but with cooler temperatures ice crystals become more frequent until at temperatures below -40°C the cloud is entirely ice crystals. Almost all clouds are found within the troposphere and are the result of cooling. This can be brought about by convection, uplift over mountains, or large-scale ascent in depressions.

cloud base. The point at which the frequency of water droplets in the atmosphere becomes sufficient to reduce visibility to that characteristic of cloud. From the ground surface this appears to be a very rapid transition but in reality it represents a zone of transition. Cloud base indicates the level at which rising air reaches saturation and condensation results.

cloud classification. Various classifications of cloud have been proposed, but the one most commonly used is based on cloud appearance and height. The major groups are divided into ten genera following plant taxonomic classification, comprising cirrus (Ci), cirrostratus (Cs), cirrocumulus (Cc), altostratus (As), altocumulus (Ac), stratus (St), stratocumulus (Sc), cumulus (Cu), cumulonimbus (Cb), and nimbostratus (Ns). The determination of cloud species is based on the appearance of the cloud, on its structure, and if possible on the physical processes involved in its formation. 14 species names are commonly used and can be referred to more than one cloud genus: *fibratus*—applied to cirrus and cirrostratus clouds in the form of filaments but without tufts or hooks; *spissatus*—denoting dense opaque cirrus cloud, often originating from the cumulonimbus anvil; *uncinus*—denoting cirrus clouds that are hooked or comma-shaped and frequently parallel; *stratiformis*—spread out into an extensive horizontal layer, applied to altocumulus and stratocumulus clouds; *nebulosus*—exhibiting a nebulous veil with no distinct details, usually cirrostratus or altostratus; *lenticularis*—lens-shaped, with sharp margins (most commonly applied to altocumulus cloud of orographic origin); *castellanus*—having a castellated or crenellated appearance connected to a

common cloud base (altocumulus show this characteristic most frequently); *floccus*—having a ragged base and a small tuft or protuberance with cumuliform character above (cirrus, cirrocumulus, and altocumulus); *fractus*—denoting stratus or cumulus clouds with a broken and ragged appearance; *humilis*—denoting fair-weather cumulus clouds, showing small vertical development and sometimes flattened; *mediocris*—denoting cumulus clouds of intermediate vertical growth; *congestus*—denoting active and developing cumulus clouds, often with the appearance of a cauliflower; *calvus*—denoting an intermediate stage between cumulus and cumulonimbus in which no cirriform part can be distinguished; *capillatus*—denoting a cumulonimbus with distinct cirriform appearance frequently in the form of an anvil. If any further distinctive properties of arrangement or transparency are apparent then these are distinguished as varieties. In this way, three names could be used to classify a particular cloud. Cirriform clouds are normally above 5000 metres, alto-clouds from 2000-5000 m, and stratiform (St, Sc, Ns) at lower levels. Cumulus, cumulonimbus, and to some extent nimbostratus develop vertically and so do not fit this height classification very well.

cloud patterns. From satellite photographs it is evident that clouds exhibit a degree of large-scale organization that produces distinctive patterns. In the analysis of these photographs, patterns such as vortices, spirals, comma-shaped masses, wave clouds, lines, and striations may be distinguished.

cloud seeding. A method of trying to induce clouds to give precipitation. It attempts to simulate the natural precipitation mechanism either by adding dry ice (frozen carbon dioxide), which causes spontaneous freezing of water droplets and increases their rate of growth, or by adding silver iodide, which has a similar crystal lattice to ice

and so acts as ice nuclei to assist the natural processes.

Whilst some success has been apparent, it is difficult to prove that seeding can increase rainfall as the clouds that were seeded may have given rain naturally and the observed increases are not sufficient to disprove this possibility.

coal. A carbonaceous deposit formed from fossil plant remains. Coalification proceeds from partially decomposed vegetable matter such as peat, through lignite, sub-bituminous coal, bituminous coal, semi-bituminous coal, semi-anthracite, to anthracite. During this process the percentage of carbon increases and volatiles and moisture are gradually eliminated. These are all woody or humic coals. Another group are termed sapropelic coals, and these are derived from algae, spores, and finely divided plant material.

coalescence. The process operating in some clouds whereby cloud droplets increase in size, eventually forming raindrops. Collision is also important in this precipitation mechanism.

Coal Measures. The uppermost of the three lithological divisions of the *Carboniferous System in Britain. It corresponds to the upper half of the Upper Carboniferous.

coastal deposits. All the deposits found at any particular coastal location are derived from one or more of the following four sources: (1) the cliffs along the coast in that vicinity; (2) inland, transported by rivers or the wind; (3) offshore, moved landwards by wave action; (4) further along the coast, transported by *longshore drift (this material must at one time have been derived from one of the other three sources). The nature of the materials and their quantities will depend upon the rock types found along the coast and inland and upon their relative contributions. A whole range of deposits, from massive boulders through shingle and sand to fine clays, can be found in different coastal sites.

coastal plain. A gently sloping plain leading from the foot of inland upland areas down to the coast, and largely continuous with the continental shelf under the sea. They are formed by the continuous processes of erosion in the inland areas, transportation of material seawards, and its deposition either on land, near the coast, or out to sea. Some coastal plains have resulted from the comparatively recent emergence of parts of a flat continental shelf due to a relative fall in sea level.

coastline. The landward limit of the beach, the boundary between the coast and the shore, or the line that forms the boundary between the land and the water. Perhaps the simplest application of the term is to take the coastline as the extreme upper limit of direct wave action, which is the limit of storm wave swash during equinoctial spring tides. The term is also used to describe the type of coast as seen from a boat, for instance a rugged coastline.

coccoliths. Minute round calcareous plates that formed part of the protective covering of a group of unicellular organisms variously assigned to the Algae, Protozoa, or Protista. They have been reported from the Upper Cambrian but were more common in the Mesozoic, especially the Cretaceous, when they contributed largely to the formation of the Chalk.

Coelenterata. A phylum of simple multicellular animals that includes the jellyfish and *corals. They are aquatic, mainly marine, and may be colonial or solitary, attached or free swimming. In the most important of the two coelenterate subphyla there are two types of individual: the *polyp*, which is cylindrical and sedentary, and the *medusa*, which is disc-shaped and free-living.

This subphylum contains three classes: the *Hydrozoa, which have both polyps and medusae in their life cycle; the *Scyphozoa (jellyfish), which have only medusae, and the *Anthozoa (e.g. corals), which contains only polyps.

The corals are geologically the most important coelenterates as many of them are colonial, forming reefs, and possess hard parts, which can be preserved.

coesite. *See* silica minerals.

Fig.1: Anticyclonic col

Fig.2: Cyclonic col

Pressure patterns in a col

col. 1. A pattern of isobars resembling a geographical col or saddle, i.e. a shallow dip at a high level. A col that is elongated along the high-pressure axis is known as an *anticyclonic col*, and if along the low-pressure axis is called a *cyclonic col*. Winds are light in this type of pressure system but the pattern is rarely long-lasting.

2. A depression forming a pass over a mountain ridge or other high ground, commonly formed by back-to-back cirque development or from the beheading of a dip-slope valley in a cuesta formation by scarp retreat.

cold front. A concentrated thermal gradient whose movement is such that warm air is replaced by cold air. They are usually found to the rear of a depression and are associated with a sudden veer in the wind, often with a marked increase in speed, a fall of temperature, a belt of cloud, and

sometimes heavy precipitation. The front slopes upwards into the atmosphere at an angle of about 1 in 50. All these characteristics refer to the ideal front, and whilst most have somewhat similar properties, each individual will have slight differences. *See also* warm front.

cold glacier (polar glacier). A glacier within which the temperature remains so low that pressure-melting does not occur. In contrast to temperate glaciers these contain very little or no meltwater to act as a lubricant for movement. The glacier may remain static, being frozen to the bed rock, and requires great shear stress to induce movement, which will be very slow.

These glaciers contain very little *englacial material. However, cold glaciers have been found with large bed loads, and since these can only become accumulated as a result of basal freezing and thawing (*see* glacial plucking) it is believed that the erosion responsible may have taken place during a period of warmer climate.

cold pole. That location in each hemisphere where the lowest air temperatures have been measured. In the N hemisphere this is the area of NE Siberia where at both Verkojansk and Oimjakon, -68°C (-90°F) has been recorded. The mean January temperature at the former station is -51°C (-60°F), which represents the coldest spot on average.

In the S hemisphere, the high-altitude research stations on the Antartic Ice Plateau have the record with a temperature of -88.3°C (-126.9°F) at Vostok. Both cold poles are in areas where radiational cooling is extreme under clear skies and low relative humidity.

cold pool. An area of cold air within the atmosphere surrounded by air of higher temperature at that level. Because this usually leads to a steepening of the lapse rate, it may lead to instability and the development of showers.

colluvium (talus). The weathered debris (scree, mud, etc.) accumulated at the foot of a slope, which has originated from the erosion of the rock face above.

colony. An association of animals of the same species having structural and physiological connections between the individuals. Examples of colonial animals are the *Bryozoa and the reef-forming corals (see Anthozoa).

colour index. An index of the relative proportions of light and dark minerals in igneous rocks. The following divisions are made according to the percentage of dark minerals:
leucocratic 0-30%
mesocratic 30-60%
melanocratic 60-90%
hypermelanic 90-100%
The terms felsic and mafic are synonymous with light and dark minerals respectively. In nearly all cases dark minerals are ferromagnesian minerals.

columnar joints. A series of hexagonal or pentagonal joints resulting in columns of igneous rock, especially basalt lava. A good example is at Fingal's Cave, Staffa, Scotland.

comagmatic. Denoting a series of igneous rocks that are derived from the same original magma through the various processes of *differentiation.

comber. A wave travelling in deep water, which has a steep and high-breaking crest. The crests, much larger than whitecaps, are blown forward under powerful wind action. The term has also been applied to certain types of spilling breakers.

comfort index. A measure of climatic comfort experienced by man. It is assumed that the ideal comfort state is between 40 and 70% relative humidity and air temperature between 60°F and 80°F. The index is subjective in that individuals may prefer lower or higher temperatures depending upon their metabolism, but it does given an assessment of climate or weather conditions relative to an ideal state.

compensation level. A hypothetical level within the earth above which all columns of rock material having a unit cross-sectional area must have the same mass. See Pratt's hypothesis.

competence. 1. The largest size of grain that a stream can move as bed load. It is determined mostly by the stream velocity at the bed, which is controlled in turn by several factors, especially stream gradient, and the ratio between width and depth: bed velocity is higher, with other things equal, in a wide shallow river than a deep narrow one. With the larger grain sizes (coarse sand and gravel) there is a sixth-power relationship between velocity and competence. In any one river, competence varies with flood discharge over time; over space it varies with turbulence in the form of eddies rising from obstructions on the bed, which exert lift, momentarily increasing the maximum size of liftable debris.
2. The degree to which beds of rock can be folded without flowage or change in thickness. Such strata respond to deformation by fracture rather than flow.

compiled map. A map that is produced from other large-scale mapping rather than original survey work. Compiled maps are usually reductions of other maps to which selected amendments have been made before reduction.

complex. A complicated body of rock that cannot be designated by any of the other formal terms used in lithostratigraphy (see stratigraphy). A complex is usually composed of a variety of rock types and it may have distinctive structural characteristics. The term may also be used informally to refer to any complicated association of rocks.

composite log. The interpreted geological column encountered in a well, reconstructed from the evidence of geological sampling and electrical investigations carried out in the bore hole.

composite map. A map, usually compiled, that brings together for ease of comparison data usually portrayed on two or more maps, e.g. land use and population distribution.

composite volcano (strato-volcano). A volcano constructed of alternating layers of lava and pyroclastic deposits, generally developed by volcanoes with fairly viscous lavas, for example, andesites.

concentric dyke (ring dyke). A roughly circular vertical dyke developing when the circular fractures produced by the upward pressure of magma in a chamber are intruded by magma. The related structures known as *cone sheets* are developed by a similar stress distribution. They surround a point source (the intruding magma) and dip inwards towards it, having the form of a series of concentric conical sheets infilled by magma.

conchoidal. Denoting a type of curving fracture marked by concentric arcuate ridges. It is characteristic of minerals such as quartz and glassy and aphanitic rocks, particularly obsidian and phonolite.

concretion. A roughly spherical body of material precipitated from a solution.

condensation. The physical process of transformation from the vapour to the liquid state. In the atmosphere, condensation refers to the formation of liquid water from water vapour as a result of the atmosphere becoming saturated; for this to take place cooling must occur. If the atmosphere were absolutely pure, no condensation would take place until extreme supersaturation existed, but throughout the troposphere there are abundant nuclei on which condensation can take place on saturation. These nuclei consist of sea salts, industrial and natural smoke particles, as well as volcanic, soil, or desert dusts. On condensation, latent heat is released equivalent to about 600 calories (2500 joules) per gram of water, which reduces the rate of cooling.

condensation level. The level in the atmosphere at which condensation takes place. It is normally used for calculating *cloud base on a thermodynamic diagram, by simulating the lifting of air of known properties of temperature and humidity.

conditional instability. The state of a part of the atmosphere in which the *environmental lapse rate lies between the dry adiabatic and saturated adiabatic lapse rates. This means that if a parcel of air rises from the ground it will cool at the dry adiabatic lapse rate (DALR) and so remain cooler than the environment; under these conditions the atmosphere is stable. However, if the parcel reaches saturation it will then cool at a slower rate and could become warmer than the environment on further uplift, and so become unstable.

conduction. The mechanism by which heat is transferred through a substance by molecular motion without overall motion of the substance itself. Air is a very poor conductor of heat and this method of transfer is only relevant when the air is absolutely calm. This may occur very close to the ground surface, but in most studies of the atmosphere, conduction can be neglected.

conduit. *See* vent.

cone sheet. *See* concentric dyke.

confidence limits. A statistical concept used to assess the degree of confidence that can be attached to estimates of true means or standard deviations when based on only a sample of the data. For example, if the annual rainfall totals for a particular location are only known for 15 years, then the mean of this sample ($\bar{x}$) will probably differ from the true mean. By placing confidence limits it can be stated that with a 95% probability the true mean for this location will be $\bar{x} \pm 2y$, i.e. between $\bar{x} - 2y$ and $\bar{x} + 2y$, where y is the standard deviation of the data set.

confining pressure (in geophysics). The pressure exerted on a point resulting from the weight of the overlying rock or water column.

confluence. The rate of convergence or approach of one streamline to the adjacent streamline relative to the direction of flow. It differs from *convergence in that it does not imply an increase of mass but simply the approach of streamlines of air flow. *Compare* diffluence.

conformable. 1. Comprising an unbroken sequence of rock strata with no angular discordance between them, marking a continuous period of uninterrupted deposition. *Compare* unconformable.
2. *See* accordant.

conformal. *See* orthomorphic.

congelifraction. The weathering of rocks through the freezing of water within pore spaces. The accompanying expansion creates stresses, which result in fracture of the rock and its consequent disintegration. The effectiveness of the process varies considerably with rock type, being dependent on the size of the pores. If these are too large, or open to the surface, the water may be forced out as temperatures fall, whilst if they are too small, the water remains in a liquid state despite supercooling. The process is most effective in schists and certain limestones, notably chalk, within which very rapid shattering is possible.

congeliturbation. The movement of soil materials in the *periglacial environment, as a result of freezing and thawing of water contained within the soil. Freezing is accompanied by an expansion in the soil, but this is irregular since in a heterogeneous material water will not be evenly distributed. Similarly, thawing takes place at uneven rates, and the result is that particles are transported considerable distances, even on flat ground. On slopes, material migrates downslope under the influence of

gravity. The ice causing the disruption tends to be concentrated in the silt and sand fraction, coarser material being moved to the surface.

conglomerate. A *rudaceous sedimentary rock in which the constituent clasts or fragments are more or less well rounded. *Compare* breccia.

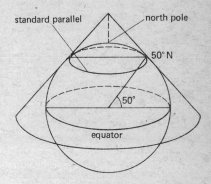

Simple conical projections

conical projection. A map projection produced by projecting the meridians and parallels onto a cone (see diagram). The centre of curvature of the cone is not one of the poles, though the meridians are drawn radiating from it. The parallels are concentric circles and are their true distance apart. The scale is only correct along the standard parallels; all others are too long. This projection is neither equal-area nor orthomorphic and is usually modified, e.g. *Bonne's and the conical with two standard parallels.

conjugate joints. A system of joints in rocks, in which the sets of joints are of related origin. It generally consists of two sets, which intersect at 90° but share a common dip or strike.

conodontophorida. Conodonts: small toothlike structures up to 2 mm long and composed of calcium phosphate. They are found in rocks of marine facies, especially shales, from Ordovician to Permian age and also in later strata, in which they are suspected as being *derived fossils. Because they are small, change in morphology through time, and are widely distributed, conodonts are particularly useful in the correlation and identification of the rocks in which they occur. They have been variously attributed to most phyla but their zoological affinities remain unknown (*see* species); their widespread distribution suggests that they may have belonged to a group of pelagic animals.

Conrad Discontinuity. A seismically detectable boundary within the earth's continental crust, separating it into a lower (basic) layer and an upper (granitic) layer. Beneath the ocean floors the upper layer is missing.

consequent stream. A stream whose course is dictated by the slope of the land. In the scarpland areas of southern and eastern Britain these streams often characterize dip slopes, and hence also conform to geology. *See also* obsequent stream, subsequent stream.

conservation of soils. The maintenance of high fertility and productivity to improve soil structure and so help to prevent soil erosion. Mechanical practices such as contour tillage, strip cropping, and terracing have been adopted to stop rill action and sheet wash. Where gullying is dominant, more stringent measures such as the building of dams are necessary. Soil conservation practices to prevent wind erosion include keeping the soil moist, roughening the surface, strip cropping, and the building of wind breaks.

conservative plate margin. *See* plate margin.

conservative property. A property of air that remains unaltered when affected by specified processes. For example, when air is cooling at the dry adiabatic lapse rate, its potential temperature remains constant and is therefore a conservative property under these conditions.

constancy of winds. An index of the degree of constancy of wind direction. It is measured by determining the ratio of the vector mean wind to the scalar wind, and converting to a percentage value. It ranges from 0 if all winds are equally strong and frequent in all directions to 100 if the winds are constant or unvarying in direction. For the British Isles, values of between 15 and 50 are typical, but in the trade wind zones it can approach 90.

Fig. 1: Initiation
Fig. 2: Growth of constant slope
Fig. 3: Domination of hill slope by constant slope

Fig. 4:
Wash of fines from constant slope evolves wash slope, which buries constant slope and ultimately dominates hill slope form
Stages of slope evolution

constant slope. The scree or talus slope, i.e. the foot slope produced by the accumulation of weathered rock debris from above. The evolution of the constant slope begins with a vertical rock face at the start of the cycle and at its peak it covers the free face and buries it. At this stage the constant slope, whose angle is defined by the *angle of rest of the debris of which it is composed, dominates and largely determines the hillslope form. Later on, the washing of fines from the constant slope leads to its burial by a wash slope, or alluvial toe-slope, which accumulates at the foot of the constant slope. *See also* colluvium.

constructive plate margin. *See* plate margin.

constructive wave. A wave that assists in the aggradation of a beach. For aggradation to occur the material moved landwards must exceed that moved seawards, so the *swash must be more efficient than the *backwash. For a powerful swash the waves must be flat, whilst their frequency cannot be too high, as the swash of a new wave would be interfered with by the preceding wave's backwash. The usual frequency of constructive waves is between six and eight per minute. *See also* destructive wave.

contact. The surface forming the boundary between adjacent and distinct bodies of rock. It may be conformable within a sedimentary succession, unconformable, or produced by intrusion or faulting. The recognition of contacts is fundamental to *lithostratigraphy and much geological interpretation.

contact (thermal) metamorphism. The changes resulting from the intrusion of hot magma into pre-existing cold country rock. The thermal effect of the magma causes a recrystallization of minerals in the country rock and the growth of new minerals. Contact metamorphic rocks have equigranular textures, have suffered little or no deformation, and in general do not possess any foliation. Thermal effects die out rapidly with increasing distance from the contact with the igneous rock. Sedimentary rocks are converted to hornfels, quartzite, and marble. Hornfels often contain porphyroblasts or spots of contact metamorphic minerals such as biotite, andalusite, cordierite, and garnet. With the exception of the expulsion of water from the country rocks, the metamorphism is largely an isochemical process.

Four facies of contact metamorphism are recognized:
albite-epidote hornfels facies
hornblende hornfels facies
pyroxene hornfels facies
sanidinite facies.

In an ideal metamorphic aureole, pyroxene hornfels rocks occur adjacent to the intrusion and pass into hornblende hornfels facies rocks farther from the contact. Inclusions of country rock caught up in the igneous magma reach the high temperatures associated with the sanidinite facies. Such rocks may become partially fused, resulting in the formation of glass, and are known as *buchites*. *See also* metamorphism, skarn.

continent. A large landmass, which rises more or less abruptly from the deep ocean floor. Associated with the exposed landmass are marginal areas (*continental shelves) that are shallowly submerged. The continents occupy about 30 per cent of the earth's surface.

continental borderland. A marine region adjacent to, or lying in place of, a continental shelf, and displaying marked topographic irregularity. A frequently quoted example lies off the coast of Southern California, a region of very diverse submarine morphology, which includes submarine ranges and basins. Some of the basins are quite deep. Often the adjacent landmass displays rather similar topography. The depths of continental borderlands are usually far in excess of the depths normally encountered over shelf areas.

continental climate. The generalized characteristic climate of continental interiors, implying a low precipitation total, a large annual range of temperature with warm summers and cold winters, and low relative humidities.

continental crust. The part of the earth's crust constituting the continents, often referred to as the *sial. It is composed of granite rocks and reaches a thickness in excess of 50 km under mountain regions, although it is generally only 33 km thick. The lower continental crust was formerly believed to be of basaltic composition, similar to that of the oceanic crust. It is now thought that it may simply be a more dense phase of the granitic rocks. *See also* oceanic crust.

continental drift. The movement of the continental blocks relative to one another across the surface of the earth, as a result of *sea-floor spreading. The hypothesis of continental drift was proposed almost 50 years ago, but it is only with the advent of the *plate tectonics theory that a viable mechanism was available to explain the movements of the continents. It is thought that the present continents were grouped together in pre-Mesozoic times into two large super-continents, Pangaea and Gondwanaland. These continents subsequently broke up to form the present continents. The presence of these supercontinents was based upon the work of Alfred Wegener in 1910. His evidence was only qualitative but included distributions of rock types, flora, fauna, geological structures, and similarity of the shape of the coastlines on either side of the Atlantic. Geophysicists of the time dismissed the hypotheses as impossible. However, in the late 1950-60s geophysical evidence supported the theory.

continental heat flow. The flow of heat reaching the surface of the earth in a continental as opposed to oceanic region.

continental margin (terrace). The combined continental shelf and slope zones, whose modes of origin are generally closely related. The depth range of the continental margin may, therefore, be taken as extending from the coast out to a depth of some 2000 metres. Some continental margins are of a constructional kind, others diastrophic. Warping, faulting, and long-continued sedimentation have been shown to have played dominant roles in their evolution. Deep seismic soundings have revealed that many have thick layers of sedimentary rocks overlying older basement rocks of a crystalline nature.

continental rise (apron). The submarine surface between the abyssal floor and the base of the continental slope. Together with the slope, the rise thus forms a separation zone between the continental shelves and the deep ocean basins. The surface of the rise is generally smooth, with gradients between 1:100 and 1:800. The minor irregularities rarely amount to more than 20 m or so in height or depth. The rise may be up to several hundred kilometres wide, for example off part of the North African coast where it is over 600 km wide. On the other hand, it may be virtually absent, as off the Bay of Biscay. In some areas, quite large seamounts are found on the rise.

continental shelf. That part of a continent that is shallowly submerged by the sea. It is a gently dipping area extending from the shoreline down to the continental slope at the *shelf edge, or to a depth of 200 metres if the slope is absent. The average shelf width is about 70 kilometres but shelves tend to be wide off low-lying regions and narrow off mountainous regions, varying from less than 1 to more than 1000 km wide. Average gradients tend to be steeper near the coast than over the outer shelf. Globally, shelves occupy some 7.6% of the ocean floor. Most shelves exhibit evidence of marine erosion, especially in shallow coastal waters. Some have carved within them valleys, troughs, and basins (*see* submarine canyon), often formed during low sea-level stands. Many are veneered with loose sediments that are being moved and sorted by wave and tidal action, and then moulded into tidal banks and channels.

continental slope. A portion of the continental margin, dipping more steeply than the continental shelf, with a gradient of more than one in forty, though this varies considerably. It is bounded by the continental shelf on the landward margin, and the continental rise on the seaward side. Globally, the continental slope zone makes up about

8.5% of the total ocean floor, but apart from some *submarine canyons that have been carefully explored and surveyed its precise form is not known. Where there is abundant sediment, especially mud, slumping and sliding is common and results in very irregular topography.

Fig. 1: Cross section of coast and hill to show contour lines

Fig. 2: Hill viewed as from above (as on maps)

Contours

contour. A line drawn on maps and charts joining points of the same elevation, above or below sea level (see diagram). This line enables the user of the map to determine the elevation and slope of the land or sea bed (contours below sea level are called submarine contours). Measurements may be in metres, feet, or fathoms (submarine).
See also contour interval, supplementary contour, hypsometric tinting.

contour interval. The difference in height between two consecutive index contours. The interval will depend on several factors: the scale of the map, the terrain the map portrays, and the purpose of the map. The scale of the map determines the maximum possible num-

ber of contours per area to retain clarity of detail; the terrain influences the number of contours required to depict accurately the true nature of the land (in level areas a few contours will show the land characteristics whereas in hilly areas more contours are needed to show the elevation variations within the area); the purpose of the map also affects the interval: plans for builders and land surveyors require the maximum number of contours per area to enable accurate measurements to be made.

contrail. Abbrev. for condensation trail. A trail of water droplets or ice crystals produced by the exhaust of a jet aircraft when the water vapour from the engine condenses and there is insufficient exhaust heat to revaporize it. The persistence of the trails depends upon the humidity conditions and wind shear, but normally they initially expand then slowly evaporate as mixing with drier air proceeds.
Some concern has been expressed about the effect of contrails on climate by reducing the input of solar radiation. Whilst being locally important, contrails rarely persist unless high-level cloud is already forming and the climatic effect is therefore small.

control point. A point on a map whose position and usually elevation are known. Control points form a network around which other map detail is plotted in its correct position, azimuth, and elevation.

Conulariidae. A family of fossil animals of uncertain zoological affinities. It has been suggested that they belong to the *Mollusca, the *Annelida, or the classes Hydrozoa or Scyphozoa of the *Coelenterata. Some authorities place them, with a few other similar groups of animals, in a separate and extinct phylum, the Conulariida. They occur in sediments of marine facies and typically have a skeleton constructed from four flat triangular plates joined at the edges to form an inverted four-sided pyramid.

The plates are formed of calcium phosphate and have an ornamentation of transverse ridges. Projections from the free basal edges of these plates fold over to protect the terminal opening. Conulariids are found in rocks dating from the Cambrian to the Triassic; in size they range from about 5 cm to over 20 cm.

convection. The most important form of heat transfer within the atmosphere. It takes place by the physical transfer of air resulting from density variations, warmer air being less dense than cool air. Two types of atmospheric convection are distinguished:
(1) free or natural convection, which is essentially the transfer of warm air from lower levels of the atmosphere through the mechanism of thermals or bubbles;
(2) forced convection, which is the vertical movement of air produced by mechanical rather than thermal forces, such as occurs through movement over uplands or irregular vegetation surfaces.

convection cell. A continuous convection system, air that rises being replaced by air from elsewhere. This can occur on a small scale with a single thermal or convection cell rising above a ploughed field heated by the sun. At the other extreme, the meridional circulation within the Tropics has been likened to a vast convection cell with zones of rising air and the trade winds linking the vertical parts of the cell. This system is called the *Hadley Cell.

convection current. A current within a fluid created by differences in temperature between layers causing differences in density. Convection currents are thought to operate in and beneath the oceans. They operate in the ocean when a portion of a water mass that is heavier than the water beneath it tends to sink, thereby being replaced by lighter water. In this context, the currents caused in such regions as the Red Sea and the Mediterranean Sea by excessive surface evaporation, increase in surface salinity, and consequent

sinking are claimed by some to constitute a convection current. Convection currents are also held, by some authorities, to occur within the earth mantle beneath the oceans. One suggestion is that the higher temperatures under the oceans at certain depths could be a consequence of convection flow that must be operating at some depth within the mantle. This could result in an increase in the temperature of certain parts of the ocean floor, such temperatures having been recorded. See *also* density current.

convective rain. Rain produced by the strong but localized vertical motion in convectional clouds found in an unstable atmosphere. This is usually produced from cumulonimbus clouds, but cumulus clouds may also give slight rain. Because of the intensity of the upward movement within the clouds, convective rainfall is normally heavy but restricted in distribution at any instant.

convergence. A measure of the rate of inflow of a fluid into a certain volume. The reverse state is *divergence. In the atmosphere, these terms are used to indicate the horizontal components of wind velocity: convergence indicates retardation and divergence indicates acceleration. Surface convergence is usually accompanied by upward air currents. In wave refraction phenomena, convergence refers to the bunching together of the various wave orthogonals in the direction of wave advance. Wave energy tends to be concentrated in a zone of convergence. In the case of opposing currents, a convergence is the boundary or zone at which these currents meet. Usually convergence zones experience the sinking of some ocean water to greater depths.

convergence zone. An area of the atmosphere in which convergence prevails and which is characterized by a belt of convectional clouds, often with rain. They can be found within otherwise uniform air streams giving a short period of heavy rain as they pass. The best known is the *intertropical convergence zone, which is frequently seen on satellite photographs and can extend for several thousand kilometres.

convergent evolution (convergence). The evolution of similar characters and structural modifications in organisms that are not closely related. For example, dolphins and ichthyosaurs, although only distantly related, have a very similar external form that is presumed to have been acquired through adaptation to similar environmental conditions. Convergent evolution also occurred in marsupial and placental mammalian groups, which were isolated on different landmasses but occupied similar habitats. Such organisms are known as homeomorphs.

convolute bedding. Highly disturbed, folded, or crumpled laminae that are found within a single well-defined sedimentary layer, resulting from deformation of the sediment by slumping, gliding, loading, upward expulsion of water, or the effect of passing eddies in the overlying water mass, whilst the sediment is still in an unlithified state.

coombe rock (head). A structureless deposit consisting of unweathered flints within a matrix of chalk mud and disintegrated chalk, resulting from *solifluction movements during the *Pleistocene period. The name is especially applied to the deposits found in the chalk areas of S England.

coordinates. Linear or angular quantities in a frame of reference such as a grid, by which positions of points on the map are determined.

coprolites. The fossilized faeces of an animal. Coprolites may contain other fossils, such as fragments of other animals, leaves, or pollen, that formed the diet of the creature concerned and they thus provide valuable information for palaeoecology.

coral. One of a group of animals belonging to the coelenterate class *Anthozoa. They secrete a hard calcareous skeleton and are important geologically in *biostratigraphy and because of their reef-building activities. See reef.

co-range lines. Lines drawn on certain hydrographic charts joining points of equal tidal range.

cordierite. An orthorhombic mineral, bluish in colour and of composition $Al_3(Mg,Fe^{2+})_2Si_5AlO_{18}$. The basal section of cordierite has a hexagonal outline and often shows concentric twinning. Cordierite is usually found in thermally metamorphosed argillaceous rocks, where it is associated with andalusite and biotite. It also occurs in some high-grade gneisses and rarely in gabbro that has been contaminated by argillaceous sediments.

core. The central sphere within the earth, separated into inner and outer units. The *inner core has the properties of a solid, whereas the *outer core prevents the passage of S-waves, suggesting that it is a liquid. It is composed of a mixture of iron and nickel, together with some dissolved silicon and sulphur, and is separated from the mantle above at a depth of 2900 kilometres beneath the earth's surface by the Weichert-Gutenberg Discontinuity.

core sampling. The collection of reasonably undisturbed sediment samples from the sea floor for oceanographic studies. The samples are corelike in form and can be split to yield a section of seabed material. A wide range of coring devices have been developed. Gravity cores drop under their own weight and drive themselves into the seabed. Piston cores are placed on the seabed and forced into it to retrieve a sample. In the case of hard-packed sand a vibro-corer may be used, the vibrator operating after the coring apparatus has reached the seabed. Some cores have been up to 20 metres in length.

corestone. A rounded hard block of rock within a matrix of soft decomposed material, occurring in well-jointed rocks, notably granites. When the jointed rocks are subjected to extensive weathering, it proceeds more rapidly in the joint areas, where water can penetrate, resulting in a series of corestones, but continued weathering will bring about their eventual disappearance. Individual corestones, however, may be especially resistant to weathering and these will remain as isolated unweathered blocks within a mass of incoherent weathered rock.

path of projectile
viewed from
ground surface

north
pole

path of projectile
viewed from space

direction of earth's rotation

Coriolis force

Coriolis force. A hypothetical force that is required to relate movement in the atmosphere to the rotating coordinate system of the earth's surface. For example, if a projectile was launched from the North Pole with a constant southward trajectory, from space it would appear to maintain this track. However, as the earth is rotating from west to east, to an observer on the ground surface it would appear to be constantly deviating to the right (see diagram). In Newtonian mechanics, a body will maintain its course unless acted on by other forces, so to explain this deflection the Coriolis force is introduced. Its magnitude is obtained from the equation $2\omega v \sin \phi$, where ω is the value of the earth's angular velocity, v is air

velocity, and ϕ the latitude. It therefore varies from zero at the equator to a maximum at the poles. Without the Coriolis force, wind flow would be at right angles to the pressure gradient, as found in equatorial areas, instead of being parallel to it. It is named after C. G. Coriolis, a French mathematician.

corona structure. The growth of a concentric mineral zone around a core mineral. The second mineral may be a *reaction rim or the result of *epitaxial growth upon the primary mineral.

corrasion. See abrasion.

correlation. A statistical technique that determines the degree of association between two sets of data. The most common method in climatology is to use the product moment correlation coefficient whose value ranges from $+1$ for a perfect direct relationship through zero for no association whatsoever to -1 for a perfect inverse correlation. The data must have a normal distribution for this coefficient, but others that do not have this constraint are available. The product moment coefficient is most frequently used for comparing rainfall values at different locations. The most famous was the work of Walker on Indian monsoon rainfall, who found significant associations between rainfall in India and sea-level pressure at various locations around the world.
In stratigraphy, correlation refers to the process of equating parts of isolated geological successions, usually in relation to time (see homotaxis, chronotaxis). Strata may be correlated on the basis of similarities in lithology or biostratigraphically on the basis of similar contained fossils. Other methods employ radiometric age determinations or palaeomagnetic information (see palaeomagnetic correlation).

corrie. See cirque.

corrosion. The process of erosion by chemical solution. All common rock-forming minerals are to some extent soluble in water, even quartz, generally considered to be highly resistant, and so removal in solution is a significant process. In humid areas, corrosion renders limestone one of the most easily eroded of rocks, while in arid zones, where water is lacking, limestone is highly resistant, demonstrating the effectiveness of corrosion. Rivers draining areas of organic materials, especially bogs, swamps, and marshes, are rich in organic acids, and these accelerate corrosive action. *See also* abrasion.

corundum. A mineral consisting essentially of aluminium oxide but minor amounts of other ions give rise to a variety of colours. The blue of sapphire is due to the presence of iron and titanium whereas the variety ruby contains chromium. Corundum occurs in some silica-poor igneous rocks such as nepheline-syenites. It is also found in hornfelses.

co-tidal lines. Lines drawn on certain hydrographic charts joining points at which average high water (or low water) occur simultaneously. These lines are often given as differences from the times of high (or low) water at a "standard port", or they may be expressed as time intervals after the time of the moon's transit. A *co-tidal chart* depicts both *co-range lines and co-tidal lines. In Britain, this information is embodied in the Admiralty Tide Tables, published annually, and on special hydrographic charts.

country rock. The pre-existing envelope of rocks into which an igneous magma is intruded. The country rock often shows the marked thermal effects of *contact metamorphism. Xenoliths contained in the solidified magma are usually derived from the country rock.

covellite. An indigo-blue copper mineral, CuS, found in metasomatic zones and hydrothermal veins.

crag and tail. A glacial erosion feature found in areas of relatively low relief, formed where a knob of particularly resistant rock exists on the floor of a

Crag and tail

valley beneath a glacier. This knob will cause deflection of the ice, protecting any less resistant rock behind it. The knob, which is invariably striated and fluted on the stoss end (facing the oncoming ice) is known as the crag, whilst the protected rock behind, which may also receive a covering of glacier-derived material, is known as the tail. Together they form a semi-streamlined form. These features only become visible on the disappearance of the ice.

crater. A large bowl-shaped depression in the earth's surface, resulting from volcanic activity, out-gassing, or the impact of meteorites.

craton. Any of those parts of the earth's crust that have been relatively stable (i.e. unaffected by orogenic activity) during the last 1000 million years, e.g. the Zambia nucleus of Africa. Frequently they represent the roots of deeply eroded ancient mountain chains.

creep. The slow movement of soil and rock debris down gentle slopes under the influence of gravity: it is the slowest of all the types of *mass movement, and it is not certain whether it is a flow, which is movement by internal deformation and overturning, or a slide whereby the whole mantle slips over the bedrock beneath. Current evidence rather supports the latter.
Creep occurs in all environments but is most important in the maritime periglacial areas, where it is of a type known as *solifluction. It is said to occur on all non-vegetated slopes of more than 5°, but in the areas subject to

solifluction it can occur on much gentler slopes.

Evidence of creep is commonly seen in structures such as tombstones and telegraph poles leaning upslope, as the material in which they stand has moved downslope. Many processes are involved, including freeze-thaw, wetting and drying, needle ice, and the preferential filling of cavities from upslope. It has been said that creep is the dominant process in shaping the convex parts of slopes. *See also* slope convexity.

crenulation cleavage. *See* strain-slip cleavage.

crepuscular rays. Optical phenomena of the lower atmosphere produced by the alternations of sunlight and shadow radiating from the sun, made visible by haze. The shadowing may be produced by gaps in low-level layer cloud, or by the irregular profile of convective cloud. A similar effect can sometimes be seen at sunset when the sun is just below the horizon and distinct rays are seen radiating from it, the dark bands indicating parts cut off from the sun's rays by clouds or hills.

Cretaceous. The final period of the *Mesozoic Era. Beginning about 135 million years ago and lasting about 70 million years, it follows the *Jurassic and precedes the *Tertiary (which marks the start of the Cenozoic Era). The lower part of the Cretaceous System consists of six Stages; the Ryazanian, Valangian, Hauterivian, Barremian, Aptian, and Albian. The six stages forming the Upper Cretaceous are the Cenomanian, Turonian, Coniacian, Santonian, Campanian, and Maestrichtian. Beginning with nonmarine deposits, the rocks of the Cretaceous System reflect a gradual marine transgression over Britain. Strata of sands and clays are followed by the characteristic Chalk, a pure fine-grained white limestone formed largely of planktonic **coccoliths. In the seas in which the coccoliths were deposited, bivalves, ammonites, belemnites,

echinoids, and bony fish also flourished. On land angiosperm plants appeared, and dinosaurs and other reptiles reached their peak of development. At the end of the period the ammonites and many other invertebrate groups and most of the reptiles became extinct.

crevasse. A crack of variable width in the surface ice of a glacier, caused by shear stresses set up by differential movements within the ice. These movements occur in *valley glaciers, the edges of which move more slowly than the centre, owing to the frictional effect of the valley sides. In this case crevasses form pointing up the glacier. Crevasses also occur where the ice moves over a steeper section of ground, in which case they are transverse to the valley. Despite the fact that their depths rarely exceed 30 metres, crevasses are very important since they assist in the downward penetration of both rock debris and meltwater.

crinanite. *See* alkali gabbro.

Crinoidea. The class of the phylum *Echinodermata that contains the sea lilies. They are typically sessile benthonic marine animals, consisting of a stem, formed of ossicles of calcite, which supports a cup (*calyx*) of calcite plates. On the upper side of this is a centrally placed mouth surrounded by five feathery arms that bear pinnae. These are used in food collection. Fossils are known from the Cambrian Period onwards and the class is still in existence today. Crinoids formed an important group in the Lower Carboniferous and contributed to the formation of bioherms and rocks. Most became extinct at the end of the Palaeozoic. Crinoids have been used biostratigraphically as *zone fossils.

cristobalite. *See* silica minerals.

critical angle. The angle of incidence of a ray which, if exceeded, will lead to total internal reflection.

73 **crystal form**

critical distance (in seismic refraction surveying). The distance between the source of seismic waves and that point in an upper rock horizon at which the arrival time of a direct wave is matched by the arrival time of a higher-velocity wave that has been refracted from a lower horizon.

crogball See ballstone.

cross bedding (cross stratification). The development of internal laminations within a stratum inclined at an oblique angle to the main bedding planes, resulting from changes in the direction of water or wind currents during deposition. It is most commonly developed in sandstones.

Crossopterygii. A group of bony fish (see Osteichthyes) whose sole present-day representative is the coelacanth. The group is important for having given rise to the *Amphibia and hence to all terrestrial vertebrates. Unlike most modern fish, the Crossopterygii had fleshy paired fins. They were common from the Devonian to the end of the Palaeozoic. Compare Actinopterygii.

cross profile. A transverse section of a river's channel or valley. A stream can adjust these parameters as well as its long profile in response to environmental changes. Valley cross profile can show such features as valley-in-valley forms, river terraces, extent of floodplains, symmetry or asymmetry of the valley-side slopes, angle of valley-side slopes, etc., all of which contain clues to the geomorphic history of the river and the region through which it flows. See also long profile.

crust. The outermost shell of the earth, varying in thickness from 5 km under the oceans to 60 km under mountain ranges. The lower boundary is marked by the Mohorovicic Discontinuity. The crust is composed of two units, the *sial (continental crust) and the *sima (oceanic crust).

Crustacea. A class of invertebrate animals of the phylum *Arthropoda, characterized by the presence of two pairs of antennae and one pair of mandibles. Crustaceans are almost exclusively aquatic and range in size from the large lobsters to almost microscopic forms. Included in the six subclasses are the *Ostracoda, important geologically in stratigraphic correlation, the Malacostraca (crabs and lobsters), and the Cirrepedia (barnacles). Fossil crustaceans, mostly ostracods, are known from the *Cambrian Period onwards.

cryoturbation. The modification of the soil through the processes of *congeliturbation and the effects of *needle ice in a periglacial environment.

cryptocrystalline. Denoting material that is crystalline yet so fine-grained that individual crystals cannot be resolved even under the microscope.

crystal. A chemical substance with a definite geometrical form, having plane faces at regular angles to each other, which is the expression of the regular arrangement of atoms composing the substance. See crystal system, crystal symmetry.

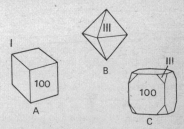

Crystal form

crystal form. A complete set of regular planes forming a crystal. The figure illustrates different forms found in the cubic *crystal system: A and B are simple crystal forms and C is a combination of the two forms cube and octahedron. The form exhibited by a crystalline mineral may be a great aid to identification.

Crystal habit   Crystal symmetry

crystal habit. The shape of a crystal arising from the shape and size of faces and the development of different forms. In the diagram the two crystals possess the same combination of crystal forms but A has a prismatic habit and B a pyramidal habit owing to the relative development of prism and pyramid faces.

crystalline rock. Rock formed by the process of crystallization, i.e. metamorphic and igneous rock.

crystallite. A microscopic embryonic crystal found in glassy rocks as a result of *devitrification. Crystallites have rodlike, stellate, or feathery forms.

crystallographic indices. A crystal face may be indexed according to a notation that depends upon the intercepts made by the face with the crystallographic axes. The distances along the axes from the origin to the points where the plane cuts are termed the intercepts. The ratios of the intercepts (referred to a standard parametral plane or axial ratio) are termed the parameters of that crystal face. According to the system of Miller, the reciprocals of the parameters of a crystal face are called the indices.

crystal symmetry. The crystal faces of minerals are symmetrically arranged and reflect the internal regularity of the atomic structure. Crystal symmetry is described by reference to the following elements:
1. plane of symmetry—a plane along which a crystal may be cut into two equal halves, one being the mirror image of the other (fig. 1).
2. axis of symmetry—a line about which a crystal may be rotated through 360° so that the crystal assumes a congruent position every 180°, 120°, 90°, or 60°. Such axes are termed *diad* (2-fold), *triad* (3-fold), *tetrad* (4-fold), and *hexad* (6-fold) axes respectively (fig. 2).
3. centre of symmetry—a central point about which every face and edge of a crystal is matched by one parallel to it on the opposite side of the crystal (fig. 3).
On the basis of these symmetry elements, 32 different crystal classes are recognized together with 7 *crystal systems.
cubic 4 triad axes
tetragonal 1 tetrad axis
hexagonal 1 hexad axis
trigonal 1 triad axis
orthorhombic 3 diad axes

monoclinic 1 diad axis
triclinic no axes.
Other symmetry elements may be
possessed by crystals in addition to
those listed. For example, a cube has
three tetrads, four triads, six diads, nine
symmetry planes, and one centre of
symmetry.

cubic

tetragonal

orthorhombic

triclinic

hexagonal and trigonal

monoclinic

Crystal systems

crystal system. A category of crystal
with reference to the position of the
crystal faces in relation to the intercepts
that the planes containing the faces
make with three (or four) axes, which
intersect at an origin. All crystals of the
32 different symmetry classes can be
referred to seven crystal systems as
follows (see diagram):
1. *cubic (isometric)*—3 orthogonal
tetrad axes of equal length, a_1, a_2, a_3.
2. *tetragonal*—3 orthogonal axes, 2

horizontal diads of equal length, and
one vertical tetrad, a_1, a_2, c.
3. *orthorhombic*—3 orthogonal diad
axes of unequal lengths, a, b, c.
4. *hexagonal*—4 axes, 3 horizontal diads
of equal length at 120° apart and one
vertical hexad at right angles, a_1, a_2, a_3,
c.
5. *trigonal*—4 axes, 3 horizontal diads of
equal length at 120° apart and one
vertical triad at right angles, a_1, a_2, a_3, c.
6. *monoclinic*—3 unequal axes, one
vertical, one horizontal diad, and a third
making an oblique angle with the plane
containing the other two, a, b, c.
7. *triclinic*—3 unequal axes, none at
right angles, a, b, c.
Different *crystal forms can be referred
to the same set of crystal axes and hence
belong to the same crystal system. For
example the cube, rhombdodecahedron,
and octahedron are different crystal
forms of the same cubic system.

crystal tuff. *See* pyroclastic rock.

crystal zoning. Many crystals, especially
in igneous rocks, are zoned such that
their composition changes systematic-
ally and gradually from the core of the
crystal to the rim. The succession of
zones reflects changes in the composition of the melt in which the crystal is
growing or changes in the physical
conditions as crystallization proceeds.

cubic (isometric). *See* crystal system.

Cuesta

cuesta. An asymmetrical ridge produced
by differential erosion of gently dipping
strata. A cuesta is characterized by its
steep scarp face, well-defined crest, and
gentle backslope, which largely con-

forms to the dip of the strata. It is constructed of a more resistant geology (e.g. sandstone or limestone) than the etched out clay vales at its foot. Good examples exist in the Weald.

culmination. The highest point on a structural feature. As the axis of a fold often undulates up and down, a series of culminations separated by depressions can develop. (See diagram at *fold*.)

cummingtonite. A monoclinic *amphibole.

cumulate rocks. Igneous rocks that are formed largely by the accumulation of early-formed *primary minerals that crystallize from a magma and sink under the influence of gravity to settle in layers on the floor of the magma chamber. Often the cumulus crystals trap small quantities of liquid in the interstices and this liquid subsequently crystallizes to produce intercumulus minerals. Cumulate rocks occur in large basic layered intrusions, often of lopolithic form. Monomineralic and bimineralic rocks are characteristic and cumulate dunites, peridotites, pyroxenites, anorthosites, and gabbros commonly occur.

cumulonimbus cloud. The main rain cloud of convective origin. It is heavy and dense with considerable vertical extent to give the appearance of a vast cauliflower, each protuberance being a tower of rapidly rising saturated air with velocities of up to 30 metres per second. At the top of the cloud there is often a more fibrous flattened cloud composed of ice crystals: this is the *anvil. Most thunderstorms are associated with this type of cloud.

cumulophyric. See glomerophyric.

cumulus cloud. A type of cloud indicating convectional activity extending above the *condensation level. Cumulus clouds range in vertical extent from shallow fair-weather cumulus clouds indicating weak convection topped by an inversion, to the much more extensive cumulus congestus, which almost approaches a cumulonimbus cloud in size.

cupola. A slender upward projection from a large igneous body into the overlying country rock. *See also* roof pendant.

cuprite. A red to black mineral, Cu_2O, found in oxidized copper deposits.

Curie point. The temperature above which permanent magnetism disappears. Each element has its own specific Curie point; in the case of iron it is $760°C$.

current (in oceanography). A horizontal flow of water, the movement affecting the whole water column or only a part or parts of it. The speed at which currents flow, and their direction, may vary markedly, or the current velocity may be remarkably constant in a temporal sense. Often variations are seasonal, or they may be due to changing meteorological factors. Permanent currents operate independently of the tides and weather, although they are indirectly affected by these. These include the general circulatory current systems in the oceans. Other currents flow on account of freshwater discharge from rivers, the action of waves and tidal motion, differences of seawater density, and wind-drag. All or certain of these currents may be superimposed, one upon the other. *See also* ocean current, density current.

current bedding. A sedimentary structure resulting from the action of either wind or water currents. It includes cross bedding and ripple bedding.

cusp. A crescentic-shaped mass of beach material, which may range from sand to quite large shingle or cobbles. The coarser material accumulates on the promontories or horns between the bays and the finer material in the bays. Cusps are regularly spaced and generally display coarser material than is found over the remainder of the beach surface. Those formed purely in sandy material are less common than those developed in shingle or in sand and shingle mixtures. They point down the beach towards the sea and the margin between coarser and finer material has a scalloped shape. They vary greatly in size, ranging between several centimetres in height to giant cusps or mega-cusps, such as those found on parts of the coast of West Africa. It seems that there exists a relationship between cusp spacing and swash length, and that a type of cellular water flow together with swash periodicity are important additional factors in their development, but their origin has yet to be explained satisfactorily. Waves breaking perpendicular to the beach are thought to be the most conducive to cusp formation.

cuspate delta. A *delta within which material is evenly deposited on either side of the river mouth. It is usually found on straight coasts where wave action is fairly strong.

cuspate foreland. An approximately triangular accumulation of beach materials, usually shingle, the apex of which extends out to sea and produces an irregularity in the coastal outline. Such forelands are created as a result of the combination of *spits or *beach ridges approaching each other from opposite directions, owing to the action of two major wave sets in the area, each being more active on one side of the foreland. The growth of these features can often be traced by the existence of many parallel shingle ridges. The maintenance of a sharp projection out to sea largely depends upon the presence of a nearby island or coastline, which provides shelter from direct frontal attack by destructive waves.

cut-off. See oxbow lake.

cut-off high. A warm anticyclone that has moved polewards from the main subtropical high-pressure belt, often producing *blocking in the westerlies. This system usually forms as a ridge in the upper westerly circulation and this intensifies into a cellular form becoming detached from the main flow like a

Cut-off high and low

meander (or oxbow lake) in a river. Its influence then extends downwards towards the surface. (See diagram.)

cut-off low. A low-pressure system of similar origin to the *cut-off high but extending towards the equator after developing from a trough in the upper westerly circulation. Cut-off lows frequently drift into the Mediterranean Sea area after cut-off has taken place further north.

cycle of erosion. A concept explaining the evolution of dissected land surfaces from uplifted areas of little relief to dissected landscapes and then to level surfaces (peneplains) via a series of stages (youth, maturity, and old age). The process is said to be cyclic since it will begin again on further uplift (see rejuvenation). The concept of strict erosional cycles is not now adhered to, since climatic changes mean that processes in any one area are not constant, and most landscapes have evidence of evolution under a series of cycles or parts of cycles of different climatic types as follows:
Arid.
The key to the cycle of arid erosion is the process of *pediment formation. Penck and King have developed this idea, and as a result arid lands are said to evolve by a process of slope retreat (see parallel retreat of slopes) not

decline, such that the trend is not the increase of relief to a maximum in maturity and thereafter increasingly subdued relief but decrease of the area of plateau and increase of the area of pediment. In youth the rivers incise themselves, and firstly retreat produces valley-side pediments; by maturity the divides have shrunk and the initial topography is nearly lost; by old age retreat of slopes has reached the point where divides are lost altogether, and pediments of individual basins coalesce to give the ultimate *pediplain.

Coastal.

This cycle, evolved by Johnson in 1919, differs on emergent (recently uplifted) and submergent (recently drowned) coasts. On both types, the general pattern is a simplification of coastal outline. In the emergent case, the coastline will be initially straight, with a shallow offshore slope. Waves break therefore offshore and build up a barrier island, with a lagoon behind. As the offshore profile is deepened, the island is attacked by larger waves which push it onshore, migrating over the lagoon, until at maturity the barrier is coterminous with the original coast. It then continues to migrate, eroding the shore, until at theoretical old age a plain of marine planation is created.

On a submergent coast, the initial outline is very complex, as existing drainage patterns are drowned. The headlands are subject to concentrated attack by refraction of waves, and as they are cut back spits begin to build out across the bays, eventually cutting them off and leading to their infill with waste. At submaturity the headlands are cut back and the bays closed; continued erosion pushes the coast to maturity, at which point the shoreline lies behind the heads of the initial drowned valleys. Thereafter the course is as in the emergent case.

Glacial.

The major process involved is the creation of cirques and the retreat of headwalls, destroying the preglacial landscape. Initiation involves the collection of snow fields and the creation of the cirques by nivation. Once created, headwall retreat eats into the original surface, eventually leaving only horned peaks and arêtes. Such features typify the passage from youth to maturity. By full maturity the main regional valleys are filled with ice, only the highest peaks projecting above the ice surface as *nunataks. The retreat of the headwall of the glacial valleys extending from the cirques eventually exceeds the rate of retreat of cirque headwalls, and the merging of the two marks the end of maturity. The old age phase has never been observed: as with the coastal cycle, only the phases of youth and maturity are well defined.

Normal (Davisian).

Developed by W. M. Davis in the latter part of the last century, this was an attempt to devise an orderly sequence for the evolution of landscapes under a humid temperate climate. The sequence involved is as follows:

1. Uplift initiates the stage of youth, when rivers begin to incise themselves into the landscape. Steep V-shaped valleys are separated by broad flat interfluves.

2. Maturity of the landscape, when widening of the river valleys has completely destroyed the original landscape and valleys meet at sharp interfluves. In the rivers, this stage occurs when the valleys are graded, and down-cutting is replaced mostly by side-cutting and floodplain creation.

3. By old age the landscape is subdued owing to *slope decline. The streams meander widely on broad floodplains, losing their adaptation to structure, a feature of maturity, due to its masking beneath debris. Only *monadnocks on rocks of great resistance in high divides rise above a peneplain.

Periglacial.

This scheme revolves around the role of frost shattering and solifluction. Originating on a dissected landscape, frost shattering attacks the valley-side slopes, producing a frost-shattered cliff, which migrates into the divide. The debris from the frost shattering is transported downslope by solifluction and meltwater to the valleys. As this process continues, the frost-shattered cliffs retreat until no solid rock remains. The scree slopes then dominate the landscape, being progressively flattened until by old age a landscape of faint relief is formed.

cyclogenesis. The initiation or development of a depression or cyclone.

cycloidal (trochoidal) wave. A wave with a flatter trough and a sharper crest than the typically smooth sinusoidal wave. It is a steep symmetrical wave with a crest angle of some 120°. The wave form is that of a cycloid or trochoid, i.e. a curve that would be described by a point rotating within a circle that itself was being rolled along a straight path. With an increase in wave steepness, the cycloidal wave sharpens its crest and increases its asymmetry. Because the flow is of a rotational type, no mass transport is possible (see mass transport currents).

cyclolysis. The process of decay or weakening of the cyclonic circulation around a low-pressure centre.

cyclone. An area of low pressure with a series of closed isobars, usually of circular or oval form, around its centre. In the N hemisphere, it is surrounded by an anticlockwise wind circulation and in the S hemisphere by a clockwise rotation, but both are known as cyclonic circulation for each respective hemisphere. *Compare* anticyclone.
In mid- and high latitudes, the cyclone is usually referred to as a *depression. In tropical areas, it is a storm system of great intensity with wind stronger than force 12 (Beaufort scale) and is synonymous with a hurricane or typhoon, though the nomenclature is not fully standardized. *See* tropical cyclone.

cyclostrophic winds. A class of winds in which there is extremely strong curvature of the airflow, such as a tropical cyclone or tornado. Under these condi-

tions, the centripetal acceleration becomes the major control of the gradient wind.

cyclothem. A series of sedimentary beds deposited as part of a single cycle. It is generally applied to Carboniferous strata, where the sequence begins with a sandstone layer, followed by shale and freshwater limestone. Above the limestone is a clay layer, above which rests a coal seam. Following the coal there is a return to marine conditions, with the deposition of a marine shale, followed by a marine limestone. Each cyclothem is separated from the next by a disconformity. The cycle represents an episode of emergence and erosion.

cylindrical equal-area (Lambert's) projection. A map projection drawn so that the scale along the equator is correct, but all the other parallels are exaggerated in length. The scale on the meridians decreases away from the equator, causing the parallels to become closer polewards. The projection is equal-area because the ratio between the meridians and parallels remains constant. It is seldom used outside the equatorial zones owing to the degree of distortion of shape north and south of about 40°.

Cylindrical projection

cylindrical projection. A map projection constructed as though a cylinder were placed around or cutting through the earth, onto which the relevant details are projected (see diagram), meridians and parallels being drawn as straight parallel lines. There are three basic types: the simple cylindrical, the equal-area (*Lambert's), and *Mercator's. In the simple cylindrical, the cylinder touches the earth at the equator, which has the effect of making the poles the same length as the equator and therefore causes considerable distortion in the higher latitudes. The scale along the meridians is correct, but directions are not true. It is a projection that is seldom used owing to the existence of more practical modified versions.

D

dacite. See rhyolite.

datum. The vertical datum is a horizontal line or a point used as the origin (zero) from which heights and depths are measured. On most maps and charts it is that of mean sea level, e.g. the *Ordnance Datum* (*O.D.*) of Ordnance Survey maps is mean sea level at Newlyn, Cornwall, calculated from tidal observations between 1915 and 1921. Horizontal datum is generally used in connection with geodetic information where it forms the basis for horizontal control. Horizontal datum is determined, using the reference spheroid, from bearings (azimuths) and longitude and latitude readings.

day. Astronomically, a *solar day* is the period of time between successive occasions on which the sun is in the meridian of any fixed place; the *sidereal day* is the time between succesive transits of a fixed distant star. As the earth varies in its rate of movement during its orbit round the sun, the solar day is not constant. The climatological day extends for a 24 hour period from 9 a.m. G.M.T. This is the time at which most climatological observations are made and so rainfall for April 21, for example, would in reality be the amount which

fell between 9 a.m. April 21 to 9 a.m. April 22.

debris load. That part of a river's total load carried as solid material. It includes material moving by suspension wholly above the bed, by *saltation, and by rolling and sliding along the bed. The total debris load is the sediment discharge of a river.
See also load, saltation.

decalcification (in soil science). The removal of lime from a soil. The process involved is carbonation, whereby rainwater percolating through humus becomes enriched with carbon dioxide, forming a powerful acid, which combines with calcium carbonate in the soil and carries it away in solution as calcium bicarbonate. It operates best at low temperatures, since the solubility of calcium carbonate decreases as temperature rises. If the content of carbon dioxide in the rainwater falls, then its ability to dissolve calcium also falls. Decalcification is said by some authors to precede *lessivage and *podzolization: in a given soil it influences the upper profile first, and so there is a point at increasing depth beyond which decalcification has not proceeded, called the *acid point.*

decile. If a series of values are ranked in order of magnitude they can be subdivided into any number of groups depending upon the amount of data. A decile represents a tenth part of the series and would normally be quoted as the first or second decile, etc.

declination. See angle of declination.

décollement. The plane marking the boundary between two different types of deformation. The rocks above are generally deformed, whereas those below may be unaffected. It is caused by the upper rock series sliding over the lower during folding.

decomposition. The weakening and break-up of a rock mass through *chemical weathering. A decomposed rock will lack its former cohesion owing to the washing away of cementing materials or the alteration of the constituent minerals.

deep ocean. One of the fundamental divisions or zones of the earth's surface. The total volume of deep oceans far exceeds the total volume of land lying above sea level. Also, the oceans are, in general, markedly deeper than the continents are high. The Pacific Ocean is the largest ocean, occupying, together with its adjacent seas, some 50% of the total ocean area, which is 361 million square kilometres. The Atlantic Ocean occupies roughly 106 million sq. km, and the Indian Ocean 75 million sq. km. The average depth of the deep oceans is 3800 m, with a large percentage of the oceans varying in depth between 3000 and 6000 m below sea level.

deep-sea trench. See trench.

deep weathering. Weathering at great depths, occurring when suitably porous, permeable, or chemically reactive rocks are subjected to humid tropical or subtropical weathering in areas where erosion is very slight. *Regoliths over 100 metres deep have frequently been reported and others up to and over 300 metres are known. There is a transition in all profiles from solid rock (at depth), through partly weathered rock (containing *corestones), to totally weathered material that has lost the former structures of the parent material. Evidence of deep weathering occurs in areas that are now totally unsuitable for its development, in which cases weathering is assumed to have occurred during former periods of warmer climate.

deflation. Wind removal of fine material (silt and clay) from areas of increased weathering. Typically, a chance depression in the desert surface increases moistness at that point, producing increased chemical weathering. This leads to clay formation. On drying, the clay is susceptible to wind action, and when picked up can be carried long distances in suspension, often in the form of

sandstorms. This fine material is dropped elsewhere, leaving behind a concentration of coarse material as a *deflation surface*. Deflation surfaces usually take the form of gravel-strewn areas, although this process can also produce large depressions, and sometimes oases may result. See also aeolian erosion.

deglaciation. The processes operating during an *interglacial period once climatic conditions begin to improve and the ice sheets that may have developed in the previous *glacial period start to shrink. Although considerable melting takes place at the margins, accumulation can still be maintained in the source zones, thereby continuing the transportation of debris by moving ice. Most melting takes place during the summer when the ice margins may recede towards the source or alternatively the whole ice mass may become shallower, resulting in the landforms characteristically created by stagnant ice. During the winter an ice sheet may remain static or even advance again slightly, causing deposition of *terminal moraines or *push moraines. Successive moraines may be distinguished in order to trace the recessional pattern of the ice sheet. The complete disappearance of an ice sheet may take thousands of years, whilst crustal adjustments and sea-level changes may continue long afterwards.

degradation. Although largely synonymous with *erosion, degradation is most usually applied to the lowering of stream beds over a time period measurable in years. It is not applied to the short-term cut and fill of stream beds extending over a period of a year or less, which is an integral part of the equilibrium régime of streams. Degradation can arise through a fall of sea level, causing *rejuvenation, or a change of flow conditions giving the river increased erosive power, such as decreased load or increased run-off. Evidence of degradation can be found in river terraces and knickpoints. *See also* aggradation.

degree. 1. A unit of measurement along the lines of latitude and longitude. One degree is equal to 1/360 of the earth's circumference on the lines of *longitude*. However, a degree of *latitude* decreases in length towards the poles. Each degree is subdivided into 60 minutes, and each minute into 60 seconds.
2. A unit of temperature. *See also* kelvin, absolute temperature, Celsius scale.

degree-day. The basic unit used for *accumulated temperature. It can refer to either degrees Fahrenheit or Celsius and is the number of degrees above (or below) a specified datum during the day.

delta. A large accumulation of sediment deposited at the mouth of a river where it discharges into the sea (or a lake). Deltas are formed as a result of the decrease in load-carrying capacity following the deceleration of river water on entering the comparatively static sea (or lake). Fine clay material, normally carried in suspension, is also deposited since the very small particles coagulate and sink in the presence of saline water. For the sediment to accumulate the amount of material deposited by the river must exceed that removed by coastal erosional processes. Deltas grow in size since the river tends to bifurcate once a certain amount of deposition has occurred; the smaller streams (distributaries) then deposit material over a wider area. They may become abandoned later, and that part of the delta no longer receiving sediment will become eroded. *See also* delta deposits, arcuate delta, bird's foot delta, cuspate delta.

delta deposits. Prior to the formation of a *delta proper, fine material is deposited on the seabed at the river mouth. These materials (*bottomset beds*) are laid down horizontally and extend a considerable way out to sea. Above these, and making up the major volume of the delta, are materials (*foreset beds*) deposited with an inclination from top to bottom of up to 35°; progressive deposits extend further out to sea and thereby cause enlargement of the delta. These beds are overlain by the *topset beds*, which are again horizontal and are a seaward extension of the river's alluvial floodplain.

demersal. Living on or near the seafloor. Flat fish, including plaice, halibut, and sole are specially adapted for life on the bottom, with special forms of camouflage. The other main types of demersal fish are the round fish, which include haddock, cod, and hake.

Dendritic drainage

dendritic drainage. The drainage pattern that develops where structural controls of slope, variable lithology, or fault and joint patterns are absent; as a result the drainage net is entirely random, with equal probability of stream flow in all directions. It characterizes areas of flat rocks with uniform lithology, notably plains, plateaux, and massive crystalline rocks. One example is the U.S. Great Plains, notably the Badlands of Dakota.

dendrochronology. The interpretation of former climates from changes in width of annual growth rings of certain tree species. By using the bristlecone pine, a long-lived conifer from the southwestern U.S., and preserved specimens, it is possible to go back as far as approximately 5000 BC. However, the width of the tree ring does not bear a simple linear relationship with one climatic factor, being related to an amalgam of many, of which temperature and amount of precipitation during its growing season are probably the most important. This limits the reliability of the method.

density. The mass of unit volume of a substance at a specified temperature and pressure. In the case of the atmosphere, density is not normally measured directly but is calculated from its relationships with temperature, pressure, and humidity through the *gas laws. For dry air at 1000 mb and 290 K, density is about 1.2 kg/m^3 (see diagram at *atmosphere*).

density current. A *current caused by differences in density. The density of a mass of water may become different from that of the surrounding water; if it is greater, the density-driven flow is usually a *bottom current or *underflow*. On the other hand, the density of a mass of water may be intermediate between that of the water above and beneath it, in which case the density-driven flow may develop as an *interflow*. A common cause of density-driven flow arises when relatively light fresh water discharging from a river rides out across and above heavier saline water entering from the sea; in this case, a saline wedge tends to drive upstream along the bed of the river or estuary, often transporting appreciable amounts of fine sediment.

density log. A subsurface logging technique, which records the variations with depth in the density of strata in an uncased bore hole.

denudation. The weathering of rocks, the entrainment of debris, and its subsequent transport and deposition. Denudation is highest in areas of high relief, heat, humidity, steep slopes, and rocks with abundant sediment yield. The highest rates of denudation recorded, reaching 3000 mm/1000 years, occur in glaciated areas; lowest rates, about 1.2 mm/1000 years, occur in hot dry lowlands. *Compare* erosion.

denudation chronology. The study of how a landscape has evolved through

time to its current state, by arranging in sequence the pieces of evidence discovered, to obtain a series of pictures of the evolution of the relief through a series of stages. For each major stage in the evolution of a regional landscape the following broad groups of features are researched. Climate, geology, and base level (the independent variables) dictate the geomorphological system, consisting of erosion, transport, and deposition. This leads to the creation of landforms, the remains of which constitute the basic research material. Partly reflecting the above factors and in turn influencing them are the flora and fauna. As flora and fauna reflect so many environmental variables, especially climate, their study in the form of pollen, insect, and mammalian remains is significant in environmental reconstruction. Once the type of environment is known, inference can often be made of the geomorphological processes operating.

Dating is done by various methods: organic matter of 60 000 years old or less can be dated by radiocarbon methods, and for greater time range other methods are available. Palaeobotany has been used to establish pollen zones through time, with similar changes occurring over wide areas allowing organic remains to be correlated between regions and assigned to a relative dating system.

Pedological methods can be used to study superficial deposits of past climates still preserved, e.g. the weathered granite of Dartmoor, which by analogy to present deposits can tell of the environment of origin.

deposition. The laying down of material subsequent to *erosion and *transport. Deposition could be described as the creative part of the geomorphological system.

In the fluid transport media of sea, rivers, and wind, deposition occurs when the forward movement and turbulence in the transporting medium falls below the settling velocity of the load, i.e. when the transporting medium lacks the *competence or *capacity to carry the load any further. Low-energy environments are therefore zones of deposition; in rivers, these occur on the inside of meander bends; on coasts, in bays and estuaries; in an air stream, in the lee of obstructions. All these environments are characterized by lack of strong upward eddies and divergent streamlines of flow.

In the solid transport medium of ice movement, most deposition occurs where changes in the climatic regime stop the advance of ice and lead to its stagnation and melting, rendering it incapable of transporting any further.

depression. 1. A mid-latitude *cyclone (*low*) or a weak *tropical cyclone with wind speeds of less than Force 6 (*Beaufort Scale). The term may also be used for smaller extratropical depressions not associated with surface fronts such as lee lows, thermal lows, or polar lows. However, its most common usage is for the main synoptic disturbances of mid-latitudes. These are areas of low pressure surrounded by several closed isobars, frequently accompanied by surface *fronts and moving towards the northeast in the N hemisphere and the southeast in the S hemisphere. They appear to undergo evolution during their movement eastwards, commencing as shallow lows with widely separated fronts (see diagram) and only moderate winds. With time the pressure at the centre of the depression falls with a strengthening of the winds and a narrowing of the warm sector. Eventually the warm sector disappears from the surface (the process being known as *occlusion), the central pressure starts rising, and the system begins to decay. This is the general pattern for depressions, but they vary appreciably in their intensity, size, direction of movement, and time of existence.

Depressions are the main source of precipitation in most lowland parts of the mid-latitudes, the amount falling being determined by distance to the depression centre, intensity of the depression, and the time taken for the depression to pass. As a result, the area of highest precipitation totals is about 50°–60° latitude where depressions are most frequent and at their most intense stage.

In the early stages of the depression, the troposphere is warm and the cyclonic

Depression evolution

circulation is shallow, but as it develops the troposphere cools and the cyclonic rotation extends to much greater heights. The origins of the depression have been disputed, but they appear to be due to *divergence in the upper atmosphere above suitable thermal gradients near the ground.
2. A structurally low area in the earth's crust, lying between culminations along a fold axis. *See* fold.

deranged drainage. A type of drainage pattern characteristic of recently glaciated areas, such as the Canadian Shield and Siberian tundra, where the drainage pattern has not yet adjusted to the structures in the relatively recent glacially deposited surface, which masks the previously adjusted drainage pattern developed on the solid geology beneath. As a result, drainage is not co-ordinated, and is characterized by many small local drainage basins and lakes.

derived fossil. A fossil that was originally preserved in a stratum older than that in which it is ultimately found, having become incorporated in the more recent stratum by processes of erosion and deposition. If its true nature is not suspected, misleading conclusions regarding age and stratigraphical relations of the deposit may be made.

desert. An area of the earth's surface where precipitation (usually taken as below 250 mm mean annual rainfall) is too low to compensate for evaporation throughout the year. This reduces the types of vegetation that can survive and the absence of surface runoff produces distinctive types of landform. The atmospheric state producing deserts is either a persistent high-pressure area, such as the subtropical anticyclones in the Sahara, or areas in which natural atmospheric stability is emphasized by surface cooling due to cold water ocean currents, such as the Humboldt and Benguela currents. Deserts are also found in continental interiors where mountain barriers prevent the passage of moisture-bearing winds; examples

are the Gobi Desert and the deserts of the southwestern U.S.
On the margins of a desert there are areas of climatic variability that experience true desert conditions in some years but not in others.
Soils are usually very poorly developed, stony, or saline (*see* sierozem). Weathering debris accumulates close to its source since surface drainage cannot be maintained. When rain does fall it is usually in the form of sudden downpours, which can cause brief surface runoff, moving considerable amounts of debris. Mechanical weathering is more important than chemical owing to the lack of water, and wind is a very active agent of erosion and transportation of fine material. Vast areas of unconsolidated sand and dunes are less typical of most deserts than stony scrublands with occasional resistant rock uplands.

desert pavement. An area of gravelly desert plain or *reg, over which the abrasive effect of wind-blown sand has created a closely packed level surface. The individual stones may be cemented together by precipitated salts drawn to the surface in solution by capillarity.

desert varnish. A thin coating, varying in colour from pale yellow to very dark red, found on the surfaces of pebbles and blocks in stony deserts. It is thought to be caused by the deposition of iron and manganese oxides from solutions drawn to the surface by capillarity and then evaporated. Highly polished surfaces of this type can occur through the extremely abrasive effect of fine sand carried by strong winds.

desiccation cracks (mud cracks, sun cracks). Cracks that develop in finegrained deposits as a result of shrinkage owing to the evaporation of the water they contain, producing polygonal patterns. These patterns are usually irregular and polygons can vary from a few millimetres up to a metre in diameter. Subsequent wetting of a dried-up sediment will cause swelling and the disappearance of the cracks. *Patterned ground may be maintained, however, if long-lasting cracks become infilled by some extraneous material, such as wind-blown sand. When preserved they act as useful indicators of palaeoenvironments and orientation.

desilication (in soil science). The removal of silica from a soil profile by intense weathering and leaching. The process is typical of tropical areas and leads to the development of *latosol profiles.

destructive plate margin. See plate margin.

destructive wave. A wave that moves more beach material seawards than landwards, resulting in a diminution in the size of the beach. Characteristic destructive waves are steep, so that on breaking their *backwash is more active than their *swash. They occur at high frequency, usually between 13 and 15 per minute, which means that the backwash of a preceding wave can interfere with the swash of the next, reducing the potential landward movement of material. Destructive waves frequently occur in association with local onshore winds, which cause the setting up of a seaward current on the sea floor, assisting in transporting the material stirred up by the breaking waves away from the beach.

detritus. Rock or mineral waste produced by the breaking up and wearing away of rock surfaces; debris.

deuteric changes. Small-scale textural and mineralogical changes brought about by a residual hot volatile phase during the final stages of crystallization of a magma. These include the alteration of feldspars to albite, analcime, and zeolites and the alteration of mafic minerals to chlorite. Deuteric changes are exceedingly difficult to distinguish from *metasomatic alteration when material is introduced from outside. Compare hydrothermal processes, pneumatolysis.

development equation. In the atmosphere there exists a high degree of compensation, so that the change in pressure observed at the surface is often only a small net effect between strong *divergence or *convergence in the surface layers and the reverse flow in the upper atmosphere. This will result in vertical motion to compensate for the changes. If there is divergence in the upper levels and convergence at the surface, the vertical motion will be upwards with the likelihood of precipitation.

The development equation, deduced by R. C. Sutcliffe, relates the difference in divergence between high and low levels to the thermal wind, vorticity, and the Coriolis force, the first two of which can be measured from charts and the last easily calculated. If the result is positive it implies cyclonic development and if negative anticyclonic development.

devitrification. The slow crystallization of natural volcanic glasses such as obsidian and pitchstone, which are metastable, often accompanied by secondary hydration. Devitrification is indicated by the presence of incipient *crystallites and *spherulitic growth of quartz and feldspar. The process often goes to completion and many rocks show little or no evidence of a former vitreous state.

Devonian. The first period of the Upper *Palaeozoic. Beginning about 415 million years ago and lasting for some 45 million years, it follows the *Silurian and is succeeded by the *Carboniferous. The Devonian System is divided into seven stages: the Gedinnian, Siegennian, and Emsian form the Lower Devonian, the Eifelian and Givetian the Middle, and the Frasnian and Famennian the Upper Devonian. These are divided on the basis of fossils from rocks of the shallow-water marine facies, where invertebrates such as corals, brachiopods, ammonoids, and crinoids flourished. Graptolites became completely extinct and the trilobites declined. Following the extensive Caledonian orogenic movements at the end of the Silurian, much of Britain was a land area during the Devonian. Extensive continental deposits accumulated, consisting of conglomerates, red silts, and sandstones. This facies is known as the Old Red Sandstone and contains remains of a large variety of ostracoderm fish. Gnathostome (jawed) fish, including placoderms, were also common. By the end of the period primitive amphibians had evolved from certain crossopterygian fishes. There is also evidence of land plants such as the Pteridophyta and of associated insects and spiders.

dew. Water droplets deposited on the ground after radiational cooling has reduced the temperature of the ground surface below the dew-point temperature of the air in contact with the surface. The source of the moisture may be either dewfall from the atmosphere during conditions of light wind and a downward transfer of water vapour to the ground, or diffusion of water vapour from the soil and condensation onto vegetation, which is also being cooled by long-wave radiation losses. The latter process only takes place when the air near the surface is calm, but is the most frequent source of dew in Britain.

dew-point. The temperature of air at which saturation will take place if the air is cooled whilst remaining at a constant pressure and moisture content. Although it can be measured directly, dew-point is normally determined indirectly from tables based on dry- and wet-bulb temperatures.

dew-pond. A shallow man-made depression lined with clay that collects water and is used in fields without running or piped water. They are particularly common on chalk or limestone rock. It was originally believed that their main source of water was dew as they appeared to be well maintained with water even during dry periods. However, later investigation showed conclusively that natural precipitation was most important and that dew was of minor significance.

dextral fault. A transcurrent (wrench or tear) fault in which the rocks on the opposite side of the fault plane are offset to the right. See diagram at *fault*. *Compare* sinistral fault.

diabase. A synonym for *dolerite used particularly by North American geologists. In Britain the term has been used to refer to altered dolerite.

diabatic. Denoting a thermodynamic process in which heat enters or leaves a system. There are many examples of this in the atmosphere, such as evaporation, turbulent mixing, and radiation absorption. *Compare* adiabatic.

diachronism. The condition of a lithological unit whose base is not a time plane, i.e. whose age is different in different successions. Diachronism occurs when the boundaries of facies move in time. It can often be detected only if suitable zone fossils are available, and failure to recognize diachronism can lead to false impressions of past events and geography.

diagenesis. A collection of processes by which loose accumulated sedimentary material becomes sedimentary rock. Diagenetic processes are post-depositional. In time, the pressure on a sediment increases owing to the increasing load of superposed material, and compaction results, involving a reduction of pore space. Chemical reactions take place between the sediment and entrapped and circulating fluids, leading to the cementation of grains by materials precipitated from the fluids. Calcite, silica, and hydrated iron oxides are common cementing materials. The diagenetic replacement of calcite by dolomite may take place in calcareous marine sediments. Such processes taking place near the earth's surface at low temperatures and pressures ultimately lead to the induration of loose aggregates and to lithification. Diagenetic changes grade into those taking place at higher temperatures within the domain of *metamorphism.

diallage. A mineral name for diopside and augite when displaying *schiller.

diamond. A cubic crystalline form of carbon found in *kimberlite pipes.

diapirism. The upward intrusion of a less dense rock mass through overlying more dense rock. It was originally applied to salt domes, but is also an important mechanism for the inplacement of granitic rock types.

diastem. A depositional break of a very short time period, with or without erosion. The beds above and below the bed have the same dip and strike. The absence of beds can only be determined by palaeontological evidence.

diastrophism. Movement within the lithosphere, including folding, faulting, orogenesis, and the formation of new ocean floor, causing large-scale deformation of the earth's crust.

diatomite. A very fine-gained siliceous rock consisting of the skeletal remains of *diatoms. They are formed under both freshwater and marine conditions.

diatom ooze. A deep-sea siliceous ooze (see pelagic ooze), containing over 30 per cent organisms. It is a cold-water deposit, especially prominent in an elongated belt in the N Pacific Ocean and flanking Antartica. On a global scale, it occupies some 9% of the total ocean floor. Living diatoms consist of siliceous algal plants belonging to the phytoplankton. They thrive in zones of upwelling water, where nutrients are abundant.

diatoms. Microscopic marine or freshwater plants classified as a subdivision of the *Algae. They form an important constituent of plankton, providing food for a great variety of aquatic animals. Their geological importance derives from the fact that many diatoms possess a case of silica, which may become fossilized, and fossilized diatoms often form extensive deposits (see diatomite). The earliest diatoms are found in rocks of Cretaceous age.

diatreme. A volcanic vent, often filled by brecciated material, that has been cut from the sides of the conduit by high-pressure gas charged with particles. The best known examples are the diamond-bearing kimberlite pipes of South Africa.

differential compaction. The reduction in volume of sediments during compaction to different degrees, depending on their porosity, grain size, and the rigidity of the particles that compose the rock. For example, shales are more compressed than sandstones.

differential erosion. The erosion of rocks subject to differential weathering. Well-weathered rocks are obviously more susceptible to subsequent erosion than resistant types. After a period of active erosion, easily weathered rocks will form lowland areas, whilst resistant strata remain as upstanding blocks. Even within a single rock type certain bands may be more or less resistant than the main mass, resulting in ridges and depressions respectively. *Tors and *inselbergs represent good examples of differential weathering and erosion within homogeneous rocks, different joint spacings accounting for the varied susceptibility.

differential shear. A type of rock deformation in which movement takes place throughout the whole rock, just as in a flow, but it occurs in distinct laminae or planes.

differential weathering. The more intensive weathering of certain parts of a rock mass even when the same weathering processes have been acting on the whole mass for the same length of time. Within many theoretically homogeneous rocks there may be variations in mineral composition or grain size, which can explain such differences. Joints play an important part, especially in the case of rocks with low porosity, as the percolation of water through them causes preferential weathering around the joints. There will be differential weathering between different rock types subjected to the same weathering processes.

differentiation. *See* magmatic differentiation, metamorphic differentiation.

diffluence. The rate of separation of adjacent streamlines in the direction of airflow. It is the reverse of *confluence.*

diffusion. The slow process by which different fluids or fluids having different densities mix together as a result of molecular movements. It obeys similar laws to thermal conduction but is too slow to be of importance in the atmosphere. Far more important is mixing achieved by eddy transfer (*eddy diffusion) in turbulent air.

dilation dyke. A discordant igneous intrusion that causes the walls on either side of a fracture to move apart. The term is also applied to swarms of dykes that have filled fractures in the earth's crust when the area has been subjected to tensional forces.

dinosaurs. A group of extinct archosaur reptiles that were the dominant form of terrestrial life from the end of the Triassic period to the Cretaceous. They evolved into a great variety of both carnivorous and herbivorous species, some of very large size. They are classified in two orders: the *Ornithischia and the *Saurischia.

diopside. A clinopyroxene with composition $CaMgSi_2O_6$. *See* pyroxene.

diorite. A coarse-grained intermediate igneous rock containing plagioclase of oligoclase-andesine composition and mafic minerals. The An_{50} (anorthite) composition of plagioclase feldspar marks the division between diorite and *gabbro. In diorites, the most common mafic minerals are hornblende and biotite although some rocks contain pyroxene. A little alkali feldspar may be present together with accessory magnetite, apatite, and sphene.

More acid varieties of diorite contain quartz up to 10% and may be called *tonalites.* With a further increase in quartz, tonalites pass into granodiorites. With an increase in the amount of alkali feldspar, diorites pass into syenodiorites. In the U.S., the term tonalite is applied to all rocks containing quartz, sodic plagioclase, and mafic minerals and is thus equivalent to the British tonalite (quartz–diorite) and granodiorite (in part).

Both leucocratic and melanocratic diorites occur. Meladiorites containing euhedral hornblende crystals are termed *appinites* and often appear to be a pegmatitic facies of more normal diorite. Diorites usually have equigranular textures. The medium-grained equivalents, microdiorites, are often porphyritic. *Markfieldite* is an over-saturated microdiorite consisting of a groundmass of graphically intergrown alkali feldspar and quartz with phenocrysts of plagioclase and hornblende. The volcanic equivalents of diorites are andesites. Dioritic rocks tend to occur in small intrusive masses associated with granodiorite and gabbro bodies and many diorites are thought to be hybrid rocks. *Compare* syenites, syenodiorites.

dip. 1. The angle made between the horizontal plane and that of the bedding plane, measured perpendicularly to the strike, in a stratified rock or any planar structure. *See also* apparent dip. *Compare* hade.
2. (Magnetic dip inclination). The angle between the earth's magnetic field at any point on the earth's surface and the horizontal. It is 90° at the *magnetic poles and 0° at the equator. It is measured using a *dip circle*, an instrument in which a magnetic needle is free to rotate, in the vertical plane, around a circular scale.

dipole field. That portion of the earth's magnetic field that can best be described as originating from a dipole magnet in the earth's interior, inclined at 11° to the earth's axis of rotation. *See also* nondipole field.

direct circulation (in meteorology). Circulation in which potential energy is converted into kinetic energy through the rising and sinking of juxtaposed lighter and denser air respectively. This occurs at scales ranging from land and sea breezes to the meridional cells of the *general circulation of the atmosphere.

direct wave. A wave that travels from one point to another along the path of shortest distance.

discharge. The volume of water flowing through a cross section of a stream. It is measured by gauging mean velocity in the cross section, which is multiplied by the cross sectional area to give an expression of flow in cubic feet per second (c.f.s.). Within a river discharge increases downstream, except in arid areas where volume is lost by evaporation. By far the greatest discharge of all the world's rivers is that of the Amazon (4000–5000 c.f.s.), which is at least as great as the combined discharges of its nearest rivals, the Congo, Yangtze, Mississippi-Missouri, Yenisei, and Lena.

disconformity (paraunconformity). An unconformity that marks a considerable time gap but where the beds of rock above and below the plane of the unconformity have a similar dip and strike (*compare* angular unconformity), the absence of beds being only detectable by palaeontological means. It is of greater magnitude than a *diastem. *Compare* unconformity.

discontinuity. 1. (In meteorology). A sharp change in the value of a meteorological variable, for example at a cold front, where there is usually a discontinuity in the temperature, humidity, and wind velocity fields across the frontal surface. Most meteorological properties are continuous functions of space and time and their values can

therefore be mapped in the forms of pressure charts or isotherm maps.
2. (In geophysics). A marked change with depth in one or more of the physical properties of the materials constituting the earth's interior. For example, a boundary at which the velocity of earthquake waves changes is a seismic discontinuity.

discordant. 1. Designating a rock unit that cuts across the bedding or foliation of adjacent rocks. Intrusive igneous rocks, such as dykes, show discordant relationships.
2. Denoting a drainage pattern characterized by streams cutting indiscriminately across structures. Discordance at a local level can be a product of various detailed factors, but at a regional level it can be due to glacial blocking (*see* deranged drainage), tectonic activity (*see* antecedence), or to superimposition of the drainage from a pre-existing cover of rocks. It is also referred to as *unconformable* drainage. *Compare* accordant.

disharmonic folding. Folding in which differences in the *competence of the various beds of rock result in variation in types of folding within the fold, the less competent beds forming numerous folds that are smaller than those formed in the more competent beds enclosing them.

dishpan experiments. Experiments conducted by D. Fultz to investigate the effects of rotation and thermal gradients on the circulation and heat exchange within fluids. The liquid was contained in a cylindrical vessel, the dishpan, which could be rotated about a vertical axis. A thermal gradient was applied by heating the exterior walls of the vessel. The mechanism of heat exchange could be seen by indicator particles, which were filmed by a camera rotating at the same rate as the vessel. Comparison could then be made with the earth's circulation, where different methods of heat transfer operate in the Tropics from elsewhere, corresponding to the low and high rates of rotation around the earth's axis.

disphotic zone. Ocean depths at which photosynthesis is not effective because of the small amount of light that penetrates to this layer, which extends from about 80 metres to 200 metres (the edge of the *continental shelf) below sea level. *See also* euphotic zone, aphotic zone.

dissolved load. That part of a river's load carried in chemical solution. Rainwater, being mildly acidic, can dissolve rocks, especially limestone, and then feed that dissolved content into a river via groundwater flow. Rivers may also be mildly acidic, especially if they pass through areas of bogs or marshes, where organic acids are produced, and they may dissolve minerals of their beds. In the Mississippi 29% of the load by weight is carried in solution, but this proportion varies in other streams according to climate and according to what proportion of runoff is contributed via groundwater flow. The major ions carried are bicarbonate, sulphate, chloride, calcium, and sodium, although in small basins there is variation according to the nature of the local rocks, and in populated areas pollution can significantly alter chemical content. *See also* load, debris load.

disturbance (in meteorology). Any small-scale synoptic feature causing a disturbance from the normal gradient wind flow, especially a shallow *depression.

diurnal variation. The changes in magnitude of any climatological property recorded during the solar or climatological *day. Most elements exhibit some variation. Temperature and relative humidity have an inverse cyclic fluctuation reaching peak and trough respectively about 1400 hrs. Atmospheric pressure also shows a daily variation, but it is based on a 12 hourly oscillation that proceeds according to local solar time. Maxima occur about 10.00 and 22.00 and minima

at 16.00 and 04.00 hours. Because the synoptic variations in mid-latitudes are large, it is only within the tropical areas that the diurnal variation of pressure is immediately apparent. Some proposals have been made for a nocturnal maximum of precipitation but this has never been proved.

divergence. A measure of the rate of outflow of a fluid from a certain volume. It is the opposite state from *convergence and the mathematical term used to describe both, convergence being negative divergence. It has important implications in the atmosphere as the cause of pressure changes and vertical motion, but is very difficult to measure directly or accurately. Values of divergence in the free atmosphere range up to 10^{-5} per second, though locally, as in fronts, it can reach higher values.

In wave refraction phenomena, divergence refers to the spreading out of the wave orthogonals in the direction of wave advance. Wave energy and wave height tend to decrease in areas of divergence. In the case of ocean currents, a divergence is the zone in which currents flow away from each other, for example at roughly latitude 10°N where the North Equatorial Current and the Counter-current associated with it separate.

divide (watershed). The area of higher ground that lies between two separate drainage systems. *See also* interfluve.

division. An informal word for any unit in any scheme of stratigraphical classification, including *lithostratigraphy, *biostratigraphy, and *chronostratigraphy. *See also* stratigraphy.

doldrums. Equatorial oceanic areas in which winds are light and variable and where navigation by sailing ships was difficult. It coincides with the intertropical convergence zone or thermal equator with frequent thunderstorms, heavy rains, and squalls. It is now only used as a graphic term for this belt of variable winds anywhere near the equator between the trade wind zones.

dolerite (microgabbro). A rock that differs little mineralogically from gabbro, of which it is the medium-grained equivalent. The term *diabase* is used in the U.S. Calcic plagioclase and augite are essential; in addition, dolerites may contain olivine, hypersthene, quartz, or feldspathoids. The characteristic texture is ophitic but many examples are intergranular and porphyritic. The term *epidiorite* is sometimes applied to altered dolerites.
Dolerites occur mainly as dykes, plugs, and sills. *See also* basalt, alkali basalt.

doline (dolina). A large *sink hole formed by solution in *karst country.

dolomite. A *carbonate mineral of composition $CaMg(CO_3)_2$. Dolomite is also used to denote a rock with a high ratio of magnesium to calcium carbonate.

dolomitization. The process by which a calcium carbonate rock is transformed into a calcium-magnesium carbonate rock through the partial or complete replacement of calcite or aragonite by dolomite.

dome. An anticlinal fold in which the beds dip in all directions away from the central point of folding. A dome may be merely structural or it may constitute an exposed landform.

Doppler effect. A change in the measured frequency of a wave due to the relative motion of the source and the recorder. As the source moves towards the recording station the wavelength decreases, whereas when the source moves away from the recorder the wavelength increases.

Doppler radar. A type of radar that relies on the Doppler effect. If the radar target is approaching or moving away from the transmitted signal, it will affect the frequency of the returning signal, being less than that transmitted if moving away or greater if approaching. In meteorology, precipitation drops are

the usual target and indicate the horizontal air motion, the fall speed of the particles, and, with certain assumptions, the vertical air motion. This technique is being increasingly used for investigations of subsynoptic levels, such as at frontal zones.

double refraction. *See* birefringence, anisotropic.

downthrow side. The side of a fault that has moved downwards relative to the other, i.e. the side that has younger beds brought down against the older beds of the other side. (See diagram at *fault*.)

drag fold. A small fold associated with a larger folding structure, often found adjacent to faults where the rock strata have been bent as a result of the movement along the fault plane.

Drainage basins

drainage basin. The area that supplies water to a particular network of drainage channels. At the edge of the basin a divide, usually in the form of hills, mountains, or a plateau, separates it from the adjacent basin. The drainage basin constitutes the unit of study for drainage pattern, rates of denudation, relation between precipitation and runoff, and various other geomorphological factors. Little is known of the controls on basin size and shape, but regional geological structure and tectonic history are clearly important.

drainage density. The ratio between the total length of stream channel in a basin, and the area that the channel occupies. Closely related is *stream frequency*, which is the number of streams divided by the total channel area. Drainage density is high on rocks yielding impermeable soils, e.g. shales and clays; it is also high where sediment yield is high, on easily erodible rocks, e.g. clays. In SW Britain drainage density on impervious culm shales is twice that on the granite, where the peat has a high water-holding capacity, and the granite gives a low sediment yield.

Other things being equal, drainage density is governed by climate, through its control on runoff via rainfall and vegetation. Relief is also significant: high-relief areas tend to have high drainage densities. Drainage density is an integral part of drainage pattern description: in particular it shows the degree of dissection of the drainage basin.

drainage pattern. The spatial arrangement of streams within a basin. It is a reflection mainly of the area's geologic structure, i.e. the nature and arrangement of faults, folds, rocks (especially lithologies), and relative relief. Past and current climate and the tectonic and geomorphic history of the basin are also important. These variables control the rate and nature of stream incision and headward erosion, the basic processes by which the pattern develops. Field studies show the pattern evolves very rapidly at first, then reaches a steady state of little further change, contrary to W. M. Davis's original idea that the rate of development was constant through time. *See also* stream ordering, drainage density, accordant, angulate drainage, barbed drainage, dendritic drainage, deranged drainage, discordant (def. 2), parallel drainage, radial drainage, rectangular drainage, trellis drainage.

dredging. The deepening of a river, port-approach channel, or other such area by excavating loose sediment or in-situ rock from the river or seabed. The dredger or dredge is a vessel specially designed to undertake this. Some dredgers actually dig up the bed using a combination of buckets or grabs; others suck up loose sediments mechanically using suction devices, as in a trailing suction-dredger. Dredging may be performed to improve navigable depths or to remove obstructions such as shoals or banks that are dangerous to navigation. Other dredgers operate farther offshore and recover useful minerals, such as sand, gravel, tin, and diamonds from the seabed. Dredging can have far-reaching environmental consequences, as when it increases turbidity, to the detriment of fish and shellfish production.

drift. Glacial and fluvioglacial deposits. Great thicknesses of this drift accumulated during the *Pleistocene period, though much has subsequently been removed by erosion. An area of glacial deposition may be referred to as one of *drift topography*. A *drift map* is a geological map on which glacial drift and other superficial deposits are shown, as contrasted with a *solid* edition showing only the underlying rocks.

drizzle. Water droplets ranging in diameter from 0.2 to 0.5 micrometres. It forms by coalescence in stratiform cloud with only weak vertical motion, otherwise the droplets would be unable to fall. It also requires a high relative humidity between cloud base and ground surface or only a short distance between cloud and surface. In both cases, evaporation of the droplets would occur without these constraints.

drought. A period of dryness due to the absence of precipitation. It is an unsatisfactory term unless very carefully specified as it implies some effect on agriculture, but this is dependent upon factors other than rainfall alone. In purely climatic terms, it can be used to indicate lack of rain. By convention, an *absolute drought* is a period of at least 15 consecutive days on none of which there is more than 0.2 mm of rainfall. A *partial drought* is a period of at least 29 days, the *mean* daily rainfall of which does not exceed 0.2 mm.

drowned valley. A river valley cut at a time when sea level was at a much lower level than it now is, usually during the *Pleistocène period, and subsequently drowned as sea level rose again on melting of the large ice sheets. These former inland valleys now exist as indentations in the coastline, their internal shapes being largely hidden underwater. Differently shaped coasts are produced by the flooding of geologically different areas. If the former drainage system was perpendicular to the general outline of the present coast a series of inlets separated by headlands will exist; if the drowned valleys lay parallel with the present coastline numerous elongate islands, the former interfluves, will be present, with narrow flooded areas between them. *See also* ria, fiord.

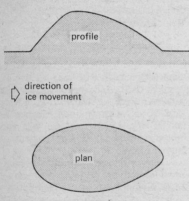

Drumlin

drumlin. A streamlined glacial form tending to occur in groups, all with their long axes parallel with the direction of ice movement. They may be composed of *till, which can vary considerably in composition, of pre-existing *drift, or of rock. Some contain stratified deposits. Since these forms are so variable a number of explanations of their origins have been suggested: there are two principal explanations. Those composed of rock or pre-existing drift materials must have involved erosion, although if erosion were the only process, one would expect shapes similar to those of *roches moutonnées, which is not the case. Drumlins composed of newly deposited till must involve deposition, and it has been suggested that they form around a nucleus of frozen till, or rock. Despite their variability, all drumlins are linked by their common shape, and the fact that their formation is associated with moving ice.

druse (drusy). A cavity in a rock or mineral vein into which large euhedral crystals project. A rounded cavity containing crystals that project towards the centre is called a *geode. See also* miarolitic cavity, vugh.

dry adiabatic lapse rate. The constant rate at which air will cool upon uplift, prior to saturation being reached. Its value of $0.98°C/100$ m depends upon the properties of the gases in the atmosphere and the gravitational force. *See also* saturated adiabatic lapse rate, environmental lapse rate.

dry valley. A typical subaerial river valley in all respects except that it contains no stream or river. They are mostly found in areas of soluble limestone where the waters responsible for the cutting of the valley, at an early stage in the erosional history of the area, have subsequently disappeared underground through enlarged joints and subsurface cavern systems, developed as a result of *limestone solution. At times of exceptional discharge the underground systems may be incapable of dealing with all the water, and surface drainage may return temporarily.
Some dry valleys may have been formed in former periglacial conditions, when permafrost rendered the ground impermeable, or in times of wetter climate, when the water table was higher.

dune. A mound or hill of sand. Dunes are characteristic landforms of deserts, in an unvegetated form, and of certain coastal and riverside areas, where they are usually vegetated. Desert dunes are simpler in form owing to the lack of moisture and plant growth, the two major forms being the *barchan (crescentic dune) and the *seif (longitudinal dune). Coastal dunes show a development inland from the young *fore-dune through the main *mobile dune to the *stabilized dune.

The major requirement for dune-building is a sand supply; in the deserts this is transported by wind from areas of erosion, notably scarps and areas of *deflation, whilst in coastal areas it is transported by the longshore drift from a source which may be a pre-existing supply or an area of erosion creating a supply, and then left on the foreshore ready for wind action to take it inland and build the dune.

Coastal dunes are hence due to a three-way relationship between littoral drift of sand, blowing of sand onshore, and vegetation growth trapping the sand and building a dune, whilst desert dunes may be wave patterns resulting from the interaction of air flow and land surface, the dunes accumulating in areas between turbulent eddies.

dunite. A monomineralic ultramafic rock consisting wholly of olivine.

Dust Bowl. An area in the western U.S. that has suffered extensive wind erosion, which has removed the fertile topsoil. It lies mainly within W Kansas, Oklahoma, and Texas and extends into Colorado and New Mexico. A smaller dust bowl occurs in central Nebraska, North Dakota, and South Dakota. With the removal of hedges in East Anglia conditions have been likened to those of the Dust Bowl but they are not of comparable severity.

dust devil. A whirlwind or small tornado in which sand and dust rise into the atmosphere and can reach a height of up to 30 m. It forms by strong convection above an intensely heated sandy surface and is only distinguished as a dust devil if the surface is sufficiently sandy for the surface material to be drawn into the rotating column.

dyke. A tabular body of igneous rock that is intruded vertically and discordantly to the structure of the rocks through which it passes. See also sill, dilation dyke, neptunian dyke, radial dyke.

dyke swarm. A large number of dykes often arranged in either a radial or parallel pattern.

dynamical meteorology. The branch of meteorology concerned with the causes and nature of motion within the atmosphere.

dynamic equilibrium (in geomorphology). The state of balance between erosion and deposition to which rivers seek to adjust. The emphasis on dynamic is because rivers never actually achieve a balance of no erosion or deposition, but are always actively adjusting to the constant changes of load and discharge, etc., by some minor erosion and deposition. See also equilibrium profile.

E

earthflow. A mass movement of soil on a steep slope, well mixed with water. They are commonest in areas with little vegetation, where rainfall comes in sharp bursts, saturating the soil, and where the soil has a high content of fines.

The difference between earthflows and mudflows is purely of degree: earthflows occur on gentler slopes and move at a lesser velocity than mudflows. The soil eventually comes to rest as a tongue at the slope foot, the thickness of the tongue becoming less as the velocity of flow increases.

Like the other mass movements, flows act on unstable slopes, reducing them to a more stable angle.

earthquake. A series of shocks, subdivided into *foreshocks, *principal shocks, and *aftershocks, which generate seismic waves within the earth, as a result of the fracturing of brittle rocks within the lithosphere. They result from the accumulation of forces within the rocks until they are strained to a point beyond which they fracture. The *magnitude* of an earthquake is the amount of energy involved. Depending on the quantity of energy liberated when the overstrained rocks fracture, the earthquake may vary from mild quiverings to violent oscillations of the land surface.

earthquake focus. *See* focus.

earthquake intensity. The degree of violence of an earthquake at a particular point on the earth's surface, expressed on a descriptive scale divided into twelve points. Point one on the scale is only detected by seismograms, whereas at point twelve objects are thrown into the air and there is total destruction.

earthquake zones. *See* seismic zones.

earthslide. The movement of the soil mantle over a shear plane. For the process to operate there must be an unstable slope and a dry soil. If the soil becomes wet, it may turn into an *earthflow. An important part may be played by water, however, in lubricating the shear plane. *See also* mass movement.

earth temperature. The temperature of the ground surface as determined by the characteristic wavelengths of long-wave radiation emission.

earthworms. The most important of the macrofauna in the soil. Under favourable conditions, as when the soil is moist and rich in lime and organic matter, there may be up to 1 000 000 earthworms per acre. They may pass as much as 10 tonnes per acre of soil through their bodies each year. This material is humified and excreted in the form of casts, which contain more humus, nitrates, and exchangeable bases than the surrounding soil. Besides their function in the chemical and physical breakdown of plants they are also important in improving the texture, aeration, and drainage of the soil.

easterlies. Any winds in which the zonal component of air flow is from the east. They are subdivided into the tropical easterlies or trade winds and the polar easterlies. The presence of easterly winds at the ground surface is an essential requirement to counteract the effect of the mid-latitude westerlies on the earth's rate of rotation.

easterly wave. A shallow trough or disturbance in the trade wind flow associated with an increase of cloudiness and precipitation to its rear. After initial debate about the status of the easterly wave, satellite photographs have confirmed characteristic cloud patterns associated with the trough although they do exhibit greater variety than was first thought. In some instances they probably act as initial disturbances for the development of hurricanes.

easting. Any of the north-south grid lines on a map, quoted before the *northing when coordinates are being given, showing distance east from the origin of the grid.

ebb tide. The outgoing of the tidal stream; the retreating tide, i.e. that part of a tide cycle following the high-water stage and preceding the low-water stage. *Compare* flood tide.

Echinodermata. The phylum of marine invertebrate animals that includes the starfish, sea urchins, and crinoids. The body of an echinoderm usually has five radii, along which are grouped hydrostatic *tube feet*, functioning in locomotion and feeding and operated by the *water vascular system*, an internal system of fluid-filled canals. These radii are known as *ambulacra* and the areas between as *interambulacra*. An external skeletal system (*test*) composed of plates of single calcite crystals is usually present and sometimes bears spines. There are five living classes: the Asteroidea (starfish), Ophiuroidea (brittle stars), *Echinoidea (sea urchins), Holothuroidea (sea cucumbers), and *Crinoidea (sea lilies). There are also a number of important extinct classes, such as the Cystoidea. Echinoderms extend from the early Cambrian Period to the present day.

Echinoidea. The class of the phylum *Echinodermata to which the sea urchins belong. They are protected by a hemispherical and usually spiny test of interlocking calcite plates, which in some later forms is flattened. Typically the anus is situated in the centre of the upper surface and the mouth is diametrically opposite. In later forms the mouth and anus may have become displaced, the anus sometimes opening on the oral surface. Echinoids are marine, benthonic, and free living and are known as fossils from the Ordovician Period onwards. The group was affected by the widespread extinctions at the end of the Palaeozoic Era but revived in the Mesozoic and extends to the present day. Echinoids are used as biostratigraphic *zone fossils in the Cretaceous System.

eclogite. A coarse-grained granular rock consisting essentially of bright green omphacite and deep red almandine-pyrope garnet. Diopside, quartz, and kyanite may also be present in small amounts.
Eclogite has the chemical composition of basalt and may be considered to be the high-pressure high-temperature metamorphic equivalent. Eclogite is found as lenses and bands in regionally metamorphosed rocks of the highest grades and also as inclusions in basalt and kimberlite.

economic basement. Strata below which there is little chance of finding economic mineral resources, particularly oil.

ecoulement. The downward sliding of large masses of rock as a result of gravity.

eddy. A rotational feature of a fluid, which retains its identity for a limited time whilst moving within the main body of the fluid and eventually amalgamating with it. Such eddies can fre-

quently be seen in river flow after the current has been disturbed by a bridge or shearing.
In the atmosphere, eddies are found in a wide range of scales. Near the ground surface they are important in transferring momentum, heat, and moisture. On the large scale, eddies in the form of depressions are a necessary mechanism for much of the meridional transfer in the *general circulation of the atmosphere.

eddy diffusion. The exchange of atmospheric matter and properties brought about by eddies. *See also* diffusion.

edenite. A monoclinic *amphibole.

edge dislocation. A defect in a crystal lattice resulting from the insertion of an extra plane of atoms.

ejectamenta. *See* tephra.

Ekman flow. The movement of surface sea water in the direction of a wind, which, as it blows, exerts a force on the sea surface in the direction of the wind and, because of frictional forces operating within the water column, causes a certain thickness of water to flow. The ocean's response is highly complicated, especially because of earth rotation and the fact that water is fluid, but also because of such factors as land-ocean configuration. In the N hemisphere, average Ekman flow is some 45° to the right of the wind, while the speed decreases and the direction swings increasingly to the right of the wind direction with increasing depth. Ekman flow has several far-reaching effects; for instance, off the coasts of California and Peru, Ekman flow tends to be in an offshore direction, thereby causing zones of upwelling of fertile deep water near the coast, which provides nutrients for fish populations.

Ekman layer. In general terms, the circulation of ocean water, viewed in the vertical column, occurs in two layers, the uppermost layer being relatively thin, probably about 100 metres deep, and beneath this and extending down to the ocean floor, the deep-water circulation involving deep water masses. The upper water masses, in the shallow surface layer, move in what is termed the *Ekman layer*, the thickness of which has been calculated theoretically. Flow within this layer is termed *Ekman flow.

Wind increases in speed and veers in direction with increasing height

Ekman spiral

Ekman spiral. The ground surface has a frictional interaction with the atmosphere and its effect decreases with height until, between 500 and 1000 m, the *geostrophic wind is observed. The spiral illustrates in vector form how the wind velocity changes with height (see diagram), blowing across the isobars at low speed near the surface and parallel at higher speeds in the free atmosphere.

elastic waves. Seismic waves that are propagated through a medium by elastic deformation.

electric log. A subsurface logging technique in which an electrode or series of electrodes are lowered into an uncased bore hole. As the sonde is raised a continuous record of the electrical properties of the rocks through which it passes is recorded. By an examination of the variations in several

Electromagnetic radiation

properties an assessment of the rock types present in the bore hole can be made.

electromagnetic radiation. The form of energy that travels in waves from its source without the necessity of an intervening medium. The waves move with the speed of light (3×10^8 metres per second) in space and only slightly slower through the atmosphere. The total spectrum of this form of radiation includes wavelengths as short as gamma rays (10^{-13}m) to long radio waves (up to 10^5m), as shown on the diagram. Within this range is visible light between 0.4 and 0.7 micrometres, to which our eyes are sensitive. The behaviour of electro-magnetic radiation is explained by the following physical laws:

(a) All matter with a temperature above absolute zero (-273°) emits radiation.

(b) Some substances emit radiation of certain wavelengths only.

(c) Substances that emit the maximum amount of radiation for a given tem-perature in all wavelengths are known as *black bodies. The amount of radia-tion emitted is then proportional to the fourth power of the substance's absolute temperature.

(d) Substances will only absorb radia-tion of wavelengths that they can also emit.

(e) The hotter a substance, the shorter will be the wavelengths at which most of the radiant energy is emitted.

(f) The amount of radiation received at a point is inversely proportional to the square of the distance of that point from the radiation source.

elevation. The vertical distance of any point on the earth's surface above the *datum level, measured in metres or feet.

El Niño effect. The periodic extension along the Peruvian coast of the warm equatorial current. This replaces the cold Peru or Humboldt Current and sea surface temperatures may increase by 10°C. Heavy rains then fall in the normally desert areas of Peru and many fish die as they are dependent on the plankton in the cold water. So much hydrogen sulphide can be released from rotting fish that it can blacken paint. This effect has been called the *Callao Painter*, after the city in Peru.

eluviation. The washing out of fine material from a soil, especially from the upper part. The eluvial horizon is the A horizon, which has less clay than the rest of the profile as a result.

emerald. A bright green gem variety of *beryl.

emissivity. The ratio of emission of radiation from a substance to the emis-sion from a *black body at the same temperature and wavelength. Values range from slightly below 1.0 to 0.85 for most substances.

enclave. An inclusion or *xenolith.

enderbite. See charnockite.

en echelon. Denoting overlapping or offset geological structures.

energy balance. A concept applied to the static energy of the earth-atmo-sphere system, rather than its dynamic energy. It relates the net radiation flux at a surface to the utilization of this available energy. This is consumed by the conduction of heat below the ground surface, the transfer of sensible heat to the atmosphere by turbulence and convection, and the transfer of latent heat by similar methods. All these processes are reversible.

The energy balance equation is often called the *heat balance equation* and is expressed in the form $R = H + LE + G$ where R is net radiation, H is sen-sible heat, LE the latent heat transfer, and G the component transferred into the ground.

englacial. Denoting materials or melt-water contained within an ice mass. Such debris or water can reach the interior ice either by movement up-wards from the bed or downwards from the surface.

enstatite. An orthopyroxene. *See* pyroxene.

entisol. One of the ten soil orders of the *Seventh Approximation classification, approximately equivalent to the azonal category of the old classification. These are recent soils without natural genetic horizons and they include lithosols (shallow stony soils), regosols (thin soils on unconsolidated drift), and alluvial soils or fluvisols (soils that are constantly being added to because of their site on active floodplains). These soils are not extensively used for agriculture but may become quite productive when managed properly.

entrainment (in meteorology). The process of mixing between the environment and a rising thermal in the updraught of a cumulus or cumulonimbus cloud. It has the effect of diluting the warmer rising air and so slightly reduces its buoyancy. This prevents the rate of cooling in the thermal from being adiabatic, but in practice the difference is slight.

Section through an entrenched meander

entrenched meander. The type of *incised meander that results from the *rejuvenation of floodplain meanders and subsequent incision into the bedrock below. They are therefore the product of a two-stage process, unlike the one-stage origin of *ingrown meanders. Entrenched meanders are often distinguished from ingrown meanders on the basis of their symmetrical valley cross profile, contrasted to the asym-

metrical cross profile of the ingrown type. However, some floodplain meanders do not incise themselves vertically into their floodplains, but at an angle, producing an asymmetric cross profile.

environmental lapse rate. The actual rate of change in temperature with height of the atmosphere, at a given time, used particularly when investigating the stability of the lower atmosphere. The differences between the *dry adiabatic lapse rate, *saturated adiabatic lapse rate, and environmental lapse rate is especially important in this respect when drawn on a thermodynamic diagram.
The lapse rate is steep in the lower layers during day-time heating, decreasing with height, so that by the upper atmosphere it approximates to the saturated adiabatic lapse rate. *Inversions are frequently present indicating a warming of the air with increasing height, but within the troposphere they are rarely very deep.

Eocene. The epoch of the *Tertiary Period that extends from the end of the *Palaeocene, 53.5 million years ago, to the beginning of the *Oligocene Epoch, some 17.5 million years later. Some classifications dispense with the Palaeocene, thus adding another 11.5 million years to the Eocene, which then becomes the first epoch of the Tertiary. Eocene rocks outcrop in S England, where they are of marine and marginal facies. During this epoch mammals were abundant, perissodactyls, including large and small horses, and artiodactyls appeared and the modern carnivore families became established. The first evidence of bats and whales also comes from this epoch.

eon. The largest interval of geological time in the Chronomeric scheme of chronostratigraphic nomenclature (*see* chronostratigraphy), formed of several *eras grouped together.

Eozoic. An era of *Precambrian time followed by the *Archaeozoic and the *Proterozoic. The term is seldom used.

epeiric sea. A shallow *inland sea.

epeirogenesis. Uplift or subsidence of large areas of continents or ocean basins. Compare orogenesis.

epicentral angle. The angular distance between the epicentre of an earthquake and a recording station, expressed in terms of the angle subtended at the centre of the earth between verticals from these two points.

epicentre. The point on the earth's surface situated directly above the focus of an earthquake.

epidiorite. A rock with a dioritic mineralogy derived from the low- to medium-grade metamorphism of labradorite-pyroxene assemblages of basic igneous rocks (gabbro and dolerite), which results in the formation of hornblende and a plagioclase of more sodic composition.

epidote. A group of minerals having the general formula $X_2Y_3Si_3O_{12}(OH)$, where X is mainly Ca but also Mn^{2+}, Ce^{3+}, and other rare earths, and Y = Al, Fe^{3+}, Mn^{3+}, and Fe^{2+}. The following compositions occur:
zoisite $Ca_2Al_3Si_3O_{12}(OH)$
clinozoisite $Ca_2Al_3Si_3O_{12}(OH)$
epidote $Ca_2Fe^{3+}Al_2Si_3O_{12}(OH)$
piemontite
$Ca_2(Mn^{3+}Fe^{3+},Al)_3Si_3O_{12}(OH)$
allanite (orthite) $(Ca,Mn^{2+},Ce)_2(Fe^{2+},Fe^{3+}Al)_3Si_3O_{12}(OH)$
The epidote minerals are monoclinic except for zoisite, which is orthorhombic. Zoisite may be grey, green, or brown in colour; clinozoisite is colourless to green; epidote is green to yellow-green; piemontite is typically red-brown; allanite is brown to black. A pink manganiferous variety of zoisite is called thulite.
Minerals of the epidote group are found in the medium-grade regionally metamorphosed rocks of the greenschist and amphibolite facies. Epidote is produced during retrograde metamorphism and may be found on joint surfaces and along fractures. Plagioclase feldspar,

clinopyroxenes, and hornblendes can all be replaced by epidote minerals and basic igneous rocks in particular may suffer extensive epidotization.
Allanite is found as an accessory mineral in some acid igneous rocks.

epipedon. A diagnostic surface horizon, constituting that part of the soil with organic matter or the upper eluvial horizon or both. Introduced by the *Seventh Approximation, there are six common epipedons: mollic, histic, plaggen, anthropic, umbric, and ochric, each being indicative of a certain class of soil. For example, *mollisols are identified by the mollic epipedon; soils influenced by human use are identified by the anthropic epipedon (>250 ppm acid soluble salt phosphate due to farming) and the plaggen epipedon (a layer >50 cm deep produced by manuring).

epitaxial growth. The parallel or orientated overgrowth of one mineral on a crystal of another such that there is some form of continuity maintained between the crystal structures of both minerals. Examples include the overgrowth of augite on orthopyroxene and idocrase on garnet.

epithermal. See hydrothermal processes.

epoch. An interval of geological time in the Chronomeric Standard scale of chronostratigraphic classification (see chronostratigraphy). The equivalent Stratomeric standard term, indicating the body of rock formed during this time, is the *series. Several epochs together form a *period and are themselves formed of a number of *ages.

equal-area projection. See homolographic projection.

equatorial currents. Among the prominent currents that flow in the oceans are those in the equatorial regions. The currents flowing at or close to the equator in the Pacific Ocean are, in general, similar in pattern to those flowing in equatorial regions of the Atlantic Ocean, there being a South Equatorial Current flowing astride the equator, which is separated from the westward-flowing *North Equatorial Current* by an eastward-flowing *Equatorial Counter-current*. However, this counter-current is much more strongly developed in the Pacific than is its counterpart in the Atlantic. There are also currents that flow at some depth; for instance, the *Cromwell Current* (also known as the *Pacific Equatorial Undercurrent*) flows as a narrow swift current in an easterly direction and at a fairly shallow depth beneath the South Equatorial Current. The flow rate in the Equatorial Counter-current probably attains some 25 million cubic metres per second, with speeds of up to 2 knots.

equatorial trough. The belt of low pressure that occurs in equatorial areas and oscillates in its mean location depending upon the position of the overhead sun. It marks the convergence zone of the trade winds blowing from each hemisphere and is most clearly observed over the ocean areas where continental modifications of airflow are least.

equatorial westerlies. A zone of rather variable winds found when the *inter-tropical convergence zone extends more than 5° from the equator. They probably represent trade-wind air that has acquired a westerly component on crossing the equator but their origins may vary depending upon the precise location of formation.

equatorial zenithal gnomonic projection. A map projection in which the tangent touches the surface of the earth at the equator. All the great circles are straight lines but the angle of intersection of the meridians and the parallels (shown by curves) becomes increasingly more acute polewards, and therefore the distortion is greater. Places best represented on this projection are those near the equator, e.g. Africa; beyond about 30° north or south the distortion is too large for the projection to be of any use.

Equatorial zenithal

equigranular. Denoting a rock that has crystals of a uniform grain size.

equilibrium (graded) profile. A long profile of a river in which there is a delicate balance between erosion and deposition. Slope of the equilibrium profile is adjusted so that the sediment load provided to the river can just be transported by the available discharge and channel characteristics. Traditionally this is thought of as being a concave profile, but in practice it need not be perfectly smooth. Streams with uneven long profiles have been found to be in equilibrium in the sense that in no part of their profile is active erosion or deposition taking place. *See also* equilibrium regime, dynamic equilibrium.

equilibrium regime. The regime of a natural system, such as a river channel, coastline, slope profile, etc., when it is in a state of balance considered over time, neither eroding nor depositing. The term is most often used in connection with rivers, where it is largely synonymous with *grade*.

equinox. The period of the year when the sun is overhead at local solar time at the equator. This happens twice a year, about March 21 and Sept. 22, when day and night are equal time periods of twelve hours. Because of refraction through the atmosphere, actual day length is slightly longer than the true astronomical day. In NW Europe, the first and second equinoxes are taken to mark the beginning of spring and of autumn respectively.

era. An interval of geological time in the Chronomeric scheme of chronostratigraphic nomenclature (see chronostratigraphy). It is formed of several *periods grouped together and a number of eras may be compounded to form an *eon. For example, the Palaeozoic Era is composed of six periods, the Cambrian, Ordovician, Silurian, Devonian, Carboniferous, and Permian, and lasted for some 350 million years, from about 590 to 240 million years ago.

erg. 1. A type of arid desert landscape consisting of a very extensive sand cover, especially in the Sahara. See also hammada, reg.
2. A unit of work or energy equal to the work done by a force of 1 dyne acting through a distance of 1 cm. 1 erg is equal to 10^{-7} joules.

erosion. The lowering of the land surface by agents that involve the transport of rock debris. Unlike degradation, erosion tends to be an episodic process, varying greatly over time and space (see cycle of erosion). For erosion to occur, the eroding medium (gravity, river flow, waves, currents, wind, ice, etc.) must exert a force on the land surface greater than its shear strength. The elastic limit of the material then being exceeded, fractures form and the material moves in the direction of the force applied to it. The movement may be sharp and sudden, as in *landslides and *rock falls, or slow and imperceptible, as with *creep. Compare denudation. See also differential erosion.
Soil erosion is a great problem because the surface part is the most fertile and plant nutrients have to be replaced artificially. Wind erosion of soil can be severe in semiarid regions (see Dust Bowl). Water erosion (sheet wash, rill action, gullying, etc.) is usually most prominent in humid lands, e.g. in the Tennessee Valley. See also abnormal erosion.

erratic. A rock that has been transported by ice and deposited in an area of dissimilar rock type. Volcanic and metamorphic rocks frequently make the most impressive erratics since they are often distinctively coloured and their high resistance to erosion permits their continued existence despite considerable transportation. By linking source outcrop with final resting place, some insight into directions of ice movement can be gained, though one erratic may, in turn, be moved by several ice masses in different directions. The existence of some erratics hundreds of metres in extent indicates the phenomenal power available in glacial transportation.

escape velocity. The initial velocity that a particle, space probe, etc., on the surface of a body such as the earth would require to overcome the gravitational influence of that body and move away from it.

escarpment. See scarp.

esker. An elongate ridge of rounded stratified *fluvioglacial deposits, consisting primarily of sands and gravels with some finer and coarser materials; they can be only tens of metres long but some extend for hundreds of kilometres. Eskers form in contact with stagnant or very slow moving ice from materials deposited by meltwater streams, which may be underneath, within, or above the ice mass. The cross-sectional shape of an esker will depend largely upon the position of the meltwater stream. If it is above the ice, the esker will have an ice core and melting will cause collapse; if it is in tunnels within the ice, collapse will also occur when the walls melt. If the tunnels are high and narrow sharp-crested ridges are produced, whilst low wide tunnels result in flat-topped and comparatively undisturbed eskers. *See also* beaded esker.

ESSA. *Abbrev. for* Environmental Sciences Services Administration, the organization formerly responsible for U.S. weather research. Several weather satellites were operated under its control and numbered ESSA (Environmental Survey Satellites) 1 to 8. Subsequently control was changed on reorganization and followed by NOAA (National Oceanic and Atmospheric Administration) satellites.

essential minerals. Certain diagnostic minerals on the presence or absence of which is based the classification and subdivisions of igneous rocks. For example, the presence of calcic plagioclase and pyroxene is implied in the term gabbro.

essexite. *See* alkali gabbro.

estuary. The part of a river mouth within which tides have an effect and therefore where fresh and saline water are mixed. Most present-day estuaries are *drowned valleys, owing their existence to the post-glacial rise in sea level, and for this reason they usually contain much deposited sediment. Deposition will continue if the river introduces more sediment than can be removed by tidal streams and by what little wave action is possible within the estuary. Many estuaries exhibit intricate patterns of channels, largely the result of erosion by both incoming and outgoing tidal streams, which give flood and ebb channels respectively.

etesian winds. Winds blowing from a northerly direction in the Aegean Sea or E Mediterranean during the summer period. They are a response to the shallow thermal low pressure over the Sahara and the northward movement of the Azores anticyclone to be centred over the W Mediterranean.

eucrite. A variety of coarse-grained basic igneous rock containing clinopyroxenes and orthopyroxenes, olivine, and plagioclase of bytownite-anorthite composition.

euhedral. Denoting crystals that are well developed and have good crystal faces. *Compare* anhedral, subhedral.

Euler's theorem. A theorem that provides a mathematical explanation for the distribution of conservative *plate margins. Plate tectonics requires that all conservative plate margins (transform faults) lie on small circles, the axes of which form the axis of rotation for the relative motion of the plates on either side. It also indicates that the velocity of relative motion across a destructive or constructive plate margin is proportional to the angular distance of the particular point from the axis of rotation and to the angular velocity about the axis of rotation for the motion of the plates. Thus velocities will vary along plate margins.

eulittoral zone. *See* littoral zone.

euphotic zone. Ocean depths to which abundant sunlight for photosynthesis penetrates, extending from the surface to about 80 metres. *See also* disphotic zone, aphotic zone.

eustasy. Worldwide movements of sea level. The origin of these movements is most commonly attributed to the withdrawal and release of water due to the growth and decay of ice masses in the Quaternary (*glacio-eustatism). But eustatic movements can also be caused by tectonic movements of the sea floors or landmasses. It may be difficult to distinguish between the two, but most effects can be attributed to glacio-eustasy. Since the last ice age there has been a gradual rise in sea level as conditions have become relatively warmer. This is a positive eustatic change. *See* base level.

eutaxitic. Denoting the streaky or banded appearance common in ignimbrites. Individual streaks or fiamme are discontinuous flattened bodies. The term *parataxitic* is applicable when the fiamme are extremely elongated. *See* pyroclastic rocks.

Eutheria. The placental mammals. Their young are born at a late stage in development, having been nourished inside the body of the mother by means of a connection called the *placenta*. Fossils suggest that the Eutheria diverged from other mammalian groups in the Cretaceous, but their main evolutionary radiation took place during the Cenozoic, after the extinction of the dinosaurs. They rapidly became the dominant land animals and now include such diverse forms as the flying bats and the marine whales (which are the largest living animals known). *Compare* Marsupialia.

euxinic environment. A marine environment in which the bottom water is poorly ventilated, deficient in oxygen, and (in extreme cases) characterized by the presence of hydrogen sulphide, i.e. reducing conditions. Such conditions apply, for example, to parts of the Black Sea and to certain of the Norwegian fiords, where seafloor basins occur at different depths. One effect is that the floor of the Black Sea is sparsely populated with living organisms. The seabed deposits in euxinic environments are characteristically fine-grained ones containing a high percentage of decomposable organic material.

evaporation. The process by which a liquid is changed into a gas. The rate of evaporation in the atmosphere represents a net effect between the removal of water molecules from the surface layers and replacement by other water molecules in the lower layer of the atmosphere, which through continual motion strike the surface and become absorbed. As the molecules are being transferred from a lower to a higher energy state through evaporation, a supply of energy must be provided for the process to be maintained. This is a very important aspect of the earth's energy balance; by this process surplus energy in tropical areas

is transferred by the flux of water vapour to the radiation-deficit areas nearer the poles.

If evaporation continued into still air, the overlying layer would very soon reach saturation and prevent further evaporation. However, air movement usually mixes lower layers by turbulence, reducing the water vapour content and enabling further evaporation to take place. Clearly, the stronger the wind, the greater will be the rate of evaporation as long as the air is not saturated. This introduces the second factor influencing evaporation, that is the requirement for the air to be capable of absorbing moisture. An index of this is the saturation deficit, which is the difference between the saturation vapour pressure and actual vapour pressure. If the saturation deficit is large, as in warm dry air, the gradient between the moist surface and the atmosphere will be high, and so the rate of transfer will be large. With moist air, the humidity gradient will be less and the rate of evaporation correspondingly smaller.

The measurement of evaporation is difficult because of the problem of adequately simulating the evaporation surface. The standard method is to measure the loss of water from an evaporation pan surface, but it is accepted that this does not equate very well with true atmospheric evaporation. Measurements of the changes in weight of soil samples are a closer approach to reality but still differ from the natural situation.

evaporite. A rock formed as a precipitate from a saturated solution. Evaporation from virtually closed bodies of saline water is the most common process involved. They are classified according to their chemical composition. Great thicknesses of evaporite deposits occur, with minerals layered in a sequence depending upon their relative solubilities.

evapotranspiration. The combined system of vapour transfer by evaporation and transpiration from the ground surface and its vegetation layer. Except in areas of sparse vegetation, such as deserts, transpiration by plants is the dominant factor in the total loss of water from the land surface.

evolution. The gradual change in organisms through time, resulting in the origin of new *species. In 1859 Charles Darwin suggested the process of *natural selection as the means by which this could come about. The diversity of extinct and modern organisms has resulted from their becoming adapted to particular habitats. Evolution is generally a progressive change, with organisms becoming more able to deal with ever more extreme environments. This theory of modification and change is opposed to the doctrine of Special Creation, which holds that species are immutable and are replaced at intervals by newly created forms. Much fundamental evidence for the various pathways of evolutionary change comes from palaeontology. *See also* convergent evolution, parallel evolution.

exfoliation. The splitting of rocks into a series of concentric shells by a number of different weathering processes: *unloading, *spheroidal weathering, and *flaking.

exhumation. The exposing by denudation of a surface or feature that had previously been buried by deposition. Theories of exhumation have been used to explain the creation of a number of landforms, such as *tors and *inselbergs. A first stage consists of progressive *deep weathering on a rock type embodying considerable variation in its susceptibility to decomposition, which largely reflects variation in its jointing pattern. A highly irregular *weathering front develops and may remain for a considerable length of time. Subsequent erosion of the *regolith, initiated by earth movements or sea-level changes, will eventually exhume the least weathered rock masses.

exotic. A boulder or large rock body that has been transported by one of a variety of processes into an area of unrelated rock types. Where the transporting mechanism is tectonic in origin the rock body is said to be *allochthonous*, whereas if ice is the transporting mechanism such blocks are called *erratics.

exposure. The degree of openness of a site and the amount of interference to airflow by natural and artificial obstacles. For climatological instruments to give representative values, they must be sited correctly with a uniformity of exposure. The correct exposure varies from element to element, but is most important for rain gauges and anemometers, where airflow can affect the recorded values. It is never measured quantitatively although attempts to do so have been made.

exsolution (unmixing). Several minerals, notably feldspars and pyroxenes, are homogeneous solid solutions of two or more chemical end-members at high temperatures. During cooling, the homogeneous mix becomes unstable and such a mineral unmixes, producing two distinct mineral phases. For example, an alkali feldspar rich in potassium may undergo exsolution to produce a perthite intergrowth consisting of separate structural units of sodium and potassium feldspar, indicated by the occurrence of blebs of albite within an orthoclase host.

external magnetic field. That part of the earth's magnetic field that results from effects produced above the earth's surface.

extinction. The disappearance of a *species or other group or organisms representing a particular evolutionary line. It may occur when an organism that has become highly specialized for living in a particular environment is unable to adapt to extreme changes in its habitat. Some extinctions affect a wide variety of habitats, as occurred at the end of the *Palaeozoic and at the

end of the *Mesozoic Eras. The latter
extinction affected the dinosaurs on
land, pterodactyls in the air, and
ichthyosaurs in the sea; many invertebrate groups, such as the ammonites,
also disappeared. The causes of these
widespread extinctions are not clearly
understood. Major climatic changes
combined with unsuccessful competition with other groups of organisms
have been suggested as likely causes:
the extinction of one group is often
broadly contemporaneous with the
evolutionary radiation of another unspecialized and often insignificant
group.

eye. The central area of a hurricane or
typhoon, where wind speeds are light,
breaks in the main cloud sheets appear,
and the driving rain stops. The diameter
of the eye varies, reaching up to 80 km
in the larger storms, though its duration
depends upon the speed of movement of
the storm. The weather in the eye feels
particularly oppressive after the strong
winds preceding it, but it is soon
followed by even stronger winds in the
opposite direction.

F

facies. 1. A collection of metamorphic
rocks that have formed over the same
range of physical conditions. Differences in mineralogy are attributed to the
variations in chemical composition of
the original rock types. For example, at
the amphibolite facies, a shale may be
represented by the assemblage staurolite
+ garnet + biotite + plagioclase +
quartz, a basalt by hornblende +
plagioclase + quartz, and an impure
limestone by diopside + calcite +
quartz. A number of metamorphic
facies and sub-facies are recognized in
both regional and contact metamorphism. Metamorphic facies and their relative temperatures (T) and pressures (P)
are as follows:
Contact metamorphic facies—low P,
low to high T.

Zeolite facies—low T, low to intermediate P, gradational from *diagenesis.
Greenschist facies—low to intermediate
P and T.
Amphibolite facies—intermediate to
high P and T.
Glaucophane schist facies—low T, very
high P.
Granulite facies—high P and T.
Eclogite facies—high T and very high P.
See also zone (def. 1), grade (def. 1).
2. A rock unit or group of associated
rock units having particular features,
lithological, sedimentological, and
faunal, that reflect some specific environmental conditions. Thus, rocks
deposited at the same time in different
regions may be dissimilar because they
are of different facies, as is the case, for
example, with the *Permo-Triassic
rocks of marine facies and continental
facies in Britain. *Correlation of one
facies with another may be difficult,
especially if the fossils they contain are
restricted to each particular facies. If
this is the case they are known as *facies
fossils.* A unit of a particular facies may
be *diachronous, that is, it is present in
different areas at different times.

Fahrenheit scale. A scale of temperature in which the freezing point of
water is at 32° and the boiling point at
212°.

fair-weather cumulus cloud. A cumulus
cloud with limited vertical extent. The
clouds are prevented from rising further
by an inversion, usually formed by
subsidence in an area of high pressure.
As high-pressure areas rarely give rain,
clouds formed in this way are known as
fair-weather cumulus.

false bedding. An obsolete term for
*cross bedding.

family. A group in the taxonomic classification of organisms. A number of
related families together form an *order,
and a family itself is composed of one or
more genera (*see* genus). For example,
the *Hominidae*, to which *man belongs,
is a family of the order Primates. *See*
taxonomy.

fan cleavage. *Cleavage in which the planes are not parallel but form a fanlike arrangement with either an upward or downward convergence. This arrangement often results from rotation of beds in the limbs of a developing fold.

fathom. A unit of depth equal to 1.83 metres.

fault. A fracture in the earth's crust along the plane of which there has been displacement of rock on one side relative to the other, either in a horizontal, vertical, or oblique sense.

fault basin. A depression separated from the enclosing higher ground by faults.

fault block. 1. An area of the earth's crust that behaves as a single unit during faulting.
2. A rock body bounded by at least two faults, which can be either elevated or depressed relative to the surrounding region.

fault breccia. The mass of broken rock fragments along a fault plane produced during dislocation.

fayalite. A mineral of the *olivine group.

feldspar. The most important group of rock-forming minerals and the most abundant minerals in igneous rocks. They have a framework structure in which $(Si,Al)O_4$ tetrahedra are linked together with calcium, sodium, potassium, and barium ions occupying the large spaces in the framework. Feldspars may be considered to be mixtures of the four components:
$CaAl_2Si_2O_8$—*anorthite (An)*
$NaAlSi_3O_8$—*albite (Ab)*
$KAlSi_3O_8$—*orthoclase (Or)*
$BaAl_2Si_2O_8$—*celsian (Ce)*.
Barium feldspars are rare and most feldspars are members of the ternary system An-Ab-Or. Members of the series between $NaAlSi_3O_8$ and $CaAl_2Si_2O_8$ are plagioclase feldspars and those

Fig. 1: Thrust fault P = principal stress

Fig. 2: Dextral wrench fault

Fig. 3 Transform fault

spreading direction

sense of fault movement

Fig. 4: Graben

Fig. 5: Horst

Fig. 6: Normal fault

Fig. 7: Reverse fault

Types of fault

between $NaAlSi_3O_8$ and $KAlSi_3O_8$ are alkali feldspars.

Plagioclase feldspars.

The replacement $NaSi \rightleftharpoons CaAl$ results in a complete gradation between the two end members of the series, calcic (anorthite 100–90% An, 0–10% Ab; bytownite 90–70% An, 10–30% Ab; labradorite 70–50% An, 30–50% Ab) and sodic (andesine 50–30% An, 50–70% Ab; oligoclase 30–10% An, 70–90% Ab; albite 0–10% An, 100–90% Ab).

Plagioclases are triclinic and exhibit multiple lamellar twinning. They are milky white or colourless. Plagioclase occurs both as phenocrysts and in the groundmass of most basic and intermediate igneous rocks. Calcic plagioclases are characteristic of basic rocks and anorthosites. Sodic plagioclases are found in intermediate rocks. Albite occurs in some granites and also in spilites. Plagioclase is also found in a wide variety of metamorphic rocks.

Alkali feldspars. At high temperatures the replacement $Na \rightleftharpoons K$ results in a continuous chemical series between $NaAlSi_3O_8$ and $KAlSi_3O_8$. In most volcanic rocks, the feldspar has crystallized at a high temperature and has been quenched, thus retaining its high-temperature crystal structure. Slow cooling under plutonic conditions or crystallization at relatively lower temperatures results in the formation of two separate feldspars, one rich in $NaAlSi_3O_8$, the other in $KAlSi_3O_8$. The homogeneous high-temperature structural state of an alkali feldspar may become unstable at a lower temperature and unmixing occurs by the rearrangement of the alkali ions in the solid state. The resulting intergrowth of the two components is called *perthite.*

Sanidine is a high-temperature monoclinic potassium feldspar found in volcanic rocks, such as trachytes and rhyolites. *Anorthoclase* is a high-temperature sodium-potassium feldspar. *Orthoclase* (monoclinic) and *microcline* (triclinic) are intermediate- to low-temperature potassium feldspars found in plutonic acid- and alkali-rich rocks.

Adularia is a very low-temerature monoclinic potassium feldspar found in pegmatites. Alkali feldspars also occur in a wide variety of metamorphic rocks. Sanidine and orthoclase exhibit simple twinning but microcline and anorthoclase have multiple twins in two directions at right angles producing a tartan effect. Alkali feldspars are colourless, white, pink, or red.

feldspathoids. A group of undersaturated minerals in which the alkali cations sodium and potassium are located in cavities within the framework structure of $(Si, Al)O_4$ tetrahedra. Feldspathoids appear in place of feldspar in rocks deficient in silica. They do not occur with free quartz since they react with silica to form feldspar.

Nepheline has an ideal composition $NaAlSiO_4$ but always contains some *kalsilite* ($KAlSiO_4$), the amount of solid solution increasing with increasing temperature. Both nepheline and kalsilite are white or colourless and hexagonal. *Carnegieite* is a high-temperature cubic form of nepheline and *kaliophilite* is a rare form of kalsilite. Nepheline is a primary mineral in many alkaline igneous rocks and is produced during the metasomatic alteration of rocks through the process of *fenitization. Nepheline also occurs as a result of the reaction between basic magma and limestone. Kalsilite is found in potassium-rich volcanic rocks.

Leucite is a white pseudocubic mineral of composition $KAlSi_2O_6$ and often shows complex twinning. It occurs as euhedral icositetrahedral crystals in potassium-rich basic lavas.

Analcime (*analcite*) is a white or pink cubic mineral of composition $NaAlSi_2O_6 \cdot H_2O$ with some replacement $K \rightleftharpoons Na$. It occurs as a late-stage mineral in basic and intermediate igneous rocks. The minerals of the sodalite sub-group are as follows:

sodalite $3(NaAlSiO_4) \cdot NaCl$
nosean $3(NaAlSiO_4) \cdot Na_2SO_4$
haüyne $3(NaAlSiO_4) \cdot CaSO_4$

These minerals are cubic, commonly

blue in colour, and are found in alkaline igneous rocks such as nepheline syenites and phonolites. *Lazurite* is the major constituent of lapis-lazuli, formed by the metamorphism of limestone.

Cancrinite is a hexagonal white or colourless mineral of approximate composition $Na_8(AlSiO_4)_6(HCO_3)_2$. It is formed as a late-stage or secondary mineral as a result of the reaction between nepheline and carbon dioxide.

felsic. Denoting light-coloured minerals such as feldspar, feldspathoids, and quartz. *Compare* mafic.

felsite. Any crystalline acid volcanic rock.

femic. Denoting the iron- and magnesium-rich minerals of the CIPW normative classification. *Compare* salic.

fenitization. The alkaline metasomatism of country rock, typically gneissose, surrounding ijolite-carbonatite complexes. Quartzo-feldspathic rocks may be completely made over to syenitic alkali feldspar-nepheline-aegirine assemblages, termed *fenites*. Fenitization precedes or accompanies the emplacement of the carbonatite magma.

fen soils. *See* organic soils.

fenster. *See* window.

ferrallitic soils (latosols, lateritic soils, red earth). Soils that are typically found on the old planation surfaces of the humid tropics. The chief soil-forming process is ferrallitization where weathering and leaching are intense. Rapid formation results in a deep profile rich in clay and hydrated oxides of iron, aluminium, and manganese. Free drainage gives a red coloration to the soils but they may be yellowish where drainage is poorer. Any plant remains are rapidly broken down and the released nutrients are immediately used again by the plants so that little organic matter accumulates. This factor plus the kaolinitic clay results in a low cation exchange capacity, which makes these soils of little agricultural value. They

fall into the *oxisol order of the Seventh Approximation.

fer(ri)siallitic soils. Tropical soils formed in a less humid climate than *ferrallitic soils. The profile differs in that weathering and leaching are not so dominant, producing a soil that is not so deep. Where the parent material is particularly resistant only an A C profile occurs but sometimes an A Bt C profile develops. The whole profile is richer in weatherable minerals and has a higher cation exchange capacity than ferrallitic soils.

ferrisols. Soils that have developed similarly to *ferrallitic and *fersiallitic soils, their profiles being less intensely weathered and leached than ferrallitic soils but more so than fersiallitic soils. Unlike ferrallitic soils these are found on sloping sites where surface erosion is an important process. The profile is similar to a ferrallitic soil, being red in colour and having a similar structure, but often clay movement results in a textural B horizon. These soils have a low cation exchange capacity but are more fertile than ferrallitic soils. They fall into the *ultisol order of the Seventh Approximation.

ferroaugite. A monoclinic *pyroxene.

ferromagnesian minerals. Minerals that are rich in iron and/or magnesium and usually dark in colour, for example olivines, pyroxenes, amphiboles, and biotite.

fertilizer. Any organic substance or inorganic salt applied to the soil to improve crop production. The nutrient elements most important for plant growth are nitrogen, phosphorus, and potassium.

fetch. The distance of the stretch of open water over which the frictional effect of a wind that is blowing in a constant direction is actually generating waves. In small sea areas, fetch distance is usually limited by the dimensions of that sea area; in the open ocean, however, the limit is usually imposed by the constantly changing meteorological situation. There is also a relation between fetch distance, wind strength, wind duration, and the maximum size of waves produced. For a given wind speed, the largest possible waves require a minimum fetch distance; and for a given fetch distance, there is an optimum size wave that can be generated, however hard or long the wind blows. In Dover harbour, for instance, easterly winds blowing across the short 35 kilometre fetch from France can only raise waves to a height of some 3 metres. Very large ocean waves may require fetch distances of the order of 1000 km or more.

fiamme. Flattened disc-shaped glassy bodies found in ignimbrites and imparting a eutaxitic structure. See pyroclastic rocks.

fibrolite. A fibrous or acicular form of sillimanite. See aluminium silicates.

field completion. A check of a map under compilation carried out in the field to ensure that all the details are shown and to make any corrections or amendments that may be necessary. Details usually affected by the field check are names and civil boundaries.

field intensity. The strength of a magnetic field at a particular point on the earth's surface.

field reversal. See magnetic reversal.

filtering (in climatology). A method of separating components of a selected time period from all other possible periodic components. It is most frequently used for investigations into changes of climate.

filter pressing. See magmatic differentiation.

fiord (fjord). A long narrow sea inlet lying between steep mountain slopes, which often reach up to several hundred metres above sea level. Fiords are glaciated valleys which, owing to a relative rise of sea level after the melting of the Pleistocene ice sheets, have become flooded by the sea. Many fiords display very considerable depths, some well in excess of 1000 metres. Because of glacial action, they are characterized by the existence of gouged basins separated from the open sea by sills of solid rock, often capped by moraine, marking the point where the glacier that cut the valley lost much of its erosive power, either through melting or slowing down. The cross section of a fiord is often U-shaped.

firn (nevé). A half-way stage in the transformation from fresh snow to glacier ice. Fresh snow is very loosely packed and has a density between 0.1 and 0.2. Compaction and recrystallization reduce the pore space between grains, increasing the density. Firn exists when the density reaches 0.5. The word means "of last year", and in this case refers to snow that has survived one summer. Further compaction continues until glacier ice of density 0.89 to 0.90 is formed, though this may take many years.

firth (in Scotland). A lengthy estuary or arm of the sea. Firths bear some similarity to *fiords and some have the closed and deep depressions and rock sills typical of fiords. They developed from river or glacial valleys that later experienced the post-glacial transgression, becoming partially flooded by the sea. Firths on Scotland's E coast are not classed as the fiord type. The lochs and firths of the W coast of Scotland are fiords but have rather flatter hillside slopes than, for example, the fiords of Norway or Alaska.

fish. One of a variety of aquatic vertebrates belonging to any of the following classes: *Agnatha, *Placodermi, *Chondrichthyes, and *Osteichthyes.

fjord. See fiord.

flaking. The splitting of rocks around their margins into curved flakes, which vary in thickness from a few millimetres to a few centimetres, depending on the process involved. The most common process is the chemical decay of minerals, especially *hydration, causing expansion. The growth of salt crystals from solution beneath the surface of porous rocks can give rise to flaking, the flakes in this case being frequently backed by a thin layer of salt. In both these cases there tends to be a series of concentric layers of flakes around one boulder. Flaking results in a rounding of the block, since there is a preferential attack on edges and corners. The process can only take place above ground level, and the final development is a flat rock surface. Flaking on concave surfaces produces hollows.

flame structure. A sedimentary structure in which an underlying bed has been squeezed up into an overlying horizon in flamelike tongues as a result of loading. Generally there is some degree of horizontal displacement.

flap structure. A structure resulting from gravity collapse, consisting of a bed originally on the limb of an anticline that has bent as it slipped downwards and come to rest in an inverted position.

flexure fold. A type of fold best developed in rocks where there is good layering. As the fold develops the beds slip over one another.

flint. A nodular variety of chalcedony formed in chalk. *See* silica minerals.

flocculation (in soil science). The process by which colloidal (i.e. clay-size) particles join together forming groups, called *floccules*. Colloidal material tends to adopt this habit in the presence of neutral salts, notably salts of calcium; in the presence of alkaline salts, especially sodium, the particles adopt the opposite habit and separate as independent units. Calcium therefore improves the structure of the soil by helping aggregation, and this in turn improves its agricultural value; flocculation of otherwise intractable clays is often encouraged by the addition of lime to make them more productive.

flood. The state of a river when the volume of water flowing in it exceeds *bankfull, and water commences to spread away from the channel over the *floodplain. Floods are produced by discharge increases due to exceptional rainfall and runoff. In hydrology, much effort has been devoted to the study of floods because of their great geomorphic significance and their cost to life and property on floodplains. Flood frequency curves have been produced for many rivers, showing the likely recurrence interval of floods of varying magnitudes, based on the analysis of past *discharge records from gauging stations. Geomorphologically, floods can accomplish great landscape modifications in short periods, since the increased velocity of flood rivers produces an increase in erosional capacity proportional to the square of that velocity: thus if velocity doubles, erosional capacity increases four times. *See also* geomorphic processes.

floodplain. A relatively level area bordering a river, subject to periodic flooding and made up of sediments deposited by the river, which bury the rock-cut valley to a variable depth. In the larger rivers it may contain the following features: the river channel itself, *oxbows, *point bars, scars of former *meanders resulting from their migration downvalley, areas of stagnant sedimenting water (*sloughs*), *levées, backswamp deposits of fine sediments in slack water away from the river, and sandy flood debris. In smaller streams all these features will not be present, but the Mississippi and Mekong, for example, display them all.
Floodplains originate from deposits within the river channel on the point bars and from overbank deposits in time of flooding. It is now thought that deposits within the river channel are the major source, constituting possibly 60-80% of floodplain material, but

actively aggrading rivers probably owe more to overbank deposits.

The existence of a floodplain does not mean a river is actively aggrading: meanders migrate downstream, depositing material on the inside of bends and eroding material on the outside. Once deposited, a particle will remain static in the floodplain for a considerable period (about 1000 years in one stream studied) until the next meander upstream had eroded its way down to the position of that grain and re-entrains it. Floodplains in streams in equilibrium therefore represent a temporary storage for sediment on its passage through the valley. See also lateral erosion.

flood tide. The incoming of the tidal stream; the rising tide, i.e. that part of a tide cycle following the low-water stage and preceding the high-water stage. Compare ebb tide.

Florida Current. A major surface current on the W periphery of the Atlantic Ocean. It forms one of two branches of the North Equatorial Current. At about longitude 60° W, the North Equatorial Current splits up into two important currents: one flows into the Caribbean Sea but then re-enters the Atlantic Ocean via the Gulf of Mexico, and thereafter flows as the Florida Current. The Florida Current extends from the Florida Staits to roughly the latitude of Cape Hatteras. As such, it constitutes the S portion of the Gulf Stream system. The discharge rate of the Florida Current is probably of the order of some 26 million cubic metres per second, but this figure varies significantly from one period to another, and almost certainly seasonally. It is a fast-flowing current that is particularly confined to the surface waters (reaching down to depths of between 600 and 800 m), probably attaining speeds in excess of 150 centimetres per second quite close to the coasts of Florida. An important factor in the generation of this current is the significant difference in water level that exists between the Gulf of Mexico coast and the Atlantic coast of Florida.

flowage. Rock deformation resulting from the stressing of the rock beyond its limit of elasticity, but without fracture.

flow cleavage. A type of cleavage resulting from solid-state flowage in a rock, accompanied by the regrowth of minerals. Traces of bedding are almost destroyed. See also slaty cleavage.

fluorite (fluorspar). A cubic mineral of composition CaF_2. The purple colour of the familiar variety blue john is due to the presence of colloidal calcium; other varieties are white, green, and yellow. Fluorite is found in hydrothermal vein deposits and as a late-stage mineral in some alkaline and acid igneous rocks.

flute. A sedimentary structure in the form of a hollow on the surface of a poorly consolidated bed of sediment, resulting from the scouring action of passing water. When this is infilled by an overlying bed of silt or sand the form of this hollow is preserved, and is exposed as a flute cast on the undersurface of the overlying bed.

fluvial (fluviatile). Of or relating to a river.

fluvioglacial. Denoting any process or resultant landform involving the present of water derived from a glacier or ice sheet. Glacial meltwater can transport and erode material just as a normal river, but if it lies within or beneath the associated ice, it may be capable of extremely efficient erosion due to increased pressures or velocities. Fluvioglacial deposits can generally be distinguished from those of purely glacial origin since they exhibit rounding, sorting, and stratification.

flux (flux density). A rate of flow of some quantity, usually some form of energy, through a unit area.

flysch. Thinly bedded marine sandstones, marls, shales, clays, conglomerates, and greywackes, which fill a trough adjacent to a rapidly rising mountain chain and represent rapid erosion and deposition prior to the main period of orogeny. The term was originally used by Alpine geologists and applies strictly to the sediments associated with the Alpine orogeny. *Compare* molasse.

focal depth. The shortest distance between the focus of an earthquake and the earth's surface.

focus. The centre of an earthquake, where strain energy is converted into elastic waves. It is the source of seismic waves produced during an earthquake. For convenience it is thought of as being a point source, although strictly speaking earthquake waves originate from a nonfinite source, such as a fault plane.

fog. A cloud near the ground surface composed of minute water droplets in suspension. It is sufficiently dense for the drops to produce a reduction in visibility to less than 1 km. Condensation of water to form the droplets in a fog can occur in many ways, and fogs are often classified by their method of formation—radiation fog, advection fog, etc. The most frequent method is by some form of cooling, such as radiational cooling at night; in advective fog the lower layers of the atmosphere are cooled through turbulent contact with the ground. More rarely, condensation can be achieved through evaporation from the surface.

In industrial areas, the greater supply of condensation nuclei and hygroscopic particles enable fogs to form even when relative humidity is less than 100%. Where smoke is abundant, this can produce a thick and particularly unpleasant type of fog, known as smog (an abbreviation of *smoke fog*).

föhn. A warm dry wind that descends the leeward side of mountain ranges to give extremely rapid thaws of lying snow in winter. They occur whenever rapid descent favours adiabatic warming, whether or not there has been cooling at the *saturated adiabatic lapse

rate on the upwind side of the mountains. However, they are of climatological significance only where the descent is sufficient to produce a marked warming, as in the Alps, Rockies, or Andes, where airflow is at right angles to the mountain barrier and the maximum rate of descent achieved.

fold. A buckling of bedded sedimentary rocks due to deformation processes or the effect of gravity. *See also* orogenesis.

fold axis. An imaginary line parallel to the *hinge line of a fold, from which the rock strata dip away in different directions (downwards from a crest; upwards from a trough). See diagram ◂

fold belt. *See* mobile belt.

fold limb. Either of the two flanks on either side of the axis of a fold. The angle between the limbs is called the *interlimb angle.*

foliation. A banded or laminated structure within a metamorphic rock, resulting from the metamorphic segregation of minerals into compositionally different layers, parallel to the schistosity. The term is also commonly used to describe any parallel planar element in a metamorphic rock, such as schistosity and cleavage.

foot wall. The surface of rock beneath a fault plane or ore body. *Compare* hanging wall.

foraminifera. A type of planktonic organism. Most species display jelly-like flesh bodies surrounded by a shell or casing of carbonate of lime. The casing is often flask- or sphere-shaped. Foraminifera abound chiefly in the surface layers of the sea, and tend to reach their maximum development near the equator. The tests or casings of dead foraminifera make up a large proportion of the organic ooze deposits, for example, *globigerina ooze, which contains some 30 per cent foraminiferal tests.

forecast (in meteorology). A statement about the probable weather events for specific areas for certain time periods.

Fig. 1: Symmetrical syncline   Fig. 2: Symmetrical anticline

Fig. 3   Fig. 4

open tight isoclinal   upright inclined overturned

axial plane

culmination

depression

trend

Fig. 5

antiform

Fig. 8 synclinal axis

plunge

Fig. 7: Recumbent fold

Fig. 6: Asymmetric fold   Fig. 9

synform

Types of fold

Forecasts are normally given at three levels of detail: (i) short-period, dealing in depth with the probable events for the next 24–48 hours; (ii) medium range, covering about one week, in which the expected movements of the main high and low pressure systems are covered; (iii) the long-range forecast for a month or even a season, in which the only details refer to climatological averages and whether the weather is expected to be warmer or cooler, wetter or drier.

The methods required for working out these forecasts differ for the time period involve. For the short-period forecast, satellite photographs show the major cloud belts, radar shows the areas of precipitation, and over land areas there are large numbers of stations continuously recording the weather elements. Together they provide a fair assessment of likely events supplemented by computer calculations of pressure fields for 24–48 hours ahead

(see numerical weather forecasting). Interpretations can then be made on the basis of these forecast maps. Medium-term forecasting for the U.S. and Europe is largely based on experience of previous weather sequences together with a knowledge of the upper atmosphere, particularly the *Rossby waves of the mid-latitude westerlies. As these to some degree control the direction of movement of low pressure systems, information about the state of the upper atmosphere aids forecasting for this time scale. However, as even quite small initial disturbances can dramatically and rapidly change the weather, success is only moderate.

For long-range forecasts, different techniques are required. In Britain, the *analogue method is used. In this method former weather charts are compared with present charts and it is assumed that similarities in the charts can be used to predict weather events. Sea-surface temperatures and their anomalies are also included as these are important in affecting depression formation and energy transfer to the atmosphere. In America, long-range forecasts are based on computer simulations of the atmosphere. Details of the present state of the atmosphere at many different levels are fed into the computer systems and then run for a time period equivalent to an one month in real time to forecast pressure movements. Neither method is entirely satisfactory and there is considerable debate as to whether it is theoretically possible to forecast movement in the atmosphere for such long time periods.

foredeep. See trench.

fore-dune. A coastal dune growing in the newest line of dunes nearest to the sea. Some authorities put a maximum size of about three metres on fore-dunes. The usual distinguishing characteristics are dominance by the grass Agropyron junceum, which is capable of tolerating the occasional drenching with salt water to which the fore-dune is subject, and a very open nature with low cover values and large areas of bare sand. Since the fore-dune is produced by the coalescence of individual grass and sand mounds, at a very early stage it will appear broken with an uneven crest line.

foreland. A stable area of older cratonic rocks marginal to an orogenic belt, generally part of the continental crust. When two continents collide the intervening wedge of sediments is squeezed between two forelands, onto which these sediments are thrust and overfolded.

foreset beds. See delta deposits.

foreshocks. A series of seismic waves recorded before the principal shock of an earthquake, resulting from small slips or fractures in brittle rocks as they reach their *yield point, as a result of a buildup in stress.

foreshore. The part of a beach that becomes covered and uncovered by water during the process of tidal rise and fall. It extends from low-water spring tide level to normal high-water springs level, and its width will naturally depend upon the tidal range and gradient of the beach.

foresight. See levelling.

formation. The fundamental unit in the lithostratigraphical classification of bodies of rock (see stratigraphy, lithostratigraphy). A formation is formally defined by a *type section at a type locality, on the basis of readily observable lithological features that distinguish it from bodies of adjacent rock. It should preferably be marked off from these by a distinct lithological change, such as might be found at an unconformity, but it may have more arbitrary boundaries in a gradually changing rock sequence. Thickness is not a criterion in its definition; a single formation will often differ in thickness at different points. Stratigraphically adjacent and related formations may be associated to constitute a *group. A formation may contain *members but need not be entirely composed of them.

form lines. Lines drawn on a map to give an impression of the terrain where there is insufficient information to construct accurate contours. They are usually represented by dashed lines rather than unbroken ones. In areas mapped by air photography there may be parts obscured by cloud and these are often covered by form lines in the absence of alternative heighting data.

forsterite. A mineral of the *olivine group.

fossil. The remains of any organism that lived in the past. The term was originally applied loosely to anything ancient and dug up and as an adjective may still be used in this sense. A fossil can be the whole or any part of an animal or plant, usually chemically altered (i.e. fossilized); it may be an impression of the shape of an organism that has been preserved in some way (*see* cast, mould) or it can be simply the remains of the effects of an organism in the past, such as fossil tracks, excrement, or burrows (*see* trace fossil). *See also* derived fossil, type fossil, zone fossil.

Fourier (harmonic) analysis. A mathematical method of analysing a data series that contains periodic variations, such as seasonal precipitation. These can be represented by a series of sine or cosine functions.

foyaite. *See* syenite.

fractocumulus cloud. Broken or fragmented cloud rising only slightly above the *condensation level. They are most frequently seen on early mornings when there has been sufficient convection for the clouds to approach the condensation level.

fractostratus cloud (scud). Cloud that is broken and ragged, rather similar in appearance to fractocumulus but found beneath altostratus or nimbostratus clouds, frequently preceding a warm front. It is the result of condensation taking place in the moist layer beneath the main cloud base, either by turbulent mixing or through the addition of moisture by precipitation falling from higher levels.

fracture cleavage. A series of closely spaced fractures and parallel joints produced in deformed rocks that have been subjected to only minor metamorphism.

free air anomaly. A gravity anomaly that takes account of altitude but does not take account of attraction effects resulting from topography and isostatic compensation.

free face. A vertical or near vertical facet of slope cut in bare rock. It is rare to find faces actually at 90°, and various writers have adopted different critical values for the minimum allowable slope; slopes of above 40-45° are usually termed free faces. They occur in consolidated materials, which can maintain their verticality when the removal of debris from the footslope exceeds the rate of debris production from the face above. Wave erosion at the foot of a sea cliff, or lateral planation by a stream at the side of its valley, are situations producing free faces. Owing to this removal of debris from its foot, the slope becomes constantly oversteepened, and slips and slides lead to stripping of material from the whole face equally, thereby maintaining the face by *parallel retreat. If the agency removing the debris at the foot ceases to do so, for example the accumulation of a beach at a cliff foot cutting off direct wave action, retreat at the foot of the free face slows down compared with its upper part, and the face will tend to be obliterated by decline to a gentle angle. *See also* basal sapping.

freeze-thaw. Denoting weathering processes involving the freezing and thawing of water within pre-existing rock fissures. When water expands on freezing, it tends to enlarge cracks: on thawing, the enlarged cracks can contain more water than before, which will cause increased enlargement on renewed freezing. Eventually, particles become broken away from the main mass of rock. Freeze-thaw processes weaken rocks before they are subjected to other agents of weathering and erosion. A notable example is *glacial plucking.

freezing level. The height above sea level of the layer of the atmosphere that is at a temperature of 0°C. More frequently, its height is quoted in terms of pressure level, e.g. 850 mb. As water does not automatically freeze at 0°C (*see* freezing nucleus), it would be more accurately called the melting level, representing the point at which solid precipitation would melt. If the ground temperature is below freezing, the freezing level would be stated as being at station level, though if there is an inversion aloft the situation may be complex.

freezing nucleus. Water droplets in clouds do not automatically freeze when the temperatures fall below freezing point. Being very small, the droplets require some form of *nucleus on which the crystalline growth can develop but such nuclei are not as effective or numerous as condensation nuclei and do not produce total freezing at $0°C$. Instead a few ice crystals will appear at between $-5°C$ and $-10°C$ and become more frequent with lower temperature. The nuclei are composed of volcanic dust or clay particles with a similar crystalline structure to that of ice, and in some cases fractures or splinters of ice crystals may themselves act as nuclei. At temperatures below $-40°C$, spontaneous freezing takes place even in the absence of nuclei.

freezing point. The temperature at which the liquid and solid phases of a substance are in equilibrium at standard pressure (1013.25 mb); for water this is $0°C$. Because nuclei (*see* nucleus) are required for cloud droplets to freeze, water can exist at temperatures far below its true freezing point. The term is therefore primarily used for ground surface temperature observations and forecasts, particularly in connection with road surface conditions.

freezing rain. Rain or drizzle that falls onto a ground surface that is below $0°C$, the water freezing to give a coating of ice. It can occur when a layer of rising warm air, such as at a warm front, is moving slowly over a cold surface where the temperature remains below freezing point. As the warm air eventually reaches the ground surface this state is normally of short duration.

friction. The mechanical force of resistance operating between two substances in contact. In the atmosphere, it is the resistance between the ground surface and the layer of air above it, though the thickness of this layer varies appreciably. The term can also be used when referring to wind shear.

The effects of friction on airflow are numerous. Wind speeds are reduced near the ground and there is a movement of wind across the isobars from higher to lower pressure, compared with the *geostrophic wind when friction is excluded. The rate of increase of speed with height away from the surface is affected by the roughness of the ground, extremes being represented by oceans and urban areas.

frigid zones. Cold areas of the earth's surface, either in polar regions or at high altitude.

front. A transition zone between air of different thermal characteristics and origins. On surface pressure charts, fronts are depicted in two-dimensional form along the line of maximum thermal gradient, where this can be determined. In cross section they represent a surface of separation between the two *air masses, sloping gently away from the surface warm air. Distinctive weather phenomena are associated with fronts and are hence very important in short-period weather forecasting. Problems of precise definition of a front occur because it represents a thermal gradient, the strength of which is not necessarily related to weather activity, so the same gradient may have quite different degrees of vertical motion. In forecasting, a front is often called a trough of low pressure. *See also* depression.

frontogenesis. The process of intensification of the thermal gradient along a frontal zone: part of the formation of a *depression. It can take place whenever the isotherms are suitably orientated during conditions of *confluence and *convergence in the lower atmosphere.

frontolysis. The weakening of the thermal gradient at a frontal zone. This is produced under the reverse conditions of frontogenesis, i.e. with surface *divergence of air and often subsidence. When frontolysis is taking place, precipitation along the front stops and the cloud sheet breaks up and eventually disappears.

frost. Frost occurs when the temperature falls below 0°C. Subdivisions are made into ground frost and air frost based on thermometer readings at grass level and screen level (4 feet) respectively. It is normally recognized by the icy deposit that usually forms under such temperature conditions, but if the air is very dry, frost may occur without forming icy deposits. For weather-forecasting purposes, grades of severity of frost are distinguished with -0.1 to -3.5°C slight, -3.6 to -6.4°C moderate, -6.5 to -11.5°C severe, and below -11.5°C very severe. Allowances are made for wind speed, which influences the sensation of cold.

frost heaving. The swelling of the ground surface through a combination of *congeliturbation and the effects of *needle ice.

frost hollow. An area that has a greater liability to frost incidence than its surroundings. As cold air has a slightly greater density than warm air, it tends to collect in hollows or low ground and so areas of high frost incidence are usually in hollows where free drainage of air is prevented. The most famous frost hollow is Gstettneralm in the Austrian Alps where temperatures as low as -52°C have been recorded. In England, an area near Rickmansworth has similar temperature conditions to Braemar in Scotland as a result of cold air drainage into a frost hollow dammed by a railway embankment.

frost-shattering. The breaking apart of masses of rock by the continued enlargement of cracks within them through *freeze-thaw action, in areas where the temperature fluctuates for considerable periods around freezing point. The resultant outcrops and debris are all highly angular in appearance, and this is the major characteristic of frost-shattered forms.

fugitive. See volatile.

fulgurite. A tubular or dendritic mass of fused silica originating when lightning strikes sand.

full. A shingle *beach ridge or a *berm composed of sand. When ridges are called fulls, the separating parallel depressions are known as swales.

fuller's earth. A clay rich in montmorillonite. See clay minerals.

fumigation. (in meteorology). The result of the influx of heavily polluted air down to the ground surface. It most frequently occurs after night-time cooling has given a temperature inversion a few hundred metres above the ground surface, beneath which industrial pollution has accumulated. When convection starts after solar heating next morning, rising air motion will resume and compensating downward flow will take the polluted air to the ground giving sudden high values of pollution.

fungi. Heterotrophic microflora that are less abundant in numbers than bacteria in the soil (up to 1 000 000 per gram of soil) but greater in bulk, as they have a filamentous nature. They require moisture and may be found in alkaline, neutral, or acid soils. Thus in the latter they number more than bacteria or actinomycetes. Although they cannot oxidize ammonium compounds or fix atmospheric nitrogen they are more important than bacteria in the formation of humus and in the promotion of soil stability. Fungi are capable of decomposing even the most resistant plant materials such as cellulose and lignin. The mycelia of certain mushroom fungi may form an association with higher trees called mycorrhizae. This association is of mutual benefit to plant and fungi and where present there is a marked increase in the uptake of nutrients.

G

gabbro. A coarse-grained basic igneous rock, the product of plutonic crystallization of basalt magma. The essential constituents are plagioclase that is more calcic than anorthite, usually labradorite, and clinopyroxene, usually augite or titanaugite. Many gabbros contain olivine in addition. Accessory minerals include magnetite, ilmenite, apatite, biotite, and hornblende.

Rocks in which orthopyroxene, usually hypersthene, predominates over clinopyroxene are called *norites*. With an increase in the proportion of plagioclase, gabbros and norites pass via leucocratic varieties into anorthosites; with an increase in olivine and pyroxene they pass via melagabbros into ultramafic rocks. With an increase in the proportion of olivine at the expense of pyroxene, gabbro passes into troctolite and allivalite. With a change to plagioclase of more sodic composition, gabbros pass into diorites.

Eucrite is a variety containing olivine, two pyroxenes, and plagioclase of bytownite-anorthite composition. Gabbroic rocks containing pyroxenes and olivines rich in iron are termed *ferrogabbros*. Alkali gabbros (syenogabbros) are marked by the introduction of feldspathoids or alkali feldspar.

Most gabbros have equigranular textures; others are ophitic or, rarely, orbicular. Reaction rims are common features and rarely multiple rims involving olivine-pyroxene-hornblende-biotite may be preserved. The medium-grained equivalent of gabbro is termed microgabbro or dolerite. Gabbroic rocks occur in stratiform layered bodies, ophiolite complexes, and as nodules in basalts.

gal. A unit of acceleration equal to one cm per second per second (named after Galileo). In practice this unit is too large and measurements of the strength of the earth's gravitational field at a point are made in milligals (one thousandth of a gal); 1 milligal is equivalent to 9.8×10^{-3}N kg^{-1}. *See* gravity units.

gale. A wind speed averaged over a 10 minute period of between 34 and 40 knots or Force 8 on the *Beaufort scale. Most statistics on gales refer to speeds of 34 knots or above, though higher speeds have other terms, such as strong gale, storm, violent storm, and hurricane. Gales most frequently occur during the passage of an intense depression.

galena. The chief lead ore (lead sulphide, PbS), found as grey metallic cubes of high density and often associated with sphalerite, barytes, fluorspar, and calcite in hydrothermal veins.

Gall's projection. A *cylindrical map projection with the cylinder cutting the earth's surface at 45° north and south. The meridians only have true scale at the points of intersection, the scale increasing polewards and decreasing towards the equator. It is neither a homolographic nor orthomorphic projection, and is not often used.

gamaray log. A logging technique run in wells that records the natural radioactivity of the formations through which it passes. High values are given by shales, whereas sandstones give low readings. It can be run in cased holes, as it does not rely upon the electrical properties of the formation.

gangue. Minerals found in an ore deposit that have no commercial value and must be removed during the refining process.

garnets. A group of cubic minerals with a general formula $R_3^{2+}R_2^{3+}Si_3O_{12}$ where the divalent metals are magnesium, iron, manganese, or calcium and the trivalent metals are aluminium, iron, or chromium. The following six end-members are recognized:

pyrope—$Mg_3Al_2Si_3O_{12}$
almandine—$Fe_3^{2+}Al_2Si_3O_{12}$
spessartite—$Mn_3Al_2Si_3O_{12}$
grossular—$Ca_3Al_2Si_3O_{12}$
andradite—$Ca_3(Fe^{3+},Ti)_2Si_3O_{12}$
uvarovite—$Ca_3Cr_2Si_3O_{12}$

Compositions corresponding to pure

end-members are rare and garnets are divided into two series, *pyralspite* (*pyr*ope, *al*mandine, *sp*essartite) and *ugrandite* (*u*varovite, *gr*ossular, *an*dradite). Little chemical variation between pyralspite and ugrandite garnets occurs.

Garnets commonly develop dodecahedral and icositetrahedral forms and are a variety of colours. Pyralspite garnets are typically pink, red, or brown. *Melanite* is a dark brown to black variety of andradite, rich in titanium and occuring in ijolites and nepheline syenites. In general, garnets are characteristic of metamorphic rocks. Almandine is found in medium- to high-grade regionally metamorphosed argillaceous sediments. Pyrope is found in ultrabasic rocks and eclogites, and grossular occurs in metamorphosed limestones.

GARP. *Abbrev. for* Global Atmospheric Research Programme. A long-term international project for studying the physical processes of the atmosphere that are essential for an understanding of its circulation. There are also a series of sub-programmes that are relevant to the main theme of obtaining full comprehension of the large-scale dynamics of the atmosphere.

gas laws. The basic physical equations that relate the pressure (p), volume (V), temperature (T), and density (ρ) of a perfect gas. These include the equation of state ($p = R\rho T/M$, where R is the Universal Gas Constant and M is the molecular weight of the gas) and Boyle's Law, which states that at constant temperature, the volume of a given mass of gas is inversely proportional to the pressure of the gas. This law controls the cooling of air as it rises and expands into regions of lower atmospheric pressure.

gastroliths. Stones and pebbles ingested by reptiles and birds to assist in the breakdown of food in the gizzard. Fossil structures associated with the remains of extinct reptiles are thought to be gastroliths.

Gastropoda. The class of the phylum *Mollusca that includes the slugs and snails. Typically they have a shell that is often coiled in a helical spiral; unlike that of the *Cephalopoda it is not divided into chambers. Most gastropods are marine but some live in fresh water and others are terrestrial. Fossils are known from the Cambrian Period onwards and the class has continued to flourish and diversify to the present day.

gazetteer. A list of names, both of places and geographical features, generally with some reference system of coordinates and an indication of the type of feature, e.g. village, stream, mountain, etc.

geanticline. A very large anticlinal structure that has developed within geosynclinal sediments, as a result of lateral compression.

gedrite. An orthorhombic mineral of the amphibole group.

general circulation of the atmosphere. The mechanism by which energy is transferred from surplus to deficit areas of the world. It is constrained by a number of processes that interact with the main driving force of the circulation to result in the observed system of winds and disturbances. This circulation is basic to an understanding of the climates of the world as it determines the direction and strength of winds in any latitudinal position.

The atmospheric circulation is very complex, but it can be simplified into a series of belts. Within the tropics there are the trade winds converging towards the intertropical convergence zone (ITCZ). Polewards of the subtropical anticyclones are the main westerly winds with a small area of easterlies near the poles. These mean winds are essentially zonal in direction and do not appear to be an effective system in transferring surplus radiational energy towards the temperate and polar lati-

General circulation of the atmosphere

tropics, air rises at the ITCZ, releasing latent heat and gaining potential energy. This is moved towards the subtropics where it descends and maintains the trade winds and where much moisture is evaporated from the sea surface to continue the convection cell towards the ITCZ. This cellular circulation has been called the *Hadley Cell. Pole-wards, the mean charts show a dominance of zonal winds, but exchange here is effected by depressions, which advect warm and cold air and aid their mixing. As this process takes place at different longitudes for only short periods of time, it is averaged out on the mean maps.

The driving force for the atmospheric circulation is the differential pattern of net radiation received at the earth's surface. If the earth were uniform and stationary this would give rise to a simple thermal cell between equator (surplus) and polar (deficit) areas. However, the effects of the earth's rotation, the presence of mountain barriers, the distribution of land and sea, and the positions of the ocean currents all help to modify the simple thermal cell into the complex general circulation of the atmosphere.

Increasingly realistic models of the general circulation of the atmosphere are being obtained now that more is known about the controlling factors and high-speed computers with large memory stores are available. Over the years the models or simulations have become more sophisticated, starting by trying to account for the primary processes responsible for maintaining the large-scale features of the circulation, using the primitive equations of motion. It is now possible to construct models of the circulation during an ice age from what we know about the controlling factors, but the large scale on which the models work makes them unsuitable for long-range forecasting. Depressions can be initiated or affected by small-scale processes and greatly change the expected weather.

tudes. However, long-term studies have shown that meridional exchange takes place as shown in the diagram. In the

genus (*pl.* **genera**). A group in the taxonomic classification of organisms that consists of one or more related *species. One or several genera form a *family. For example, the genus *Homo*, to which man belongs, is placed in the family Hominidae. A generic name always begins with a capital letter and is italicized. It is always included with the specific name in naming a species, when it is often abbreviated to the initial letter. Thus, the species to which modern man belongs is *Homo sapiens* or *H. sapiens*. A genus is defined on the basis of the species it contains, the most typical of which is designated as the *type species. See* taxonomy.

geocentric. At or relating to the centre of the earth.

geochronology. The science of age determination of parts of the earth. It has two branches: absolute dating and relative dating. The former is more modern, and involves techniques such as carbon-14, potassium-argon, and radioactive decay methods to put actual ages in years B.P. (before present) on organic remains, rocks, or sediments. Relative dating includes fossil correlations, pollen analysis and correlation, matching of tills from different areas on the basis of weathering or geological content, archaeological indicators, and several lesser used techniques that help establish stratigraphy. Relative dating seeks to put events in order; absolute dating tries to give precise dates of occurrence. In geomorphology both are used, especially in studies of the Pleistocene and post-Pleistocene periods.

geode. *See* druse.

geodesy. The science concerned with determining the exact shape and size of the earth and the exact position of points on the earth's surface. In addition it investigates the earth's gravitational field, variations in tides, and the earth's rotation. It provides the reference surface from which astronomical observations are made.

geodetic surveying. The large-scale surveying of the earth's surface, taking into account its curvature. Precise measurements from geodetic surveys provide the horizontal control points for more detailed surveying.

geodimeter. A modern surveying instrument used for the accurate measurement of distance. The measurement is indirect, being obtained by timing the period required for a beam of light to travel from one end of a line to the other and return. Since the velocity of light is known, the distance can then be calculated. The instrument sends out a light beam, which is reflected by a mirror at the other end of the line to be measured. Suggested maximum ranges are 5 to 10 kilometres in daylight and 15 to 25 kilometres in darkness, depending on the light source. The geodimeter is ideal for rapid *base-line measurement.

geology. The study of the structure and composition of the earth. *See* petrology, geomorphology, geophysics. For geological time scale *see* chronostratigraphy.

geomagnetic equator. A great circle equidistant between the geomagnetic poles. It connects all points of zero geomagnetic latitude and its plane is at right angles to the earth's magnetic axis.

geomagnetic field. The earth's magnetic field, which causes a compass needle to align north-south whatever its location on the earth's surface.

geomorphic processes. The chemical and physical interactions between natural forces (e.g. running water, waves, ice, gravity, biological phenomena, etc.) and the earth's surface, which act to modify the landscape. An increasing trend in geomorphology is towards the study of processes, inferring from these the landforms being created, as contrasted with more traditional geomorphology, in which processes were merely inferred from landforms. Processes are determined by the environmental variables of climate, geology, and base level; a change in one or some of these will change the nature or rate of processes. Processes fall into the broad categories of weathering, erosion, transport, or deposition, within each of which many different types can be recognized. Rates of process, as shown by measurements or inference, are characterized by great spatial and temporal variation.

A central concept in geomorphology is the relative significance, in terms of work done in landscape formation, of infrequent but highly destructive events such as storms, floods, and gales and the very frequent but far less effective events of average conditions. In storms, whole beaches can come or go overnight; rivers can change their courses and expand their floodplains during floods; sand dunes can be built and eroded in a single severe gale. This is because capacity for work increases as a power function of the increase of the agency concerned; erosional capacity of rivers is proportional not to velocity, but the square of velocity; wave energy is proportional to the square of wave height; the transporting power of wind increases as the cube of its velocity. Major landscape features are largely shaped by the infrequent severe events, but Leopold, Wolman, and Miller (1964) conclude that moderate events of moderate frequency are responsible for most work done.

A better understanding comes from actually measuring the processes: this shows the rates at which the same process operates in different environments, and the comparative effectiveness of different processes in the same environment. It also shows the spatial and temporal distribution of changes, and once this is understood, prediction to the future is easier and more reliable, and the formation of existing landforms is more easily appreciated. Measurements of processes are taken as they operate, by the use of rods inserted into slopes and river banks for example, recording losses, or by the use of map evidence recording, for example, the

successive growth of a spit across a river mouth, measurements from which can show variation in rates at different periods.

geomorphology. The study of the evolution of landforms, excluding the major forms of the earth's surface, such as mountain chains and ocean basins. It includes the study of the relationships between structures and landforms at the basic level, but then has two major branches: the inductive study of existing landforms, from which the processes of their evolution are inferred, and the deductive study and measurement of actual processes operating, inferring their ultimate influence on the landscapes on which they are acting. These two are complementary, as they approach the cause and effect relationships between landforms and processes from two contrasted viewpoints. The inductive branch is older than the more scientific deductive branch.

geopetal cavity (spirit level structure). A *way-up structure produced within a closed cavity in a rock, generally within a fossil. On death some mud-sized material entered the fossil and settled out with its upper surface parallel to the horizontal. Once the cavity was closed no further sediment could enter. The trapped sediment hardens and leaves a record of the past horizontal level. The empty space above the sediment is generally later infilled, usually by coarse calcite crystals.

geophysics. The science that combines the principles of mathematics and physics with the use of sophisticated equipment to examine the earth's interior and the properties of its various internal constituents.

geostrophic wind. A theoretical wind representing a balance of forces between the pressure gradient and the *Coriolis force. This produces a wind flow parallel to the isobars. As the effects of *friction are ignored, the real wind only approximates to the geostrophic wind above the *boundary layer. At these levels the geostrophic wind can easily be calculated from the pressure gradient.

geosyncline (geotectocline). A large linear trough developed along the margin of a continent, within which a considerable thickness of stratified sediments including turbidites accumulates, with occasional extrusive volcanic rocks. After a long period of accumulation the trough is folded and uplifted to form mountain chains. In the light of the theory of plate tectonics and sea-floor spreading, this term is falling into disuse. *See also* trench.

geotectocline. *See* geosyncline.

geothermal gradient. The increase in the earth's temperature with depth from its surface, expressed either in depth units per degree, or more generally degrees per unit depth.

GHOST. *Abbrev. for* Global Horizontal Sounding Technique. A scheme for obtaining information about atmospheric circulation from 0.5 to 35 km in the troposphere and stratosphere. The system consists of a series of balloons, which are located by satellite and provide information on their height. From this the circulation can be deduced. It is especially useful in such areas as the S hemisphere where ground stations are sparse.

glacial maximum. The greatest extent of *Pleistocene ice existed about 200 000 years ago, during the penultimate glacial period. Ice extended across the Arctic Ocean and joined with the ice sheets that covered much of North America, Greenland, N Russia, and NW Europe (the Baltic, Norway, Sweden, Denmark, and Finland were completely covered). This ice is believed to have extended across the North Sea to engulf all but the very south of the British Isles. Iceland was covered by an isolated ice cap. Antarctica was concealed by ice, as today, and mountainous areas in both hemispheres underwent glaciation. At this maximum an area of some 46 million square kilo-

metres was beneath ice, over three times that of the present day.

glacial phase (glacial). The period during an ice age when ice sheets expand to lower latitudes. This would normally be associated with a global drop of temperature and changes in position of the main circulation belts. *See also* interglacial, interstadial, glacial maximum, deglaciation.

glacial plucking. The erosive process by which rock material can be included within the ice of a glacier, later becoming a tool of glacial *abrasion. It entails the freezing of the glacier ice onto bedrock and the subsequent plucking out of blocks on movement. For this to occur *freeze-thaw activity must be taking place at the ice-rock interface, thereby restricting the process to *temperate glaciers.
A prerequisite for plucking is the presence of already loosened blocks, since the tensile strength of consolidated rock is far greater than that of ice. Well-jointed rocks are most susceptible (an optimum mean joint separation of from one to seven metres has been suggested). Freeze-thaw activity both before and after the appearance of the glacier will assist, whilst *unloading joints can also form as a result of the replacement of eroded rock by less dense ice, providing more susceptible layers.

glacial wastage. A reduction in thickness or areal extent of an ice mass resulting from more material being lost by ablation than is added by accumulation.

glaciated sea floors. One of the most characteristic types of *continental shelf is found off coasts that have been heavily glaciated. Such shelves tend to have highly irregular surfaces and in their deepest parts may have 200 metres or more of water covering them. Glaciated shelves are, in general, very wide, averaging 160 kilometres; the average shelf-edge depth is around 220 m. Shelf areas that have been heavily glaciated, such as that off the Norwegian coast, often display enclosed basins and trough features. Such submarine topographic forms are analogous to lake basins found in many glaciated valleys on the continents. Not all of the sea-floor features testify to erosion; there may also be accumulations of morainic material and other deposits, built into or retaining a constructional form. Drumlins have been found off the coast of Maine, while concentric stone deposits on part of the floor of the North Sea are probably of morainic origin. Many glacially-eroded features have become buried by shifting sediments and can only be found by seismic measurements. Many of the banks and channels formed in glacial debris have been shaped by a combination of wave and tidal action, for example, in the southern North Sea.

glacier. An accumulation of ice of limited width moving downslope, under the influence of gravity, from a source area. They are formed by the accumulation and compaction of snow (*see* firn). They may be contained within basins (*see* cirque glacier) or within pre-existing valleys (*see* valley glacier). *See also* cold glacier, temperate glacier.

glacier regime. The pattern of relative gaining or losing of ice from a glacier or ice sheet. A glacier having a positive regime is gaining ice and will therefore advance and thicken, whilst one with a negative regime loses ice (*see* ablation) and will be reduced in size.

glacio-eustatism. Worldwide change in sea level due to the effect of ice. During the *Pleistocene glacial periods sea level was much lower than at present, owing to the presence of much water on the continents in the form of ice. Estimates give values for this lowering of around 100 metres. During the *interglacial periods the ice sheets melted and sea level rose again, sometimes to higher levels than those of today. Such changes would have a worldwide effect on erosional processes, because of the lowering of *base level. However, these changes were not exclusively the result of the reduction in the volume of sea water, since deformation of the earth's crust at the same time also had an appreciable effect.

glauconite. A bright green authigenic mica-like mineral with an approximate formula $(K,Na)_{1.2-2.0}(Fe,Al,Mg)_4(Si_{7-7.6}Al_{1-0.4}O_{20})(OH)_4 \cdot n(H_2O)$, which is found only in marine sediments, particularly greensands.

glaucophane. A monoclinic *amphibole common in certain kinds of metamorphic rock.

glazed frost. *See* black ice.

gleying. The permanent or seasonal presence of either perched water or groundwater within a soil profile. This creates anaerobic conditions, leading to a dominant process of *reduction of ferric iron to its ferrous form, giving the soil a blue-grey colour. The water may either be perched on a heavier impermeable horizon below, as in the *peaty gleyed podzol, or the result of a high groundwater table in areas near drainage lines. If the gleying is seasonal, the profile may have ochreous mottlings due to periodic oxidizing conditions, changing the iron back to its ferric state. The lack of oxygen inhibits microbiological breakdown of humus, which accumulates as acid peat. Anaerobic bacteria tend to produce gases toxic to large plants, such as hydrogen sulphide, ammonia, and marsh gas. Together, the effects of hydromorphism are sufficient to completely change the direction of development of the soil profile.

gley soils. Intrazonal hydromorphic soils that may be found in tundra, temperate, or tropical regions where there is excessive moisture in the soil profile. The characteristic poor drainage may be a result of the profile characteristics, i.e. a fine-textured parent material, or the site of the soil, i.e. a low-lying area. Two main types of gley can be recognized: the surface-water gley and the groundwater gley. The former is found where, because of a poorly drained subsoil, water is held within the upper part of the soil, giving water-logged conditions for part of the year. A typical profile would consist of a very dark AI horizon rich in humus. Below this there would be Eg and Bg horizons with typical gleyed characteristics (see gleying). The C horizon would not show any gleying and would be similar to the parent material. The groundwater gley often occurs where there are permeable sands overlying impervious clay. The high groundwater table that is formed results in increased gleying with depth. The surface horizons are typically aerobic, grey or brown in colour, and rich in humus. With depth a mottled Bg and a grey/blue G horizon are common. Most gley soils are under grassland vegetation and are used mainly for grazing.

glide twinning. A complex form of crystal twinning resulting from deformation. It results from one layer of atoms changing its position so that the lattice is reversed. This results in broad lamellae within the crystal. It is commonly shown in the calcite crystals of marble.

globigerina ooze. A calcareous deep-sea ooze (see pelagic ooze) containing over 30% organisms. It is very widespread on the deep-sea floor. The organisms largely comprise the calcareous skeletons or tests of minute *foraminifera. Globally, globigerina ooze represents some 130 million sq. km, covering something like half of the Atlantic Ocean floor, being widespread in the Indian Ocean, particularly on the W side, and very conspicuous in the S Pacific Ocean.

glomerophyric (glomeroporphyritic, cumulophyric). Denoting a *porphyritic texture indicated by the occurrence of phenocrysts in aggregates or clumps set in the groundmass of an igneous rock.

GMT. See Greenwich Mean Time.

Gnathostomata. Vertebrates possessing jaws. The Gnathostomata include most fish and all higher vertebrates. Compare Agnatha.

gneiss. A coarse-grained metamorphic rock in which quartz and feldspar predominate over micas. The schistosity is poorly defined and segregation banding is irregular and discontinuous. Coarse granular bands of quartz and feldspar alternate with thin often undulating schistose bands in which micas and amphiboles are concentrated.
Parageneiss has an unambiguous sedimentary composition. Orthogneisses are metamorphosed igneous rocks. Rocks of granitic composition containing a planar or linear orientation of minerals, imparted by stress, are termed granite-gneiss. Gneisses are formed during high-grade regional metamorphism.

gnomonic projection. A form of azimuthal map projection in which the great circles of the earth are shown as straight lines. Great circle routes can thus be plotted for navigation purposes. This projection is not often used because of its limited application.

goethite. A yellow-brown mineral, FeO.OH, formed by the oxidation and hydration of iron minerals or as a direct precipitate. See limonite.

Gondwanaland. The S hemisphere super-continent, which takes its name from the Gondwana system of India, thought to have existed over 200 million years ago. Since then it has been fragmented as a result of *sea-floor spreading into the present continents of Africa, Australia, India, South America, and Antartica. See also Pangaea.

goniatite. One of the earlier molluscs of the subclass *Ammonoidea, whose shells had simply folded angular suture lines. Goniatites are used as *zone fossils in the Devonian and Carboniferous System but were replaced by the *ammonites in the *Permian.

gossan. A mass of quartz and hydrated iron oxides that often marks the outcrop of a sulphide-bearing vein, the sulphides having been oxidized to soluble sulphates. Metalliferous material removed in solution may be redeposited at depth in a zone of secondary enrichment. *See also* hydrothermal processes.

graben. A generally elongated block of rock that has been downthrown between two parallel faults relative to the surrounding area. It differs from a *rift valley in that it is a structural feature and not necessarily also a topographical one. *Compare* horst. (See diagram at *fault*).

grade. 1. The degree of metamorphic change undergone by a rock. When such changes can be traced from unmetamorphosed rocks to highly metamorphosed rocks, the grade of metamorphism is said to increase. High-grade rocks are produced under conditions of high temperatures or pressures; likewise low-grade metamorphic rocks form at low temperatures and pressures. *See* zone.
2. The condition reached in the later stages of a normal *cycle of erosion when a river or slope has an *equilibrium regime, with a smooth concave long profile. Since the theory was proposed by Davis, other factors besides the modification of the long profile have been taken into account, especially adaptation to changes in the controlling environmental factors of base level, rainfall, and the quantity and type of the load supplied to the stream. A river that is at grade is able to maintain its *competence so that it is just able to transport its load at a given discharge. It does this by adjusting its long profile, cross section, channel pattern, and bed roughness: any environmental changes will be met by changes in some or all of these factors, so that the river uses up its available energy and no more.

graded bedding. Sedimentary bedding in which particles show a size distribution. The coarsest material forms the base

and then the sequence becomes progressively finer upwards. It is often present in turbidity deposits. On a larger scale such upward fining sequences are developed in braided river channels, as they are infilled.

graded profile. *See* equilibrium profile.

gradient wind. An extension to the concept of the *geostrophic wind. Isobars in the upper atmosphere are rarely straight, so to account for the curved flow, following Newton's laws of motion, another force must be included. This is the *centripetal acceleration. The equilibrium wind for these three forces is known as the gradient wind. Curvature of the isobars can be either in the cyclonic or anticyclonic sense.

granite. A family of acid coarse-grained plutonic igneous rocks containing essential quartz, alkali, and plagioclase feldspars and small quantities of mafic minerals. The rocks of the granite-granodiorite suite and their volcanic equivalents, rhyolites-dacites, are divided according to the proportions and compositions of the feldspars.
Granites contain on average about 25% quartz and contain either a single feldspar, a perthitic intergrowth, (*hypersolvus granites*) or two kinds, oligoclase and potassium feldspar (*subsolvus granites*). All are *leucocratic rocks, the only common dark mineral being biotite. Accessory minerals include muscovite, zircon, apatite, and tourmaline. The typically granular texture in which most of the crystals are subhedral is often termed granitic. Porphyritic varieties containing large zoned phenocrysts of white, grey, or pink feldspar are common. Many granites exhibit graphic, orbicular, and rapakivi textures and contain miarolitic cavities. Some strongly alkaline granites are chemically distinctive, having low aluminium and calcium contents and characterized by the presence of the soda pyriboles, aegirine and riebeckite, and an abundance of otherwise rare

Granite-granodiorite Rocks

dominant feldspar	*coarse-plutonic*	*medium*	*fine-volcanic*
alkali feldspar	granite	microgranite	rhyolite
alkali feldspar = plagioclase feldspar	adamellite	microadamellite	rhyodacite
plagioclase feldspar	granodiorite	microadamellite	dacite

accessory minerals. With a decrease in the amount of quartz, granites pass into quartz-syenites and syenites.

Adamellites, of which Shap granite is an example, contain oligoclase and potassium feldspars, quartz, and possibly hornblende in addition to biotite. With a decrease in the amount of quartz, adamellites grade into monzonites; the term quartz-monzonite is sometimes used as a synonym for adamellite.

Granodiorites that are almost devoid of alkali feldspar are called *trondhjemites*.

Granitic rocks are particularly susceptible to the pneumatolytic (*see* pneumatolysis) processes of alteration, greisening, tourmalinization, and kaolinization.

Microgranites are the medium-grained equivalents of granites. Porphyritic varieties have been termed quartz-porphyries or granite-porphyries. Granophyre is a microgranitic rock exhibiting a micrographic (granophyric) texture.

Granodiorites are volumetrically the most abundant plutonic rocks and constitute the bulk of the batholiths in orogenic regions. Granodioritic magma may be produced by anatexis at deep crustal levels. When such sites of magma generation become exposed at the surface, the association of granites, migmatites, and high-grade regionally metamorphosed rocks is apparent. Once generated, granitic liquids rise up in the crust and undergo *differentiation to produce the more chemically extreme

members of the suite. At high crustal levels, intrusive granite plutons produce marked metamorphic aureoles. Although most granites crystallize from a magma, some granitic rocks may be produced by granitization, the pervasive metasomatism of pre-existing rocks. *See also* aplites, pegmatites.

granitization. The process of metasomatic transformation of pre-existing rocks into granite due to the action of granitic fluids (*ichors*) arising from depth.

granodiorite. A plutonic igneous rock containing plagioclase feldspar of oligoclase-andesine composition, subordinate potassium feldspar, biotite, or hornblende. *See* granite.

granophyre. A microgranite exhibiting a micrographic (granophyric) texture. *See* granite.

granular disintegration. The separation of individual grains from the main mass of a rock. It most frequently occurs in coarse-grained rocks, notably granite, and both mechanical and chemical weathering processes can be responsible. Mechanically, the differential expansion and contraction of different mineral grains due to *insolation may cause disintegration, whilst crystallization of salt from solution, within the surface pores of a rock, may prise grains apart. Chemically, *hydration usually involves a considerable volume change, and granular disintegration may occur where there is differential expansion of various mineral grains. The usual product of this type of weathering is a coarse sand.

granulite. A granular textured metamorphic rock occurring in areas of regional metamorphism of the highest grade. Granulites lack the hydrous minerals, micas and amphiboles, but may contain pyroxene, garnet, kyanite, or sillimanite. Characteristically the quartz and feldspar crystals are flattened and their parallel alignment gives rise to a foliation. *See also* charnockite, metamorphic facies.

graphic. Any map, chart, or photomosaic produced by cartographic techniques.

graphic intergrowth. An intergrowth of alkali feldspar and quartz commonly found in pegmatites and granitic rocks. The quartz is orientated along preferred directions within the feldspar and on a flat surface resembles hieroglyphic or runic writing.

graphite. A soft iron-grey massive or laminar form of pure carbon, which is characteristically greasy to the touch. Graphite is found mainly in metamorphic rocks.

Graptolithina. A primitive group of invertebrates of the phylum *Chordata that is included in the subphylum Hemichordata. Graptolites are totally extinct, fossils being confined to the Palaeozoic. The body consists of a number of minute cups (*thecae*) of chitinous material, which house individual polyps. The thecae are arranged along a stem (*stipe*) and graptolites show great variation in the arrangement and orientation of the thecae and the disposition of the stipes. Biseriate forms have thecae on both sides of the stipe, uniseriate forms along only one, and there may be a single stipe or many. Graptolites were benthonic and planktonic marine organisms and the planktonic forms attained a wide distribution.

This, coupled with their great morphological variation and rapid evolution, makes them of considerable importance in biostratigraphy and they are used as *zone fossils throughout much of the Ordovician and Silurian Systems. Graptolites are first known from rocks of the Cambrian System; they suffered widespread extinctions at the end of the Silurian but some groups continued to the early Carboniferous.

graticule. The network of lines on a map projection representing the lines of latitude and longitude. On some maps the graticule may not be shown over the entire face of the map; in these cases the lines shown have graticule ticks representing lesser lines not shown.

gravel. According to the British Standard code of particle size classifications, gravel is unconsolidated material (usually rock fragments rather than individual mineral crystals) in the 2-60 mm size range. It is the size of material lying immediately above sand, and below cobbles. In practice, however, the term tends to be loosely used in geomorphological literature for all material of an unconsolidated nature of greater than sand size and less than boulder size (i.e. from 2-200 mm in diameter).

gravitational constant. The constant (G) used in the law of universal gravitation. It has the value 6.670×10^{-11} N m^2 kg^{-2}.

gravitational gradient. A regional shift in the measured value of gravity across an area.

gravity. *See* acceleration of free fall.

gravity anomaly. On the assumption of uniform density, calculations can be made to predict the value of gravity for a particular point on the earth's surface. Where this value differs from that actually measured an anomaly exists. A *negative gravity anomaly* is an area in which gravity is less than that predicted; it is an area out of isostatic balance. An area of greater gravity than that predicted is a *positive gravity anomaly* and usually results from a large mass of basic rocks near the earth's surface.

gravity collapse structure. A tectonic structure produced mainly as a result of downward movement under the influence of gravity.

gravity fault. *See* normal fault.

gravity fold. A fold structure resulting from sliding in response to gravity, as distinct from vertical or horizontal compressional forces operating during an orogeny.

gravity gliding. The movement of a large rock mass downhill as a result of gravity.

gravity meter. An instrument used for measuring variations in the strength of the earth's gravitational field.

gravity unit. One gravity unit (gu) equals 10^{-6} m s^{-2} and is often used in place of the milligal (*see* gal). One gravity unit is roughly equivalent to one ten millionth of the value of gravity at the earth's surface.

gravity wave. A wind-generated wave at sea whose length exceeds 50 mm and whose speed of propagation is influenced mainly by gravitational forces.

Great Barrier Reef. A *coral reef lying off the NE coast of Australia, extending for some 1900 kilometres and varying from 30-160 km in width. It is an example of a barrier reef found off a continental coast in contrast to those reefs that circumscribe volcanic islands. It is separated from the mainland by a discontinuous channel 40-90 metres deep and therefore too deep for coral growth. On the seaward side of the reef, the shelf attains depths of at least 420 m. The coral composing it covers about half of the Queensland shelf region. The reef is considered one of the best coral features in the world, and fears are now being expressed concerning serious damage to the reef caused by certain species of starfish. Borings have indicated that recent coral extends down to depths of between 120 and 140 m, and

that sand and mud intercalations occur within the coral. The coral tends to be of two quite different types, the dividing line between the two being the *Trinity Opening*. The reef may be based on a step-fault platform.

great circle. A circle round the earth's surface whose plane passes through the centre of the earth. Great circle routes, broken down into a series of *rhumb lines, are often used in navigation because they represent the shortest distance between two points on the earth's surface.

green flash. When the sun sinks below the horizon, the last rays may be seen to change from pale yellow, to orange, then to green. The rapidity of the process has given this phenomenon the name of the green flash. It only occurs when the air is exceptionally clear and it is caused by differential refraction of the spectral colours by the atmosphere. Normally the colours complement each other when the sun is high in the sky, but as the sun disappears the individual colours may very occasionally be identified.

greenhouse effect. The presence of the atmosphere maintains the temperature of the earth's surface at a much higher level than would be expected on the basis of equilibrium with solar radiation input. This is because the gases are transparent to short-wave radiation but almost opaque to long-wave radiation. Glass has similar properties and the effect of the earth's atmosphere was likened to that of a greenhouse. Detailed work has since shown that the higher temperatures in a greenhouse depend more on reduced turbulence than on radiation differences. The analogy is still used, albeit erroneously.

Greenwich Mean Time (GMT). Local time at Greenwich, London, which is located on the 0° meridian and from which the standard times of different areas of the globe are calculated. 15° longitude represents one hour in time from the Greenwich meridian.

greenstone. Basic volcanic rock that has suffered low-grade *metamorphism or alteration.

greisening. *See* pneumatolysis.

grey-brown podzolic soils. Soils found covering large areas of the northeastern U.S. to the south of the brown podzolic zone. They are more mildly podzolized soils, less acid conditions resulting in more abundant soil fauna incorporating humus deep into the AI horizon. An Ea horizon is present but it is darker (grey-brown) in colour than the typical eluvial horizon of a podzol. Clay is illuviated in the B horizon, which normally exhibits a blocky structure.

grey desert soil. *See* sierozem.

grey forest soils. Soils found in the transition zone between forest and steppe in North America and Russia. The typical profile consists of a thin litter below which is a dark grey A horizon with a crumb structure. Organic and mineral matter have been well mixed. Below is the Ea horizon, with its nutty structure, which is light grey in colour due to silica coating the ped faces. Clay and humus have been removed from this horizon and deposited in the illuvial Bt horizon, which has a prismatic structure. The gradation to parent material, which is often loess, is usually characterized by calcium carbonate concretions. Thus the soil exhibits the leaching characteristics of a podzol and the calcification of a chernozem. From the profile characteristics it has been suggested that these soils originally developed under steppe vegetation, which was replaced by forest when there was a change from a warm dry to a cool humid climate. These soils may be subdivided zonally. Westwards from E Russia to European Russia these soils change from dark grey forest soils to normal grey forest soils and finally to light greyish-brown forest soils. The humus content decreases westwards from 10% to 3% owing to more podzolic conditions.

They fall into the *alfisol order of the Seventh Approximation.

greywacke. An *arenaceous sedimentary rock in which fairly angular particles of *sand grade, mainly lithic fragments, are suspended in a matrix of much finer material. *See also* turbidite.

grey wooded soil. A soil belonging to the podzolic group, morphologically resembling a podzol but chemically resembling a grey-brown podzolic soil. It is typically found in the mid-continental states of Canada on a base-rich parent material under boreal forest. It has a well-developed Ea horizon with a platy structure and a Bt horizon with a blocky structure. Leaching is less intense than in a podzol, resulting in less movement of sesquioxides in the soil profile and a soil with a higher pH value. Grey wooded soils fall into the *alfisol order of the Seventh Approximation.

Grid

grid. A network of parallel lines intersecting at right angles and forming reference squares over the face of a map. Grid lines are numbered, therefore each square has unique easting and northing readings. Grids are used to enable identification of points on the map with respect to other points, or distances between points. (In the diagram the junction of stream Y and river X has a grid reference of 545 315). They are also used to determine the accuracy of a map: by knowing the true position of a point in relation to the grid and the position as shown on a map the discrepancy between the two can be calculated. *See also* national grid.

grid zone. The earth's surface can be arbitrarily divided into grid zones, which are areas of different grid systems, each with its own origin. Grid zones enable the identification of points on the earth's surface without the use of geographical coordinates, i.e. longitude and latitude.

grike (gryke). *See* limestone pavement.

grossular. A calcium-rich *garnet.

Grosswetterlagen (large-scale weather patterns). A concept devised by Baur to identify the major trends in atmospheric events over a particular area. It has subsequently been modified and is now used in Germany as a method of assisting long-range weather forecasting. In the classification the main anticyclone or depression centre is located and this is used to predict the likely wind and weather systems.

ground frost. The outcome of a fall in temperature below 0°C, measured by a thermometer at ground level on a grass surface. In climatological statistics, note is made of whether a ground frost occurred, not its intensity. Data prior to January 1 1961 took 30°F as the base for ground frost.

groundmass. The finer-grained bulk of crystalline or glassy material that composes an igneous rock and into which the coarser components (*phenocrysts, *xenoliths) are set.

ground moraine. A sheet of *till, usually some tens of metres thick, with a surface characterized by very low relief. Ground moraine was deposited from the base of an ice sheet or glacier on the melting of the ice, and forms a cover that tends to mask former bed-rock features, since where hollows existed the greatest thicknesses of till were deposited.

ground swell. 1. Swell waves as they enter shallow water, i.e. water with a depth approximately that of half the wavelength. This causes the swell waves to decrease in length and increase in height. In this sense, the waves are beginning to be influenced by the ground (seabed).
2. Swell waves in deep water that possess considerable height and length.

groundwater. Water precipated from the atmosphere that has percolated into the ground and become trapped within pores, cracks, and fissures. Its presence is essential for practically all weathering processes and for this reason more weathering takes place in well-jointed rocks than in massive types. In the upper layers of permeable rock, groundwater can flow through the strata quite easily; however, at depth a level is reached below which all pore spaces are water-filled (the *water table*). Weathering still occurs below the water table, in the form of reduction and hydrolysis.

group. A division in the hierarchy of the lithostratigraphic classification of bodies of rock (*see* stratigraphy, lithostratigraphy). It is formed of two or more adjacent and related *formations; adjacent groups may be aggregated to form *supergroups*.

growing season. The period of the year during which plant growth can proceed without temperature restriction. By temperature latitude convention, a daily mean temperature at screen level of 6°C is the critical lower limit; the growing season can then be determined from the monthly variation of mean temperature. It is not a very precise concept as a mean temperature of 6°C could be produced by a variety of diurnal ranges, and different plants respond to different critical temperatures.

groyne. A man-made barrier constructed on beaches and extending seawards perpendicular to the coastline in order to trap beach materials moving along the shoreline. They are usually built in groups, their length, height, and separation varying with type of beach material and desired results. Though very effective at building up the beach in their immediate vicinity, by halting or at least slowing down longshore movement of material, they may cause considerable erosion of that part of the beach down-drift of the groynes.

grumusol. *See* tropical black soil.

grunerite. A monoclinic *amphibole.

gryke (grike). *See* limestone pavement.

guano. Seabird excrement found in large amounts on certain of the Pacific Islands and along part of the coast of South America. It is of great economic interest since, being rich in nitrogenous matter and phosphates, it serves as a valuable land fertilizer.

Gulf Stream. The largest and most important permanent ocean current in the N hemisphere. It is most prominent in its southern portion, beyond the meeting-point of the Florida Current and the Antilles Current. In this region, it attains its greatest depth, probably some 1000 metres, and achieves a maximum width of some 50–70 kilometres. Further north, it becomes less effective at depth, while to the south of the Newfoundland Banks it begins to split up into several branches. It is not a very warm current, differing only little in its thermal characteristics from the Sargasso Sea region which lies close to its path. Indeed, as it spreads out northwards, it tends to mix with colder surrounding waters and is fed also by the rather cold Labrador Current. Where strongly developed, its sharply defined left-hand flank contrasts markedly with its more diffuse right-hand flank, where it is common for large eddies to be thrown off. *See also* North Atlantic Drift.

gully erosion. A type of erosion in which gullies, which are meandering rectangular vertical-walled channels, develop from *rills when *sheet flow of water becomes concentrated into distinct channels. They originate naturally near the head of the drainage pattern, but they are better known as the most widespread and obvious signs of human influence on geomorphology due to the removal of vegetation cover in farming. Ploughing down the slopes aids the concentration of sheet flow into gullies, which then erode their headwalls and advance upslope, as well as widening their valleys and developing tributaries. Gullies remove great volumes of sediment, especially topsoil, and are known and feared in many currently settled areas, such as central southwestern U.S.A. and southern Australia. There is evidence that they were also once widespread in Europe. Today it is known that the simple conservation practice of ploughing parallel to contours will retard gully development. *See also* abnormal erosion, arroyo.

gust. A sudden increase of wind speed of short duration. Gusts are due to mechanical interference by the ground surface, so that where the surface is aerodynamically rough, as in cities, gustiness is increased. Conversely, winds in exposed coastal sites tend to experience fewer gusts, though their mean wind speed would be high.

guyot. A relatively smooth flat-topped *seamount or tablemount. Guyots are best known in the Pacific and Atlantic Oceans. Their flat tops are interpreted as being planation surfaces eroded by a combination of marine and subaerial processes. The tablemount is more or less conical in shape, and the summit surface usually lies in fairly deep water. The summit depths often range between 1000 and 2000 metres; others have been sounded between 2000 and 3500 m. Few guyots with summit depths less than some 1000 m have been located. Guyots may be veneered with sediments such as volcanic sand, gravel, and globigerina ooze.

Gymnospermae. A class of primitive seed-bearing plants that differ from the *Angiospermae in having seeds that are not protected by an outer covering. They include the conifers, cycads, and ginkgos. Gymnosperms are known as fossils from the Carboniferous Period and flourished during the early Mesozoic. Most gymnosperms became extinct during the Cretaceous, presumably due to unsuccessful competition with the angiosperms.

gypsum. A monoclinic mineral of composition $CaSO_4.2H_2O$. Euhedral colourless crystals of tabular habit are known as *selenite*. Gypsum is an evaporite mineral found in shales and limestones. *See also* anhydrite.

H

haar. A local term for advection fog on the east coast of Britain. It is also called *sea-fret* or *sea-roke*. In spring and early summer the North Sea is relatively cold and quickly cools moist air to saturation point giving low stratus cloud. Whenever winds are onshore, the low cloud drifts inland where it is gradually dispersed by heating. It is most frequent under anticyclonic conditions when vertical motion and mechanical turbulence are weak.

habitat. The place where an organism lives, as defined by those aspects of its total environment that affect it and to which it is adapted. For example, sponges have a benthonic habitat.

haboob. An Arabic word applied to any dust storm in the Sudan, occurring chiefly in the summer, raised by strong winds, without reference to its origin. Many of them result from the downdraughts of cumulonimbus clouds with wind speeds reaching 90 knots in extreme cases, and they are often followed by heavy rain or thunderstorms.

Hachures

hachures. Short lines drawn on a map to show the relief of an area without the use of contours. They point downhill and are thicker and closer together where the gradient is steepest. Before cartographic techniques were sufficiently advanced to enable the construction of contour lines this method was extensively used. It can be of particular effect in mountainous areas.

hade. The angle measured between the vertical plane and that of the incline of a structural surface, generally applied to faults but applicable to any structural surface. *Compare* dip.

Hadley Cell. A cellular wind circulation in tropical latitudes with surface winds blowing from the sub-tropics at about 30° to the equator and winds in the upper atmosphere blowing in the reverse direction. This corresponds with the surface temperature gradient from the thermal equator towards the poles. This simple circulation was first suggested by Hadley in the 18th century. Although it is modified by the effects of the earth's rotation, it is still believed to be a reasonable approximation to reality. *See also* general circulation of the atmosphere.

haematite. Ferric iron oxide (Fe_2O_3), an important iron ore. It occurs in two main forms, as a massive red botryoidal or reniform ore and as metallic crystals known as *specular iron ore*. Haematite often occurs as a cement in sandstones producing a red coloration. Most ore deposits result from the alteration of iron carbonates and silicates in sedimentary rocks.

hail. Approximately spherical particles of ice that fall from cumulonimbus clouds. The pieces of ice can be irregular in shape and have been known to weigh up to almost 1 kg, though they are normally far less. They often have a concentric structure with alternating layers of clear and opaque ice providing some evidence of their evolution within the cloud.

It is believed that this structure is the result of the stone being transported into different parts of the cloud during its development. Beginning with an ice nucleus, opaque ice will form around it when it is in the colder parts of the cloud. Small cloud droplets freeze rapidly to produce a spherical aggregation of ice with many air enclosures to give the characteristic white and opaque appearance. In the lower parts of the cloud with temperatures only slightly cooler than 0°C, the relatively larger droplets there tend to spread over the hail surface before freezing so that little air is trapped and the ice is transparent. The distribution of hail in relation to the main path of the storm will depend upon the nature of updraughts and cloud structure.

Hailstorms occur most frequently in the continental interiors of temperate latitudes and decrease towards the poles and equator, and over the sea. This is because conditions most favourable to cumulonimbus development are found here (intense surface heating, sufficient concentrations of cloud water, and strong thermal gradients).

halite. Common salt, NaCl. It occurs as an evaporite deposit from sea water or salt lakes.

halomorphic soils. Soils dominated by sodium salts. There are three main types: the solonchaks or saline soils, which are dominated by chlorides and sulphates of sodium; the solonetz or alkali soils, dominated by carbonates of sodium; and the leached or degraded *solod. There are also many arid zone soils subject to some salinization. These halomorphic soils are not true *intrazonal soils, but tend to occur in certain climates, e.g. the arid to semiarid transition zone; they are often related to the beds of former lakes or seas, such as the area north of the Caspian Sea, or to depressed areas where a water table is near enough to the surface to feed salts upwards by *capillarity. In highly irrigated but poorly drained areas, e.g. the San Joaquin Valley of California, the water table may be artificially raised by irrigation leading to salinization of formerly fertile soils, through increased capillary rise of water bringing up dissolved salts.

hammada (hamada). A type of arid desert plain, consisting of an extensive almost bare rock surface, especially in the Sahara. *See also* erg, reg.

hanging valley. A tributary valley in a glaciated area, the gradient of which becomes much steeper on entering the main valley. A large glacier will cause greater deepening of a pre-existing valley than will a smaller glacier, and therefore where glaciers invade a major valley and its tributaries the major valley will be deepened to a greater extent. On the disappearance of the ice, the floor of the major valley will be at a lower altitude than those of the tributaries, which will hang above the main valley. Subsequent rivers will reach the main valley from these hanging valleys as waterfalls.

hanging wall. The surface of rock above a fault plane or ore body. *Compare* foot wall.

harbour. A sheltered stretch of water where ships may anchor or tie up to buoys or jetties, in order to be safe from storms or other adverse conditions, or to load or unload their cargoes. Some are formed by natural features, including sheltered bays and estuaries; others are created by the construction of jetties, breakwaters, moles, and other man-made structures. Man-made harbours are usually built, sometimes after careful scale hydraulic model tests, so as to minimize wave action, *seiche action, and undesirable currents. Many harbours, both natural and artificial, have to be dredged (see dredging) in order to maintain or to impove limiting depths.

hardness. See Mohs' scale.

harmatome. See zeolites.

harmattan. A dry wind blowing from between north and east over West Africa. As the air has had a long trajectory across the Sahara, it is very dry, cool by night but warm by day, and is laden with dust. It represents the normal dry season state of the area, oscillating in its extent with the seasons, occasionally reaching the Gulf of Guinea in January but rarely south of 15°N in July.

harmonic analysis. See Fourier analysis.

harzburgite. An ultramafic rock consiting largely of olivine and orthopyroxene.

hastingsite. A monoclinic *amphibole.

haüyne. See feldspathoids.

hawaiite. See trachybasalt.

haze. Atmospheric obscurity due to minute suspended solid matter, such as dust or smoke particles, in the sky. It is not a very precise term; when visibility approaches 1 km, the phenomenon is called mist, especially when it is produced by water droplets.

head. See coombe rock.

heat. The form of energy to which all other forms will eventually revert. Heat can be transferred by conduction, convection, or radiation and may lead to an increase of temperature, but it can cause

a change of state from liquid to vapour without any corresponding alteration in temperature. Heat is normally measured in joules, though the former unit, the calorie, is still often used.

heat balance. The static *energy balance between the earth and atmosphere. It indicates the utilization of net radiation by evaporation, sensible heat, and advection.

heat island. An urban area that has a higher temperature than its rural surroundings: on calm clear nights excesses of up to 10°C have been recorded. They are the result of the different nature of the surfaces in a city, which in turn affects the heat balance and airflow. See also urban climate.

heave. The horizontal displacement along a fault.

hedenbergite. A monoclinic *pyroxene.

Fig. 1: Distribution of maximum velocity in a meandering stream due to helical flow

deposition / erosion

maximum current velocity as directed by helical flow

Helical flow

Fig. 2: Section through the outside of a meander bend

deposition (inside of bend)

helical current   erosion (outside of bend)

helical (helicoidal) flow. The most significant type of turbulence in streams. Superimposed on the primary downstream flow, a secondary flow moves across the surface of the stream towards the outside of the meander bends, compensated by a reverse flow along the bed towards the inside of the meander bends. This gives the streamflow a net cork screw movement, concentrating erosion on the outside of the meander bends, with deposition on the insides, causing downstream propagation of the meanders.

helicitic structure. Curved or S-shaped trails of inclusions occurring in *porphyroblasts, especially garnets, and representing an earlier foliation.

helm wind. A local wind that blows down the Pennine escarpment slope into the Vale of Eden. It is a strong cold gusty northeasterly wind, which is topographically induced below strong inversions. The escarpment acts in a similar manner to a river weir and standing waves, indicated by the helm bar, develop over the Eden Valley. It has its maximum frequency in spring when the suitable easterly airflow is most common.

Hercynian orogeny. A phase in the Variscan orogeny affecting Europe and characterized by a northwest fold trend. The term is used without time significance and covers the Carboniferous and Permian.

hercynite. *See* spinel.

heterogeneous strain. The changes in shape or dimensions occurring when a body of rock does not deform equally in all directions. A linear structure would become curved and parallel structures would diverge after deformation.

heterolithic unconformity. *See* nonconformity.

heulandite. *See* zeolites.

hexagonal. *See* crystal system.

hiatus. A break in a stratigraphic sequence, either as a result of nondeposition or erosion. It represents the period of time missing between beds above and below an unconformity.

high. An area in which atmospheric pressure is higher than surrounding areas. It is used as a more general term than an *anticyclone, which is centred on a closed isobar. Areas of high pressure are normally associated with dry weather, though the skies may be either cloudy or clear.

high index circulation (in meteorology). The phase of the *index cycle when the westerly circulation reaches its maximum intensity in specified areas. This represents a strong surface westerly flow with Rossby waves of long wavelength and small amplitude. Meridional exchange is at a minimum value.

hill shading (plastic shading). A means of showing relief on maps, shading the east- and south-facing slopes (the steeper the slope, the darker the shading) to give the effect of an oblique light shining from the northwest over a relief model.

hinge line. 1. (In folding) An imaginary line joining points of maximum curvature of the folded strata.
2. The boundary between a stable region of the earth's crust and one undergoing changes in elevation, generally as a result of isostatic readjustment but also including areas of tectonic deformation.

hinge (pivot) fault. A normal fault that dies out along its trend by a gradual decrease in throw. (See diagram at *fault*.)

histosol. One of the ten soil orders of the *Seventh Approximation classification, which includes bog soils such as peat. Histosols are characterized by accumulations of organic matter, which remains more or less undecomposed owing to the waterlogged conditions. The histic *epipedon (surface horizon) has at least 20% of its weight in organic matter, or over 30% if half the weight of the horizon is clay. Histosols are divided into four suborders on the basis of the degree of decomposition of the organic matter.
Although found throughout the world, histosols occupy the least area of all the ten orders of the Seventh Approximation (under 1% of all soils). They tend to

develop particularly in cooler, poorly drained, more humid areas.

hoar frost. A silvery-white deposit of ice crystals formed on surfaces cooled below freezing point by radiation. It may result from the freezing of dew or by the direct sublimation of ice crystals from water vapour in the atmosphere when temperatures are less than 0°C.

Hodograph

hodograph. A diagram used to analyse the wind field above an observing station. Winds at different pressure levels are drawn as vectors from the origin and so give an indication of the changes in wind speed and direction with height. It is then possible to make deductions about the thermal patterns at these upper levels and about the advection of warm or cold air. (See diagram.)

Holocene (Recent). The present epoch, covering the last 10 000 years or so of geological time from the end of the *Pleistocene. In Britain it follows all the major Pleistocene glacial episodes and is therefore often known as the *Post-*Glacial.* However, some authorities consider it to be no more than an interglacial phase of the Pleistocene. At the beginning of the Holocene Britain was isolated from the rest of the continent of Europe by a general rise in sea level. Representatives of most fossil species of this epoch are still alive today.

holocrystalline. Denoting a rock composed wholly of crystals.

homeomorphy. Similarity in structure between organisms that are not closely related as a result of evolutionary adaptation to similar habitats (*see* convergent evolution). The term is often restricted to similarities between more closely related species, in which homeomorphy leads to confusions in taxonomy (*see* parallel evolution).

homocline. A series of beds of rock all of which have a similar dip and strike, including monoclinal structures and isoclinally folded beds. The term is applied only to small areas of the earth's crust.

homogeneous strain. The changes in shape and dimensions that occur when a body of rock deforms equally in all directions. It results in straight-line and planar structures.

homolographic projection. A map projection possessing the property of equal area, i.e. the area bounded by adjoining meridians and parallels on the map is equal in area, by ratio, to that area bounded by the same meridians and parallels on the ground, e.g. Mollweide's and Bonne's projections.

homotaxis. The occurrence of *divisions of rock occupying the same position in the stratigraphic sequence in separate successions. Such divisions are said to be *homotaxial.* Although the divisions may be of the same age, the concept does not take account of considerations of time and simply reflects the order of deposition. *Compare* chronotaxis. *See also* correlation.

honeycomb weathering. Weathering within jointed rocks in which joint infillings are more resistant to weathering than the main mass of the rock, so that after erosion they project and surround recesses in the rock. Typical infilling materials are iron oxides, secondary silica, calcite, and manganese oxides. Migration of rock cements into the joints may produce a corresponding decrease in the resistance of the rock itself, thereby increasing the effectiveness of honeycomb weathering.

Hooke's Law. A stressed body deforms to an extent that is proportional to the force applied. Materials that obey Hooke's Law are considered to be elastic.

horizon. 1. (In soil science). One of a number of layers of soil arranged in a vertical sequence in the *profile. Each layer is reasonably uniform. Most soil-forming processes result in this layered arrangement but some, e.g. the action of earthworms, are destructive in this respect.
2. (In stratigraphy). A plane within a rock sequence that is assumed to be a time plane. In practice, a horizon is not a sharp plane but a thin bed characterized by some distinctive feature of lithology or fossil content. A particular horizon is sometimes merely theoretical, and it may be regarded as extending through a contemporaneous succession that carries no internal evidence of its presence.

horizontal equivalent. The distance between two points on a slope projected onto a horizontal plane, as they would be represented on a map.

hornblende. A monoclinic mineral of the *amphibole group, common in both igneous and metamorphic rocks.

hornfels. A fine-to medium-grained nonfoliated rock composed of equidimensional mineral grains showing no preferred orientation. *Porphyroblasts of minerals such as biotite, andalusite, and cordierite may occur and their incipient development is often indicated by a spotted appearance to the rock. Hornfels are the product of contact metamorphism and are found in aureoles bordering intrusive plutonic igneous rocks. *See also* contact metamorphism.

horn (horn peak). *See* pyramidal peak.

hornito. A small volcanic structure resulting from the accumulation of small blebs of lava thrown out around a parasitic vent; a spatter cone.

hornstone. A very fine-grained volcanic ash. *See* pyroclastic rocks.

horse latitudes. The zone of light and variable winds between 30° and 40° N and S where the subtropical anticyclones are dominant. The name arose during the days of sailing ships when unfavourable winds could prolong the journey; when food became short, horses would be thrown overboard or eaten.

horst. An elongated block of rocks bounded by faults. The sense of movement of the block is upwards relative to the surrounding rocks. *Compare* graben. (See diagram at *fault*.)

hot spots. Areas on the earth's surface that have a higher than average heat flow, e.g. volcanoes. Hot spots are also thought to develop within the mantle, giving rise to *mantle plumes. These plumes are thought to be important features in the mechanism of plate tectonics.

Hudson Canyon. One of numerous *submarine canyons that cut into or across the wide continental shelf lying off the E coast of the U.S. It is one of the best known submarine canyons in the world and has been carefully sunveyed several times. It cuts well into the shelf opposite the Hudson River and has been traced seawards as far as a wide submarine fan. The cross section of the canyon tends to be V-shaped, while flanking it are what appear to be small tributary valleys.

Core samples have yielded a variety of deposits (rock, gravel, and clay), certain of which suggest that some sort of powerful turbidity flow may have operated, perhaps when sea level was significantly lower.

human influence on geomorphology. In the 8000 years of the Recent (Holocene) geological period during which man has become established, his activities have had considerable geomorphological impact, principally in accelerating existing processes but to a lesser extent in creating new landforms. The major effects are those consequent on destruction and removal of the vegetation cover. Clearing the land for agriculture can cause gullying and soil erosion, leading to destruction of valuable farmland, and wind erosion of bare soil can create dustbowls. In coastal areas, human use of sand dunes leads to vegetation destruction and creation of *blowouts. River basins heavily used by man have higher sediment yields than those not so much used, owing to the increased erosion from farming, etc. Brown (1970) found erosion rates could locally increase a hundredfold from human influence.

Landforms created by human action include lakes due to subsidence of the land surface in mining areas, the Norfolk Broads, created by peat-cutting in medieval times, and reclaimed land from the sea, severely changing the coastline, as with the Zuider Zee in Holland. Spoil heaps, railway cuttings, and the blowing out of hillsides to build towns are other deliberate results. Sometimes human action can produce quite unexpected results, especially in the coastal zone where the erection of groynes, harbour arms, and other artificial structures severs the littoral drift leading to the decay or growth of beaches in quite unnatural situations. Large-scale recharge schemes may be used to overcome these problems, with convoys of lorries shuttling beach materials that can no longer be moved by natural agencies. *See also* arroyo.

humic acids. Resynthesized organic materials that dominate the soil humus along with the fulvic acids. Humic acids are polysaccharides and contain more carbon and nitrogen and less oxygen than fulvic acids. Fulvic acids tend to be more important in newly formed humus but eventually they are overtaken by the humic acids.

humidity. The amount of water vapour in the atmosphere. It can be measured or calculated in a variety of ways. The most frequently used measure is the *relative humidity*, which is the mass of water vapour in a given volume of air expressed as a percentage of the mass of water vapour in an equal volume of saturated air at the same temperature and pressure. As its name implies, this is only a relative index and it varies in opposite phase to temperature, even though the absolute amount of moisture in the air may not change. A better system from the meteorological point of view is the use of *vapour pressure, which indicates the water vapour content of the atmosphere irrespective of temperature. The *absolute humidity* is the mass of water vapour per unit volume of air, given in grams per cubic metre.

humification. The formation of *humus from organic matter.

humites. A group of orthorhombic and monoclinic minerals consisting of layers of Mg_2SiO_4, which have an olivine structure, alternating with layers of composition $Mg(OH,F)_2$. Humite minerals are found in metamorphosed limestones.

humus. Amorphous colloidal material in the soil, dark in colour and composed of resistant plant tissues, such as lignin, and new compounds, such as polysaccharides, synthesized by microorganisms. It is important to the soil both physically and chemically (its cation exchange capacity far exceeds that of the clays). *See also* moder humus, mor, mull.

hurricane. A *tropical cyclone with surface wind speeds in excess of 64 knots, found in the Caribbean and Gulf of Mexico. They are identical to similar cyclones in the W Pacific, Bay of Bengal, and Queensland areas, which have their own local names. At the centre of a hurricane is an area of light winds and higher temperature known as the *eye about which clouds and rain bands spiral with the associated winds. The term is also used in the *Beaufort Scale for wind speeds above 64 knots, whether or not they are linked to a tropical cyclone. Such speeds rarely occur over land.

Huygen's Principle. A principle stating that each wave front acts as a source of secondary wavelets.

hyaline. Denoting a rock that is glassy.

hyaloclastic rocks. See palagonite.

hyalocrystalline. Denoting a rock composed of both crystals and glass.

hybridization. See assimilation.

hydration. The chemical addition of water to a mineral, usually involving a fairly considerable expansion in the mineral grains. This may be important in producing subsequent mechanical weathering, in the form of *exfoliation and *granular disintegration. Minerals affected by hydration are prepared for further chemical weathering processes, such as *oxidation and *carbonation, whilst the process is also very important in the formation of clay minerals.

hydraulic action (hydraulicking) (in geomorphology). The removal of loose, incoherent, or weathered material by flowing water, assisting in stream bed and bank erosion. Material carried can range from single minerals or aggregate of crystals to pieces of layered bed strata, e.g. slate or shale, if the materials dip downstream. See abrasion.

hydraulic jump. A sudden increase in mean water level in the direction of flow, which is of a rapidly varying type and leads to a form of stationary wave.

In the simplest terms, a surface flow at high velocity confines a deeper flow, thereby resulting in the dissipation of energy through turbulence.

hydrography. 1. The study of the oceans, seas, rivers, and other water bodies, together with the strip of land bordering these. It involves description and measurement and the subsequent presentation of this information on hydrographic charts.
2. The shape of the sea floor and the deposits of which it is composed, including navigational information.

hydrolysis. A form of chemical weathering involving a reaction between the H and OH ions formed by the decomposition of water and the ions of rock minerals; it occurs wherever rocks and water are in contact. Hydrolysis is a particularly important process in the weathering of feldspars; when water comes into contact with orthoclase feldspar, potassium hydroxide and alumino-silicic acid are produced. These react with atmospheric carbon dioxide giving potassium carbonate and water, whilst the acid breaks down into clay minerals and easily removable soluble colloidal silica. Kaolin (china-clay) is produced by weathering in this way.

hydromorphic soils. Soils found in a wide range of environments where drainage is poor, e.g. alluvial flats, and therefore they are classified as intrazonal. Reduction is a more dominant process than oxidation, resulting in a blue/grey subsoil, with red/brown mottles. The most important soil of this group is the gley but also included are peaty gley podzols, peaty gleys, meadow soils, planosols, groundwater podzols, and groundwater latosols. With increasingly poor drainage these soils grade into the organic soils.

hydrostatic equation. An equation relating the variation of pressure with height to the density of air and the force of gravity: $dp/dz = -\rho g$, where dp/dz is the rate of change of pressure with height, ρ is the density of air, and g is the acceleration of free fall. It is a useful approximation when considering horizontal movement relative to the earth and is used as one of the basic equations in models of the *general circulation of the atmosphere.

hydrothermal processes. Following the pegmatitic stage during the crystallization of an igneous melt is the hydrothermal stage, when the residual fluid is a relatively low-temperature aqueous solution. Such a fluid may effect considerable alteration of the crystallized portion of the magma by such processes as *saussuritization, *kaolinization, and the alteration of mafic minerals to serpentine and chlorite.
Many mineral deposits are formed by precipitation from hydrothermal solutions. A characteristic hydrothermal deposit is the sulphide-bearing vein filling rock fissures. Hydrothermal deposits may be divided into three groups: hypothermal deposits formed at temperatures of 300–500°C at considerable depth and including cassiterite, wolfram, and molybdenite veins; mesothermal deposits including sulphides of iron, lead, copper, and zinc and formed at temperatures of 200–300°C; epithermal deposits formed at the low temperatures of 50–200°C and including stibnite, cinnabar, sulphur, silver, and gold. See also pneumatolysis.

Hydrozoa. A class of the phylum *Coelenterata. As few hydrozoans possess hard parts they are not common as fossils, although the Palaeozoic *stromatoporoids may belong to this class.

hyetograph. A type of rain gauge that records the amount and duration of rain as it falls. Rain is collected in a cylinder with a float on the water surface. As the water level rises during precipitation, the float rises in proportion to the rate of rainfall and this is recorded by pen on a rotating chart.

hygroscopic nuclei. Atmospheric particles that have an attraction for water vapour and help in the initiation of precipitation processes.

hypabyssal. See plutonic.

hypersthene. An orthorhombic *pyroxene.

hypidiomorphic. Denoting a rock consisting of *euhedral and *anhedral crystals or in which the majority of crystals are *subhedral. Compare idiomorphic, allotriomorphic.

hypothermal. See hydrothermal processes.

hypsographic curve. A curve showing the proportion of a landscape lying at, above, or below particular elevations. The percentage of the landscape between successive contours is calculated from a relief map, and the results expressed either as simple proportions between different heights, or as a cumulative measure showing the percentage of area lying above each level, starting with 100% at sea level and working up to nil at the absolute peaks. It has been used to look for development of erosion surfaces, e.g. terraces and former peneplains, which appear on the curve as extensive areas at their particular elevation. It is also used to display the proportions of the earth's surface at particular elevations above and depressions below sea level.

hypsometer. An instrument for determining atmospheric pressure or altitude by measuring the boiling point of water. The air pressure can be deduced directly from the temperature at which boiling occurs, but altitude must then be obtained from the altimeter equation. Accuracy is not very high: the boiling point must be known to within 0.01 K to obtain the height to within 3 metres.

hypsometric tinting. The differential colouring of elevation bands on a map to enable the user to determine quickly the higher and lower areas of the land portrayed. Greens usually portray lowland areas; as the land rises so the colours change from yellows to browns to purples. This technique is common in small-scale maps, e.g. atlases and wall maps.

I

ice. The solid state of water. It melts at 0°C, requiring approximately 340 000 joules per kilogram (80 calories per gram) of ice (latent heat of fusion) or 2.8 × 10^6 J/kg (677 cal/g) if converted directly from ice to vapour (latent heat of sublimation). Pure water does not necessarily freeze to ice when the temperature falls below 0°C, especially if it is in the form of small droplets such as those found within clouds. This has very important implications in the *Bergeron-Findeisen theory of precipitation formation. Even when *freezing nuclei are present, droplets may still remain in the liquid phase to temperatures of -30°C or less. By -40°C the water will freeze spontaneously irrespective of the presence or absence of nuclei.

At the ground surface, ice can take many forms: rime, hail, black ice, and on a vast scale glaciers. As ice reflects solar radiation, and requires heat for melting, it is a very important aspect of the heat balance in high latitudes.

Ice Age. A period in the earth's history when ice spread towards the equator accompanied by a general lowering of surface temperatures, especially in temperate latitudes. The *Pleistocene period, ending about 10 000 years ago, experienced at least four major ice advances (*see* glacial maximum), with the margin reaching about 52°N over NW Europe and about 45°N in NE America. With this change in location of ice surfaces the whole atmospheric circulation altered, the main climatic belts being compressed and pushed towards the equator. At present we appear to be in an interglacial circulation but it is assumed that further ice ages will be experienced in the future; as the true cause or causes of ice ages are not known it is impossible to predict when this will be. It is possible that changes in landmass altitude and variations in the quantity or quality of solar radiation are at least partially responsible.

From geological records, it has been deduced that ice ages also existed in Permo-Carboniferous times about 250 million years ago, one in late Pre-Cambrian times some 500 million years ago, and possibly several earlier. These former ice age deposits have even been found in present tropical latitudes, as the continents have since changed their relative positions.

Between 1550 and 1850 temperatures in much of the N hemisphere fell to their lowest since the last ice age, and this period has been called the *Little Ice Age*. Alpine glaciers advanced and settlement in many northern areas, such as Greenland, Iceland, and N Norway, had to be abandoned.

iceberg. A mass of ice in the sea that has moved from a land area to the coast, and thence into the sea, and which exceeds 5 metres in height. These ice masses, many of which result from the calving off of fragments of glacier ice, float partly above but largely beneath the surface of the sea. They vary greatly in shape one from the other: some are dome-shaped, some are sloping or pinnacled, while others have a more tabular form. Glacier bergs display very irregular shapes.

ice cap. A permanent mass of ice such as might cover a highland area; a small-scale *ice sheet.

ice floe. An area of sea ice that measures 20 metres or more across and is essentially flat. Small floes are 20 to 100 metres across, big floes are 500 to 2000 metres across, and giant floes are over 10 kilometres.

ice fog. When visibility falls to less than 1 km as a result of ice crystals, an ice fog is said to exist. Such fogs have increased in frequency in recent years as human activities extend to colder latitudes. When the air is very cold, only a little water is required before saturation takes place. If the temperature is below -40°C the ice crystals will form directly on saturation. Normally little evaporation takes place, but the release of water vapour from car exhausts or power station cooling systems can quickly saturate calm air, as often happens in the Fairbanks area of Alaska.

Icelandic Low. The mean low pressure system of the North Atlantic. Depressions form in the latitude of Newfoundland, move northeastwards as they intensify, then gradually decay. Although their tracks vary quite considerably, on average they are most frequent and at their most intense in the Iceland area. As the circulation of the atmosphere varies with time, the precise location of the Icelandic Low changes. Recently it has been moving further south than its position during the 1930s.

Iceland spar. A transparent variety of calcite of optical quality. *See* carbonate minerals.

ice-rafting. The transport of debris in sea ice. Widespread at high latitudes are sediment deposits that have been rafted by ice, either icebergs or ice floes. They reached the ice from meltwater streams or by being frozen into the base of ice that later became waterborne. These materials range from very large boulders to clays and silts. They may be transported over considerable distances to be deposited among material of an entirely different character. Icebergs and floes reach nearer to the equator in the N hemisphere than they do in the S hemisphere. Ice-rafted pebbles and boulders seem to be capable of making pits or dents in soft sea-floor deposits, presumably as they fall to the sea floor, as was shown by underwater photography in the Arctic.

ice sheet. An accumulation of ice hundreds of metres thick and covering vast areas. Many developed during the *Pleistocene period, and are represented by the present Greenland and Antarctic ice sheets. The ice develops at high altitudes, spreading outwards and submerging all the underlying topography. Being unrestricted by rock walls, unlike *cirque and *valley glaciers, the directions of ice movement within these ice sheets reflect the slopes of the ice surface, which depend upon relative accumulation rates within the various parts of the sheet.

ichor. *See* granitization.

Ichthyosauria. An order of extinct reptiles that became secondarily adapted to a marine life. In shape they were similar to dolphins (mammals): they had fishlike tails and the limbs were modified as paddles. Ichthyosaurs were totally aquatic and the young were probably born alive. They were prominent throughout the Mesozoic, especially in the Jurassic period, becoming extinct at the end of the Cretaceous. *Compare* Plesiosauria.

iddingsite. The red-brown alteration products of forsteritic olivine consisting largely of iron oxides and clay minerals.

idioblastic. Denoting a metamorphic rock consisting largely of crystals having euhedral form.

idiomorphic. Denoting a rock in which the majority of crystals are anhedral. *Compare* allotriomorphic, hypidiomorphic.

idocrase (vesuvianite). A yellow, green, or brown tetragonal mineral with an ideal formula $Ca_{10}(Mg,Fe)_2Al_4Si_9O_{34}(O-H,F)_4$, found in thermally metamorphosed limestones.

igneous rocks. Rocks that have crystallized from a high-temperature molten silicate (or rarely carbonate) liquid or magma. Igneous rocks include plutonic, hypabyssal, volcanic, and pyroclastic rocks. The compositional range of igneous rocks is described by the terms acid, intermediate, basic, and ultrabasic. Classification may also be based upon the *silica saturation principle. *See* andesite, basalt, carbonatite, diorite, gabbro, granite, ijolite, lamprophyre, rhyolite, syenodiorite, syenite, trachyte, layered igneous rocks.

ignimbrite. See pyroclastic rocks.

ijolite. A suite of strongly alkaline undersaturated plutonic rocks often associated with carbonatites. They are characterized by varying proportions of nepheline and clinopyroxene, an abundance of accessory minerals, and the virtual absence of feldspar. Members of the suite are classified in terms of *colour index as follows:

urtite <30 (% dark minerals)
ijolite 30–70
melteigite 70–90
pyroxenite >90

Thus an ijolite may consist of about equal proportions of nepheline and aegirine-augite. Accessory minerals include apatite, melanite, phlogopite, sphene, and calcite. *Uncompahgrite* is a melitite pyroxenite and *jacupirangite* consists largely of titanium-rich augite, magnetite, and biotite.

illite. See clay minerals.

illuviation. The accumulation of fine material in a soil, or a part of a soil, washed down from above. The *illuvial horizon* is the B horizon: the degree of development of the B is therefore a guide to the time and effectiveness of operation of the illuvial processes. The materials involved are sesquioxides, bases, clays, and colloidal organic matter.

ilmenite. A black metallic mineral ($FeTiO_3$) found as an accessory in igneous and metamorphic rocks and as a detrital mineral in sands.

imbricate structure. A series of thrust sheets all dipping in the same direction and displaced by roughly the same amount.

inceptisol. One of the ten soil orders of the *Seventh Approximation, covering soils that are better developed than entisols but not so advanced in formation as the alfisols, i.e. there is no horizon of iron and aluminium ac-

cumulation. They are young soils in which the horizons present have developed quickly. They are equivalent to the humic gley soils, acid brown soils, and andosols of the old classification system.

incised meanders. Meanders of a stream that are cut deeply into bedrock. This incision could arise from original development, as meanders can develop before a stream has completed downcutting (*ingrown meanders*). Alternatively, incision may result from *rejuvenation of typical floodplain meanders causing them to cut down and incise themselves into their floodplain (*entrenched meanders*).

inclination. See dip (defs. 1 and 2).

inclusion. The occurrence of one substance enclosed within another, e.g. a pre-existing rock fragment caught up in a later rock (xenolith) or crystals of one mineral contained in another. Small volumes of volatile constituents trapped during the growth of crystals are termed *fluid inclusions.* Inclusions of gabbro and peridotite within alkali basalt are often called *nodules.*

incompetent. Denoting beds of rock that deform plastically and flow when stressed during folding, or folds in which the thickness of the beds changes during folding. See also competence.

index contour. A contour line that is accentuated by its width, in order to facilitate the reading of elevations on a map. It is usually every fourth line, e.g. where the contour interval is every 25 ft. then the 100 ft. contour is accentuated (on metric Ordnance Survey maps the interval remains in feet, with the metric equivalent shown).

index cycle (in meteorology). The *zonal index is believed to undergo a cyclic variation from a high-index circulation, with its strong zonal westerlies, to the low-index state, with much meridional transfer, then back to the high-index phase, with a wavelength of about 28 days. However, further work has cast doubt on the validity of a true cycle.

index fossil. *See* zone fossil.

Index map

index map. Usually a small-scale map forming a base upon which certain information concerning larger scale maps, or other data, may be portrayed for easy reference. In series mapping the individual sheet lines are drawn on a small-scale outline map and such information as sheet numbers, dates of publication, and edition numbers are shown for each sheet. This enables the user to ascertain immediately which sheets cover any part of the area.

index mineral. *See* zone.

Indian clinometer. A surveying instrument used in *plane tabling for determining the heights of points fixed by intersection or radiation methods. The height of the plane table and of the point over which it is set up must be known. The clinometer is placed on the plane table and an adjustable sight is used to view the points for which heights are required. This adjustable sight indicates a tangent value, positive for an elevation, negative for a depression, which is multiplied by the distance between the points, measured from the table, to find the height difference.

Indian summer. Any period of warm settled weather in October or early November. The term was first used in New England when under such weather conditions the Indians made preparations for the coming winter by storing food and repairing tents. Most years do have at least one spell that could be called an Indian Summer but it has no precise meaning.

induration. The hardening of porous rocks or of soils through the deposition of minerals, which act as a cement, on or within the surface layers. Chemical weathering usually causes the weakening of rocks through the removal of elements in solution. Where strong evaporation occurs, as for instance in the semiarid regions, these elements are brought to the surface by capillarity, where they combine to cement the soil or weathered rock. There are three main types of induration rock forms. The cement in calcrete consists mainly of calcite ($CaCO_3$), that in ferricrete is of haematite (Fe_2O_3), whilst silcrete is cemented by silica (SiO_2).

infrastructure. A structure produced deep within the earth's crust under conditions of high temperature and pressure. It is characterized by plastic folding, migmatites, and granites. Overlying this area are the less highly deformed rocks of the superstructure.

Cross section through an ingrown meander

ingrown meander. The type of *incised meander that develops from origin. If a winding course develops in a stream before it has completed downcutting, it will meander and cut down simultaneously, lowering its course into bedrock. As with floodplain meanders, lateral erosion on the outside of meander bends, complemented by deposition on the inside of bends, produces an asymmetric cross profile of the valley and downstream migration of the meanders. *Compare* entrenched meander.

inland basin (bolson, playa). A closed depression within an upland desert region towards which material is moved whenever rain falls in sufficient amounts. The material is moved both down wadis and as sheet wash on broad slopes. The finest grains and material in solution are moved farthest, so that there is a gradation from vast accumulations of unsorted material at the basin margin, through sand and loam, to clay and salts in the centre. Many of the mineral grains also exhibit salt or calcareous coatings. The basins have a very flat surface when dry, though extensive cracking may be produced by the heat. Salt lakes or salt marshes may form during periods of rain.

inland sea. A category of *adjacent sea (see also* marginal sea) consisting of an extensive water body lying in the interior of a landmass, often remote from the ocean. Inland seas may or may not have access to the open coast; where they do have access it is usually restricted to a single or a few narrow sea passages. Inland seas display a large depth range. Those with depths generally less than 250 metres are called shallow inland (or *epeiric*) seas, e.g. the Baltic Sea. Far greater depths are encountered in the deep inland seas, for example the Mediterranean, where depths range from 2000 to 5000 m. Very large lakes have some of the characteristics of inland seas. All inland seas and lakes experience wave action, *seiche movements, and wind-induced flow. Waves on a large lake such as Lake Kariba can be over 3 m high, and very much larger waves affect some inland sea areas. The shores display many of the morphological forms typical of sea coasts in general.

inlier. An area of exposed rock surrounded by stratigraphically younger strata, usually a result of folding, faulting, and erosion (such as the erosion of the crest of an anticline). *Compare* outlier.

inner core. The earth's innermost shell, believed on geophysical evidence to consist of solid iron and nickel and separated from the *outer core at a depth of 5000 kilometres. It has a diameter of 2600 km.

Insecta. The largest class of the phylum *Arthropoda, comprising the only invertebrate animals adapted for flight. They are air-breathing, have three pairs of legs, and all but the most primitive have one or two pairs of wings. This highly successful and diverse group occupies an enormous range of habitats. Many fossil species are known, despite the rarity of suitable environments for preservation. Fossil insects have been found in the Devonian and some Carboniferous dragonflies attained a wing span of nearly 80 cm.

Insectivora. The order of the class *Mammalia that includes the shrews, hedgehogs, and moles. Modern insectivores are small and usually very unspecialized in their anatomy and feeding habits. In these primitive features they resemble the first Mesozoic placental mammals, which are generally regarded as early insectivores and the ancestors of most modern placental groups. The tree shrews (family Tupaiidae) are thought to have given rise to the *Primates and are often classified with that order.

inselberg (bornhardt). A large domelike residual hill of hard rock, characterized by very steep slopes rising abruptly from the surrounding surface. Inselbergs were formerly believed to be semiarid landforms, but it is now widely believed that they are more typical of humid tropical climates. The main reason for their occurrence is differential *deep weathering followed by subsequent *exhumation, which exposes the more massive, less weathered parts of the weathering profile as inselbergs. Some large forms extend to a height of over 300 metres and are possibly formed by successive stages of weathering, which proceed at the same time as *regolith removal. As an inselberg is exposed at the surface, *unloading joints usually develop, and movement of rock slabs along such partings can bring about the destruction of these domed forms.

insolation. (From *in*coming *so*lar *radiation*). The intensity of either direct or global (direct and diffuse) solar radiation on a unit area at a specified time on a specified surface. Its value is dependent upon the *solar constant, the time of year, the latitude of the receiving surface, the slope and aspect, if any, of the surface, and the transparency of the atmosphere. In S England, measured maximum values of insolation on a clear summer day amount to about 30 MJ m^{-2} (720 cals cm^{-2}).

insolation weathering. Weathering resulting from the expansion and contraction produced by temperature changes. It was formerly believed that in arid areas practically all rock fragmentation was caused by the extreme variations in temperature and consequent differential expansion between the outside and inside of blocks, which set up stresses producing cracks. However, experimental work in the 1930's suggested that the process was extremely overrated, although there are many examples of fragmented rocks for which this process seems to be the best explanation. In addition to large-scale cracking, *granular disintegration may be produced by the differential expansion and contraction of several mineral types in one rock.

instability. The state of the atmosphere when thermals are able to rise freely by their own buoyancy forces. This occurs when the *environmental lapse rate is steeper than the *dry adiabatic lapse rate and is known as *absolute instability*. This normally is only found near the ground surface. Other states of

instability depend on the relative rates of cooling of the environment and dry and saturated thermals. Once condensation has taken place and the atmosphere remains unstable, cloud development will be extensive and heavy rainfall probable.

insular shelf. The shelf zone surrounding large islands. The shelf extends from low-tide level out to the shelf-edge zone where, as with all shelves, there occurs a marked and fairly steep descent to the deep-sea floor. Insular shelves, like continental shelves, may be broad or narrow, but they tend to contrast with the zone surrounding coral reefs and oceanic islands, for in these cases the sea floor plunges steeply to the deep-sea floor from close to the shore. The shelf edge of insular shelves usually lies at a depth of some 200 metres.

Interfluves

interfluve. The higher ground between one river and the next in the same drainage system: an upstanding area not yet subject to fluvial denudation. Interfluves become lowered and narrowed as denudation proceeds, until at the stage of peneplanation they are almost insignificant. *See also* divide.

interglacial. A period of warmer climatic conditions separating *glacial phases of the *Pleistocene. Temperatures were probably similar to those of today, or perhaps a little warmer. They are believed to have lasted longer than the glacials and very much longer than the 10 000 years or so since the last glacial phase.

intergranular. Denoting a texture common in basic lavas in which the spaces between plagioclase crystals are occupied by relatively small grains of pyroxene and olivine. *Compare* ophitic.

intergrowth. An interlocking growth of two minerals that crystallize simultaneously from a melt. Intergrowths may also result from the *exsolution of a homogeneous mineral to form two discrete phases, one included in the other. *See* graphic intergrowth, myrmekite, perthite, symplectite.

intermediate contour. A contour line that falls between the *index contours.

intermediate rocks. Strictly, rocks containing 55-66% silica (by weight); in current usage intermediate rocks contain less than 10% free quartz, sodic plagioclase, and/or alkali feldspar. Typical intermediate rocks are syenite, diorite, trachyte, and phonolite. *See also* acid rocks, basic rocks, ultrabasic rocks.

intermontane. A basin of deposition enclosed by mountains.

internal magnetic field. That portion of the earth's magnetic field that originates within the earth itself.

internal waves (boundary waves). Waves that occur within a water mass, which may be stratified or in which density may vary with depth. Internal waves have quite different characteristics from those of waves that develop at the sea's surface. The density variations sometimes occur abruptly, at sharp surfaces of discontinuity called *interfaces*, and sometimes quite gradually. The amplitude of internal waves often far exceeds that of waves on the sea's surface; for example, one measurement recorded in the Atlantic Ocean several decades ago amounted to some 60 metres.

International Date Line. A line corresponding to the 180° meridian, deviating to some extent around island groups.

The date immediately to the east of the line is one day earlier than to the west, since 180°E is 12 hours ahead of *GMT and 180°W is 12 hours behind.

International Map of the World projection. A modified polyconic map projection having two standard parallels and a scale of exactly 1:1 000 000. Straight lines joining points on the truly divided top and bottom parallels of the projection represent the geographic meridians. Arcs of the same circle, rather than concentric circles, form the parallels.

intersection. A type of *plane tabling in which points of detail are fixed by setting up the plane table at two or more stations for each detail point and drawing lines of sight to it, the point of intersection of these lines representing the location of the point.

intersertal. Denoting a texture common in basic rocks in which interstices are filled by a glassy *mesostasis or a fine-grained aggregate of quartz, alkali feldspar, and deuteric minerals.

interstadial. A warmer stage within a *glacial phase, in which the ice receded, to be followed by a readvance on the return of colder conditions. *Compare* interglacial.

interstices. The angular spaces inside a meshwork of lathlike crystals. In basalts, interstices between feldspar crystals may be occupied by grains of pyroxene or alternatively glass. *See also* intersertal, intergranular.

intertropical   convergence   zone (I.T.C.Z.). The zone of convergence between the airstreams from the N and S hemispheres. It oscillates in position with the thermal equator, reaching its maximum northward extent in July and maximum southward extent in January. Over the ocean areas it marks the meeting point of the trade winds, but over the continents it becomes affected by the monsoonal circulation and has somewhat different properties.
The I.T.C.Z. can be clearly seen over ocean areas from satellite photographs

as a narrow band of enhanced convectional activity indicating upward motion and cloudy showery weather at the surface. Sometimes two bands are found separated by about 3-5° latitude, each exhibiting the usual I.T.C.Z. characteristics. Many theories have been proposed to account for this feature, but as yet the real origin remains in doubt. As the dual convergence zone is only found over the oceans, it is presumed that it must be connected with sea-surface temperatures and upwelling.

Reference to this zone as the intertropical front still remain, but as it has dissimilar features to temperate latitude fronts and is not really frontal, the use of this term is discouraged.

intraclast. An *allochem that is a penecontemporaneously eroded fragment of calcareous material. Intraclasts are not derived from pre-existing limestones.

intraformational. Existing or formed with a formation. For example, an intraformational conglomerate is one in which the clasts are eroded fragments of newly consolidated sediment. These clasts are then incorporated immediately into the accumulating sediment.

intrazonal soils. Soils differing from surrounding *zonal soils owing to the dominance of local drainage or parent material over the zonal influence of climate and vegetation. These include hydromorphic soils (poor drainge), halomorphic soils (salinization), calcimorphic soils (calcareous parent material), soils dominated by human influences, soils on organic matter, and various horizons in zonal soils regarded as intrazonal. They differ from *azonal soils in that they have more or less well developed horizons, whilst azonal soils still have little horizonation. They are often linked to zonal soils in catenary sequences, with poorly drained soils occurring downslope from the well-drained zonal types. In the *Seventh Approximation, these soils are linked with the nearest zonal soils as aquic or

halic variants, for example there is no separate group of gleys.

intrusive. Denoting igneous rocks that have been injected into the earth's crust and have solidified beneath the earth's surface.

inversion. An increase in temperature with height in the atmosphere. This can act as an upper limit to convection, hence inversions are associated with atmospheric stability and usually dry weather. They can be formed by cooling beneath the inversion or warming at the inversion level and above. The former method occurs most frequently as a result of radiational cooling at night from the ground surface, an extreme case being over the Antarctic ice cap, and the latter by subsidence of air under anticyclonic conditions. In these circumstances the air may be extremely dry, as occurs above the trade wind inversion, and quickly evaporates any saturated thermals reaching this level. It acts therefore as a very effective lid to convectional cloud.

Invertebrata. Animals that do not possess a jointed backbone formed of vertebrae. The members of all animal phyla except the *Chordata belong to this group. *Compare* Vertebrata.

inverted relief. Topographic relief that is the opposite of the geological structure, as for example where anticlines form valleys and synclines form high ground. It is the result of prolonged denudation.

involution. 1. A lobe of one type of material projecting upwards or downwards into material of another type, produced by the effects of *cryoturbation. These involutions are seen in the upper sections of bedded deposits and are a clear indication of former *periglacial conditions. The exact cause of this type of movement is not yet fully clear.

2. The refolding of a nappe structure resulting in very complex fold patterns.

ionosphere. The layer of the atmosphere above the stratopause in which free ions and electrons occur as a result of ionization of gas molecules by solar ultraviolet and X-radiation. It consists of several layers, indicated by the letters D to G, which reflect electromagnetic waves back to earth and thus it is very important in radio communications. There is, as yet, no evidence that surface weather is in any way influenced by conditions in the ionosphere.

irradiance. The quantity of radiant energy received in unit time on unit area of surface. It is expressed in watts per square metre.

isallobar. A line on a chart connecting places of equal pressure tendency. Such lines are used in forecasting the movements of pressure systems, particularly depressions.

isarithm. A line on a map joining points of equal value. There are many forms of isarithm, depending on the values concerned (*see* isobar, isogon). A contour is also a form of isarithm joining points of equal elevation.

island arc. A long chain of islands, usually arcuate or bow-shaped. Many of them are bordered on their ocean flank by deep slits or *trenches in the deep-sea floor. The E seaboard of Asia, for example, has a whole series of island arcs—the Aleutians, the Kurils, the Japanese, and the Marianas—flanked on their ocean side by a series of trenches: the Aleutian Trench, Kuril Trench, Japanese Trench, Ryukyus Trench, and Philippine Trench. On a global scale, the island arcs can be seen to continue the great folded mountain chains on land such as the Himalayas and Western Cordilleras. The arcs usually include lines of active volcanoes; moreover, they are associated with many of the world's most severe earthquakes and with very pronounced gravity anomalies. The theory of *plate tectonics provides an explanation for the distribution of these features, together with their associated volcanic

and seismic activity: they mark the boundary between two of the plates that make up the earth's surface. At this margin ocean floor is being destroyed as one plate overrides the other. The friction between these plates accounts for the series of earthquakes whose foci increase in depth away from the ocean side of the arc. The volcanic activity is the result of the increased thermal energy present as a result of the friction, which leads to partial melting of one or both plates. The trench on the oceanward side marks the surface expression of the junction between the plates.

isobar. A line on a chart joining points of constant barometric pressure. At the ground surface, observing stations are often at different altitudes and corrections have to be made to pressure readings to provide a common level, normally sea level. In some countries, e.g. South Africa, much of the land surface is well above sea level and surface pressure readings are corrected to differences from the 850 mb pressure level.
The patterns produced by joining points of equal surface pressure represent synoptic systems, such as anticyclones, depressions, troughs, ridges, and cols, from which interpretations of the weather can be made.

isochemical. Denoting metamorphic processes that involve little or no change in chemical composition of a whole rock. However, the addition or subtraction of water and carbon dioxide usually occurs during metamorphism.

isoclinal folding. Generally upright tight folds whose axial planes and limbs are parallel. (See diagram at *fold*.)

isogon. 1. A line joining points of constant wind direction.
2. A line joining points of equal magnetic variation.

isograd. *See* zone (def. 1).

isohaline. A line drawn on certain oceanographic charts and diagrams joining points of equal salinity.

isohyet. A line joining points experiencing the same amount of rainfall. This can be used for any time interval from a single period of rain to mean annual totals.

isomeric line. A line that joins points having the same average monthly rainfall expressed as a percentage of the mean annual rainfall. It is helpful in displaying similarities in rainfall regimes by removing the effects of large totals over mountainous areas.

isometric. See cubic.

isopach (isopachyte). A line on a geological map joining points of equal thickness for a particular rock bed.

isopleth map. A map showing quantitative spatial distributions indicated by lines of equal value, such as isotherms.

isopycnic (isopycnal). A line drawn on certain oceanographic and meteorological charts joining points of equal density.

isoseismal line. A line on a map joining points on the earth's surface of equal earthquake intensity.

isostacy. A condition of theoretical balance for all large portions of the earth's crust, which assumes that they are floating on an underlying more dense medium. As a result of erosion or deposition, this balance is put out of equilibrium and has to be compensated for by movements of the earth's crust. Areas of deposition sink, whereas areas of erosion rise. In this way the roots of old mountain chains formed many kilometres beneath the earth's surface are brought up to the surface. See also Airy's hypothesis of isostacy.

isotach. 1. A line of constant wind speed.
2. A line joining points of equal distance travelled in a period of time.

isotherm. A line joining points of equal temperature. Isotherm maps are the most common methods of showing temperature changes on a climatic scale.

As with pressure, the effects of altitude are important and corrections to sea level are normally made.

isothermal layer. Any vertical section of the atmosphere in which the temperature remains constant with height, i.e. there is a zero lapse rate, as revealed by an upper-air sounding. Isothermal layers are frequent but are usually transitory. The term formerly referred to the stratosphere but it has now been superseded as more information about the thermal structure of that layer became available.

isotropic. Having the same physical properties if measured in different directions. The term usually pertains to optical properties, particularly the velocity with which light is transmitted in crystals. Crystals of the cubic system are isotropic. Compare anisotropic.

J

jacupirangite. See ijolite series.

jade. A green or white semiprecious stone. Jade is a tough compact variety of either jadeite or nephrite.

jadeite. A *pyroxene of composition $NaAlSi_2O_6$, found in high-pressure metamorphic rocks such as glaucophane schists. See also jade.

jasper. A red opaque variety of chalcedonic quartz. See silica minerals.

jet. A type of *coal that can be carved and polished for decoration.

jet stream. A narrow band of winds at high altitudes, with speeds above 60 knots and having strong vertical and lateral shear. Two main regions of jet streams are known in the troposphere, one in the subtropical westerly circulation, which is fairly constant in location for any given season and so appears clearly on mean charts, and a second associated with the polar front. This is highly variable in its location, being dependent on the transitory thermal gradients of mid-latitude depressions.

As surface depressions form where divergence in the upper atmosphere is strong, they are frequently initiated downstream of a trough in the upper westerly circulation, with anticyclones forming in areas of upper air convergence upstream of the trough. This development takes place in zones of large surface temperature gradient, which in turn causes marked temperature contrasts in the upper atmosphere as depressions intensify. The jet streams are the response to this upper atmospheric thermal gradient, and frequently encourage further development of surface pressure features by the marked convergences and divergences that are experienced in different parts of the jet.

Easterly jets have been reported between India and Africa, and low-level jets in East Africa, but these are weaker and less persistent than those of the westerly zone. Above the troposphere, a *polar night jet stream occurs around high latitudes in winter at about 50 mb level (40 km).

jointing. The system of cracks in a mass of rock constituting, in many rock types, the only means by which water can infiltrate the rock mass. Consequently, within an area of a single rock type in which there are variations in the extent of jointing, well-jointed areas will become weathered more quickly and to a deeper level than the more massive parts of the outcrop, which may even remain as solid rock.

joule. The unit of work or energy in the Système International (SI), equal to the amount of work done by a force of one newton in moving an object one metre in the direction of the force. It is equivalent to 1 watt second or 0.239 calories.

junction. The plane of contact between two adjacent and distinct bodies of rock. Such a junction may be conformable, unconformable, or produced by intrusion or faulting.

Jurassic. The period of the *Mesozoic Era that follows the *Triassic and precedes the *Cretaceous. It lasted for about 65 million years, from 200 to 135 million years ago. The Jurassic System is subdivided into eleven stages. The Lower Jurassic consists of the Hettangian, Sinemurian, Pliensbachian, and Toarcian Stages; the Middle Jurassic consists of the Bajocian and Bathonian Stages; the Callovian, Oxfordian, Kimmeridgian, Portlandian, and Purbeckian Stages form the Upper Jurassic. Following a marine transgression, the characteristic rocks of the Jurassic System in Britain are clays and limestones, some of them oolitic. There were coral reefs, and other important invertebrates included brachiopods, bivalves such as oysters, ammonites (on which much of the system is zoned), and irregular echinoids. On land, dinosaurs continued to flourish and diversify and other reptiles included aerial pterosaurs and marine forms. Fossils of both *Archaeopteryx*, the earliest known bird, and the first mammals come from Jurassic rocks. A marine regression towards the end of the period resulted in nonmarine deposits.

K

kaersutite. A monoclinic *amphibole.

Kainozoic. See Cenozoic.

kaliophilite. See feldspathoids.

kalsilite. See feldspathoids.

kame. An isolated hummock of stratified *fluvioglacial sediments, mainly sands and gravels, associated with slow-moving or stagnant ice. Kames may be formed in a variety of ways. Debris-laden meltwater streams may emerge from the snout of a decaying glacier, depositing their load into an ice-dammed lake. On melting, that part of the accumulation formerly adjacent to the snout may form a steep ice-contact slope, though a certain amount of slumping will occur. Alternatively, material may be deposited in meltwater pools on the surface of a stagnant glacier. The accumulated sediments will be lowered to ground level on melting, forming a kame.

kame terrace. An accumulation of *fluvioglacial sediments deposited by meltwater flowing between a decaying glacier and its valley sides. As with *kames, the ice contact slope suffers collapse on melting of the ice. Kame terraces can be continuous or discontinuous, deposition only occurring where meltwater channels could widen, thereby reducing velocities of flow. These features are flat-topped and steepsided, sloping gently down-valley. Long continued existence of these terraces after deglaciation depends upon the extent of subsequent fluvial and slope processes.

kaolinite. See clay minerals.

karren. Relatively small irregular hollows and elongated grooves cut on limestone surfaces as a result of solution. At the most basic level they may be divided into *rundkarren*, having rounded separations between grooves, and *rillerkarren*, with sharp separations. It is believed that whilst the latter are the result of running water, the former may be at least partially created beneath a cover of snow, soil, or peat. The term is also used for the whole dissected surface and is the German equivalent of *limestone pavement, the French equivalent being *lapiés*.

karst. Denoting any area within which limestone solution landforms such as *sink holes, *uvalas, and *limestone caverns have become well developed. The term stems from the regional name for the massive limestone area of Yugoslavia, where practically all the landforms have been produced by solution and almost all the drainage is underground.
Prerequisites for a fully developed karst landscape include a considerable thickness of strong soluble well-bedded and well-jointed limestone, moderately heavy rainfall, and sufficient altitude to allow an extensive flow of underground water.

katabatic wind. On calm clear nights the ground surface cools by radiational losses and the air in contact with the ground also cools. The density of air increases when the temperature falls, and if the ground surface is sloping, these heavier layers will give rise to a downslope gravitational flow. Where concentrated in a valley, night-time mountain breezes can be quite strong, but the most extreme form of katabatic wind is off the Greenland and Antarctic ice caps. A mean hourly speed of 156 km per hour (97 mph) was reported at Cape Denison (67.9°S, 142.7°E) under such conditions. See also anabatic wind.

katafront. Any frontal surface at which the warm air is descending relative to the cold. As a result of this subsidence, weather activity at a katafront is normally weak with only a belt of stratiform cloud indicating its presence. Some fronts vary in character along their length and may take the form of an *anafront near the depression centre and a katafront further away.

katophorite. A monoclinic *amphibole.

kelp. Certain species of seaweed of considerable length and thickness. These seaweeds, which are usually brownish in colour, thrive below lowtide level, and may be luxuriant enough to form *kelp forests*. Of particular importance are the large laminarians, which anchor themselves to rocky or stony bottoms and, depending on their rigidity, either stand fairly erect or move with the tidal currents. They influence the movement of bottom materials, and may, if uprooted by strong tidal flow or wave action, carry their stony attachments shorewards or alongshore. They are also effective at times in damping wave action. Kelp forests are important as fish feeding grounds.

kelvin. The unit of thermodynamic temperature in the Système International (SI), equal to 1/273.16 of the temperature of the triple point of water. 1 kelvin is equal to 1°C and a temperature expressed in kelvins is the same as the *absolute temperature.

Kelvin-Helmholtz instability. The development of waves at the surface separating two layers of the atmosphere having different temperatures and wind speeds. These waves sometimes increase in amplitude and become unstable, rolling into vortices, which break and give *clear air turbulence. Very occasionally moisture conditions may be such that clouds form on the waves and make the vortices visible.

Kelvin wave. A tidal phenomenon in which a progressive wave travelling along a tidal channel is affected by the earth's rotation to the extent that the tidal range (in the N Hemisphere) is increased along the right-hand side of the channel and decreased on the left-hand side (with the observer facing the direction in which the progressive wave is travelling). Usually, the energy of the progressive wave is much diminished, so preventing a true *amphidromic tidal system from operating. The Kelvin wave phenomenon can be observed in the English Channel, where the tidal range along the English coast is small compared with that along the French coast. During any tidal state, the sea surface slopes from one side of the Channel to the other.

kelyphitic rim. *See* reaction rim.

kentallenite. A *syenogabbro containing olivine and augite together with plagioclase and orthoclase feldspars and large poikilitic crystals of biotite.

kenyte. A *trachyte containing large rhombic orthoclase phenocrysts. Medium-grained varieties may be termed *rhomb-porphyry.*

keratophyre. *See* spilites.

Kerguelen-Gaussberg Ridge. A large ocean feature extending southwards from the East African coast, reaching almost to Antarctica. The ridge branches out, one branch reaching westwards to the *Mid-Atlantic Ridge, and another trending eastwards, thence circumscribing the Australian continent and extending towards the East Pacific Rise. Surveys conducted off the continent of Antarctica show that the continental slope south of the Kerguelen-Gaussberg Ridge is in places made up of several tilted plainlike features with gentle undulations. Rocks dredged from the Kerguelen-Gaussberg Ridge yield samples of basalt and also samples of continental-type rock.

kernlose winter. In Antarctica, temperatures decrease towards winter, as in most parts of the world, but by the end of the long winter night, temperatures are little lower than they were at its commencement. This peculiarity has been called the kernlose (or coreless) winter. It represents a balance between surface radiational cooling and atmospheric counter radiation from above the intense surface inversion. Some theories suggest that advection of warmer maritime air may play a part in the kernlose effect, but this is disputed.

kettle hole. A depression in the ground surface in a glaciated area. As a mass of ice stagnates, material is deposited from above the ice surface, whilst *fluvioglacial deposits also accumulate. In this way masses of ice can become buried beneath *drift. Once buried the ice takes a considerable time to melt, and when this finally happens, collapse occurs and a depression is formed, which may subsequently become filled by a lake or by sediments. Not all kettle holes are associated with stagnant ice, since small lakes and streams may freeze whilst sediments are accumulating, but those that are will be found in association with *kames and *eskers.

key. *See* cay.

khamsin. A hot dry southerly wind blowing across Egypt from the Sahara desert. It precedes depressions passing eastwards along the North African coast and hence is most common between April and June. According to the Arabs it blows for 50 days.

kimberlite (blue ground). A brecciated carbonate-rich phlogopite-bearing *peridotite found in pipes and diatremes piercing very old metamorphic rocks. Many kimberlites contain diamonds.

kinetic energy. The energy of a body derived from its movement. Its magnitude is expressed as ½ mv^2 where m is the mass of the body, and v is its velocity. The atmosphere possesses large amounts of kinetic energy by virtue of its motion, but this is constantly being lost through surface friction and turbulence. It is replenished by conversion of potential energy derived originally from solar radiation and upward motion of air.

kingdom. The largest group in the taxonomic classification of organisms. Two kingdoms are usually recognized, the Plantae and Animalia. Unicellular organisms are sometimes placed in a third kingdom distinct from the plants and animals, called the *Protista. The kingdom Animalia is composed of several phyla (*see* phylum); the Plantae is made up of a number of equivalent groups called divisions. *See* taxonomy.

kink plane. A deformation structure in which the orientation of a foliation is changed as a result of slippage or gliding.

klippe. Originally, any rock body isolated by erosion. The term is now restricted to the outlier or erosional remnant of a nappe.

knee fold. A *gravity collapse fold, generally zigzag in shape. (See diagram at fold.)

knickpoint (rejuvenation head). A break of slope in the long profile of a stream, resulting from a fall of base level re-

Knickpoint

juvenating the seaward portion of the stream. This *rejuvenation leads to renewed downcutting, and the creation of a new lower long profile; the point where this profile meets the established profile is the knickpoint.
Knickpoints are often marked by waterfalls if the break of slope is steep, or rapids if less steep. Once created, the knickpoint tends to migrate upstream and be lowered in height; the rate at which it advances and the degree to which it loses its height depends on the lithology in which it is cut. In unconsolidated material it will rapidly disappear. The increased turbulence associated with break of slope accelerates erosion and rapidly lowers its height.

knot. A unit of speed, being one nautical mile per hour. In spite of not being part of the metric system, it is still used for reporting wind speeds and sometimes ocean currents in most countries. 1 knot is equal to 0.515 metres per second.

Kuroshio Current. An ocean current constituting one of the important western *boundary currents in the world's ocean circulation system. It develops following a gradual deflection of part of the North Equatorial Current in the Pacific Ocean, being at first rather diffuse, but in more northern tracts becoming concentrated between the shelf region off the Ryukyu Islands and a submarine ridge. At about 35°N, the current swings away from the Japanese mainland and flows for some 8000 kilometres before again splitting up into branches. In contrast to the water beneath the Gulf Stream, water that is relatively warm and fairly saline because of its continual replenishment of very saline water from the European Mediterranean Sea, the water beneath the Kuroshio Current is only partially saline and cold, being of sub-Antarctic origin. The Kuroshio Current and the Florida Current have roughly the same flow rates.

kyanite. *See* aluminium silicates.

L

Laborde projection. A map projection resembling Mercator's transverse, the only difference being that Laborde uses a spheroid and not a sphere. It is generally restricted to areas of east-west extent, for which it is orthomorphic.

Labrador Current. One of several major surface currents in the N Atlantic Ocean, bringing cold water southwards from the Arctic Ocean region. The Labrador Current flows in on the W flank of Greenland, and is matched on the E flank by the East Greenland Current. These influxes of cold water meet, in the surface layers, with the relatively warm and saline Gulf Stream and North Atlantic Drift water. Both cold currents carry icebergs southwards, and these tend to become concentrated in the "Gateway of Icebergs" east of the Grand Banks. This assembly of bergs is most common between mid-March and mid-July. Another climatological feature of the region is the high frequency of fogs, especially off the coast of Newfoundland. Winter cooling of the combined waters from the North Atlantic Drift, the Labrador Current, and the East Greenland Current may increase their density sufficiently to cause the surface waters to sink, perhaps to depths in excess of 1000 metres.

labradorite. A variety of plagioclase *feldspar.

laccolith. A concordant intrusive igneous body with a dykelike feeder, usually forming small lenslike features less than five kilometres in diameter. As the magma is injected it has sufficient pressure to arch up the overlying strata. Therefore although it has a flat base, its upper surface is convex.

lacuna. The time interval missing between beds above and below an unconformity, including both the non-depositional and erosional components.

lagoon. A stretch of water that is more or less enclosed and often shallow, protected from the open sea by a spit, tombolo, bay-mouth bar, or other kind of barrier. These barriers are not complete, for lagoons invariably possess a free connection with the open sea, however narrow this may be. The barrier provides protection from waves, although wave overwash is common to many lagoonal areas. Tidal current action is usually minimal within the lagoon itself. The water may be fresh, saline, or brackish. Moreover, the salinity level in a lagoon may vary with time. The deposits of lagoons are characteristically fine-grained, with a significant proportion of organic matter.

lahar. A mudflow composed mainly of volcanic debris. If the unstable debris accumulating on the sides of a volcano is lubricated by heavy rain, it will flow under gravity. The flow that covered Herculanium in AD 79 may have been of this type.

Lambert's zenithal projection. An equal-area map projection used mainly in polar areas, where the pole is the centre of the projection and the meridians are straight lines radiating from it, making the bearings true. The parallels are concentric circles. Lambert also constructed an oblique (again equal-area, showing countries within 40° with good shape) and an equatorial projection (used for countries astride the equator, equal-area).

Lamellibranchia. *See* Bivalvia.

laminar flow. The nature of movement of a fluid over a smooth surface at very low velocities, whereby parallel "slabs" of air or water move by sliding over each other, with no mixing. Energy is transmitted from one layer to the next by the viscosity between the layers, while at the boundary (ground surface, stream bed, stream wall, etc.) movement is nil. Laminar flow is rare in natural streams or air flows, except at boundary contacts.

lamprophyre. One of a group of medium-grained basic alkali-rich igneous rocks occurring as dykes and sills. They are characterized by the presence of mafic phenocrysts, biotite, amphibole, or augite, and a groundmass containing orthoclase or sodic plagioclase feldspar.
Minette and *vogesite* are varieties containing orthoclase feldspar and in which biotite and hornblende respectively is the predominant mafic mineral. Analogous rocks containing plagioclase are called *kersantite* and spessartite.
Camptonite contains plagioclase and a brown amphibole called *barkevikite*. *Monchiquite* is a feldspar-free lamprophyre containing phenocrysts of biotite, augite, amphibole, and olivine in an analcime-rich matrix.
Lamprophyres are melanocratic hypabyssal equivalents of diorites and syenites and are associated with such plutonic intrusions.

land breeze. The weaker nocturnal equivalent of the *sea breeze. It results from the unequal cooling of the different surfaces at night, but as the temperature difference is small, wind speeds are low. It is most evident when the pressure gradient is weak and skies are clear, so allowing radiational cooling over the land to be at a maximum.
The surface wind is part of a larger convection cell, which maintains air continuity. Above the land breeze is a weak airflow from sea to land.

landslide. The sudden downslope movement of rock and debris due to failure along a shear plane. The movement is started when the stress in the *free face exceeds the resisting power of the potential shear plane: this loss of resistance may be due to increased weight of the face, e.g. if it becomes wetted; it may be due to undercutting of support at the foot of the slope by some process of *basal sapping, or it may be due to a sudden triggering by an earthquake.
As a result, a convex scar is left upslope, with a mass of jumbled debris at the base in a tonguelike form. Areas of rapid downcutting by rivers, or with variable lithologies, or swelling clays that expand on wetting are susceptible; so too are undercut sea cliffs and river banks, and areas of ice formation. Like all *mass movements, the effect is to render an unstable slope more stable.

landslide surge. A large and often destructive wave caused by the falling of a mass of rock, or perhaps parts of a glacier, from cliffs or hill slopes bordering a body of water. Such events have been witnessed on the open coast and in lakes. Because of the generally unpredictable nature of rockfalls and rockslides, detailed studies of landslide surges have rarely been possible. One rockfall in Lituya Bay, Alaska, which resulted from a 1958 earthquake, caused the fiord water to swamp some 500 metres up the mountainside on the opposite shore of the fiord. A 15 metre high wave was generated along the fiord, travelling at an estimated 160 kilometres per hour. Somewhat similar occurrences have been recorded in Japan, Norway, and elsewhere, but they are comparatively rare.

Langley. A unit of energy equal to 1 calorie per square centimetre. It is mainly used for radiation, but as the calorie has been largely superseded by the *joule, the Langley is decreasing in use.

lapiés. The French word for *karren.

lapilli. *See* pyroclastic rocks.

lapis-lazuli. The semiprecious variety of lazurite. *See* feldspathoids.

lapse rate. The change of temperature in the atmosphere with height. Distinctions are made between the decrease of temperature in the free atmosphere, the *environmental lapse rate, and the decrease of temperature under adiabatic conditions in thermals, the *dry adiabatic lapse rate and *saturated adiabatic lapse rate.

larvikite. *See* syenite.

latent heat. The energy required or released on a change of phase. In the atmosphere, water can exist as a solid, a liquid, or a vapour, representing increasing energy states respectively. Thus freezing and condensation release latent heat, melting and evaporation require heat. Latent heat is extremely important in atmospheric processes, enabling energy to be transferred within the general circulation, from ground to atmosphere, and as a reservoir of heat in the atmosphere.
Specific latent heat is the latent heat required or released per unit mass.

lateral erosion. River erosion in a horizontal direction. Within the meandering reach of a river, erosion on the outside of bends leads to downstream migration and constant paring away of the bluffs at the side of the valley; this effectively erodes the valley width laterally. In floods, the elevated water level fills the channel and raises the water table, saturating the banks. When the floods subside, the support on the weakened (wetted) banks is removed and mass slumping occurs, hence widening the channel laterally. By these processes, some *floodplains are eroded rather than deposited; they consist of a rock-cut bench with a thin veneer of alluvium, unless they form owing to a base level rise, when a deep purely aggradational floodplain will result.

lateral moraine. A ridge of material along the side of a glacier (or along the side of a valley formerly occupied by a glacier), primarily composed of angular and unsorted material that has fallen from overhanging rock outcrops as a result of *freeze-thaw weathering, although it is believed that a certain proportion of the material is derived from within the glacier itself. The ridge may consist extensively of ice, since once a layer of waste about 0.5 metres thick has developed, the ice beneath is protected from melting and hence it stands above the surface level of the rest of the glacier.

laterite. A layer of deposits formed from the weathering of rocks in humid tropical conditions and consisting mostly of iron and aluminium oxides. It hardens on exposure to the atmosphere and is therefore used for building. It is not a soil, as it is produced by processes operating on a far larger scale than typical pedologic processes. It can occur in two forms, either buried and soft or as a superficial capping (cuirass) of hardened red material on uplifted areas that have had their overburden stripped off. Most laterites developed in the Tertiary period, and are hence relic. In profile they display a strong hardened reddish surface horizon, dominated by ferric oxide, which breaks up with depth into a mottled horizon, which in turn passes down to a depleted pallid zone, which may be 50 metres thick and reach to the bedrock. In a pure laterite, the red horizon will be composed of 90-100% iron, aluminium, and titanium oxides. *See also* laterization, limonite.

lateritic soil. 1. A soil developed on part of a relic *laterite, or with an indurated layer within its profile.
2. Red tropical soils developing into laterites. They undergo leaching of silica and bases, the concentration of aluminium and iron oxides increasing, as happened in the formation of the relic laterites. As leaching of silica proceeds, the silica:sesquioxide ratio falls; in 1927 Martin and Doyne calculated that while

laterites had a ratio of <1.33, lateritic soils had a ratio of 1.33-2.0, showing that they were following the same development trend but had not yet been desilicified as much as true laterite. However, relic laterite probably developed by much larger-scale processes and the term lateritic soil has now been replaced by latosol (ferrallitic soil) or, in Australia, red loam.

laterization. The concentration of iron and aluminium oxides in the upper layers of the soil and the removal of silica and bases, either in the formation of relic *laterites or in current soil-forming processes in the tropics. In the case of relic laterites, laterization is thought to be a result of a fluctuating water table. Opinions vary: the rising and falling groundwater (resulting from seasonal dryness and wetness) either brings up iron and aluminium from the pallid zone and concentrates it at a point of maximum upward extension, or it causes iron and aluminium being washed down in percolating rainwater to be precipitated on meeting the alkaline groundwater, or it causes a combination of the two. It is a large-scale process, operating over geologic time scales. In the case of current tropical soil formation laterization denotes the process of individualization of iron and aluminium oxides, and to a lesser extent oxides of titanium, chromium, and nickel, by intense weathering and leaching, removing bases and silica. This process now tends to be called ferrallitization, leading to the development of *ferrallitic soils (latosols).

laterolog. A subsurface logging technique, which measures variations in the conductivity of strata.

latite. See syenodorite.

latitude. The angular distance of a point on the earth's surface north or south of the equator, measured as the angle subtended at the centre of the earth by an arc along a meridian between the point and the equator. The equator has no angle whereas the poles are at 90

Latitude

degrees. Latitude is measured in degrees, minutes, and seconds. Parallels of latitude form approximate concentric circles, with the poles as the centre (see diagram). See also longitude.

latosol. See ferrallitic soils.

laumontite. See zeolites.

Laurasia. The N hemisphere supercontinent believed to have been present prior to 200 million years ago. This super-continent subsequently fragmented to form the present Greenland, Europe, Asia (excluding India), and North America. See also Pangaea.

lava. A molten or partially molten mass of *magma extruded from a volcano or volcanic fissure and the rock that forms as a result of cooling and solidification. The accumulation of single extrusions, termed *lava flows*, produces a volcano or lava pile.

Basic lavas are fluid and cover large areas, whereas acid lavas are viscous and do not flow great distances.

There are numerous textural terms used to describe lavas, such as aphyric, porphyritic, vesicular, glassy, holocrystalline, etc. See also aa, block lava, pahoehoe, pillow lava, columnar jointing.

lawsonite. A white mineral of composition $CaAl_2(OH)_2(Si_2O_7)H_2O$, found in low-temperature regionally metamorphosed rocks, particularly *glaucophane *schists.

layer cloud. A cloud having little vertical development. Such clouds are formed under conditions of zero or weak uplift; precipitation may be extensive from nimbostratus clouds but as uplift is weak, intensity is low. Clouds of this type are cirrostratus, altostratus, stratus, stratocumulus, and nimbostratus.

layered igneous rocks. Many large intrusions of gabbroic igneous rocks are stratified, containing layers in which different minerals are concentrated, which suggests that the dominant *differentiation process was the gravitational settling of early-formed crystals. Often mineralogically similar layers are repeated in a rhythmic fashion. Systematic changes in mineral composition from the bottom to the top of a layered sequence are termed *cryptic layering*. Typically, olivines and pyroxenes become progressively richer in iron (relative to magnesium) and plagioclase trends to more sodic compositions, changes which are compatible with crystallization from residual liquids that are differentiating towards more acid compositions.

lazurite. *See* feldspathoids.

leaching. The action of water moving down through a soil profile carrying soil materials with it in suspension or solution. It includes the mechanical action of water, e.g. *lessivage, its chemical action, as in the weathering processes of *hydration, *hydrolysis, and *carbonation, and its partly biochemical action, as when it contains leaf leachates and moves material by *cheluviation. Leaching removes bases, clays, organic matter, and the various sesquioxides; in its varying forms it is responsible for the processes of lessivage, *podzolization, and *laterization. Soils subject to leaching become increasingly acid with strongly developed eluvial and, if the leached material is redeposited, illuvial horizons.

lechatelierite. A rare silica glass. *See* silica minerals.

lee waves. Under certain conditions of atmospheric stability, stationary waves may be generated on the leeward side of

hills or mountain ranges. Their wavelength is usually between 3 and 30 km. Lee waves are frequently seen when the crests of the wave reach saturation point to give a lens-shaped cloud outlining the upward motion. This cloud is constantly forming on the upwind side and being dissipated in the area of descent whilst remaining stationary; it is classified as *altocumulus lenticularis*. Lee waves occur when a stable layer of air is sandwiched between layers of lower stability above and below, with a strong and steady wind flow.

lepidolite. *See* micas.

lessivage. The mechanical movement of clay down a soil profile under the influence of water and its redeposition lower down. It occurs in soils subject to *leaching but where acidity is neutral or slight, so that the clay is not broken down into its constituents but moves as a whole. It does nevertheless operate better in less alkaline conditions, and *decalcification generally precedes lessivage.

Diagnostic signs include an increase in the heaviness of texture with depth, and micro-morphological examination can show clay skins on ped surfaces and along channels. Clay skins are evidence of redeposition of clay; increased heaviness alone is only suggestive, as Bt horizons (texturally heavier B horizons) can be due to a lighter horizon above or increased weathering in the B due to increased moisture.

leucite. *See* feldspathoids.

leucitite. *See* nephelinite.

leucocratic. *See* colour index.

levée. A berm or bank elevated above the general level of the floodplain, bordering many streams in their alluvial floodplain sections. Usually made of coarser material than the rest of the floodplain, they originate in times of flooding when the overbank flow decreases in speed and volume away from the stream, depositing the coarse materials first as it rapidly loses *competence. If the river lacks a coarse fraction, alluvium being mostly silt and clay size, levées may be absent.

levéed channel. A submarine channel in the deep ocean flanked by marked levées, not unlike some of the levée features that border many river channels on land. Such submarine channels usually lie at the lower ends of *submarine canyons, such as the La Jolla Canyon off the coast of California. Here, at a depth of some 600 metres, the true canyon terminates in a channel flanked by natural levées. At its seaward extremity, the channel merges into a submarine fan. Sand layers have been found in the fan and on the levées on either side of the channel. Channels with levées are also strongly developed across many abyssal fans.

level. A surveying instrument used in conjunction with a *levelling staff to determine heights. A level is basically a telescope fitted to an adjustable base, which clamps onto a tripod. Before use the instrument must be adjusted until the line·of sight is perfectly horizontal, by centering a bubble that moves as the basal footscrews are turned. Once levelled it can be used to sight onto the staff. The telescope incorporates a diaphragm with engraved lines, the reading at the central line being that used for heighting calculations.

levelling. A method of surveying used for obtaining heights of points in relation to that of a point of known height. A *level is set up between a point of known height and one for which a height is required; it is then adjusted to give a horizontal line of sight. A sight, known as a *backsight*, is made onto a *levelling staff at the known point and the staff reading noted. A reading is then obtained by making a *foresight* onto the staff at the other point. The difference between the two staff readings gives the difference in height between the two points. The process continues by moving the level between the second

point, now of known height, and another unknown one, and so on. A levelling *traverse returns to the first known point, as a check on accuracy.

levelling staff. A staff used in surveying in conjunction with a *level for determining heights. Most staffs consist of three sections, which are either telescopic or simply clip together, to reach a height of 4 metres at their full extent. They embody a small bubble to enable the user to hold them vertically. The staff has heights marked clearly in black or red on white or yellow, which can be read to the nearest millimetre. However, when viewed through the telescope of a level, the figures appear upside-down, and care must be taken in reading them.

lherzolite. An ultramafic rock consisting largely of olivine together with orthopyroxenes and clinopyroxenes.

lightning. The visible discharge of a thunderstorm and the natural mechanism for neutralizing the high electrical fields that build up. Air is a good insulator but as charge production increases the potential gradient in a thunder cloud, and water droplets decrease the insulational properties of air, eventually the insulation is overcome and the lightning flash results. It consists of a line of highly ionized air molecules along which electricity can flow for a very short time.

High speed film recordings of lightning discharges have clarified the development of a flash. A cloud-to-ground discharge is started by a streamer, which develops downwards from the cloud in a series of steps. It is of low luminosity. When this streamer has approached to within about 5 to 30 m of the ground, a highly luminous return stroke comes up to meet it and travels up the ionized channel to the cloud. This is the main visible flash, which travels at speeds of about 0.1 times that of light, passing a current of 10 000 amperes but only lasting for about 100 microseconds. Several more streamers and return strokes may develop.

lignite. Low-grade brown coal with a high moisture content.

limb. *See* fold limb.

limburgite. An undersaturated basic igneous rock occurring as flows and dykes and consisting of phenocrysts of augite and olivine embedded in a matrix of brown basaltic glass.

lime. *See* calcium carbonate.

limestone. A rock formed from carbonate minerals, principally *calcite but including others such as *dolomite. Limestones can be classified broadly on a genetic basis as *clastic, organic, precipitated, or metasomatic. Organic limestones are formed from the calcareous skeletons of living organisms, and include in situ *bioherms and accumulates such as *chalk. Among the various precipitated limestones are those that are part of an *evaporite sequence, and *oolites. Clastic limestones are those derived from pre-existing calcareous rocks. Metasomatic limestones are other limestones that have undergone diagenetic change. The most common change involves the alteration of calcite to dolomite. Descriptive classifications employing the relative proportions of *allochems, *micrite, and *sparite, are increasingly used.

limestone cavern. A subterranean cave developed in limestone as a result of the enlargement of joints and fissures by solution, larger caverns occurring in less resistant well-jointed limestone. Most cave systems comprise both large open caves and small restricted passages, all of which continue to grow in size as long as unsaturated water flows through them. Some caves are considerably extended horizontally, which may reflect a position corresponding to the present or a former water table. The finest caves are found in hard well-jointed limestones of low porosity; soft limestones, such as chalk, are unsuitable for major cave development.

limestone pavement. A flat exposure of bare limestone resembling a rough pavement and consisting of flat or ridged irregularly sized and shaped blocks (*clints*), separated by clefts (*grikes* or *grykes*) formed by the widening of joints by solution. Grikes can measure up to half a metre across and frequently two to three metres deep.

limestone solution. Limestone is the only common rock type in which *solution is important in the development of its characteristic landforms. Since it is composed of calcium carbonate, solution is easily achieved by very weak carbonic acid (formed from water and dissolved carbon dioxide from the air and soil). Many limestones possess a well-developed system of joints and bedding planes; the vast majority of the water flowing through the rock passes along these fissures, in which solution takes place and they therefore become enlarged, forming better water courses.
In theory more limestone is dissolved as the temperature or acidity of the solution increases, but it is probably more effective to have a rapid turbulent flow of ample supplies of water over a large surface area of rock.

limonite. The yellow to brown amorphous and cryptocrystalline oxidation and hydration products of iron. Goethite and haematite are important constituents together with colloidal silica and clay minerals. Limonite is found as an alteration product in all kinds of rocks, as a precipitate in bog iron ore, and as a major constituent of gossan and laterite.

lineament. A large-scale linear topographic feature that is structurally controlled. They often appear as long linear features on aerial photographs and frequently result from faults, where erosion has worked selectively on the softer material of the fault zone.

line scale. A divided scale given on a map to enable distances to be directly measured and read off in terms of distances on the ground.

linkage analysis. A statistical procedure used to group individuals into clusters. The measures of similarity used are coefficients of association, coefficients of correlation, or distance measures depending upon the type of data and the nature of the problem being analysed.

litchfieldite. See syenite.

lithification. The process by which sedimentary deposits develop into sedimentary rocks.

lithosol. *Azonal soil with an AC or (A)C profile (i.e. no illuvial B horizon) developed on fresh and imperfectly weathered rock or rock debris. These soils often form on steep slopes where runoff erodes developing soil and little water percolates down through the profile to promote *leaching and soil development. The surface horizon is typically dark due to organic matter accumulation, but may be coarse-textured and light coloured if slope wash is intense. On eroded land, subject to poor agricultural practices, these soils can be man-made. A special type is the *ranker* developed on acidic rocks. These soils are part of the entisol order of the *Seventh Approximation.

lithophile. The elements can be divided into 4 groups based upon their geochemical affinities, as follows:
1. *lithophile*—an element occurring mainly in oxygen compounds and forming silicate minerals. The 8 elements oxygen, silicon, aluminium, iron, copper, sodium, potassium, and magnesium make up nearly 99% of the earth's crust.
2. *chalcophile*—an element occurring mainly as a sulphide: silver, arsenic, copper, mercury, lead, sulphur, and zinc.
3. *siderophile*—an element occurring mainly in the native state: gold and platinum.
4. *atmophile*—an element occurring in the gaseous state: nitrogen and the inert gases.

lithosphere. That part of the earth including the crust and the upper mantle above the *asthenosphere.

lithostratigraphy. The branch of *stratigraphy concerned solely with lithological features and with naming and elucidating the spatial relations of rock units. It is the most purely descriptive of the systems of stratigraphic classification, incorporating the least amount of inference, and does not take account of the evolution of organisms as shown by contained fossils (see biostratigraphy) or of time (see chronostratigraphy). Hence lithostratigraphic units are often *diachronous. The hierarchy of lithostratigraphic divisions consists of *supergroup, *group, *formation, *member, and *bed (see also complex). Formally designated lithostratigraphic units (formations) are given geographical names with capitalized initial letters.

lit-par-lit gneiss. A coarsely banded or foliated gneiss consisting of alternating layers of quartz-feldspar and mafic minerals. The felsic material, which may have originated by partial melting, has intruded along the schistosity planes of the metamorphic rock. See also migmatite.

litter. The accumulation of leaves and twigs on the surface of the soil. It is the raw material for the formation of the soil humus; beneath the fresh litter there is a fermenting layer and below this the humus.

littoral drift. See longshore drift.

littoral zone. The region immediately flanking the coast on its seaward side, strictly the combination of the intertidal and *breaker zones, i.e. the region lying between highest high water and the outer edge of the breaker zone. The width of the littoral zone varies according to the prevailing wave conditions and the slope of the sea floor. The term *eulittoral* refers to the zone that extends between high water and the limit of attached plants, which is usually at a depth between 40 and 60 metres. In

Load

major division	subdivision	nature of load
(1) solution load		chemical content, dissolved in water
(2) solid debris load	(a) suspension load	finest solid particles, supported by water
	(b) saltation load	sand/fine gravel, bouncing along bed
	(c) bed load	coarsest material, rolling and sliding on bed

global terms the littoral zone occupies an area of about 150 000 sq. km.

load. The material carried along by a river. Material is incorporated into a river by its erosive action on the valley bed and walls. It can also be supplied by groundwater flow, or direct from valley sides by wash, *creep, or *landslides. Once in the river, load can be split up as in the table. The predominance of the different types of load varies between rivers and in the same river over time, e.g. *dissolved load is important in rivers receiving a steady groundwater flow and little overland runoff; in floods, transporting ability is increased owing to velocity increases, and debris that at low flow moves as bed load may start to saltate, and saltating load may be carried in suspension. Generally bed load is the least important part: in the Mississippi, only 8% of load moves as bed load, compared with about 65% in suspension and saltation.

lodestone. *Magnetite that is strongly magnetic.

lodgement till. Unstratified glacial material deposited directly from beneath a glacier or ice sheet. Such deposits tend to be somewhat compacted due to the weight of ice at one time above them. *Compare* ablation till.

Lomonosov Ridge. A vast submarine ridge that effectively divides the Arctic Ocean into two separate basins. The ridge was first discovered by Russian scientists while they were conducting their oceanographic surveys from field stations set up on drifting pack-ice. The ridge runs directly underneath the North Pole, stretching from Ellesmere Island, north of Canada, across to the Novo Sibirsk Islands off the Siberian mainland. Such data as has been collected suggests that the ridge may be a faulted feature rather than volcanic. Soundings across the ridge have revealed what appears to be a truncated upper surface lying at a depth of some 1400 metres.

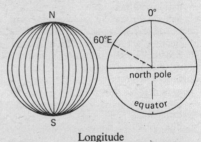

Longitude

longitude. The angular distance of a point on the earth's surface east or west of a central meridian (see diagram), measured by the angle between the plane of the meridian through the point and that of the central meridian. In 1884 it was internationally agreed that the meridian from which the readings would be taken would be the one passing through Greenwich, now considered as 0 degrees east, west. In passing through 15 degrees of longitude at the equator there is a local time difference of one hour. *See also* latitude.

longitudinal waves. *See* primary waves.

long profile. A section drawn from source to mouth along a stream or river, showing the changes in gradient throughout its length. The ideal form is

Ideal long profile

an exponential concave curve, with far greater gradients at the head than at the mouth. This profile is due to the fact that discharge increases downstream and hence velocity increases, so less gradient is needed to transport the load supplied. Simultaneously the size of debris decreases downstream, most probably owing to abrasion of the debris, but possibly owing to sorting, and so there is a further reduction in energy needed, allowing a further reduction in gradient.

Surveyed profiles in fact rarely appear as the ideal profile; rather they are a series of partial curves, due to past base level changes, with further irregularities due to lakes, pools, bars, hard rock bands, etc. Insufficient time to grade a smooth profile is a general cause of irregularity, as well as the fact that if a river flows over different lithologies, the size of debris supplied will vary: the coarser the debris the steeper the slope needed, so gradients over sandstone are steeper than those on shale and limestone.

See also cross profile.

longshore bar (ridge, full). A sand *bar lying roughly parallel to the coastline, in the intertidal zone or in the breaker zone.

longshore current. The current that is generated over the whole width of the *breaker zone at those times when waves approach and break at an angle to the shore. Longshore currents tend to flow parallel to the shore, and probably attain their maximum rate when the wave crests near breakpoint are angled

approximately 30° to the shoreline. Field measurements have revealed that such wave-induced currents are roughly of uniform speed across the whole width of the breaker zone, but that they rapidly weaken seaward of the breaker zone. Tidal and other currents may be superimposed upon the longshore currents, tending either to strengthen or to nullify them.

longshore (littoral) drift. The movement of beach materials, sand or shingle, along the shore parallel with the coastline. This process is basically due to the effects of waves breaking on the beach obliquely. Despite *wave refraction, waves infrequently break perfectly perpendicularly to a beach and their *swash tends to move material landwards diagonally. However, the returning water, in the form of the *backwash, moves directly down the beach and the net effect of swash and backwash is a small longshore movement. Longshore currents aid this process. In most areas one set of waves predominates, resulting in an undirectional longshore movement, but some coasts may be influenced by two sets in opposition, causing the material to move to and fro along the same stretch of beach.

long wave (Rossby wave). The smooth broad wave-shaped contour patterns on a pressure chart of the upper atmosphere. They have wavelengths up to about 2000 km and there are usually either four or five such waves around the westerly wind belt of the N hemisphere. Both heat and momentum are transferred polewards by the long waves and they also have a significant effect on *convergence and *divergence at the surface.

lopolith. A large concordant igneous intrusion, which is saucer-shaped in cross section. The type example is the Duluth gabbro, Canada, which has a volume of approximately 200 000 km^3.

love waves. Surface waves produced by an earthquake in which the particle motion is in a horizontal direction, perpendicular to the direction of wave propagation. *See also* Rayleigh waves.

low. *See* depression (def. 1).

low index. The state of the westerly circulation when flow is weak and there is appreciable meridional transfer, as in a *blocking situation.

low-velocity zone. *See* asthenosphere.

loxodrome. *See* rhumb line.

lustre. The appearance of the light reflected from the surface of a mineral, which is a qualitative characteristic often providing an aid to identification. The kinds of lustre are:
1. metallic—displayed by galena and pyrites.
2. vitreous—displayed by glass and quartz.
3. resinous—displayed by amber.
4. silky—displayed by gypsum.
5. pearly—displayed by talc and muscovite.
6. adamantine—displayed by diamond.

luxullianite. A *tourmaline-quartz-feldspar rock produced by the boron pneumatolysis of granite.

M

macroclimate. The general climate of a large area. Observations of the macroclimate are normally recorded in Stevenson screens to provide a standard exposure of the instruments and to reduce the effect of the local ground surface. In this way it is easier to obtain more comparable values between observing stations, which are determined by the larger-scale features of the climate rather than local conditions.

macrometeorology. The study of the atmospheric processes responsible for the differentiation of the macroclimates on the earth's surface.

mafic. Denoting dark-coloured minerals. Mafic minerals are approximately equivalent to *ferromagnesian minerals. *Compare* felsic.

magma. A hot silicate liquid beneath the earth's surface containing suspended crystals and dissolved gases. *Igneous rocks are formed from the crystallization and solidification of magma and are said to be magmatic. A lava represents magma extruded at the earth's surface whereas magma solidifying at depth gives rise to *hypabyssal and *plutonic rocks. During the solidification of magma, the volatile constituents escape and thus compositions of igneous rocks are only approximations of the compositions of the magmas from which they originated.

magma chamber. A reservoir within the earth's lithosphere in which molten rock accumulates prior to being emptied at the earth's surface through a volcano. Such a chamber exists beneath most volcanoes, and is replenished from below after being emptied during a volcanic eruption.

magmatic differentiation. A number of processes causing the gradual evolution of the composition of an igneous melt and the separation of the *magma into two or more fractions of contrasting compositions. Several mechanisms are recognized:
1. *Fractional crystallization.* One of the main processes producing compositional variation in igneous rocks is the gravity settling of early-formed minerals. Such crystals having densities higher than the enclosing magma sink to the bottom of the magma chamber. In some cases, light minerals such as leucite float upwards. The composition of the residual liquid differs from that of the original melt because of the removal of the solid crystalline material.
2. *Filter pressing.* During the later stages of crystallization, residual liquid may be squeezed out from a crystal mush and rise upwards in the crust.
3. *Flow differentiation.* The movement of a magmatic liquid within a dyke or lava flow often concentrates phenocrysts towards the centre of the body.
4. *Liquid immiscibility.* During cooling, two liquid fractions of a magma may

become immiscible and separate. Sulphides separate from a silicate magma during the early stages of crystallization. The role of liquid immiscibility in igneous petrogenesis is limited but this process may account for the segregation of carbonate liquids from mafic alkaline magma.

5. *Gaseous transfer.* The upward streaming of gas bubbles and dissolved materials results in the concentration of volatiles near to the top of a magma body.

magnesite. See carbonate minerals.

magnetic anomaly. A departure from the predicted value of the earth's magnetic field at a point on the earth's surface.

magnetic division. A stratigraphical unit (*see* stratigraphy) consisting of the rocks formed during one *magnetic interval (*see also* palaeomagnetic correlation). The establishment of magnetic divisions constitutes an important method in the *calibration and *correlation of stratigraphic sequences, especially in the Quaternary and late Tertiary.

magnetic elements. The seven parameters of the geomagnetic field at a particular locality on the earth's surface. They include a value for the field with respect to geographic north (X), east (Y), the vertical (Z), the horizontal (B), the total induction (F), its *declination (D), and inclination (I) (*see* dip).

magnetic field. A field of force that exists as a result of a circuit carrying an electric current, or the presence of a permanent magnet.

magnetic interval. The variable period of time between *magnetic reversals in the earth's polarity. The palaeomagnetic scale must be calibrated by some independent method of assessing time, such as radiometric dating. The rocks formed during a magnetic interval are known as a *magnetic division, which can be used in the correlation of stratigraphic successions. *See also* palaeomagnetic correlation.

magnetic meridian. An imaginary line on the surface of the earth joining the magnetic poles. It indicates the direction of the horizontal component of the earth's magnetic field.

magnetic poles. Either two of the points on the earth's surface at which the lines of magnetic force are vertical. These points are slowly changing with time and do not coincide with the geographical poles.

magnetic reversals. Palaeomagnetic studies (*see* palaeomagnetic correlation) have shown that the direction of the earth's magnetic field's induction has periodically changed by 180°, that is north became south and vice versa. Based upon these reversals, which have been recorded in rocks forming at that time, a polarity/time scale has been established for the last 4.5 million years of the earth's history.

magnetic stripes. The roughly parallel bands of ocean floor with alternating directions of induction: a normally magnetized stripe will be enclosed by two reversely magnetized stripes. These patterns can be picked up by shipborne instruments and used to correlate areas of ocean floor offset along transform faults.

magnetite. See spinel.

magnetometer. An instrument used for measuring the strength of the earth's magnetic field.

magnetosphere. The area around the earth in which the earth's magnetic field is present. The field is confined to this area as a result of the interaction between the earth's magnetic field and the solar wind. The magnetosphere extends out away from the earth's surface for a much greater distance on the side away from the sun.

malachite. See carbonate minerals.

malignite. See syenite.

Mammalia. A class of warm-blooded vertebrates that nourish their young on milk secreted by mammary glands in the mother. Mammals have a relatively large brain, morphologically differentiated teeth, and (in most) a body covering of hair or fur. They are skeletally distinguished from reptiles by having only one bone in each lower jaw, which also differs in its articulation with the cranium.

Mammals evolved from mammal-like reptiles in the late Triassic; the earliest forms were small flesh-eating active creatures similar to modern shrews. Fossils of these primitive Mesozoic mammals are rare and consist mainly of teeth. Mammals existed throughout the dominance of the dinosaurs but did not achieve supremacy on land until the Cenozoic, after the extinction of most reptilian groups, when their main radiation took place. The two main mammal groups, the Marsupialia and Eutheria, separated from the ancestral stock by the late Cretaceous. They both give birth to living young (as opposed to laying eggs). The most primitive group is the Monotremata, which comprises egg-laying mammals whose modern representatives are the duck-billed platypus and echidnas (spiny anteaters).

man. Modern man, *Homo sapiens*, belongs to the family Hominidae of the mammalian order *Primates. Animals sometimes classified as hominids are known from the Miocene and perhaps even earlier. In the Pliocene and early Pleistocene of Africa the remains of a variety of manlike creatures have been found; they are usually placed in two genera, *Australopithecus* and *Homo*. Some authorities believe that *Homo* evolved from one of the species of *Australopithecus*, others contend that man belongs to a separate lineage. *Homo erectus*, a hominid of robust construction, was present in Africa, Asia, and possibly Europe during the mid-Pleistocene. In the later Pleistocene two subspecies of *Homo sapiens* are recognized: modern man, *H. sapiens sapiens*, and Neanderthal man, *H. sapiens neanderthalensis*. Primitive

stone tools have been found from rocks dated as Pliocene in age.

manganese nodules. Somewhat similar in form to *phosphorite nodules, manganese nodules (one of the *authigenic minerals) are the only potential deep-sea mineral deposit that could be economically recovered from the deep ocean floor utilizing present-day technological methods. They seem to be largely confined to deep-sea clays, but have also been found in association with oozes. The nodules are surprisingly heavy, averaging some 24% manganese, 14% iron, 1% nickel, 0.5% cobalt, and 0.5% copper. The various minerals frequently form roughly concentric layerings on stones and other hard objects, such as sharks' teeth, present on the sea floor. These layerings build up gradually on account of the slow precipitation from sea water of manganese oxides and other mineral salts. Surveys have revealed that the nodules are widely distributed on the deep ocean floor and are sometimes surprisingly abundant. For example, in certain parts of the Pacific Ocean, concentrations of 20 000 tonnes per sq. km have been located.

mantle. That part of the earth's interior beneath the base of the *crust and above the earth's *outer core, roughly between 30-2900 km beneath the earth's surface. It is thought to consist of ferromagnesian silicate minerals such as olivine and pyroxene. Essentially it behaves as a solid, although within the asthenosphere it may be partially molten.

mantled (gneiss) dome. A structure present in Precambrian shield areas, consisting of a central core of granite rock surrounded by regionally metamorphosed rocks, mainly gneisses, that has been exposed by erosion and covered by a series of younger sediments. The area was then subjected to orogenesis, during which the granitic core was remobilized and rose up, causing the overlying strata to be arched upwards.

mantle plumes. A mechanism which may account for the formation of volcanoes and constructive plate margins. Mantle rock begins to melt, thereby becoming less dense. As a result this material rises towards the surface as a plume. In so doing it causes the overlying crust to be domed up. *See also* hot spots.

map. A graphic representation on a plane surface of the earth's surface or part of it, showing its geographical features. These are positioned according to pre-established geodetic control, grids, projections, and scales.

map scale. The ratio of the distance measured on the map to the distance on the ground between the same points. The old Ordnance Survey one-inch-to-the-mile maps had a scale of 1:63 360, where one mile on the ground was shown by one inch on the map. Most maps now are metric and therefore have ratios such as 1:50 000, 1:100 000. The larger the ratio, the smaller the scale of the map.
The scale used is largely determined by the purpose of the map: for index maps and wall charts of the world a small-scale map would normally be used; for town plans the larger the scale the more accurate and detailed the plan can be.

map series. A collection of maps, usually at the same scale, using the same specifications and generally identified by a series number. Map series normally cover individual countries but can cover the entire earth's surface, e.g. the International Map of the World 1:1 000 000.

marble. A rock composed largely of calcite or dolomite, produced by the regional or contact metamorphism of limestones. During the metamorphism of a pure limestone, calcite recrystallizes to produce coarser interlocking grains, often with a preferred orientation imparting a weak schistosity. A variety of minerals may form when impure limestones are metamorphosed, including quartz, diopside, forsterite, grossular, tremolite, micas, and epidote.

marcasite. A pale bronze-yellow mineral, FeS_2, polymorphous with pyrite but having orthorhombic symmetry. Marcasite is found mainly as a replacement mineral in sedimentary rocks and as radiating nodules, especially in chalk.

margarite. *See* micas.

marginal sea. A category of *adjacent sea (compare* inland sea) consisting of a sea area that is significantly open to the adjacent ocean. Marginal seas may be of the deep type or the shallow (shelf sea) type. The deep marginal seas usually lie between the continental blocks and offshore submarine ridges, which may or may not have islands, and often display depths well in excess of 200 metres. The shallow marginal seas occupy the continental shelf areas and are thus generally less than 200 m deep. There is an obvious contrast between the open ocean and those sea areas juxtaposed between mainland and groups of offshore islands.

marigram. The graphic record obtained from the use of an instrument that monitors the rise and fall of water level throughout a tide cycle. From this, an average water-level curve, known as a tide curve, can be plotted. Such curves or records enable oceanographers to identify the types of tidal motion affecting particular areas.

marine ecosystem. The *littoral and *sublittoral zones are characterized by an enormous diversity of plant and animal life which, taken with their physical environment, constitute the marine ecosystem. The system is highly dynamic. Most sublittoral plant life occurs as plankton but there are also a number of bottom-living seaweeds. The range of species of sublittoral animals is enormous. The cycle of sublittoral life begins with plant plankton (phytoplankton), which consume nutrient salts present in the sea water and also carbon dioxide. Animal plankton (zooplankton) feed actively on the phytoplankton and are themselves eaten by the smaller species of fish. The small fish are consumed by larger fish, and so on. Decomposition of dead fauna and flora refurbishes the supply of nutrients. Thus, the individual organisms in the marine ecosystem are interdependent. The marine ecosystem is highly susceptible to damage from marine pollution and other forms of human intervention.

maritime climate. The generalized characteristic climate of the temperate parts of the earth's surface that are affected by the sea. The sea acts as a vast storehouse of the sun's energy and only changes its temperature slightly from winter to summer. Hence areas experiencing a maritime climate have low annual ranges of temperature (cool summers and mild winters) and an even distribution of precipitation throughout the year with no dry season. Some coastal areas may not experience a maritime climate if the prevailing winds are offshore.

marker bed (marker horizon). A bed of rock having some distinctive characteristic of lithology or contained fossils that permits its easy recognition wherever it occurs. Such a bed can often be inferred to represent a very short period of time or, in the case of beds resulting from certain kinds of volcanic eruption, to be virtually instantaneous in its formation. Marker beds thus have great use in *stratigraphy and in the *correlation of strata.

markfieldite. A porphyritic microdiorite. See diorite.

marl. An *argillaceous sedimentary rock in the form of *mudstone that has a high proportion of calcareous material in its composition.

Marsupialia. Mammals whose offspring are born at an immature stage and continue their development within a special pouch (*marsupium*) on the belly of the mother. This and other (skeletal) differences distinguish them from the placental mammals (*see* Eutheria). Fossils show that the marsupials diverged from the placentals in the Cretaceous, when they appear to have been much more abundant than they are today. They are known from the Tertiary of Europe and America, but as the placentals became the more successful group, the marsupials gradually became confined to isolated areas such as Australasia and South America. In these regions marsupial species evolved to resemble placental species elsewhere (*see* parallel evolution).

mass movement. On unstable slopes, that is slopes whose angle is greater than the natural *angle of rest of the constituent material and whose *shear strength is not capable of maintaining this angle, gravity along with the help of other agents such as wind and water may act to produce a mass movement of some kind, whereby slope angle becomes reduced to a more stable value. Mass movements constitute flows, slides, and falls of rock material from a slope; they may be sudden and short-lived, as in the case of *rock falls, or very slow and long-lived, as in the case of *creep. Slides and falls act along a shear plane within the rock. Flows, on the other hand, involve internal deformation and movement by overturning of the material. Commonly mass movements are compound: flows on gentler slopes often start on steeper slopes above as a slide or fall.
See also basal sapping, earthflow, earthslide, landslide.

mass transport current. The slow drift of water beneath waves, in the direction of wave propagation, that arises from the nature of *orbital motion beneath waves. Because, in the case of deep-water waves, the orbits of water particles are almost circular but not quite closed loops, each particle of water in motion not only orbits but also moves slowly forward in the direction of wave propagation. This asymmetry or orbital motion in deep water becomes even

Fig. 1: Slope angle becomes too steep to be stable

Fig. 2: Shear plane develops

Fig. 3: Slide/fall lowers slope angle

Mass movement

more pronounced in shallow water, for here the orbits become increasingly elliptical with decreasing depth. Theoretically a cork placed on the sea surface in deep water should both bob up and down and shift slowly in the direction of wave travel.

matrix. The fine-grained component of a rock into which the coarser components are set. In sedimentary rocks, the matrix is often the material that cements the larger grains or pebbles together. In igneous rocks the *groundmass is equivalent to the matrix.

maximum temperature. The highest value recorded by a thermometer in a specified time. The normal period between observations is the day, but the mean monthly maximum and mean annual maximum are often calculated from the daily data. The maximum temperature is recorded by a mercury thermometer, which has a constriction near its bulb. As the temperature rises, the force of expansion is strong and pushes the thread of mercury up the column. If the temperature then falls, the contraction force is weaker and the constriction prevents the mercury returning to the bulb. It remains at the position of the highest temperature. In Britain, the highest maximum air temperature was recorded at Tonbridge, Kent, on 22 July 1868 when the temperature was 38.1°C (100.5°F). On a world scale, 57.8°C (136°F) was reported from Azizia, Libya, on 13 September 1922.

meadow soil. *See* gley soils.

mean. The arithmetic mean or average is a statistical method of representing the magnitude of a data set. It is obtained by summing the individual values and dividing by the number of individuals. It only gives meaningful results when the data have a normal distribution. For example, the mean rainfall in desert areas is often calculated on the basis of many years without rain interspersed with exceptionally heavy falls and may indicate an annual total that has never been experienced.

meander. A marked curve in a river channel. W. M. Davis stated that meanders originated when a river used up excess energy by side-cutting when it could no longer cut down, but since Davis other causes have been put forward:
1. Local erosion and deposition patterns will lead to the development of one meander, which will then influence the stream flow pattern, propagating the system of bends down river. The initiation of local erosion and depositions is

due to a chance abrasion in the channel, e.g. a fallen tree or stream bed shoals.
2. Long profiles of rivers characteristically develop *pools and riffles. Shallowness over the riffles leads to increased velocity and bed roughness, and hence greater energy loss over the riffles than the pools. Since rivers try to distribute energy loss as evenly as possible throughout their lengths, it may be that meander development in the pools would be one way of equalizing energy loss. Others have said the riffles are the site of initiation.
3. Irrespective of the cause, the divergence of primary downstream flow will set up a secondary *helical flow concentrating erosion on the outside of bends with deposition on the inside, hence continuing meander development downstream. Individual meanders will tend to migrate downstream by this process of erosion of the outside of meander bends, and deposition on the insides. If the erosion and deposition exactly complement each other, the meander train retains its form but migrates down valley. However, erosion rates typically exceed deposition rates in some meanders, leading to modifications.

The distribution of velocity of stream flow in a meandering reach is not even: owing to the pattern of helical flow, velocity is highest on the outside of meander bends, least on the inside. There is therefore active erosion in the former areas, deposition in the latter.

max. erosion

deposition as point bar

deposition as point bar

streamline of maximum flow

migration of meander

Meander

As the outsides erode and move downstream, so the insides of the bends sediment and move downstream as well. Thus the whole reach migrates down valley.

mean sea level. The level of the surface of the sea averaged over all tide states, being actually determined from the average of hourly heights. The periods over which readings are recorded vary; computations have been based on a month, a year, and even a 19-year period. All levels, including those of the sea surface, coastal land elevations, and the levels of coastal structures are referred to a chosen datum plane known as the *tidal datum. See also* sea level.

mechanical (physical) weathering. The breakdown of solid rock either through the development of cracks produced by strain as a result of internal or external stresses, or by the movement away from each other of the individual grains within a rock. The cause of stresses within rocks are many and mechanical weathering can operate at a number of different scales. The major types of mechanical weathering are: *freeze-thaw weathering, *exfoliation, *granular disintegration, *unloading phenomena, *wetting-and-drying weathering, *flaking, and *insolation weathering.

medial moraine. A ridge or spread of angular material extending lengthwise along the centre of a glacier. They may be formed as a result of the joining of two *lateral moraines as two glaciers converge, or of material originating at a spur between two confluent glaciers. Beaded forms occur, reflecting a greater availability of rock waste in summer periods. On the melting of the glacier the medial moraine may be left as a ridge running down the middle of the valley.

median ridge. *See* mid-ocean ridge.

median valley (median rift, axial rift zone). A deep cleft that follows the axis of an *mid-ocean ridge, marking the site of a constructive *plate margin.

Mediterranean climate. In Köppen's climatic classification, the Mediterranean basin was shown to have a distinctive climate of hot summers and mild wet winters, which he designated a Cs climate. Similar climatic regimes are found in California, Chile, S Africa, and W and S Australia.

mega-ripple. *See* sand wave.

melange. A sedimentary rock consisting of a jumbled mass of various rock fragments including schists, limestones, cherts, quartzites, greywackes, and a wide range of other rock types. They are thought to have been deposited as a result of the slumping of large masses of unstable rock debris, associated with destructive plate margins.

melanite. *See* garnet.

melanocratic. *See* colour index.

melilites. A group of minerals with composition $(Ca,Na)_2(Mg,Fe^{2+},Al,-Si)_3O_7$ found in thermally metamorphosed limestones and some strongly undersaturated basic igneous rocks such as *nephelinites.

melilitite. *See* nephelinite.

melteigite. *See* ijolite series.

meltwater. Melted ice from a glacier, which may travel over the surface of the ice, within it, or beneath it, carrying material with it and achieving a certain amount of sorting and rounding of rock fragments in the process. At ice margins meltwater is responsible for the formation of distinctive landforms, such as *kames and *eskers, whilst the presence of meltwater at the ice-rock interface is essential for successful glacial erosion in the form of *glacial plucking. *See also* meltwater channel.

meltwater channel. A channel cut by glacial meltwater in either solid rock or drift deposits, the most favourable locations being beneath the ice, where water restricted to tunnels can move at high velocity, carrying an erosively powerful load, and marginal to the ice, where

large volumes of water derived from the ice surface can accumulate and flow. After the disappearance of the ice, these channels bear little similarity to normal fluvially-developed ones. They may start abruptly, frequently in unlikely locations, crossing present-day drainage divides; they may be unusually straight and steep-sided and may contain only a small stream compared with the channel size, or sometimes no stream at all.

member. A division in the lithostratigraphic classification of bodies of rock (*see* stratigraphy, lithostratigraphy). It is part of a *formation, distinguished by some particular lithological characteristic.

Mercator projection. An *orthomorphic cylindrical map projection most commonly used for navigation charts (see diagram). Though there is great exaggeration of area in the higher latitudes, the straight-line bearings are correct. It is therefore used for portraying information of a directional nature, e.g. ocean currents. Similar to the Mercator is the *transverse Mercator.

meridian. A line of longitude passing through any given point and the north and south poles. Meridians are semicircles of equal length and cut the equator and all other parallels at right angles. The Greenwich meridian is taken to be the *prime meridian* from which all others are measured. Distance between two adjacent meridians decreases with distance from the equator. *See also* magnetic meridian.

meridional circulation. Any large-scale air movement from south to north or vice versa. *Compare* zonal circulation.

mesa. An isolated flat-topped hill with steep sides most frequently found in old-established landscapes based on horizontally bedded strata. This often exhibits alternate layers of comparatively hard and soft rocks, which on dissection produce steep and flat slopes respectively. Mesas often have almost vertical upper slopes, developed on the

poles cannot be shown

loxodrome or rhumb line

Mercator map projection

resistant cap rock, followed by much flatter slopes extending down to a general plain. The cap rock may be a lava flow or the same effect can be produced where a resistant soil horizon has been created.

mesocratic. *See* colour index.

mesolite. *See* zeolites.

mesometeorology. The study of the atmospheric processes that give rise to weather phenomena having scales intermediate in size between those of *macrometeorology and *micrometeorology. The actual size is a matter of some dispute but it is somewhere from approximately 10 to 150 km. Mesosystems can be subdivided into those topographically induced, free-atmosphere convective, and free-atmosphere nonconvective, depending upon their mode of origin. A denser network of observing stations is required to obtain adequate data for this scale of investigation than would be needed in macrometeorology.

mesopause. The upper limit of the mesosphere at a height of about 80 km (50 miles). It represents a temperature minimum (-80°C) between the mesosphere and the ionosphere.

mesosphere. 1. The layer of the upper atmosphere between 50 km and 80 km above the earth's surface. Through the layer temperatures decrease from values of about 0°C at the stratopause, its lower boundary, to about -80°C at the mesopause, its upper boundary. It is not thought to affect weather conditions in the troposphere.

2. That part of the earth's interior lying beneath the *asthenosphere.

mesostasis. Glassy or late-stage crystallization minerals, such as quartz, alkali feldspar, zeolites, or calcite, which infill *interstices in igneous rocks.

mesothermal. See hydrothermal processes.

Mesozoic. The era of *Phanerozoic time that follows the *Palaeozoic and precedes the *Cenozoic, comprising three periods: the *Triassic, *Jurassic, and *Cretaceous. It lasted about 175 million years, from 240 million years ago to the beginning of the Palaeocene, about 65 milion years ago. It is often known as the age of reptiles, for it was during this time that the Reptilia underwent their major evolutionary radiation, producing such diverse forms as the dinosaurs, pterosaurs, and ichthyosaurs. Most reptiles became extinct before the end of the era, and the mammals, birds, and flowering plants first appeared. Invertebrate groups important during the Mesozoic include the Ammonoidea and Belemnoidea. The Alpine episode of orogenic activity began at the end of this era. See also chronostratigraphy (for table of the major divisions of geological time).

metabasite. Any metamorphosed basic rock.

metamorphic differentiation. In medium- to high-grade metamorphic rocks some constituents, especially quartz and feldspar, migrate by a diffusion process into preferred zones, leaving behind micas and amphiboles. Layers of contrasting mineralogical and chemical compositions result and constitute a *foliation parallel to the *schistosity.

metamorphism. The process by which mineralogical and chemical changes take place in the solid state in pre-existing sedimentary or igneous rocks as a response to the imposition of new physical or chemical conditions. Metamorphic changes take place at temperatures ranging from 100°C to those in excess of 600°C, when rocks begin to melt. The mineral assemblages produced when rocks have attained chemical equilibrium are dependent upon the chemical compositions of the original rocks and the temperature and pressure conditions prevailing, provided that the metamorphism was isochemical and involved no *metasomatism.

Different types of metamorphism are recognized:

1. Contact metamorphism, i.e. the thermal metamorphism developed in rocks that are intruded by hot magma.

2. Regional or dynamothermal metamorphism, developed over large areas that have suffered intense deformation and the regional emplacement of granitic bodies. The temperatures and pressures associated with regional metamorphism are those incurred at depth within the earth's crust.

3. Dislocation metamorphism, developed as a result of the mechanical deformation or *cataclasis of pre-existing rocks and localized along shear belts, fault planes, and thrust planes.

Prograde metamorphic assemblages are formed in response to an increase in intensity or grade of metamorphism. Retrograde mineral assemblages are formed in metamorphic rocks that have become subjected to a lower grade as the intensity of the metamorphism wanes. See also facies (def. 1), zone (def. 1).

metasomatism. A metamorphic process by which mineralogical and chemical changes occur in rocks as a result of interaction with migrating fluids introduced from an external source. Metasomatic changes must be distinguished from those produced by pneumatolysis. See fenitization, granitization.

Metazoa. A group of animals whose bodies are formed of many cells, as opposed to the *Protozoa, which are unicellular.

meteoric dust. Extra-terrestrial fine dust that reaches the earth's surface through entering the earth's gravitational field. It contributes to a small degree to marine sediments. Some deep-sea cores have been found to contain meteoric dust, often in the form of magnetic spherules, perhaps only 0.1 to 0.5 mm in diameter. Meteoric dust may be transported in the atmosphere for considerable distances across the oceans, and, if present in significant amounts, may later be identifiable in certain seabed samples. One estimate suggests that some five million tons of meteoric dust fall onto the earth's surface annually. Meteoric dust is probably a small though important part of some deep-sea *red (brown) clay deposits, and meteoric spherules have been found to be plentiful in some slowly deposited deep-sea lutites.

meteorite. A solid body that has fallen to the earth's surface from an extra-terrestrial source. Meteorites are composed of a nickel-iron alloy (typically 90% iron and 10% nickel) and silicate minerals, mainly olivine and ortho-pyroxene. Three main types are distinguished:
1. Stony meteorites containing mainly silicate minerals plus some nickel-iron alloy. They are divided into chondrites and achondrites depending upon the presence or absence of small rounded bodies consisting of olivine or ortho-pyroxene, termed chondrules.
2. Stony-iron meteorites contain about equal proportions of silicate minerals and nickel-iron alloy.
3. Iron meteorites consist largly of nickel-iron with only accessory silicates. Certain nonvolcanic glasses, termed *tektites*, are also thought to be of extra-terrestrial origin. These are small bodies composed of acid glass and containing lechatelierite. No tektite fall has been witnessed and their origin remains controversial.

meteorology. The science of the atmosphere. It is concerned with the physics, chemistry, and movement of the atmosphere and its interactions with the ground surface. Some meteorological interest has also developed in studying the atmospheres of other planets by applying the principles obtained from the earth's atmosphere to different environmental conditions. As the main emphasis of meteorology has been on explaining and forecasting surface weather, meteorology is primarily concerned with the troposphere and stratosphere. Higher levels of the atmosphere, where different techniques of data collections are needed, tend to be regarded as part of geophysics. *See also* micrometeorology, climatology, synoptic meteorology, mesometeorology, macrometeorology.

miarolitic cavity. An irregular cavity within a plutonic rock into which large euhedral crystals project. *Compare* druse, vugh.

mica. A mineral that has a layered structure in which cations are sandwiched between sheets of $(Si,Al)O_4$ tetrahedra and hydroxyl ions. The general formula is $X_2Y_{4-6}Z_8O_{20}(OH,F)_4$, where X = K,Na,Ca; Y = Al,Mg,Fe,Li, and Z = Si,Al. The main mica minerals are:

muscovite $K_2Al_4(Si_6Al_2O_{20})(OH,F)_4$
paragonite $Na_2Al_4(Si_6Al_2O_{20})(OH)_4$
margarite $Ca_2Al_4(Si_4Al_4O_{20})(OH)_4$
phlogopite $K_2(Mg,Fe^{2+})_6(Si_6Al_2O_{20})(OH,F)_4$
biotite
$K_2(Mg,Fe^{2+})_{6-4}(Fe^{3+},Al,Ti)_{0-2}(Si_{6-5}Al_{2-3}O_{20})(OH,F)_4$
zinnwaldite
$K_2(Fe^{2+},Li,Al)_6(Si_{6-7}Al_{2-1}O_{20})(OH,F)_4$
lepidolite $K_2(Li,Al)_{5-6}(Si_{6-7}Al_{2-1}O_{20})(OH,F)_4$

Clintonite and *xanthophyllite* are related to phlogopite by the substitution of calcium for potassium.

All micas have a perfect basal cleavage, which reflects their layered structure. "Books" of mica, found in pegmatites, are so called because they have the appearance of piles of pages. The cleavage flakes of micas are flexible and elastic. Muscovite and paragonite are colourless whereas biotite and phlogopite are usually dark shades of red, brown, and black.

Muscovite and biotite are common in schists, gneisses, and granitic rocks. Biotite is also found in basic and intermediate igneous rocks. Phlogopite occurs in some peridotites and metamorphosed limestones. The lithium micas are found almost exclusively in pegmatites.

micrite. Chemically precipitated calcite having microscopic grains of less than 0.01 mm in diameter, present in some *limestones; the terminology used in the petrographic description and classification of limestones is based on the presence of micrite, *sparite, and *allochems.

microclimate. The climate within a few metres of the ground surface, resulting from the interaction between soil, atmosphere, and vegetation.

microcline. A variety of alkali *feldspar.

microfossil. A fossil so small that a microscope is required for its study. Microfossils include bacteria, diatoms, Protozoa, some Crustacea, the larvae of certain animals, and also the isolated skeletal parts or fragments of organisms. Apart from their taxonomic and evolutionary interest, microfossils are important in the correlation of rocks of which only small samples are available, such as the cores from boreholes. The study of microfossils is known as *micropalaeontology.*

microgabbro. *See* dolerite.

microlite. A small incipient crystal found in glassy rocks. Unlike *crystallites, microlites are sufficiently large for their nature to be determined under the microscope.

micrometeorology. The study of small-scale atmospheric processes, usually operating near the ground surface. Experiments and research in this subject require large numbers of accurate instruments, which result in most studies being limited to small areas and short duration under ideal conditions. The enormous variety of surface conditions results in a complex interaction between the atmosphere and the ground to give multitudinous microclimates; in fact each instrumentation site could be classed as unique.

micropalaeontology. The study of *microfossils.

microseisms. Small irregular earth tremors and quaverings, which make up the background pattern recorded on seismometers. They can result from natural sources such as waves breaking on a beach, or from the passing of heavy traffic.

Mid-Atlantic Ridge. A very large relief feature forming part of the *mid-ocean ridge system, which trends north-south through the Atlantic Ocean, connected by Kerguelen Island and St. Paul Island with the Indian Ocean Ridge. The relief of the elevation above the adjacent ocean basin floor is 1 to 3 km, and the width in most places is more than 1000 km. It is essentially a wide fractured arch taking up the centre third of the Atlantic Ocean. Along the crest region are the rift mountains and high fractured plateau, jointly making up a strip 80 to 300 km wide. Some of the higher parts of the ridge rise above sea level to form islands.

mid-ocean ridge (median ridge). A massive submarine elevation that extends, in global terms, over a distance of about 60 000 km. It traverses all of the major oceans. Its general form is that of a broad arch that stands, on average, 1 to 3 km above the adjacent deep sea floor, and which has experienced fracturing along its crest region. Along much of its length, the ridge is over a 1000 km wide. Parts of the ridge crest region are gashed by a steep-sided rift feature (*see* median valley), while other fracture zones (some of them known as *transform faults) trend perpendicular to the main axis of the ridge. The rift is coincident with a belt of shallow earthquake epicentres. The floor beneath the ridge is generally hot and the basaltic rocks of the ridge-crest and ridge-flank region appear to be quite young in geological terms.

In terms of the *plate tectonics theory, such mid-ocean ridges mark the site of constructive plate margins. It is at this point that basaltic lava from the earth's mantle reaches the surface to be added to the oceanic crust in the form of pillow lavas and dykes. As these eruptions are frequent by geological scales the area does not have time to adjust immediately to regain isostatic balance but sinks as the sea floor spreads away from the ridge.

migmatite. A coarse heterogeneous gneissose rock consisting of bands and patches of quartz-feldspar granitic material and mafic material consisting mainly of biotite or hornblende. Migmatites have the appearance of mixed rocks, comprising portions that resemble granitic igneous material and mafic portions that are metamorphic and possess a *schistosity. They are associated with metamorphic rocks that have formed at the highest grades. Under such conditions, partial melting takes place producing mobile granitic material, which invades and reacts with the metamorphic rocks.

Milankovitch radiation curves. The earth does not revolve in a circular orbit round the sun at a constant velocity, but over a period of many years changes take place affecting the amount and distribution of solar radiation received by the earth. First, the tilt of the earth's axis of rotation relative to the plane of its orbit varies between $21.8°$ and $24.4°$ over a period of 40 000 years. This affects the seasonality or thermal range between summer and winter. Secondly, the ellipticity or eccentricity of the earth's orbit varies over a period of about 100 000 years. This results in a greater seasonal range of radiation receipt. When the orbit is at its most eccentric, there will be a 30% difference between aphelion and perihelion, compared with 7% at present and none when the orbit is circular. Finally, the season when the earth is nearest the sun

changes over a period of about 21 000 years. At present it is nearest in the N hemisphere winter (January 7) and farthest in N hemisphere summer (July 7).

The effects of these radiation changes vary from latitude to latitude. The variations likely to be produced were calculated by Milankovitch in 1940. It is believed that these cyclic changes may have great importance for the commencement of ice ages, but the association is not as close as might be expected.

millibar (mb). One thousandth of a bar, a C.G.S. unit of pressure. As 1 bar is equal to a pressure of 10^6 dynes per sq.cm, one millibar is equal to 1000 dynes/cm^2 or 100 newtons/m^2 (pascals). The millibar is still in use in meteorology.

milligal. See gal.

Millstone Grit. The middle of the three lithological divisions of the *Carboniferous System in Britain. It corresponds to the lower half of the Upper Carboniferous (or Namurian) Stage.

mineral. Any naturally occurring substance having a definite chemical composition. When a mineral of commercial value is present in some rock body in economically sufficient quantity to merit extraction, the body constitutes a mineral deposit.

minette. See lamprophyre.

minimum temperature. The lowest temperature recorded during a given period either in a Stevenson screen (minimum air temperature) or on the ground (grass minimum temperature). Both temperatures are normally measured by an alcohol thermometer in which the meniscus drags a metal index to the lowest temperature then leaves it as the column rises when temperatures increase. Global minimum temperatures are found on the Antarctic ice caps; in Britain, Braemar holds the record for the lowest air temperature with -27.2°C (-17°F), recorded on Feb. 11, 1895.

Miocene. An epoch of the *Tertiary period extending from the end of the *Oligocene, about 22.5 million years ago, for 17 million years to the beginning of the *Pliocene. There are probably no rocks of this age in Britain. Grasses evolved and spread and, by their effects on the environment, may have contributed to changes in the mammals, which became more modern in appearance. Miocene mammals included pigs, deer, horses, rhinoceroses, elephants, monkeys, apes, and possibly hominids. Alpine orogenic movements took place during this epoch.

miogeosyncline. A geosyncline in which there are no volcanic products or processes associated with its sedimentation.

mirage. An optical phenomenon resulting from the refraction of light through layers of air having very large temperature gradients. The rapid change of temperature vertically produces varying refractive indices of the air and so light appears to travel in curved paths. The most common is the inferior mirage above a heated ground surface. Light is strongly refracted upwards near the surface so that the apparent pools of water on the ground are, in reality, refractions from the clear sky. A superior mirage may occur above a flat surface of much lower temperature than the air above, as over ice or a cold sea in summer. Light in this case is bent downwards from the object towards the viewer.

misfit river. A river that is apparently too small for its valley. It is characterized by meander bends in its channel of smaller amplitude and greater intricacy than the meanders in the valley itself. The length of the valley meanders is ten times that of the current meanders. There is an established relation between meander length and discharge in rivers, and on that basis it has been calculated that the rivers that eroded the valley meanders must have had a bankfull discharge 80-100 times the current streams. This probably occurred at the end of the Ice Age, when the glaciers thawed; the periglacial climate of that period would have reduced vegetation and soils to a minimum, allowing all the meltwater to flow off the land to the rivers, with none lost by infiltration into the soil. The resulting torrents cut the current valley.

Misfits could also evolve through the capture of a river's headwaters, reducing its volume, and leaving it a misfit in its valley. *See* river capture.

mispickel. An old name for *arsenopyrite.

Mississippian. A period within the American classification of geological time that extends from the end of the *Devonian, about 370 million yers ago, for about 45 million years to the beginning of the *Pennsylvanian. The Mississippian System corresponds approximately to the Lower *Carboniferous elsewhere.

mist. The state of atmospheric obscurity intermediate between fog and haze. It is composed of suspended microscopic water droplets with an atmospheric relative humidity of at least 95%. Mist is also used for dense but shallow condensation phenomena at ground level when the ground surface may be totally obscured, but hedges or animals can be seen quite clearly.

mistral. A strong cold dry northerly wind that is funnelled down the Rhône Valley in S France and then blows across the delta into the Mediterranean Sea. Its frequency and strength have necessitated agricultural adaptations to prevent crop damage. These take the form of hedges or screens oriented east-west to protect plants. The winds are linked to intensification of depressions in the Gulf of Genoa.

mixed tide. Any tide that is not clearly of the diurnal or semidiurnal type. Such tides might be referred to as intermediate tides. The tidal wave is characterized by a significant inequality in either the low–water or the high-water levels and a double low water and a double high water occur during each tidal day.

mixing ratio. The ratio of the mass of an atmospheric gas to the mass of air with which the gas is mixed. It is most frequently used for water vapour, the *humidity mixing ratio*, and is expressed in g kg^{-1}.

mobile belt (orogenic *or* fold belt). A long linear area of the earth's crust undergoing intense deformation, often accompanied by seismic and volcanic activity. These structures originate as deep trenches, which fill up with a thick wedge of sediment. As two continents later collide this wedge between them is compressed and deformed to form a mountain chain.

mobile dune. A coastal sand dune at the stage when its vegetation (mainly marram grass) is open, leaving sometimes 50% or more bare sand subject to wind movement and hence mobile. These dunes vary greatly in size, reaching over 30 metres at Cubbin Sands in the Grampian region of Scotland, the largest in the British Isles. Their appearance is of a confused mass of sandy depressions and grassy knolls superimposed on a profile that shows a gentle windward slope and a steep lee slope.

mock sun (parhelion). An optical phenomenon seen in the sky as a result of the refraction of sunlight by hexagonal ice crystals with vertical axes. This is most frequent with cirrostratus clouds. Usually two mock suns are seen, equal distances on either side of the sun, and appear as brighter areas of the cirrostratus clouds.

mode. The percentage of each of the component minerals contained in an igneous or metamorphic rock. *Compare* norm.

moder humus. Humus intermediate between mull and mor.

Mohole project. An abandoned project originally proposed in order to obtain samples of the rocks of the upper mantle. It was hoped to drill down through the earth's crust to the Mohorovicic Discontinuity.

Mohorovicic Discontinuity. The seismic boundary that marks the junction between the base of the earth's crust and the top of the mantle. This boundary varies in depth below the earth's surface from 5-10 km beneath the ocean and between 55-70 km beneath the continents. The boundary is marked by an increase in the P wave velocity from 6.9 to 8.2 km/sec.

Mohs' scale. A scale of hardness devised to aid the identification of minerals. Ten reference minerals were chosen, the softest, talc, being assigned a hardness of 1 and the hardest, diamond, 10. Each mineral on the scale can be scratched by those of higher numbers. 1. talc. 2. gypsum. 3. calcite. 4. fluorite. 5. apatite. 6. orthoclase. 7. quartz. 8. topaz. 9. corundum. 10. diamond. Other common substances are useful in testing hardness: finger nail (2.5), copper coin (3), glass (5.5) and a pen knife (6.5). The hardness of many minerals varies with direction. For example, the hardness of kyanite varies between 5.5 and 7.

molasse. A term originally used by Alpine geologists for a particular sequence of Miocene sediments. The term has since been used to denote sequences of sediments deposited under continental or freshwater conditions after a period of mountain-building. *Compare* flysch.

mollisol. One of the ten soil orders of the *Seventh Approximation classification. They are soft calcimorphic soils, developed in subhumid to semiarid conditions, characterized by a dark strongly structured surface horizon, often almost one metre deep and more than 50% saturated with bases (mainly calcium), which is termed a *mollic epipedon*. It includes the *chernozem, *chestnut, *prairie, *rendzina, *brown earths, brown calcareous soils, and associated types such as humic gleys and solonetzic soils.

Mollusca. The phylum of invertebrate animals that includes snails, mussels, and octopuses. Molluscs are unsegmented creatures having a head, a visceral region, a muscular ventral organ for locomotion known as the *foot*, and a *mantle*, which generally secretes a hard calcareous shell. The geologically important classes of this phylum are the *Gastropoda, the *Bivalvia, and the *Cephalopoda, which includes important extinct forms such as the *Ammonoidea and *Belemnoidea. Molluscs seem to have been marine animals inhabiting shallow waters and their shells are known as fossils from the Cambrian Period onwards. Some, such as the Bivalvia in the Carboniferous, have been used in stratigraphic *correlation.

Mollweide's projection. A map projection showing the entire earth's surface on an ellipsoidal base. The major axis (equator) is twice the length of the minor axis (central meridian). The geographic parallels are straight lines, as is the central meridian; the other meridians are curved, the curvature increasing towards the outside limits of the projection. The distortion of shapes and directions is therefore considerable, though the projection is homolographic and consequently used for distributions. This projection is sometimes interrupted (see diagram): each continental area has its own central meridian, with different ones north and south of the equator; the interruptions are in the oceans.

molybdenite. A silver-grey molybdenum mineral, MoS_2, found as an accessory in acid igneous rocks and in hydrothermal veins.

monadnock. Any hill standing up above the surface of a flat or gently undulating plain. These hills may be composed of

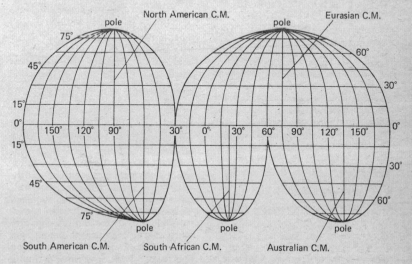

Mollweide's interrupted projection

rocks that are more resistant to weathering than those around them; alternatively they may be lócated in former watershed positions. In the latter case they will have been subjected to active fluvial erosion for a shorter period of time than the rest of the area and it is for this reason that they remain as upstanding masses.

monazite. A rare-earth mineral of composition $(Ce,La,Y,Th)PO_4$ found as an accessory in acid igneous rocks and as a detrital mineral.

monchiquite. See lamprophyre.

monocline. A bending of rock strata produced in sedimentary sequences that have deformed under conditions favouring the development of a normal fault. Two areas of horizontally bedded sediments are left at different elevations but still connected by a steeply inclined series of the same beds. See diagram at fold.

monoclinic. See crystal system.

monogeosyncline. See trench.

monomineralic. Denoting a rock consisting almost wholly of one mineral, e.g. dunite, anorthosite.

monsoon. A large-scale reversal of winds in the tropics (from the Arabic word for season) due to differential heating of continent and ocean, but as the circulation can be affected by many other factors, the monsoon varies in character from one area to another. It is best developed in India, SE Asia, and China but N Australia and E and W Africa all show similar wind reversals. The summer season is normally the rainy period of the monsoon with southwesterly winds in the N hemisphere, the dry season having winds from the N sector.

Monsoon Current. In the N part of the Indian Ocean, the surface currents reflect closely the seasonal changes in the wind direction as the monsoon season develops. The North Equatorial Current is clearly apparent during February and March, at the time when the northwest monsoon is blowing. An Equatorial Counter-current is also strongly developed, with its axis aligned roughly along latitude 7°S. However, when the southwest monsoon commences in August-September, the North Equatorial Current is replaced by the Monsoon Current and flows eastwards. These currents are generally located within the uppermost layers of water. See also equatorial currents.

monticellite. A calcium-bearing variety of *olivine.

montmorillonite. See clay minerals.

monzonite. See syenodiorite.

moraine. A depositional feature composed of glacial *till, which may be in association with active ice or deposited by former glaciers and ice sheets. This material may be transported on the surface of the ice, within the ice (englacial), or beneath the ice (subglacial). See lateral moraine, medial moraine, terminal moraine, push moraine, ground moraine.

mor humus. Acid humus, which forms in wet lime-deficient environments, e.g. podzolic conditions. Most of the organic breakdown is achieved by the fungi in the soil but it is a slow process with the result that the L, F, and H layers (see profile) are clearly differentiated.

morphogenetic zone (in climatic geomorphology). An area of the earth in which climate and relief are distinctive, through the control of climate on geomorphic process and the control of process on landform. These zones run roughly parallel to major climates, which conform to latitude. Early attempts to divide the earth into such zones used very simple climatic data (mean annual rainfall and mean annual temperature) but modern attempts use much more sophisticated parameters. Tricart and Cailleux have identified four major world zones, running from a cold zone in the north, through a forested zone and subarid zone to the equatorial tropical zone; within each, climates and landforms are in sympathy through the link of process. ·

mould. A fossil in which the original skeletal parts have been dissolved away, leaving a space that preserves their shape. In some cases a mould may preserve features of only the outer or inner surfaces of such structures as shells. These are known respectively as *external* and *internal moulds*. The infilling of a mould with secondary material produces a *cast.

mountain wind. A form of *katabatic wind in mountainous areas where, after night-time radiational cooling, strong breezes are concentrated in the valleys as the cold air has subsided downslope.

mud. Sediment having a preponderance of particles measuring less than 0.06 mm in diameter. Under natural conditions, muds generally form very plastic masses comprising sediment particles admixed with water. The term applies to both silty and clayey particles. Mud may be deposited, according to prevailing conditions, in both shallow water and deep-sea areas. Sheltered environments are particularly susceptible to mud deposition, as for example in sheltered lagoons and estuaries, and along low-energy beaches and tidal flats. Once partially consolidated into mud banks, the material tends to be remarkably cohesive and therefore resistant to scour; many mud banks are eroded primarily through side-scour because of the gradual migration of tidal channels.

mud cracks. See desiccation cracks.

mudflow. See earthflow.

mudstone. An *argillaceous sedimentary rock that is less fissile along bedding planes than *shale.

mud volcano. See sand volcano.

mugearite. See trachybasalt.

mull humus. Alkaline humus, which commonly forms in a mild, moist, and base-rich environment, e.g. chernozem conditions. It is rapidly incorporated into the soil by the abundant soil fauna, particularly earthworms.

mullions. Tectonically produced structures in metamorphic and sedimentary rocks that resemble rods or columns.

mullite. See aluminium silicates.

multiple reflections. On a seismic profile a seismic wave may be recorded more than once as a result of it having been reflected more than once.

muscovite. See micas.

mylonite. A rock formed during dislocation metamorphism by extreme granulation and shearing. Mylonites are banded or streaky rocks and may contain augen of undestroyed crystals or rock fragments in a fine-grained matrix. They are commonly found at thrust planes along which extensive movements have taken place. See cataclasis, pseudotachylite.

myrmekite. Wormlike intergrowths of quartz in plagioclase feldspars produced as a result of the replacement of potassium feldspar by sodium feldspar, during which excess silica is liberated.

N

nappe. A large tectonic feature that owes its origin to a combination of folding and thrusting. They are basically large horizontal recumbent folds that have travelled for many tens of kilometres along thrust planes. They are well developed in the Alps where they were first described.

national grid. The *grid used by the Ordnance Survey, enabling any point within the British Isles to be given its own unique coordinates. The grid consists of 500 kilometre squares designated by a letter, divided into 100 kilometre squares indicated by a second letter and further subdivided into 1 kilometre squares. The value of such a national grid is that on beginning to map an area, any previously fixed features, such as trigonometric pillars and bench marks, may be located initially and used as primary control stations before continuing with detail mapping.

native. Denoting the state of occurrence of certain minerals when they are uncombined with other minerals.

natrolite. *See* zeolites.

natural selection. The process proposed by Darwin in 1859 to explain the *evolution of organisms from one species to another. It attempts to account for the origin and diversity of all organisms. Plant and animal species produce relatively large numbers of offspring that differ in various ways. If an organism possesses certain variations that make it better suited to its environment, this organism is more likely to survive and reproduce. If these variations are heritable the likelihood of its offspring also possessing them is increased. In this way, and over many generations, radical changes may arise.

Nautiloidea. An almost extinct subclass of molluscs of the class *Cephalopoda. The external shell of the nautiloids is similar to that of the related *Ammonoidea, except that in fossil forms it is straight or only slightly coiled and in all types the suture lines are simple curves, showing none of the complex convolutions characteristic of the Ammonoidea. The oldest fossils come from upper Cambrian rocks and their shells sometimes reached a length of up to 4.5 metres. These straight-shelled forms were extinct by the end of the Triassic Period. The group as a whole declined from the Devonian Period onwards; very few genera existed during the Mesozoic and only one, *Nautilus*, has persisted to the present day.

neap tide. A *tide of relatively small range that occurs near the time of quadrature of the moon (i.e. near the time of the moon's quarters). The tidal range falls below the average range by

about 10 to 30%. Because of this low range, the tidal current speeds during neap tides are significantly less than those attained during *spring tides.

nearshore circulation system. The system of currents, notably those induced directly or indirectly through wave activity, that operate within and closely adjacent to the *breaker zone. These currents include the shoreward-directed *mass transport currents beneath waves, the wave-induced *longshore currents, the powerful seaward-flowing *rip currents, and other currents associated with the expanding rip-head zones. Superimposed on these currents, there is invariably a reversing tidal current, and, on those occasions when local winds are blowing, wind-induced currents. In the vicinity of rivers and estuaries, there may also be density-induced currents. The relative importance of the various types of current varies both spatially and temporally.

Nebular Hypothesis. An idea proposed by the Marquis de Laplace in 1796 in which he suggested that the material now forming the sun and planets originated as a disc-shaped nebula or gas cloud, which contracted into discrete bodies.

neck (plug). An erosional remnant representing the former conduit that fed a volcano. This conduit was filled with lava and pyroclastic material that was more resistant to erosion than that of the enclosing volcanic cone, which has since been eroded away.

needle ice. Needles of ice, often several centimetres long, growing beneath the surface layer of debris and able to lift frost-shattered rock fragments and soil particles perpendicularly from the ground surface. On melting of the needles (often called *pipkrakes*), the fragments are deposited a little way downslope. Material can progress considerable distances and, as the process tends to be more effective in coarser material, it also achieves a certain amount of sorting. Needle ice occurs in periglacial environments, most effectively where there is diurnal freezing and thawing.

negative gravity anomaly. *See* gravity anomaly.

negative movement of sea level. A rise of the land relative to the sea due either to an actual rise of the land through tectonic movements, or a fall in sea level through the locking up of water in the form of ice, as happened in the Pleistocene period. Whatever the cause, more land is created, and the relative relief of the land, from sea level to mountain tops, is increased. The major result is the extension of river systems out across former sea bed areas and their *rejuvenation. Raised beaches, marine beaches, knickpoints, river terraces, and incised meanders are all evidence of past negative movements. *See also* positive movement of sea level.

nekton (nektonic organisms). Pelagic organisms that swim and move actively, such as fish. *Compare* plankton.

Neogene. The upper part of the *Tertiary Period, comprising the *Miocene and *Pliocene Epochs. It lasted for about 20.7 millions years, from the end of the *Oligocene Period, 22.5 million years ago, to the beginning of the *Pleistocene. Some authorities suggest that the Neogene should be considered as a period, with the Tertiary as a sub-era.

nephanalysis. The analysis of cloud patterns on weather satellite photographs. The photographs cover large areas of the earth's atmosphere and surface and new techniques were required to describe and analyse the larger features of cloud patterns compared with the apparently random distribution seen by the surface observer. On a nephanalysis the following information can be portrayed: cloud elements, cloud masses, cloud patterns, cloud systems, cloud bands, cloud types (stratiform, cumuliform, cirriform, cumulonimbus,

or stratocumuliform), percentage cloud cover, cloud boundaries, and synoptic interpretations of these features.

nepheline. *See* feldspathoids.

nephelinite. A strongly undersaturated basic to ultrabasic feldspar-free volcanic rock, having a plutonic equivalent within the *ijolite-melteigite series. Nephelinites consist of *nepheline, which may occur both as euhedral phenocrysts and as anhedral groundmass grains, together with a variety of mafic minerals, typically titanaugite, biotite, olivine, and magnetite.
Assemblages of *leucite plus mafic minerals constitute the *leucitites*. Ugandite is an augite-rich olivine-leucitite. *Melilitites* are composed of melilite plus mafics and often contain small amounts of nepheline and calcite in addition. *Alnoite* is a dyke rock largely composed of melilite and biotite together with pyroxene, calcite, and olivine. Mafurite is an olivine-kalsilite rock.
Nephelinites and leucitites are compositionally related to phonolites and leucitophyres. These volcanics are restricted to stable continental areas and occur in association with ijolites and carbonatites.

nephrite. A tremolitic *amphibole. *See also* jade.

neptunian dyke. A roughly vertical body of sediment, usually sandstone, that has infilled a fissure in a pre-existing rock body exposed at the earth's surface or on the sea floor.

neritic. Denoting the shallow-water marine environment lying between low-tide level and a depth of some 200 metres. The environment rarely covers a distance from the shore in excess of several hundred kilometres; on a global scale, it covers roughly 30 million sq. km or about 10% of the total ocean area. The environment is characterized by very diverse sediments (of which fine to coarse terrestrially-derived sediments admixed with what are mostly calcareous organic remains tend to predominate) and *benthos, and a wide array of environmental conditions, as for example in the degree of light penetration. The whole of the seafloor in the neritic zone probably experiences some measure of wave disturbance and almost certainly tidal current action.

neutron logging. A subsurface logging technique used in uncased bore holes to record the presence of fluids. When used in conjunction with a gamma-ray log it can be used to calculate the porosities of the formations encountered. It measures the intensity of radiation in the bore hole after it has been exposed to a radioactive source.

nevé. 1. See firn.
2. The area in which firn exists; firn field.

New American Comprehensive Soil Classification. See Seventh Approximation.

New Red Sandstone. A succession of red sandstones forming the continental facies of the *Permian and *Triassic Systems in Britain.

nimbostratus cloud. The main rain-bearing cloud of temperate latitudes. It consists of a grey cloud layer of appreciable depth beneath which are frequently low ragged clouds, called *scud. They are most often associated with low-pressure areas and precipitation may be prolonged, although it is not usually heavy.

NIMBUS. A weather satellite launched in 1964 that succeeded the TIROS system. It maintained a constant camera angle with the earth's surface and obtained good quality visible and infrared photographs. It only functioned for 26 days but it represented an advance in remote sensing by satellite.

nitrification. The conversion of nitrogen by bacteria to a form usable by higher plants. When material decays ammonia is often liberated and this is toxic to many plants. Some bacteria, namely *Nitrosomonas*, can oxidize ammonia to

nitrite and in turn it may further be oxidized, by *Nitrobacter*, to nitrate, which can be used by plants. *Denitrification*, a conversion of nitrates back to nitrogen gas, most of which is unusable, may occur when soils become poorly aerated and acid.

nitrogen. The most abundant gas in the atmosphere and a critical constituent in the soil, which can only be used directly by a few specialized bacteria. To be of widespread value it has to be converted into the nitrate form (see nitrification). In nature, nitrogen is involved in cyclic changes termed the *Nitrogen Cycle*, which is basically a change from animal life to nitrites to nitrates to plant life to animal life.

nitrogen fixation. The absorption of atmospheric nitrogen by some heterotrophic bacteria. There are two groups: 1) the nonsymbiotic, e.g. *Azotobacter*, which make the nitrogen part of their tissue so that when they die it is made available by nitrification; 2) the symbiotic bacteria, e.g. *Rhizobium*, which fix the nitrogen and pass it on to their host.

nivation hollow. A hemispherical hollow of variable size produced by *nivation processes. These hollows can be described as transverse, longitudinal, or circular, depending on the shape of the associated snow patch and its relationship with the slope. The downslope part of the hollow is generally flat or gently inclined, whilst the upslope part is steeper. It is considered that this backslope recedes gradually upslope, increasing in height, and that in this way the hollows may develop into cirques, as more and more snow can be accommodated, and *firn begins to form.

nivation (snow patch erosion). Any of a number of processes associated with a patchy snow cover over unconsolidated rocks, such as glacial deposits. The most important erosional process is *freeze-thaw, the role of the snow being to supply meltwater to assist in the process. The thickness of snow is an important factor, since if it is too thick it will tend to protect surface materials from the effects of atmospheric freeze-thaw cycles. The most active nivation takes place around the edges of snow patches. The presence of *permafrost greatly increases efficiency since it stops the meltwater soaking away. In order to achieve any erosion, weathered material must be removed, and consequently the process is most efficient on slopes, where *solifluction and meltwater runoff are the principal transportation agents. The characteristic form produced by nivation is the *nivation hollow.

NOAA. *Abbrev. for* National Oceanic and Atmospheric Administration. It gave its name to the 1974 range of operational satellites. Visible wavebands and various wavebands in the infrared are filmed.

noctilucent clouds. Clouds observed in the high atmosphere when it is almost dark at ground level. Sometimes they show brilliant colours, although they more usually have a bluish-white or yellow appearance. Almost all other clouds are limited to the troposphere, but the height of noctilucent clouds has been shown to be about 80 km (50 miles), sometimes reaching speeds of 300 knots. Their true nature and origins are not completely understood, but they are believed to consist of ice particles, saturation being reached through orographic wave development resonated from the surface.

nodule. 1. A rounded concretion in sedimentary rocks.
2. *See* inclusion.

nonconformity (heterolithic unconformity). An unconformable contact between overlying younger sedimentary rocks, and underlying older igneous or metamorphic rocks.

nondipole field. That small part of the earth's magnetic field that is superimposed upon the main *dipole field. This small additional component is responsible for the irregularities of the earth's magnetic field. It is irregular in its distribution and is different in each hemisphere; as a result the earth's magnetic dip poles are not antipodal, the north magnetic dip pole being at $75°$N, $101°$W, whilst the south magnetic dip pole is at $67°$S, $143°$E.

nonsequence. A short break in sedimentation, causing a type of unconformity only detectable by palaeontological techniques.

nordmarkite. *See* syenite.

norite. *See* gabbro.

norm. A chemical analysis of an igneous or metamorphic rock expressed in terms of standard minerals (the *normative minerals*), the proportions of which form a basis for comparison and classification. The norm is distinct from the *mode, which is the actual mineral composition of a rock. A quantitative classification for igneous rocks was devised in 1903, based upon a normative calculation by Cross, Iddings, Pirsson, and Washington, and termed the C.I.P.W. classification.

normal. 1. (In climatology). Denoting the average value of any climatological element over a specified time period. The usual time period is 30 years, which is believed to be sufficiently long to average out year-to-year variations but not long enough to contain trends in the value of the elements, such as temperature or precipitation.
2. (In statistics). Denoting a distribution of data that corresponds to an accepted frequency distribution about a population mean.

normal (gravity) fault. A type of fault in which the predominant displacement is downwards in the same direction as the inclination of the fault plane. This results from a stress configuration in which the principal maximum stress is vertical with the other two principal stresses (minimum and intermediate) being horizontal. See *fault*.

North Atlantic Drift. The portion of the major surface current in the North Atlantic that is an extension of the Gulf Stream current. The flow of the North Atlantic Drift is generally in a north-easterly direction. It tends to be more diffuse than the Gulf Stream, being characterized by several shifting bands of water. Each band displays large meander flows that appear, disappear, and reappear in a constantly altering kaleidoscope of flow patterns. Large eddies are often thrown off the main stream. In its more easterly portion, the North Atlantic Drift bifurcates, one stream trending north-northeastwards towards the Polar Seas, the other stream (the Canary Current) trending east-southeastwards. Being a relatively warm current, especially on account of being partially replenished at depth by fairly warm water from the Mediterranean Sea, it has an important ameliorating influence on the climate of Northwest Europe's ocean flank.

northing. Any of the east-west grid lines on a map, quoted after the *easting when coordinates are being given, showing distance north from the origin of the grid.

nosean. *See* feldspathoids.

nucleation (accretion). A process by which it has been suggested that continents grow, younger fold belts being added to their margins. This is consistent with the present theory of plate tectonics as these fold belts originate in the deep trenches bordering continents that are overriding the adjacent ocean floor.

nucleus (in meteorology). Any minute solid particle suspended in the atmosphere. They have been classified on the basis of size into Aitken nuclei (smaller than 2×10^{-5} cm), large nuclei with radii between 0.2 and 1×10^{-4} cm, and giant nuclei with radii greater than 1×10^{-4} cm. The Aitken nuclei are most abundant in the atmosphere' reaching about 10 000 per cm³, but there are far more in industrial areas than over the oceans. Identification of the nuclei is very difficult, even with electron microscopes, unless they possess a distinct crystalline form.

Some nuclei have an attraction for water and are known as hygroscopic, others are nonhygroscopic. This is very important in enabling nuclei to act as favourable points for condensation as part of the precipitation process. There are undoubtedly sufficient such nuclei in the atmosphere as condensation always takes place as soon as saturation is reached. *Compare* freezing nuclei.

nuée ardente. An incandescent cloud of gas and volcanic fragments emitted during certain types of volcanic eruptions. *See* pyroclastic rocks.

numerical weather forecasting. A system of computing expected values of selected isobaric surfaces. In operational terms this is used for up to 48 hours ahead, as beyond that time differences between observed and computed values become unacceptable. This is because future pressure fields will be influenced by many factors, not all of which are included within the modelling system. Interpretation of the predicted chart has to be made to obtain the weather forecast for that time. For 24 hour periods, numerical methods are as good as if not better than forecasts based on years of experience by professional forecasters.

nummulites. Benthonic marine Protozoa forming a family of the *Foraminifera. Their skeleton, up to 80 mm in diameter in some species, consists of a smooth flattened disc-shaped spiral divided into many separate chambers. Nummulites are known from the Cretaceous Period but were most abundant in the Eocene and Oligocene Epochs; they are used locally in stratigraphic correlation.

nunatak. A rock peak sticking out above the surface of an ice sheet. In many instances these peaks were formerly ice-covered and only subsequent reduction in the extent of ice cover has brought about their emergence.

nutation. The small oscillation superimposed upon the precessional motion of the earth. This results from the gravitational attraction on the earth's equatorial bulge from the sun and moon. This attraction varies continuously as the sun and moon change their positions with respect to the earth.

O

objective analysis (in meteorology). A method of interpreting a two-dimensional scalar field of some meteorological element, usually pressure, so that the results from a particular data set are independent of human subjectivity. The usual way is by fitting a two-dimensional surface to the data by means of a least-squares method, which is a statistical process in which the sum of the squares of the difference between actual and predicted values is reduced to a minimum.

Obsequent, subsequent, and consequent streams

obsequent stream. A stream that flows in the opposite direction to a *consequent stream, often against the direction of dip. In scarpland areas, the obsequent streams develop after the consequent and subsequent pattern has dissected the strata to produce the characteristic sequence of limestone and sandstone scarps, with clay vales; obsequent streams will flow down the scarp faces, tributary to the subsequent master streams.

obsidian. *See* rhyolite.

Fig. 1: Warm occlusion

Fig. 2: Cold occlusion

Occlusions

occlusion. A front that develops during the later states of the evolution of a *depression when the air of the warm sector is no longer at the ground surface. As the cold front normally travels more quickly than the warm front, it slowly reduces the area of the warm sector until it merges with the preceding front to complete the occlusion process. The occlusion is therefore a compound zone with warm and cold front characteristics. If the air behind the original cold front was colder than that ahead of the original warm front it is known as a *cold occlusion*, and if warmer, as a *warm occlusion*. The frontal structure of the occluded system is shown in the diagram. In reality individual occlusions are more complex. Sometimes as the depression moves eastwards along the occlusion, the line of airmass contrast to the north of the depression swings anticlockwise giving a further period of rain. This is known as a *back-bent occlusion*.

ocean. The water mass (excluding lakes and seas completely surrounded by land) that covers part of the surface of the earth. The water mass as a whole constitutes the hydrosphere. The interface between the hydrosphere and the atmosphere is thus the sea surface, while the interface between the hydrosphere and the lithosphere is the sea bottom. The *deep ocean lies beyond the shelf edge or shelf break.

ocean basin floor. The ocean basin floor, the *continental margin on the continental flank, and the *mid-ocean ridge on the oceanic flank constitute the three major morphological divisions of the ocean floor. The ocean basin floor has been further subdivided into a number of physiographic provinces, two of which (the elevated oceanic rises and the very deep abyssal floor zones), are of particular importance. The ocean basin floor occupies very extensive areas: approximately a third of the Atlantic Ocean floor, a third of the Indian Ocean floor, and three quarters of the Pacific Ocean floor. The ocean basin floor is also highly important for its *seamounts (either occurring individually or in large groups), and its linear-type archipelagos.

ocean current. A distinct flow of water in the ocean. Almost all the water in the ocean is in a constant state of movement, true stagnation occurring only at the bottom of certain deep basins hemmed in by rock sills. Generally, currents in the oceans occur at fairly low speeds, especially within the deep water masses, but there are also well-defined currents (like part of the Gulf Stream) that may flow as rapidly and strongly as some of the largest rivers on land. Neglecting those currents that flow within the breaker zone, ocean currents are due to three particular sets of circumstances: wind stresses acting on the sea surface, tidal motion, and differences in the density of seawater. The density differences arise because of differential heating and cooling, differential salinity (perhaps because of evaporation, ice

melting, river dishcarge, and so on), and changes in turbidity levels. The wind-induced ocean currents may be directly or indirectly driven.

ocean floor. The whole of the seabed seaward of lowest low-water mark, including the continental shelf, slope, and deep-sea floor. It is characterized by diverse relief forms, some of them of immense size. Significant tracts of the deep-sea floor are remarkably flat and smooth. In spite of considerable depths of water in the *abyssal zone, most of the ocean floor experiences some current action. In global terms, the ocean floor is vast: some 360 million sq. km out of a total of some 510 million sq. km for the earth's surface as a whole. Ocean floor occupies about 61% of the N hemisphere and 81% of the S hemisphere. In general, the ocean floor arches upwards rather than downwards. Truly concave basins are rare.

oceanic crust. That part of the earth above the Mohorovicic discontinuity forming the floor of the ocean basins. It is usually up to 15 km thick and consists of three layers: layer one composed of young and poorly consolidated sediments, layer two composed of basalt pillow lavas and dolerite dykes, and layer three composed of dolerite dykes and gabbro. The ocean crust is generated at the constructive plate margins and destroyed at the destructive plate margins. *See also* continental crust.

oceanicity. The degree of oceanic influence on the climate of an area. This is indicated by low annual and diurnal ranges of temperature, and abundant precipitation throughout the year.

oceanite. A basaltic rock containing a high proportion of olivine phenocrysts. *Compare* ankaramite.

oceanography. The study of the oceans, with particular reference to their overall form, the nature of the sea floor and associated sediments, the characteristics of the ocean waters, and the types of fauna and flora living within the oceans.

This field has widened its scope to embrace aspects of human intervention in the ocean environment, since the oceans have assumed such importance economically and strategically. It is a multidisciplinary subject, embracing physics, mathematics, biology, and others.

ocean waves. Ocean waves of some kind are operating all the time, some affecting the surface of the sea, others the internal water masses. Some waves are generated by wind blowing over the sea's surface, often travelling far beyond the generation area as *swell. Large waves with long periods may spread from storm centres and travel thousands of miles before affecting distant coasts. Some waves or wave energy may be reflected, or generated, in a seaward direction, as with *surf beats or the occasional catastrophic *landslide surges. *Tsunami waves are relatively rare and result from submarine earthquakes or explosive submarine volcanic eruptions. Like landslide surges and very big storm waves, they may cause damage and loss of life along coasts. Oceans also experience tidal waves: these waves operate as standing oscillations that are modified by the earth's rotation and move around nodal centres known as amphidromic points (see amphidromic system). Within the water masses of the oceans, there occur interfacial waves known as *internal waves. See also wave.

ocellar. Denoting a texture of some volcanic rocks in which *phenocrysts are enveloped by small radially or tangentially arranged crystals of another mineral.

ocelli. Small spherical or droplet-like bodies found in certain alkaline igneous rocks. Ocelli contain mineral assemblages supposed to have crystallized from a liquid that was immiscible with the host magma.

offlap. The disposition of sediments laid down as a sea regresses, the progressively younger sediments being deposited seaward of the shore line that marked the maximum extent of the former marine transgression. In this way instead of older rocks being covered by younger deposits they are exposed. The beds that mark the maximum extent of the former transgression have the largest areal development. See also overlap.

offset. See chaining.

offshore bar. A *bar that is partially or completely submerged beyond the *breaker zone. Considerable littoral transport of sediment, especially sand, may occur along the crest of nearshore bars and offshore bars that lie in fairly shallow water because of wave and tidal action. See also barrier beach.

offshore zone. The zone extending from the outer limit of the *breaker zone to the depth at which waves cease to influence the seabed. But since experimental evidence suggests that such wave influence occurs almost everywhere over continental shelves (with the exception, possibly, of shelves that have been abnormally deepened), the offshore zone effectively extends out to the *shelf-edge zone.

ogive. A cumulative frequency curve. It constitutes one of the most effective ways of representing a frequency series, as uneven class intervals do not distort the curve and interpolation is easy. Calculation and plotting are also easy. The accumulated values for each class interval are determined as a percentage of the grand total, or simply plotted as frequency against the element concerned.

Old Red Sandstone. A succession of conglomerates, red shales, and sandstones forming the continental facies of the *Devonian System in Britain. These rocks contain abundant remains of ostracoderm and gnathostome (jawed) fish.

Oligocene. The epoch of the *Tertiary Period that follows the *Eocene and precedes the *Miocene. It began about

36 million years ago and lasted for some 13.5 million years. Oligocene rocks outcrop in S England and most are of brackish or freshwater facies. Many mammalian groups common in the Eocene became extinct but others continued to flourish, including camels, rhinoceroses, and the first pigs. The main phase of Alpine folding began at the end of the Oligocene.

oligoclase. A sodic plagioclase *feldspar.

olivines. A group of orthorhombic rock-forming minerals consisting of (SiO_4) tetrahedra linked by divalent metal cations. The general formula is R_2SiO_4, where R = Mg, Fe^{2+}, Mn, or Ca (in part). A complete gradation in chemical and physical properties exists between the two end-members, *forsterite* (Mg_2SiO_4) and *fayalite* (Fe_2SiO_4).
Olivines are green, brown-green, and yellow-green and show little or no cleavage but possess a chonchoidal fracture. Peridot is a pale green gem variety. Magnesium-rich olivine is common in basic and ultrabasic rocks whereas fayalite occurs in acid igneous rocks. Forsterite and monticellite $(CaMgSiO_4)$ are found in metamorphosed limestones.

omphacite. *See* pyroxene.

onion weathering. Small-scale expansive *exfoliation in which the splitting away of layers of rock resembles that of onion skins.

onlap. *See* overlap.

oolite. An allochemical *limestone formed predominantly from *ooliths.* These are more or less spherical bodies formed by the precipitation of carbonate in concentric layers around a nucleus. They are usually small, up to about 2 mm in diameter. Ooliths larger than this are often known as *pisoliths.* Oolites are common in the *Jurassic system of Britain. Some noncalcareous oolites are known, such as those formed from iron minerals.

ooze. *See* pelagic ooze.

opal. A hydrous cryptocrystalline variety of silica. *See* silica minerals.

open fold. A fold in which the interlimb angle is in excess of 70°. See diagram at *fold.*

ophiolite. The sequential association of ultramafic rocks, gabbros, dolerite dykes, pillow lavas, and cherts, occurring within eugeosynclinal environments. Ophiolites are thought to represent slices of the basaltic ocean crust that have been tectonically emplaced onto continental margins. *See also* spilites, Steinmann trinity.

ophitic. Denoting a texture of common occurrence in basalts and dolerites in which large plates of clinopyroxene completely envelop earlier-formed euhedral plagioclase plates. The term *subophitic* may be used when the pyroxenes only partially enclose the plagioclases. Ophitic texture is a specific example of *poikilitic texture.

orbicular. Denoting certain plutonic rocks that contain large ovoid bodies made up of concentric shells of alternately light and dark minerals. The orbs are the result of rhythmic crystallization around *xenoliths, which have acted as nuclei. *Compare* rapakivi structure.

orbital motion. Waves on the sea's surface experience orbital motion of the water particles beneath each wave; concurrently, the wave form is propagated along the sea's surface, in the direction of wave advance, at speeds that are dependent on the length of the waves. Beneath the waves, the orbital motion of water particles takes place at much lesser speeds. The orbits of the water particles are nearly circular and have their greatest diameter just below the sea's surface, but the diameters decrease rapidly with increasing depth. The orbital paths are referred to as open, because the circular orbits are not completely closed loops; with each wave period, a water particle moves slightly in the direction of wave propagation. On entering shallow water orbital motion becomes distorted, the orbital paths becoming increasingly elliptic as waves run into increasingly shallow water. Beneath a given shallow water wave, the long diameter of the ellipses decreases with increasing depth, while at the bed the water particles no longer orbit but merely oscillate to and fro along a straight line, though again with a slight asymmetry shorewards. See also mass transport currents.

order. A group in the taxonomic classification of organisms. Several related orders constitute a *class, and an order itself is composed of one or more *families. For example, the Primates and Carnivora are two orders of the class Mammalia. See taxonomy.

Ordnance Datum. See datum.

Ordovician. The period in the *Palaeozoic Era that follows the *Cambrian and precedes the *Silurian. It began about 515 million years ago and lasted for some 70 million years. The Lower Palaeozoic marine *transgression continued in Britain; a deep-water facies of shales and mudstones and a facies of sandstones and shallow-water rocks can be recognized. In the former, graptolites are an abundant and rapidly evolving group and are used to divide the system into Upper and Lower Ordovician. The Lower Ordovician consists of the Arenig, Llanvirn, and Llandeilo series; the Upper Ordovician consists of the Caradoc and Ashgill series. There is evidence of extensive volcanic activity during the period. Common fossils include brachiopods (articulate forms were dominant), trilobites, and gastropods. The first corals, echinoids, crinoids, and Bryozoa appeared and the straight-shelled nautiloids reached their peak. The first fossils of ostracoderm vertebrates are found in Ordovician rocks.

organic acids (in soil science). When organic matter is attacked by the soil microorganisms certain simple products such as oxalic acid, $(COOH)_2.2H_2O$, acetic acid, CH_3COOH, and lactic acid, $CH_3CH(OH)COOH$, are released. These acids greatly increase the power of leaching in soils. See podzolization.

organic horizons. The L, F, and H layers in a soil *profile, which lie above the mineral soil. However, humified organic matter is also usually found intermixed with the mineral matter in the A horizon and may also be present lower down the soil profile in the B horizon.

organic matter (in soil science). Organic matter rarely forms more than 5% by weight of the soil yet it is highly significant in promoting a productive soil as it improves the structure and provides a source of important mineral nutrients. It forms as a result of the incorporation of plant and animal remains in the soil and their breakdown by the microorganisms present. Some of this material is broken down completely into soluble substances but the more resistant tends to remain, and with the new resynthesized compounds this forms the soil *humus.

organic reef. See reef.

organic soils (bog soils). Soils with an accumulation of peat more than about 70 cm in depth. They form in water-saturated environments where the decomposition is slow. In upland regions with high rainfall, rapid leaching of bases results in the formation of an acid peat called blanket bog. Similar acid soils, called raised bogs, may occur in lowland sites where rainfall is sufficient. The most characteristic lowland organic soil, however, is fen peat, which is neutral to alkaline in reaction as a result of saturation by base-rich waters. When this black peat is drained rich agricultural soils are formed.

organic weathering. The breakdown and decomposition of rocks due to plants and animals. Both mechanical and chemical breakdown are involved. Burrowing animals and plant roots can physically separate rock particles and can mix or transfer material elsewhere. Through the respiration of vegetation, the carbon dioxide content of the soil may be substantially increased, having a marked effect on weathering, whilst soil bacteria can also be very important, especially in reducing conditions. Lichens can exist on bare rock surfaces and are frequently responsible for the initial decomposition of rocks, by the removal of nutrients. Larger plants can affect the surface atmosphere through shading whilst even in areas of only shallow soils, weathering has been seen surrounding roots at great depths, owing to their localized ability to alter the constituent minerals chemically.

Ornithischia. An order of dinosaurs characterized by a pelvis similar to that of birds, although they were not bird ancestors nor very closely related to them. They were all herbivorous and had correspondingly modified dentitions; some ornithischians had a horny beak. For avoiding saurischian predators some developed rapid bipedal locomotion, while the more slow and bulky forms evolved horns and other types of armour. Ornithischians became extinct at the end of the Cretaceous period. *Compare* Saurischia.

orocline. An orogenic belt that has a marked change in trend. This is thought to have resulted from horizontal forces operating within the crust.

orogenesis. The process by which mountains are formed, i.e. the deformational processes such as thrusting, folding, and faulting, which result from the collision of two continents. The sediments between these continents are then strongly deformed, causing them to spill out onto the older stable continents and be compressed into long linear mountain chains. There is frequently associated igneous activity. *Compare* epeirogenesis.

orogenic belt. *See* mobile belt.

orogeny. A mountain-building period. Major orogenic phases that have affected the British Isles since the Precambrian are the Caledonian, Variscan, and Alpine orogenies.

orographic clouds. Clouds that owe their formation to rising air resulting from airflow over mountains. As air is forced to rise over high ground there will always be some upward component in the wind field. If the air is already moist, or vertical motion extensive, then the condensation level may be reached and orographic cloud formed. If there are stable layers within the air stream, *lee-wave clouds may be seen. These are the most easily recognizable type of orographic clouds.

orographic rainfall. Rainfall resulting from the vertical motion of an air stream, caused by the presence of uplands. However, it is fairly rare for orographic rain to fall without either convective or cyclonic processes also acting. The orographic component is normally weak and merely acts as an enhancement to the other two mechanisms.

orthite (allanite). *See* epidote.

orthoclase. A potassic alkali *feldspar.

orthoferrosilite. *See* pyroxene.

orthogeosyncline. A geosyncline that is associated with both continental and oceanic environments, and contains both volcanic and nonvolcanic areas in association with the accumulating sediments.

orthogonal (wave ray). A line that is constructed perpendicular to a series of wave crests. This is usually done on the basis of a wave refraction diagram, which shows a series of wave crests in the vicinity of the coast or a harbour. In theory, the wave energy between any two orthogonals remains roughly the same as they are traced shorewards into decreasing depths. For this reason, where orthogonals bunch together at the coast, or conversely when they tend to spread out, one can delimit zones of wave energy concentration (zones of *convergence) and zones of energy dissipation (zones of *divergence) respectively.

orthomagmatic. Denoting the stage in the crystallization of a magma during which the early-formed primary minerals having high crystallization temperatures are formed. The orthomagmatic stage is followed by periods of pegmatitic, pneumatolytic, and hydrothermal crystallization.

orthomorphic (conformal) projection. Any map projection on which the shape of an area of the map is the same as the corresponding area of the earth's surface.

orthopyroxene. See pyroxene.

orthoquartzite. See quartzarenite.

orthorhombic. See crystal system.

orthotectonics (alpinotype tectonics). Mountain belt structures having the characteristics of the Alps, i.e. their deep-seated areas have deformed plastically, with associated igneous activity and metamorphism, whilst their shallower regions have deformed brittly and are characterized by faults, thrusts, and several small folds.

oscillation (in meteorology). Any cyclic variation of a climatic element above and below its mean value or position. Its most frequent use is as the Southern oscillation where an oscillation with a period of 2.33 years was found in the seasonal distribution of pressure and to a lesser extent temperature and rainfall over the oceanic areas of tropical latitudes.

oscillatory current. The type of current that waves induce at the seabed arising from the *orbital motion of the water particles beneath waves. The larger the waves, the deeper one might expect such currents to operate. As waves, especially long waves, enter shallow water, the orbital motion of the water particles tends to be elliptic, while at the seabed the particles oscillate to and fro about a mean position along a straight line. This gives rise to an oscillatory current at the bed. Beneath the wave crest there occurs a short sharp acceleration shorewards, while beneath the flattish trough of the wave, there is a more protracted seaward movement of water. Such an oscillating type of flow beneath waves often has a profound influence on the movement of bed materials (though far less an influence on materials moving continually in suspension), and may cause pebbles to move rapidly shorewards.

oscillatory wave. A wave, often of the progressive oscillatory type, in which only the wave form on the sea's surface advances in the direction of wave propagation, while the water particles beneath the wave orbit in almost closed loops. Whereas the wave form may be propagated across the sea's surface quite rapidly, at a speed that is largely dependent on the length of the wave, the gradual shift of the water particles in the direction of wave travel may be quite slow.

Osteichthyes. The class constituting the bony fish. It includes the *Actinopterygii (teleosts and more primitive ray-finned fish) as well as the fleshy-finned *Crossopterygii. Some early groups had a body armour of closely fitting scales of complex construction; these were reduced and simplified in later forms. The class is characterized by the development of some kind of lung, which may be converted into a swim bladder for maintaining hydrostatic equilibrium in advanced forms. Fossil fish first appeared in the late Silurian, since when the class has continued to expand in diversity and abundance. Compare Chondrichthyes.

Ostracoda. A group of aquatic arthropod animals that belong to the class *Crustacea. The body is completely enclosed within two calcareous valves forming a carapace. Unlike the shells of the *Bivalvia, these have no growth lines; they are periodically completely replaced as the animal increases in size.

They are usually very small, less than 1 mm in length, but some species reach up to 20 mm. Varied ornamentation of the shells is of use in taxonomy. Ostracods range from the Cambrian Period to the Recent and because of their small size, distinctive forms, and widespread distribution, they are valuable in the calibration and correlation of the rocks in which they occur, especially in the cores from boreholes.

Ostracodermi. Fossil jawless fish (see Agnatha), having an outer protective covering of bony plates and scales. Usually not more than one foot long, they were common inhabitants of Silurian and Devonian ponds and rivers and a few fossil fragments are known from the Ordovician. This group probably gave rise to the jawed fishes.

outcrop. The area on the earth's surface where a particular rock type or body is present. This includes both exposed areas and others covered by drift.

outer core. The layer of the earth between 2900 km and 5000 km beneath its surface. It is bounded at 2900 km by a seismic discontinuity that separates it from the overlying mantle. On geophysical evidence it is thought to have a composition of iron alloy and nickel and to behave essentially as a liquid, unlike the *inner core, which is solid.

outlier. An area of exposed younger sediments completely surrounded by older rocks, usually as a result of folding, faulting, and erosion. *Compare* inlier.

outwash plain (sandur). A widespread area of fluvioglacial deposits produced by deposition from meltwater streams emerging from the margins of an ice mass. The material decreases in size with distance from the ice and is frequently well bedded. Some unstratified till may be found amongst the gravels, indicating a period of readvance of the ice margin. These outwash plains may exhibit irregular surfaces, resulting from the presence of kettle holes, and are frequently found in association with other fluvioglacial landforms, such as *kames, *kame terraces, and *eskers.

overland flow (wash, rain wash, sheet erosion). The movement of water as a shallow unchannelled sheet over the soil surface. Overland flow, which is intermediate between flow of water through the soil and surface channelled flow, occurs once the infiltration capacity, or ability to hold and store water, of the soil is exceeded. Water then collects in depressions on the surface and begins to flow as a broad shallow layer, often giving a glistening sheen to the surface. The flow is not even but turbulent, moving as a series of waves, although *laminar flow in sheets 8 cm deep has been recorded. Speeds and depth of flow are limited but soil particles can be entrained and moved. The thickness of the sheet determines the size of material moved. Overland flow is most devastating on bare soils of limited permeability, especially on long steep slopes. The depth of flow increases downslope from nil at the hill crest until at the downslope end the sheet becomes channelled into rills and ceases to exist. It tends to erode a hydraulic concave curve, and as such is important in *pediment evolution. Most authorities attribute to it a major capacity to shape the landscape.

overlap (onlap). The disposition of beds lying above an unconformity, where they were deposited by a transgressing sea. Each successively younger bed extends further onto the previous land surface than its predecessor. *See also* offlap.

oversaturated rocks. Igneous rocks that contain free quartz. Examples include granites and rhyolites. *See* silica saturation.

overstep. The disposition of strata associated with an unconformity where younger transgressive marine beds encroach onto progressively older beds of the underlying sequence.

Fig. 1: Pattern of erosion and deposition in a meandering reach

Fig. 2: As a result of the pattern of erosion and deposition, meander migrates as shown

Fig. 3: In a storm, the narrow neck is breached leaving the oxbow

Oxbow lake formation

oxbow lake (cutoff). A crescent-shaped lake that was formerly part of a river meander. Oxbow lakes are typical features of meandering rivers, and result from the river's abilty to erode laterally being concentrated on the outsides of meander bends. Once created the oxbow rapidly silts up.

An alternative origin of cutoffs has been suggested by laboratory experiments, which showed that cutoffs develop when stream gradient falls below a critical limit, since the stream needs a minimum gradient to flow, and meanders effectively decrease gradient by increasing length over a given fall. If the meanders develop to such an extent that they rob the stream of its minimum necessary gradient, cutting off that meander will restore the gradient needed. *See also* meander.

oxidation. The chemical weathering process involving the reaction between rocks and atmospheric oxygen, the oxygen usually being dissolved in water. The products of oxidation are oxides and hydroxides, iron being the mineral most frequently affected and its oxidation products give many weathered rocks their reddish or yellowish colour. A certain amount of oxidation may also result from bacteriological activity. *Compare* reduction.

oxisol. One of the ten soil orders of the *Seventh Approximation classification characterized by the presence of free iron and aluminium oxides (Fe_2O_3 and Al_2O_3) and possibly other oxides of titanium and chromium, as well as a high proportion of simple clays (especially kaolin) and some quartz. This includes the currently developing ferrallitic soils and the relic laterites of tropical areas. Oxisols are highly weathered and leached, generally lacking in fertility, and in the case of the relic laterites may well include deposits of a more geological than pedological origin.

oxygen. One of the main gases of the atmosphere (about 20% by volume). From the meteorological point of view, oxygen is most important as an absorber of radiation in the ultraviolet wavelengths (0.13 - 0.17 μm). It dissociates at high levels of the atmosphere into monatomic oxygen (O), which combines with oxygen molecules (O_2) to give ozone (O_3).

oyster reef. A *reef largely formed from the consolidation of dead oysters. The maximum development of oysters tends to be in the brackish water areas skirting coasts, as within certain estuaries, or in bays with fairly narrow inlets. A reasonable supply of fresh water from rivers, to reduce salinity levels, is also an important factor. On the other hand, oysters do also occur in the open sea, though in lesser numbers. The reefs they give rise to are common to many lagoonal areas in the humid zone. The reefs may attain a significant thickness, for instance, commonly 10 metres or more along parts of the coast of Texas.

ozone. Triatomic oxygen (O_3), which forms in the upper atmosphere especially at about 20–25 km level (sometimes called the *ozonosphere*). It results from the dissociation of molecular oxygen into single atoms of oxygen, which then combine with other oxygen molecules to give ozone. Below this level of formation, it gradually disperses towards the ground surface, but being a chemically active gas it is quickly reduced to oxygen. Ozone absorbs strongly in the 0.23–0.32 μm waveband, preventing potentially damaging ultraviolet radiation from reaching the ground surface. It also absorbs in other wavelengths, but these are of less importance.

The distribution of ozone would be expected to correspond to its rate of production under conditions of prolonged exposure to ultraviolet radiation. However, it seems to reflect vertical and horizontal movements in the stratosphere rather better. High latitudes have the maximum levels of ozone in spring with a minimum in autumn.

P

pahoehoe. A lava having a surface that resembles coils of twisted rope. *Compare* aa, block lava.

palaeobotany. The branch of *palaeontology that deals with the nature and evolution of plants through geological time, as shown by fossil remains.

Palaeocene. The first epoch of geological time in the Tertiary. Beginning about 65 million years ago and lasting for 11.5 million years, it follows the *Cretaceous Period and is succeeded by the *Eocene Epoch. Occasionally the time represented by this epoch is included within the Eocene. Palaeocene rocks occur in S Britain and are of both marine and nonmarine facies. Following the extinction of the large reptiles at the end of the Cretaceous, mammals became abundant and diversified into a variety of primitive and now mainly extinct groups. Insectivores

were common and by the end of the epoch primates and rodents had evolved.

palaeoclimatology. The study of the climates of earlier geological periods. The evidence for the former climate is obtained from sediments and fossils. Complications arise from the fact that the continents have been changing their latitudinal positions through time, so the time period and location of deposition have to be determined before atmospheric circulations can be deduced.

palaeoecology. The study of the ecology of fossil organisms, i.e. the relationships of organisms in past geological ages with their nonliving environment and with other animals and plants. Palaeoecology involves the investigation of the rocks in which the organisms are found to determine palaeoenvironmental information and details of *taphonomy. *Trace fossils often provide information regarding the behaviour of an animal.

Palaeogene. The lower part of the *Tertiary Period, comprising the *Palaeocene, *Eocene, and *Oligocene Epochs. It lasted for about 42.5 million years from approximately 65 to 22.5 million years ago, when it was followed by the *Miocene Epoch of the *Neogene. Some authorities suggest that the Palaeocene should be considered as a period, with the Tertiary as a sub-era.

palaeomagnetic correlation. The correlation of the residual magnetism in rocks. The direction of polarization of the magnetic field of the earth changes periodically. It is possible to measure the residual magnetization of suitable rocks and to discover the direction of polarity at the time of their formation. By this means a sequence can be established showing normal and reversed periods in the earth's magnetic field. It may be calibrated by some means, such as radiometric dating (*see* calibration), to provide a valuable tool for the *correlation of stratigraphic sequences of rock. *See also* magnetic division, magnetic interval.

palaeontology. The study of all aspects of ancient organisms, including their *taxonomy, anatomy, ecology, and *evolution. The evidence for this comes from *fossils preserved in rocks, which are either the remains of the organisms themselves or *trace fossils. Much palaeontological work is applied to the elucidation of the stratigraphical relationships between bodies of rock by means of *biostratigraphy. The branch of the subject that deals with microscopic organisms is known as *micropalaeontology*; fossils of such organisms are *microfossils.

Palaeozoic. The first era into which *Phanerozoic time is divided. It follows the *Precambrian and consists of the following periods: the *Cambrian, *Ordovician, *Silurian, *Devonian, *Carboniferous, and *Permian. Systems of the first three periods constitute the Lower Palaeozoic, and the second three the Upper Palaeozoic. It lasted for about 350 million years from 590 to 240 million years ago, when it was followed by the *Mesozoic Era. The fauna of the Paleozoic is characterized by an abundance of invertebrate types, many of which, such as the rugose corals (*see* Anthozoa) trilobites, graptolites, and productid brachiopods, became extinct at the end of the era. In the course of the Palaeozoic fish evolved and the first amphibians appeared, flourished, and declined. Two episodes of major orogenic activity occurred, giving rise to mountain ranges and associated tectonic activity. The *Caledonian was the earliest, occurring at the end of the *Silurian and the beginning of the *Devonian; the *Variscan orogeny took place towards the end of the era. *See also* chronostratigraphy (for table of the major divisions of geological time).

palaeozoology. The branch of *palaeontology concerned with the nature and evolution of animals through geological time by the investigation of their fossil remains.

palagonite. Hydrated basaltic glass, usually yellow or orange, formed when basalts are erupted beneath water or ice. Palagonite breccias or tuffs produced by the fragmentation of the glassy material are termed *hyaloclastic rocks*.

palynology. The study of fossil spores, especially *pollen. As spores are usually adapted to resist destruction and to be dispersed over large distances, they are valuable for use in the *correlation of the rocks in which they occur. They are also important environmental indicators and have been used in monitoring climatic change during the Quaternary Period. Palynology forms part of micropalaeontology.

Pangaea. A hypothetical super-continent that is thought to have existed in the very distant geological past. This single continent was composed of all the present-day continents, which have since been derived from it as a result of repeated episodes of *sea-floor spreading. This super-continent is thought to have fragmented initially into two segments, Laurasia to the north and Gondwanaland to the south.

paragonite. *See* micas.

parallel. A line of latitude, running parallel to the equator round the earth through any given point. The plane of each parallel is at right angles to the earth's axis. Parallels range in length from a point at each pole to the circumference of the earth at the equator, which is the only parallel that is a *great circle. They are uniformly spaced along the meridians.

parallel drainage. A type of drainage pattern that develops where there is strong structural control in one direction, streams being strictly guided in that direction. A uniform regional slope, rigid alternation of hard and soft lithologies, or parallel folds will produce parallel streams; recently glaciated areas may also have parallel drainage nets if the surface is covered in fluted ground moraine or drumlin fields.

parallel evolution. The *convergent evolution of closely related and anatomically similar organisms, which undergo nearly identical evolutionary changes through time.

parallel retreat. As contrasted with *slope decline, parallel retreat involves a slope eating into a rock but maintaining its original angle as it does so, hence remaining parallel in new positions to its previous positions. W. Penck and later L. King used this principle as the basis for their scheme of the *cycle of erosion. As a method of *slope evolution it is strongly related to geomorphic processes, in that a slope will only remain parallel if the debris being eroded in its retreat is removed at an equal rate from its base. If the debris accumulates, the slope declines.
The idea was first formulated in relation to the tropical scheme, with the original work being in Africa; since then, Dury claims to have identified it as a viable process in the humid temperate lands, and it can be seen in areas of *basal sapping, e.g. active sea cliffs. S. Schumm has suggested it operates preferentially on certain lithologies through their control on process: on sandstones, dominated by overland flow, parallel retreat operates, whilst on clays, dominated by creep, the slope declines.
It seems that a number of situations can favour parallel retreat, not merely certain climates; lithology and processes, in various permutations, are also vital.

parameterization (in numerical weather prediction). The inclusion of the effects of meteorological systems that are smaller than the grid on which the model is based. It involves approximating the statistical effects of these small-scale processes in terms of the large-scale factors.

parasitic cone. A small cone on the flank of a major volcanic cone. These cones develop frequently and indicate that the magma trying to reach the surface has found an easier route than via the main vent. They are usually several tens of metres beneath the main vent.

parataxitic. See eutaxitic.

paratectonics. The tectonics of stable areas, such as old fold belts and cratons.

paraunconformity. See disconformity.

parautochthonous. Denoting rock bodies that are midway between *allochthonous and *autochthonous, i.e. that have been displaced only short distances.

parent material. The material from which the soils forms, which may not be the same as the underlying bedrock. Before the importance of climate was recognized, parent material was thought to be the dominant soil-forming factor. Certain features of the parent material, such as texture, mineral composition, and porosity, have a considerable influence on the soil-forming processes, e.g. a limestone soil rich in calcium will delay the process of acidification in a humid climate. Parent material is likely to have a greater influence in temperate regions where soils have been forming for a relatively short time, e.g. in Scotland brown earths have been recorded on basic igneous rocks and podzols on acid igneous rocks.

parhelion. See mock sun.

partial pressure. In a mixture of gases, such as the atmosphere, the partial pressure of one constituent is the pressure it would exert on its own whilst occupying the same volume as the whole mixture. The integration of all the individual partial pressures of the components is equal to the pressure of the whole mixture.

particle size. The effective diameter of a particle. Particle size analysis is the technique of determining the proportion of the different particle sizes present (each particle size is termed a *separate*) in a sample. There are several classifications in use; the main classes in one of them are shown in the diagram. There are three main techniques of analyzing particle size: by sieving in a stack of

British Standards Classification of Particle Sizes

class	size range (mm)
boulder	>200
cobble	60–200
gravel	2–60
coarse sand	0·6–2
medium sand	0·2–0·6
fine sand	0·06–0·2
silt	0·002–0·06
clay	<0·002

sieves of decreasing mesh size, by allowing particles to settle in a tube of water, the rate of settling being proportional to size, and by micrometric methods. It is a technique commonly used in soil science and geomorphology, e.g. to describe texture classes in soil, or to infer the origin of a sedimentary deposit in geomorphology.

patina. A film or skin on the surface of a boulder, produced by chemical weathering. Patinas are distinctive in colour and physical properties, their thicknesses often reflecting age.

patterned ground. A distinctive geomorphological feature mostly found in periglacial areas. Where the ground surface is flat, *stone polygons or circles may develop, either in groups or in isolation, which may grade into *stone stripes even on very gentle slopes.
In nonperiglacial climatic areas the most likely cause of patterning is cracking due to heat shrinkage (see desiccation cracks).

peat. A mass of fibrous plant debris, which is only partly decomposed, and is often dark brown in colour. This is a result of wet anaerobic conditions, which retard microorganism activity. Certain soils such as peaty gleys and peaty gleyed podzols have peat as one of their main horizons; other soils may have a thicker accumulation of peat. (See organic soils).

Peaty gley podzol

peaty gley podzol A hydromorphic variant of *podzol, characterized by a blue-grey waterlogged area above the impermeable iron pan, capped by a thick peat horizon. Above and below the gleyed area the colour is orange-brown owing to the free drainage and oxidation, as contrasted with the reducing conditions in the gleyed area. They are most probably polygenetic, being originally *brown earths that became degraded to podzols with forest clearance, and subsequently became gleyed when the iron pan developed to the point where it became impermeable. Once gleying had set in, microbiological activity was inhibited and so litter was not broken down but accumulated as peat. It is characteristic of many gently sloping uplands, e.g. Dartmoor, where it occupies ground above brown earth soils that have not been degraded to podzols.

ped. An aggregate of soil particles, forming a crumb of soil.

pedalfer. A leached soil in which iron and aluminium increase relative to silica during *pedogenesis. Pedalfers are soils of humid climates, including *podzols, *brown forest soils, *laterites, and *prairie soils.

pediments. Surfaces of low relief that slope away from residual uplands at angles of between 9° and 0.5° or less, being bounded on their upslope ends by a sharp break of slope, the *piedmont angle, at the point where they meet rock residuals. Such features are said to be typical of arid and semiarid regions, although some would attribute this type of surface with a much wider occurrence.
Pediments have a concave long profile, with the angle of slope decreasing away from the piedmont angle. They are cut in bedrock, often with a capping of gravel or alluvium, and display great regularity of form over wide areas. Pediments have been identified at various scales, ranging from valley-side types to the continental-scale forms that L. King has identified in Africa.
Pediments evolve by *parallel retreat of the upstanding residuals, leaving a broad area of low relief as they retreat. L. King and W. Penck, who see this as the usual tendency for landscape evolution, therefore see pediments as the end products of denudation.
The processes responsible are not certain, but much discussion has centred on erosion by running water. As the pediments have a concave profile, analogies have been drawn between their evolution and that of the long profiles of rivers: both are hydraulic curves. The form of this water erosion is disputed: some authorities consider that the scarp retreats by headward erosion of streams emerging from the upland, leaving the low-level surface as it retreats; others consider that pediments are due to lateral planation of streams, while a major school of thought has stressed the importance of sheet wash, which has been recorded up to a metre deep on pediments. L. King states that

pediments begin on weak rocks and then extend into harder rocks as the scarp retreats by stream erosion at the base. Several different processes may be responsible, with different emphases in different areas.

pediplain. The coalescence of a number of pediments towards the end of the cycle of erosion produces a pediplain, which is a broad landscape of low relief broken by isolated residual uplands, which meet the pediplain in a sharp *piedmont angle. According to L. King and W. Penck a pediplain is the logical final product of subaerial denudation in an area of *parallel retreat (compared with a *peneplain in areas of *slope decline). Pediments tend to be smooth with gentle concave profiles, broken by few stream lines. It is difficult to be categorical as to whether a surface of low relief constitutes a true pediment, owing to the fact that landscapes have not evolved under constant climates and hence a single cycle, but are *polycyclic in origin.

pedocal. Unleached soil in which lime accumulates during pedogenesis, e.g. *chernozems, *chestnut soils, and *sierozem.

pedogenesis. *See* soil formation.

pedon. A three-dimensional body of soil, including the full *solum and the *parent material, with a circular or hexagonal cross section, ranging in size from 1–10 square meters. Introduced by the *Seventh Approximation method of classification, it replaces the earlier use of the two-dimensional profile as the lowest unit of classification. It includes all the properties formerly noted from the profile, plus notes on interfingering of horizons. Similar contiguous pedons are grouped into *polypedons*, which can then be amalgamated into soil series, and hence mapping of soil is dovetailed into classification.

pegmatites. Very coarse-grained igneous rocks occurring as segregations, veins, and dykes within and emanating from granite bodies. They consist largely of alkali feldspar and quartz, often graphically intergrown, and contain abundant accessory minerals such as micas, tourmaline, topaz, spodumene, beryl, cassiterite, and wolframite. The largest crystals occur in pegmatites, occasionally measuring metres in length, and because of the concentration of rare elements, pegmatites may be of economic importance. Coarse-grained facies of igneous rocks other than granite may be termed pegmatitic. Pegmatites represent a stage in the crystallization of a magma during which a residual silicate melt and an aqueous gas phase coexist over the temperature range 500–700°C. The growth of large crystals may be ascribed to conditions of slow crystallization, rapid diffusion, and low viscosity due to the high concentration of volatiles. *See also* aplites.

pelagic. 1. Denoting the environment of the open ocean. A classification of ocean sediments, based on distance from the coast, might include beach, shelf, hemipelagic, and pelagic sediments. The latter have been precipitated from the open ocean or have accumulated from the organic remains of planktonic marine animals. The main types of pelagic sediment are the *pelagic oozes and *red clay. The hemipelagic-abyssal environment is taken to lie within several hundred kilometres of the coast, at depths of over 1000 m. The pelagic-abyssal environment also occurs in depths greater than 1000 m but is further from the coast. Similar sediments occur in the hemipelagic environment but in this case they are often admixed with land-derived material.
2. Denoting communities of marine organisms (free-swimming nekton and floating plankton) that survive within the ocean waters quite independent of shore or seabed environments. *Compare* benthos.

pelagic ooze. Organic deposits made up of shells and other hard parts of marine organisms, which cover large tracts of

the deep-sea floor. The nature of the skeletons of the various organisms determines the kind of deposit ultimately formed, the deposits being named after the most prominent organisms present. They include the calcareous *globigerina and *pteropod oozes, and the siliceous *radiolarian and *diatom oozes. Nearly all the oozes are soft and are easily disturbed by crawling or burrowing organisms and deep-sea currents, a fact confirmed by deep-sea photographs. The radiolarian and pteropod oozes occupy very limited areas of deep-sea floor; diatom ooze, a cold-water deposit, occupies some 9% of the total ocean floor, while globigerina ooze, the most widespread of the oozes, globally occupies some 130 million square kilometres.

Pelecypoda. *See* Bivalvia.

Pele's hair, Pele's tears. *See* pyroclastic rocks.

pelite. A metamorphosed *argillaceous rock. *Compare* psammite, psephitic rock.

pellet. An *allochem that is well rounded but has no internal structure. Pellets may be produced by algae or they may be the faeces of invertebrates.

pendant. *See* roof pendant.

penecontemporaneous. Designating geological events that appear to have occurred at almost the same time. For example, the deposition and erosion of a bed of sediment are described as penecontemporaneous if the bed underwent erosion during, or just after, its deposition.

peneplain. An extensive area of low relief dominated by broad floodplains and gentle interfluves, with isolated residuals (monadnocks) left upstanding in areas of resistant rocks.
According to W. M. Davis's original *cycle of erosion scheme, the peneplain is the end product of subaerial denudation. His scheme being formulated mostly in the humid temperate climate

of New England, he regarded this as the normal cycle, with the *pediment and *inselberg landscapes of arid and semiarid areas being deviations due to climatic controls.

There are no large peneplains on the earth, as no landscape has evolved under just one cycle. All have polycyclic origins, interrupted by base level movements and process variations.

The peneplain concept is developed from the theory that .slopes evolve by decline, such that as the cycle nears its end the remaining interfluves gradually become inconspicuous as weathering and rill wash continue to erode them, with the slope foot zones in the valleys being areas of little activity, mostly accretional in nature. Relative relief diminishes therefore leaving an almost flat plain. This contrasts with the ideas of King and Penck, who stated that slopes evolve by *parallel retreat, leaving broad *pediplains and small upstanding residuals as the final products.

Pennsylvanian. A period within the American classification of geological time that follows the *Mississippian, and precedes the Permian. It began about 325 million years ago and lasted for about 45 million years. The Pennsylvanian System corresponds approximately to the Upper *Carboniferous elsewhere.

pentad. A period of five successive days. It is often used in climatological work as the period divides exactly into the number of days in a year, leap years excepted.

percentile. The percentage division of a ranked data series. For example, the upper five percentile indicates the value that is exceeded by five percent of the data, and the lower five percentile is the value above which ninety-five percent of the values occur.

perfect elasticity. The property of a material that can regain its original form after an applied force has been removed.

perfect plasticity. The property of a material that retains a new form after an applied force is removed.

periclase. A pale-coloured cubic mineral of composition MgO, found in metamorphosed dolomites and limestones.

pericline. A fold structure, such as a basin or dome, in which the beds dip around a central point. In a basin they dip towards the centre (*centroclinal*); in a dome they dip away from the centre (*quaquaversal*).

peridot. A gem variety of *olivine.

peridotite. An ultramafic rock consisting wholly or largely of olivine together with other ferromagnesian minerals and devoid of feldspar.

periglacial. Denoting the climate, physical processes (*see* altiplanation, congelifraction, congeliturbation, freeze-thaw, frost shattering, needle ice, solifluction), and resultant landforms (*see* involution, patterned ground, permafrost, pingo, stone polygons, stone stripes) characteristic of an area bordering an ice sheet. Though ice sheets and glaciers do not occur in the periglacial zone, it is still extremely cold, temperatures remaining below freezing throughout the winter and only rising slightly above during the summer. Periglacial zones are restricted to high latitudes today but were far more widespread during the *Pleistocene glacial periods.

perihelion. The point on the earth's orbit that is nearest the sun. It is also applied to the nearest point to the focus of any orbiting body. *Compare* aphelion.

period. An interval of geological time in the Chronomeric Standard Scale of chronostratigraphic classification (*see* chronostratigraphy). The equivalent Stratomeric Standard term, indicating the body of rock formed during this time, is the *system. Period and system are usually known by the same name; for example, rocks constituting the

Jurassic System were formed during the Jurassic Period. Periods are formed of a number of *epochs grouped together and are themselves compounded to form *eras. Thus the Triassic, Jurassic, and Cretaceous Periods together constitute the Mesozoic Era.

periodicity. An oscillation in a time series of a climatic element that is found to recur at approximately equal time intervals. There have been numerous searches for periodicities in climatic data because they would be of great assistance in long-range forecasting. Unfortunately, whilst periodicities can be found for short time periods, they are rarely persistent.

Perissodactyla. The order consisting of hoofed mammals having an odd number of toes, such as the horse and rhinoceros. Horses evolved from eohippus, a small dog-sized five-toed animal of the Eocene, by increasing in size and, as an adaptation to fast locomotion of the plains, by gradually losing all but one toe on each foot. They acquired high-crowned teeth with a complicated enamel pattern, well suited for chewing a coarse diet of grass. Horses originated in North America and spread to Europe, Asia, and Africa. Other, now extinct, types of perissodactyl lived in the early Tertiary, some reaching a large size, but the order has not achieved the success of the Artiodactyla.

perlitic. Denoting glassy rocks that contain concentric onion-like cracks caused by contraction during cooling.

permafrost. Permanently frozen soil occurring in *periglacial areas, where the winter temperatures rarely exceed freezing point and the soil is frozen to considerable depths. In summer only the top metre or so of soil thaws, that beneath remaining frozen and acting as an impermeable barrier to percolating water. This top layer, which is subject to freezing and thawing, is known as the *active layer* and when melting occurs it rapidly becomes saturated and hence mobile (*see* solifluction). Pedogenic and cryoturbation processes are confined to this layer.

permeability. The ability of a rock to allow pore fluids and gases to pass through it. This is governed by the extent to which the pore spaces within the rock are connected.

Permian. The final period of the *Palaeozoic Era. Beginning about 280 million years ago and lasting some 40 million years, it followed the *Carboniferous and was succeeded by the *Triassic (which marks the start of the Mesozoic Era). The lower part of the Permian System consists of three stages: the Sakmarian, Artinskian, and Kungurian. The Kazanian and Tatarian Stages compose the upper division. Over much of Britain continental conditions prevailed, producing red sandstones difficult to distinguish from similar rocks in the overlying Triassic System (*see* Permo-Triassic). In N England there is a marine facies of limestone and marls with a limited fauna of brachiopods and bivalves, giving way to important evaporite deposits. The period saw the extinction of many animal groups, including the tabulate and rugose corals (*see* Anthozoa), productid brachiopods, trilobites, and blastoids, and a great reduction in others. Reptiles became abundant and pteridophyte plants were superseded by gymnosperms.

Permo-Triassic. The rocks of the *Permian and *Triassic periods in Britain, considered as a single unit. Because continental conditions prevailed for much of the Permian and Triassic Periods in Britain recognition of any boundary between the two systems is difficult.

perovskite. A black or brown cubic mineral of composition $CaTiO_3$ but with some substitution of rare earth elements for calcium and niobium for titanium. It is found as an accessory mineral in some highly undersaturated alkaline igneous rocks and in thermally metamorphosed limestones.

persistence. The continuance of any synoptic event or climatic element beyond its expected duration; it is frequently used for sea-surface temperatures or pressure anomalies. In a time series of climatic data, persistence also indicates a nonrandom tendency for relatively high or low values to occur in succession.

perthite. An intergrowth of orthoclase and albite feldspar in which the albite occurs as patches or lenticles in the orthoclase host. Perthite may be produced by the reaction of potassium feldspar with sodic fluids or by the unmixing of an originally homogeneous alkali feldspar. See exsolution, antiperthite.

perthosite. See syenite.

petrogenesis. The origin or mode of formation of rocks.

petrography. The study of the mineralogical and textural relationships within rocks revealed by observation of thin sections and hand specimens.

petrology. The study of rocks, involving mineralogy, chemistry, petrography, and petrogenesis.

phacolith. A minor concordant igneous intrusion, usually lensoid (the concave surface facing downwards) and present in folded strata.

phanerocrystalline (phaneritic). Denoting an igneous rock in which the constituent crystals can be seen with the naked eye. Compare aphanitic.

Phanerozoic. The geological time that has elapsed since the end of the *Precambrian, comprising the *Palaeozoic, *Mesozoic, and *Cenozoic Eras. It has lasted for some 590 million years, from the *Cambrian Period to the present. The name, meaning visible life, refers to the fact that clearly recognizable fossils are found in rocks laid down during these periods. In Precambrian rocks fossils are extremely rare and often of obscure biological affinities.

phase boundary (boundary line) (in geophysics). The line along which two constituents meet where only two are present. In a more complex system it is the line along which any two liquid phases meet.

phenoclast. A large fragment or clast set in a finer-grained matrix of a sedimentary rock.

phenocrysts. Large generally euhedral crystals contained in many igneous rocks and set in a fine-grained matrix or groundmass. Such rocks are said to be porphyritic. The phenocrysts are the first crystals to form as a melt cools and are minerals having the highest crystallization temperatures.

phillipsite. See zeolites.

phlogopite. See micas.

phonolite. A strongly undersaturated lava, the volcanic equivalent of nepheline-syenite. Phonolites are leucocratic rocks containing a high proportion of sanidine or anorthoclase feldspar and nepheline. Mafic minerals include soda pyriboles and biotite. Most phonolites are porphyritic and possess phenocrysts of feldspar, nepheline, and aegirine-augite. The typically aphanitic groundmass has a flinty appearance and the rocks ring when struck with a hammer and fracture sub-conchoidally.
Trachytes containing accessory nepheline up to 10% are termed phonolitic trachytes. In many phonolites, analcite, sodalite, or leucite accompany nepheline. With an increase in the content of leucite and the disappearance of nepheline, leucite-phonolites pass into leucitophyres.
Tinguaite is an obsolete term for phonolite when it occurs as a medium-grained dyke rock.
Phonolites often occur with strongly undersaturated basic lavas, nephelinites, and in association with nepheline-syenites in oceanic islands and continental rift environments.

phosphorite (phosphate rock). A calcic phosphate deposit that occurs as a marine deposit in roughly nodular form and (according to sampling and photographs) sometimes in quite large concentrations. It is mainly used for the manufacture of fertilizers. It is found on some shelf areas, and over parts of the continental slope. It is currently dredged at a number of offshore sites, for example, off the E coast of the U.S.

photocontour map. A topographic map produced from air photography. All the detail normally apparent on topographic maps is shown, the information being extracted from the air photographs using stereoscopic equipment. This technique is now extensively used for 1:50 000 series mapping of level underdeveloped areas of the world, e.g. Saudi Arabia and Botswana, especially if a fairly rapid result is required.

photogrammetry. The technique of producing maps and charts using stereoscopic equipment to obtain reliable measurements from aerial photography. See photomap.

photomap. A map prepared by adding grid information, names, boundaries, and other map data to a reproduction of photographs or photomosaics. It is a quick method of producing maps, and is often used in areas of little relief, e.g. deserts, or for towns. Contours can be added to these maps for use in areas of relief difference, though this greatly lengthens the time taken to produce the map.

photoperiodism. The response of plants to variations in day length. Some plants flower only when the day length (*photoperiod*) exceeds a specific time; others will flower only in photoperiods of less than ten hours. This is obviously important in the natural distribution of plants.

phreatic activity. The violent reaction that results from hot lava coming into contact with cold water. The surface of the lava chills and forms a glassy skin. The pressure of gasses such as water vapour present within the lava then cause this surface to fracture. Small fragments are hurled into the air, the reaction continuing until a tuff ring has built up, which separates the lava and water.

phreatic eruption. A volcanic eruption caused by escaping steam generated when a lava flow comes into contact with groundwater.

phreatic water. *Groundwater, esp. that occurring below the water table, i.e. where all fissures are filled with groundwater. Phreatic water may supply springs and wells. *Compare* vadose water.

phyllite. A metamorphosed rock resembling slate but of a coarser grain size. The cleavage or schistosity surfaces have a lustrous sheen given off by muscovite and chlorite. Phyllites may possess incipient banding due to the segregation of quartz and feldspar into layers parallel to the cleavage. The characteristics of phyllites are essentially intermediate between those of slates and schists.

phylum (*pl.* **phyla**). A major group in the taxonomic classification of the animal *kingdom. There are about 25 phyla, including the Mollusca, Coelenterata, and Chordata. Each phylum is composed of one or more *classes. The corresponding category in the plant kingdom is known as a *division*. See taxonomy.

physical weathering. See mechanical weathering.

phytoplankton. Small, often microscopic, plants that float passively in the sea or other bodies of water (*see* plankton).

picotite. *See* spinel.

picrite. An ultramafic rock consisting of *ferromagnesian minerals and accessory calcic plagioclase feldspar.

piedmont. A gentle slope leading from the foot of a mountain range down to comparatively flat land. In arid and semiarid areas, where these features most frequently occur, they consist of an eroded upper segment (known as a *pediment*), which makes an abrupt angle with the mountain front, followed by an accumulation form or *bajada, consisting of transported debris from the mountains. This merges into a flat *inland basin or playa.

piedmont angle. The sharp inflexion between lowlands and uplands in pediment and inselberg landscapes. Characteristically, the scarp of the upland slopes at 25–35°, passing to the slope of the pediment at 9° or less over a very short distance, leaving an abrupt angle. This angle can be very sharply defined, but usually it is a concavity, with the break of slope spread over a considerable horizontal distance.
Its origin is closely linked with the processes of *parallel retreat of the upland and bevelling of the pediment. Some have found that the angle is maintained by intense weathering in the scarp foot zone, caused by runoff from the pediment and through flow emerging at the angle; in other cases it coincides with a tectonic or geologic boundary. Some consider it to be a product of contrasted processes, e.g. unconfined wash on the residual with channelled water on the pediment (Bryan), or turbulent wash on the residual with laminar wash on the pediment (King); others have explained it by slope process, the increased volume of water in the scarp foot area undercutting the slope of the residual, leading to mass movements which keep the angle sharp. It is almost definitely produced by different mechanisms in different areas. *See also* pediment.

piemontite. *See* epidote.

pigeonite. A calcium-poor monoclinic *pyroxene.

pillow lava. A lava extruded under water and having the appearance of pillows piled one upon another. The outer skin of the lava is chilled on extrusion and a bubble of lava grows, flattening under its own weight and producing the characteristic pillow shape.

pilotaxitic. Denoting a close-packed felted arrangement of acicular *microlites. In many trachytes and andesites, feldspar laths exhibit parallelism due to flow and are deflected around phenocrysts in the direction of flow, this texture being called *trachytic.*

pinch and swell. A deformation feature developed when competent rocks are squeezed. The more competent beds extend and thin towards their margins and eventually break. The less competent beds deform plastically to fill any space. *See* boudinage.

pingo. A dome-shaped hill found in *permafrost areas. Pingos vary in size but seldom exceed 60 metres high and 300 metres in diameter. The top may be broken, so that it resembles a crater, and often contains a lake. Internally they frequently consist of outward dipping beds of stratified sand or silt. Many have a visible or supposed core of ice. They are believed to have been formed as a result of bulging, produced by sub-surface pressure build-up within isolated groundwaters prior to the complete extension of permafrost over the area.

pipkrake. *See* needle ice.

pitch. The direction of dip of the axis of a fold, measured by the angle between the axis and the horizontal on the axial plane.

pitchblende. A massive form of *uraninite.

pitchstone. *See* rhyolite.

pivot fault. *See* hinge fault.

placentals. Placental mammals (*see* Eutheria).

Placodermi. A class of extinct jawed fish comprising a number of primitive but varied groups common in the Devonian. They had paired fins and in the arthrodires and antiarchs, an armour of protective bony plates. Some placoderms were of great size, reaching a length of up to 10 metres.

plagioclase feldspars. A series of minerals with compositions varying between two end-members, albite ($NaAlSi_3O_8$) and anorthite ($CaAl_2Si_2O_8$). *See* feldspar.

planation surface. A surface of low relief, the end product of a cycle of subaerial or marine erosion. Characteristically such surfaces bevel indiscriminately across structures; they may be *pediplains, *peneplains, or surfaces of marine erosion. In order to develop, a planation surface needs a long period of base-level and climatic stability: such conditions have not existed since the end of the Tertiary period, owing to the base-level and climatic oscillations of the Pleistocene and post-Pleistocene periods. Those planation surfaces that do exist therefore are relic and much dissected. They have been reconstructed by analysis of relief, which shows in general concordance of summit levels at the level of former planation surfaces. In Wales and Scotland three or four such surfaces at decreasing elevations have been recognized.

plane tabling. A rapid surveying method for fixing detail in fairly open areas. The plane table is a flat board with an attached sheet of paper onto which a base line is drawn to scale between two known points. The whole stands on a tripod, which is set up over one end of the base line, with the drawn line aligned with the actual line. Points of detail are then sighted using an *alidade and rays to them drawn directly onto the paper. Once sufficient points have been covered, the plane table is set up at the other end of the base line, aligned, and rays drawn to the same detail points. Their actual positions on the

map occur at the points of ray intersection on the paper. More accurate fixing can be achieved by drawing rays from three known points.

planimetric map. A map on which, unlike topographic maps, no vertical information such as contouring is shown.

plankton. Aquatic and usually microscopic organisms that float and drift passively in the water (*compare* nekton). Plankton consists mainly of animal larvae, *protozoa, and plants such as *diatoms. *Phytoplankton* refers to plant forms, on which all other marine organisms depend, directly or indirectly, for their survival; *zooplankton* refers to the immense variety of animal forms. The distribution of both phytoplankton and zooplankton throughout the oceans is very patchy; plankton-rich areas form highly fertile zones in the oceans, for example where *upwelling currents occur.

Plankton is of considerable geological importance as it contributes to rock-building; for example, much of the Chalk (*see* Cretaceous) consists of *coccoliths, the skeletal remains of past planktonic organisms. Fossil plankton is studied in micropalaeontology (*see* microfossil), which has important stratigraphical applications.

planosol. An *intrazonal soil developed in flat areas, principally under humid continental warm summer climates. Planosols are characterized by a whitened A_2 horizon passing abruptly to a B horizon of high clay content, either due to in situ weathering or *lessivation from the A horizon. Periodic waterlogging results from the poor drainage due to the high clay content in the B horizon and lack of relief. They intergrade with a number of soils, including *grey-brown podzol, *prairie soils, and surface water *gleys. In the *Seventh Approximation classification they are split between a number of orders, including mollisols, alfisols, and ultisols.

plant cover. The geomorphological significance of the plant cover is as a balance between the soil and weathered rock beneath and the processes acting on the surface from above. Its loss greatly accelerates rates of erosion, e.g. in areas of cultivation, overgrazing, human trampling, or destruction of vegetation by pollution. The beneficial effects of vegetation include the binding action of the roots, the diverting action of its mass on water flowing on the surface, shelter from wind action, and the increase in organic matter on the soil surface, which improves aggregation and hence the ability of the soil to hold water, thereby reducing runoff. Vegetation can hold soil on a slope that would otherwise be too steep for stability and hence be eroded; it also intercepts rainfall, preventing *rainsplash erosion.

plastic deformation of ice. A process operating in glacier flow. Glaciers do not move down their valleys as rigid masses simply sliding across the bed rock. Ice is a crystalline solid and as such changes shape (or *deforms*) at temperatures near its melting point. Movements between adjacent crystals are limited but individual crystals can deform internally, though little change in shape appears to occur over a period of time: this indicates that recrystallization accompanies the deformation. Individual crystal deformation is achieved by relative movements of layers, one above another, parallel to the basal plane. Field evidence has shown that ice is moulded as it moves across its bed, but that resultant features are maintained within the ice beyond the location of moulding. This suggests that the ice acts plastically under pressure, but that it remains rigid on removal of the pressure.

plastic relief map. A three-dimensional map produced by printing a topographic map on plastic and then moulding the plastic to fit the relief. It is generally used only for demonstration purposes as there are still certain inaccuracies involved in this method.

plastic shading. *See* hill shading.

plate. One of a series of large blocks of continental or oceanic material of which the earth's crust is composed. These plates, whose base is marked by the asthenosphere, move across the surface of the earth as a result of *sea-floor spreading. The six major plates are named Eurasian, Indian, Pacific, American, African, and Antarctic.

plate margin. The edge of a lithospheric plate. There are three types of margin:
a. *Constructive*, where new sea floor is added to the plates on either side of the margin, e.g. at the Mid-Atlantic Ridge.
b. *Destructive*, where sea floor is destroyed through subduction. This is usually marked by a deep ocean *trench and results from one plate overriding another. *See also* subduction zone.
c. *Conservative*, where plates slip passively past one another without destroying or adding sea floor. This occurs along *transform faults.

plate tectonics. A theory arising from a series of ideas developed in the early 1960s proposing that the surface of the earth is composed of a number of relatively thin *plates of rigid material. These plates extend down to the low-velocity zone of the upper mantle. They are all in motion relative to one another and it is through these movements and the consequent collisions between the plates that the present distribution of almost all volcanic, seismic, and orogenic activity is controlled. The plates are bounded by *plate margins. The plates themselves are composed of either oceanic or continental crustal types, or a combination of both. Only the oceanic parts of the plates grow or are destroyed; the continental areas ride along on these plates and grow only slowly by the addition of volcanic material and sediment deposition along their margins. These sediments are compressed and folded when two continental regions collide by orogenic

processes, which result in the formation
of fold mountain chains. These have a
central nucleus of older rocks, frequently cratons.

playa. See inland basin.

Pleistocene. The earlier epoch of the
*Quaternary, extending from the end of
the *Pliocene, about 1.8 million years
ago, until the beginning of the *Holocene. During this period, often referred
to as the *Ice Age, the world experienced great fluctuations in temperature,
resulting in cold periods (glacials),
separated by warmer periods (interglacials). In the Alps, four main
glacial episodes can be recognized: the
Gunz, Mindel, Riss, and Würm.

Plesiosauria. A group of Mesozoic
reptiles that were secondarily adapted
to an aquatic life but, unlike the
*Ichthyosauria, were not fishlike. They
had a rigid flattened trunk and well-
developed powerful paddles for propul-
sion. A long neck provided the necessary rapid flexibility for catching the
fish on which they fed. Some plesiosaurs
attained a length of 17 metres. The
group became extinct by the beginning
of the Cenozoic.

Pliocene. The final epoch of the *Tertiary Period, preceded by the *Miocene
and followed by the *Pleistocene. It
began about 5.5 million years ago and
lasted some 3.7 million years. There are
few rocks of this age in Britain; some of
the crags of shelly limestone in East
Anglia are placed in this system. Mammals similar to modern forms existed,
and there were definite hominids, including species of Australopithecus and
Homo (see man).

plug. 1. Any roughly cylindrical vertical
body of intrusive igneous rock, usually
relatively small.
2. See neck.

plunge. The tilt of the axis of a fold
from the horizontal, the value of plunge
being the angle between the axis and the
horizontal lying in the same vertical
plane. See diagram at fold.

pluton. A deep-seated major intrusive
body of coarse-grained igneous rock,
generally of granitic composition.

plutonic. Igneous rocks of the same
composition may show striking textural
differences dependent upon their mode
of occurrence. Rocks that crystallize at
depth and cool slowly, resulting in a
coarse grain size, are termed plutonic.
Those that are extruded on the earth's
surface as lava flows and cool rapidly,
producing a fine grain size, are volcanic.
Hypabyssal rocks are those that have
crystallized at levels intermediate
between those of plutonic and volcanic
conditions. They are medium-grained
and occur mostly as sills and dykes.
Gabbro and dolerite are respectively the
plutonic and hypabyssal equivalents of
basalt.

pluvial period. A period of time experiencing greater rainfall than preceding or succeeding periods, usually on
a geological time scale. Many of the
semidesert areas of the tropics experienced pluvials during full glaciation in
polar regions. This was a response to
the southward movement of the circulation belts and depression tracks.
Evidence for these wetter periods comes
from greater water erosion, increased
plant growth, and animal remains found
in areas in which they would not be
found under present conditions.
However, this has been disputed as
lower temperatures could have reduced
evaporation, making the same rainfall
amounts more effective.

pneumatolysis. A process occurring
during the final stages of the crystallization of acid igneous rocks when residual
borofluoric gas escapes along joints and
fissures and brings about mineralogical
changes in the crystalline parent rock
(compare metasomatism). Three kinds
of pneumatolysis are recognized:
1. Greisening. Alteration at the margins
of granites to assemblages of muscovite,
quartz, and topaz (greisen) is the result
of the action of fluorine-bearing vapours.
Original feldspars are pseudomorphed

by aggregates of mica, often varieties rich in lithium such as zinnwaldite. The end product of the process is a quartz-topaz rock known as topazfels.

2. *Tourmalinization.* The boron pneumatolysis of granitic rocks results in the growth of *tourmaline at the expense of feldspar and biotite. The rock, luxullianite, contains radiating aggregates of black tourmaline but some feldspar survives. The final stage is a quartz-tourmaline assemblage known as *schorl rock.*

3. *Kaolinization.* Feldspars in granitic rocks may be altered to aggregates of kaolinite and sericite under the action of high-temperature aqueous fluids. The end product of this pneumatolytic/hydrothermal process is china clay.

podzol. A soil characterized by an ashen coloured acid eluviated A horizon and a B horizon illuviated with iron or humus, possibly in the form of a compact pan. The A horizon is depleted of bases and sesquioxides by *leaching processes, especially *cheluviation, while the B horizon is divided into an upper part (Bh) dominated by the redeposited humus and a lower part (Bs or Bfe) dominated by the redeposited iron, and to a lesser extent, aluminium. If both the Bh and Bs horizons are present, the soil is an iron-humus podzol; if the Bh only is present, a humus podzol; if Bs only, an iron podzol.

Podzols are zonally developed soils in the taiga zones of Russia and North America, where they form a mosaic with regosols, gleys, and peats, and develop from initiation directly on the parent material. Elsewhere podzol is intrazonal, e.g. on coarse deposits such as the Bagshot Beds, or man-induced by forest clearance. Most British podzols are of the latter type, being originally brown earths, but forest clearance and subsequent climatic deterioration led to the spread of heath or coniferous vegetation to formerly deciduous forest areas and increased leaching, thereby degrading the brown earths to podzols.

As the profile matures, the Bh-s horizons may become impermeable and lead to *gleying, producing hydromorphic variants such as *peaty gleyed podzols.

podzolic soil. A soil with certain features of morphology and genesis akin to true podzols. There are a large number of varieties: in North America there are grey-brown podzolics in a belt below the true podzols, which develop slowly by increased leaching, destruction of the Bt horizon, and greying of the A_2 horizon to brown podzolics. In the south, in the subtropical areas, are red-yellow podzolics, which have free aluminium and ferric oxides like other tropical soils but also clay skins in the B horizon. In Britain, a common sequence as leaching continues is for a brown earth to develop a distinct Bt horizon owing to clay movement and then as leaching continues this develops to a sol (brun) lessivé, the equivalent of the American grey-brown podzolic.

podzolization. The movement of clays and sesquioxides down the soil profile and their deposition in the B horizon. The dominant process is *cheluviation by organic acids, but opinions vary as to the other processes involved. Some believe that podzolization operates best in acidic and anaerobic conditions, so that the cheluviation is preceded by *decalcification, *lessivation, and clay destruction by weathering. Others have suggested that acidic conditions are not necessary, and decalcification is therefore not a necessary preliminary; it has also been argued that anaerobic conditions (i.e. waterlogging) are not necessary as the organic acids can reduce the sesquioxides themselves, and do not rely on the anaerobic reduction of iron from its insoluble ferric to its soluble ferrous state. Podzolization is a zonal process in areas of natural *leaching and coniferous vegetation, which together favour intense cheluviation, the chelates of pine litter being amongst the most powerful. Intrazonally, it is the dominant process on coarse-textured

215

parent materials, or where forest clearance has increased leaching.

poikilitic. Denoting igneous rocks in which large crystals of a mineral completely enclose crystals of earlier-formed minerals. *Poikiloblastic* denotes a similar texture in metamorphic rocks. *See also* ophitic.

poikiloblastic. *See* poikilitic.

point bar. A depositional feature that develops on the inside of meanders, complementing erosion on the outside of meander bends. Point bars extend downstream from the point of maximum curvature of the meander bend, leaving a trough between themselves and the bank, which eventually becomes filled up by the sedimentation of fine material. *See* meander.

Poisson's ratio. The ratio between the fractional longitudinal strain and the fractional lateral strain in a deformed material. It is equal to the ratio of change in diameter divided by change in length.

polar air depression (polar low). A small depression that forms within cold north or northwesterly air streams between Iceland and Scotland. It was formerly thought to be the result of thermal contrasts between warm sea and cold air, but more recent radar investigations have shown that these depressions are very similar to the normal baroclinic depression, although on a smaller scale. The small scale prevented the frontal positions being identified in the sparse network of observing stations over sea areas.

polar easterlies. The easterly wind belt found between the weak polar anticyclone and the westerly depression tracks. Because of the variability of the intensity and tracks of the mid-latitude depressions and the weakness of the polar anticyclone, the polar easterlies are rarely strong or persistent.

polar front. The major frontal system, situated in the N Pacific and N Atlantic,

separating tropical and polar air masses. Depressions are often initiated on this pronounced thermal gradient and Bjerknes based his theory of frontal evolution on it. In summer the thermal contrast across the front is less and its position is much more variable than in winter.

polar glacier. *See* cold glacier.

polarization colours (interference colours). *See* birefringence.

polarized light. In ordinary light the electromagnetic vibrations take place in all directions in a plane at right angles to the direction of propagation of the ray of light. When vibrations are confined to a single direction in this plane the light is said to be plane-polarized. Certain crystals constrain ordinary light to vibrate in only two directions at right angles to one another. *See* anisotropic, birefringence.

polar night jet stream. A very steep thermal gradient in winter giving correspondingly very strong westerly winds, situated around the stratospheric cold pole at levels of 20-30 km. During summer the stratosphere at this level warms up owing to absorption of ultraviolet radiation and a reversal of the wind system takes place to give stratospheric easterlies.

polar wandering curve. A theoretical line produced for a particular point on the earth's surface by joining successive palaeomagnetic pole positions through time.

polar zenithal gnomonic projection. A map projection in which the centre of the projection is the pole, from which the straight lines representing the great circles radiate (see diagram). The parallels are portrayed as concentric circles. It is commonly used to show the Polar areas, the exaggeration becoming too great in areas further away from the centre.

poles of rotation. Poles about which the lithospheric plates rotate during seafloor spreading and continental drift.

Polar zenithal

polje. The largest type of solution depression found in limestone areas, extending up to 250 sq. km. The floors support a certain amount of surface drainage, are alluvium-covered, and often uneven, reflecting the collapse of former cave systems. Poljes are frequently surrounded by steep marginal walls, up to 100 metres in height, whilst considerable numbers show signs of being tectonically bounded basins.

pollen. Microscopic spores of the higher plants (gymnosperms and angiosperms). As pollen is very resistant to destruction and may be carried for large distances by the wind, fossilized pollen provides a valuable means of correlating the rocks in which it occurs. Pollen may also be used as a sensitive environmental indicator and has proved particularly useful in monitoring climatic change during the Quaternary Period. The study of pollen and other spores is known as *palynology.*

pollen analysis. A technique of both relative dating and environmental reconstruction, consisting of the identification and counting of pollen types preserved in peats and lake beds. It is based on the assumption that the vegetation in an environment is in equilibrium with it, and hence reflects its conditions; dispersal of pollen leads to some of it being preserved in reducing environments, such as peat beds and lake bottoms. Subsequent careful close sampling and analysis allows the structure of the vegetation at each particular horizon in the deposit to be worked out. Reference to the present-day vegetational assemblages in different conditions allows deduction, by analogy, of the environment that the vegetation lived in. This method has shown well-defined sequences of changes for each of the interglacials and the postglacial period, which allowed relative correlation between different sites and hence dating.

polyconic map projection. A modified *conical projection in which each parallel is treated as a standard parallel on a normal conical projection. All the parallels and the central meridian are truly divided, the meridians being constructed by joining the divisions on the parallels. This projection is neither *orthomorphic nor *homolographic and is therefore restricted to showing small areas.

polycyclic landscape. A landscape that has evolved under a number of geomorphic cycles (*see* cycle of erosion) or part cycles of different types. The independent variables of geomorphology are climate, geology, and base level: a change in any one starts a new cycle. Regional studies of landscape evolution emphasize that most if not all landscapes have experienced changes in these factors and have hence evolved under several different cycles. This realization has led to the abandonment of the youthful, mature, and senile labels for landscapes, since they assume each landscape is a product of only the current cycle, variation being due to the *stage of that cycle. Instead each landscape can be seen as composed of elements from several different cycles, only some of which are related to current conditions.

polygenetic (in geomorphology). Denoting a soil or landscape that has evolved under a number of differing conditions that occurred in successive phases of its history. Each of these conditions has played a part in influencing its current appearance. With landscapes, a change in base level, climate, or geology will institute a new cycle and hence superimposition of varying conditions in its evolution; with soil, a change in climate, vegetation, topography, or drainage will institute a new set of soil-forming conditions and hence change the direction of the soil's evolution. Some writers consider this term to be synonymous with *polycyclic when applied to landscapes; others consider that polygenetic should be used only to describe the influence of minor changes in conditions, leaving polycyclic for the major changes.

polymorphic transitions. Changes in minerals which involve a change in their atomic structure but not their chemical composition, e.g. aragonite ($CaCO_3$) to calcite ($CaCO_3$).

polymorphism. The ability of some substances to exist in two or more structurally distinct forms, each having its own characteristic properties but having identical chemical compositions. Calcium carbonate, $CaCO_3$ occurs as aragonite and calcite. Andalusite, kyanite, and sillimanite are polymorphs of the aluminium silicate, Al_2SiO_5. Graphite and diamond are mineral polymorphs of the element carbon.

polyphase deformation. Folding and faulting occurring in several periods during a single orogeny.

Polyzoa. *See* Bryozoa.

pools and riffles. In detail, the long profiles of many streams have alternating gravel bars (riffles) and pools: these features are regularly spaced, usually such that the distance between successive pools is 5-7 times the channel width. In meandering streams, lengths of meanders are about twice the distance between pools, and there may be a relationship between the pool and riffle formations and *meander creation.

Porifera. The sponges: a phylum of simple sessile aquatic (mostly marine) multicellular animals with a saclike body, often containing small calcareous or siliceous skeletal elements known as *spicules.* Water is drawn into the body through small holes and expelled from an opening, the *oscula*, during which food particles are filtered off. The spicules may become fossilized. Fossil sponges are useful environmental indicators and have contributed to the growth of bioherms and formation of rocks. They are known to have extended from the Cambrian Period to the present day, and structures found in Precambrian rocks have been attributed to this group.

porosity. The extent to which a body of soil, rock, or sediment is permeated with cavities between grains, usually expressed as a percentage of the volume. These pores are filled by air and water (air is mainly in the larger macro pores and water in the micro pores), which impede air movement and allow water to move by *capillarity only. In sands and compact soils, where the particles lie close together, porosity is low (25-30% in compacted soils); conversely, where organic matter content is high, promoting good aggregation, porosity is high, reaching possibly 60%. Cropping, which removes organic matter, eventually lowers porosity, and hence aeration.

porphyritic. Denoting an igneous rock that possesses large crystals called *phenocrysts* set in a finer-grained groundmass.

porphyroblastic. Denoting a metamorphosed rock containing large crystals set in a fine-grained matrix. The large crystals are called *porphyroblasts* by analogy with the igneous term, *porphyritic.

porphyry. A medium- or fine-grained igneous rock containing numerous *phenocrysts. The porphyritic mineral may be indicated by the prefix of a mineral name, e.g. quartz-porphyry. A rhomb-porphyry is so called on account of the distinctive shape of the feldspar phenocrysts.

positive area. A large area of the earth's crust that has remained above sea level for a long period of geological time.

positive gravity anomaly. *See* gravity anomaly.

positive movements of sea level. A fall of the land relative to the sea, usually due to sea level rise, as has happened since the end of the Ice Age. The results are basically twofold: flooding, and deposition of material creating broad low plains.
Flooding produces estuaries or rias from inundated river valleys; estuaries characterize lower-lying areas (e.g. in E and S Britain), rias the more rugged areas (e.g. in SW Britain, SW Ireland). If the valleys inundated are glacial in orgin, fiords result (e.g. in Norway). Low-lying parts of the land may be flooded wholesale, creating new seas and severing islands from the mainland (Britain was severed from the continent by the post-glacial sea-level rise).
The effect on rivers is that *capacity and *competence are reduced, leading to *aggradation in the lower reaches, which fills up the newly created estuaries and creates broad alluvial floodplains. The lengths of drainage systems are reduced, leaving buried portions beneath the elevated sea level. Most of the coastal geography of Britain today is directly attributable to the effects of the post-glacial sea-level rise. *See also* negative movement of sea level.

post-kinematic. Denoting minerals developed after a period of deformation (usually metamorphic minerals).

potential energy. The energy possessed by a body as a result of its position. It is measured by the amount of work re-quired to move that body from a position of zero potential energy, usually sea level, to its new position. Stationary air at high levels of the troposphere would therefore have a high potential energy.

potential evapotranspiration (PE). The evaporation from an extended surface of short green crop, actively growing, completely shading the ground, of uniform height, and possessing an adequate supply of soil moisture. It is essentially a function of climate rather than the nature of the vegetation, and as such has been used by Thornthwaite as a method of climatic classification. It can be estimated or measured more easily and accurately than actual evapotranspiration and so has achieved more universal acceptability in studies of evaporation.

potential temperature. The temperature of a parcel of air if it is uplifted or subsides at the *dry adiabatic lapse rate to a standard pressure, usually 1000 mb. Use is also made of the wet-bulb potential temperature by changing the temperature of the parcel of air at the *saturated adiabatic lapse rate from the wet-bulb temperature of the original level to 1000 mb. This is useful as the wet-bulb potential temperature is a conservative property in such processes as evaporation, condensation, and both dry and saturated adiabatic temperature changes.

pot-hole. 1. A circular hole worn in rock in an eddy of a stream or river, often at the foot of a waterfall, by moving pebbles and gravel. **2.** *See* sink hole.

prairie soil (brunizem). Dark soil of subhumid grasslands in which the profile has been decarbonated but leaching has not produced any movement of sesquioxides. The carbonate appears as flecks in the C horizon. These soils develop under tall grass vegetation and have a brown or grey-brown A horizon grading to a yellow-brown B horizon, with blocky structures and a light parent material at around one metre. Their exact status is not certain. They may be degraded *chernozems or more related to the podzolic group, with which they intergrade at their boundary, or their distinctive profile may be due to a water table standing in the profile producing *gleying. In the *Seventh Approximation classification they fall in the order of *mollisols.

Pratt's hypothesis. A proposed mechanism of hydrostatic support for the earth's crust. This hypothesis relies upon crustal density being greater under mountain chains than under oceans. If this was true at a datum level, called the *compensation level by Pratt, rock columns of equal diameter would have equal mass.

Precambrian. The geological time prior to the Cambrian Period or the rocks stratigraphically below the Cambrian System. As the age of the earth's crust has been estimated at about 4500 million years, and the beginning of the Cambrian is dated around 590 million years ago, the Precambrian represents most of geological time. Precambrian rocks are practically devoid of *fossils and, because of their extreme age, have often been subjected to a great deal of subsequent alteration. The original stratigraphical relationships are therefore frequently obscure. The old division into *Archaean and *Proterozoic, corresponding to crystalline rocks and largely unaltered sediments respectively, seems now to be of little significance. Calibration and correlation of isolated successions is achieved mainly by radiometric dating. There are several small outcrops of Precambrian age in England and Wales and more extensive outcrops occur in NW Scotland. The remains of organisms have been found in a few Precambrian rocks, but the taxonomic affinities of most of them remain problematical.

precession. A form of motion of a rotating body that results when a couple having its axis at right angles to the axis of rotation is applied to a body, which then turns about a third mutually perpendicular axis. As a result of the gravitational attraction of the sun and moon, the earth's axis traces out a conical figure in space.

precipitable water. The amount of water that could be obtained if all the vapour in a standard column of air was condensed onto a horizontal surface of unit area. It is a useful index of the moisture content of air above a specified point, although precipitation processes are never so efficient that all the water would be precipitated and it neglects the effects of vapour advection. It is calculated by the formula:

$$M_W = \frac{1}{g} \int_{p_2}^{p_1} r\,\mathrm{d}p$$

where M_w is the precipitable water, g is the acceleration of free fall, p_1 and p_2 are the pressures (mb) at the top and bottom of the layer, r is the mixing ratio, and $\mathrm{d}p$ is the depth of the individual layer of mixing ratio.

precipitation. The deposition of water in solid or liquid form from the atmosphere. It therefore covers a wide range of particles including rain, drizzle, sleet, snow, and dew. Precipitation is initiated within clouds by the *Bergeron-Findeisen process, by the coalescence process, or by a combination of both operating together. For precipitation to reach the ground a number of other conditions must be satisfied. The droplet or ice crystal produced by one of the above mechanisms must be sufficiently heavy to overcome upward vertical motion and large enough to withstand evaporation beneath the cloud base. Thus, some clouds can be seen to be giving precipitation that does not reach the ground.

precipitation effectiveness. A measure of the usefulness of the annual rainfall total for agricultural purposes or for hydrology. For example, 600 mm of rain in temperate latitudes with low evaporation maintains humid vegetation and surplus runoff for river flow. In the tropics, such an annual total would give semidesert. Precipitation effectiveness has been used by Thornthwaite as a basis for climatic classification. However, the sparsity of data of both measured and calculated *potential evapotranspiration, from which precipitation effectiveness is obtained, has prevented its use on a global scale.

precipitation variability. The annual variation in rainfall totals, though shorter time periods can be used. It is assessed by many statistical methods but the most common is the *coefficient of variation*, which is the standard deviation of the annual totals divided by the mean annual value, multiplied by 100 to be expressed as a percentage. In Britain, values range from below 10% in the northwest to 20% in S England, but these are low compared with many other parts of the world. Malden Island in the central Pacific is believed to have the highest rainfall variability with annual rainfall totals varying between 30 mm and 1422 mm in a thirty-year period.

prehnite. An orthorhombic mineral of composition $Ca_2Al_2Si_3O_{10}(OH)_2$ found chiefly in basic lavas as a secondary mineral associated with *zeolites. It is also found with pumpellyite in low-grade regionally metamorphosed rocks.

pre-kinematic. Denoting minerals formed before deformation.

pressure (in meteorology). The weight of air vertically above a unit area centred on a point. It is measured by balancing the force exerted by the atmosphere with a dense liquid, usually mercury. As a result of this, atmospheric pressure was formerly quoted as a number of millimetres of mercury representing the length of the mercury column required to balance air pressure. It is now measured in *millibars. Sea-level values range from extremes of about 890 mb in hurricanes to 1060 mb in strong anticyclones.

pressure gradient force. The force that acts on an air molecule by virtue of the spatial variations in pressure at any horizontal level. It is the primary motivating force of air movement in the atmosphere.

pressure release. See unloading.

pressure system. A pattern of isobars that exhibits coherent weather characteristics. It normally denotes low-pressure areas or anticyclones.

pressure tendency. The local rate of change of surface pressure. It is recorded at most observing stations with a 10 point code to distinguish various trends of the pressure trace in the preceding time period, usually 3 hours. It is very useful for indicating future movements of pressure systems.

prevailing wind. The most frequently occurring wind at any site. In most parts of the globe this will correspond with the climatic zone, so that the British Isles, being in the westerly circulation, have prevailing winds from between southwest and west. Occasionally local factors, such as wind funnelling in a valley, become dominant. Also for shorter time periods, the prevailing wind may be different from its annual value, as in monsoon areas.

primary (P) waves. A type of seismic wave, the first to be recorded on a seismogram of an earthquake. These waves travel by a series of compressions and rarefactions (pushes and pulls) in the direction of propagation, i.e. each particle vibrates backwards and forwards along the direction in which the wave is travelling. P waves can pass through solids, liquids, and gases. See also secondary waves.

Primates. The order of mammals that includes man, apes, monkeys, and lemurs. They are characterized by adaptations for an arboreal habitat, such as flexible limbs and hands, anteriorly directed eyes providing stereoscopic vision, often a long tail for balance, a relatively large brain, and an unspecialized dentition. Fossil primates are known from the beginning of the

*Tertiary onwards; they probably evolved from the *Insectivora. Monkeys appeared in the Oligocene and the remains of manlike forms have been found in Pliocene strata (*see* man).

prime meridian. *See* meridian.

primitive equations. The physical equations governing momentum in the atmosphere. They have been used most extensively in models simulating the general circulation of the atmosphere.

principal shock. The suite of waves produced by the main movement in an earthquake. *See also* foreshocks, aftershocks.

prismatic. Denoting the habit of some crystals that are elongated and show well-developed prism faces. *See* crystal habit.

prismatic compass. A magnetic compass within which the needle, or the zero of a 0° to 360° scale, always points towards magnetic north. Also incorporated is a sighting arrangement, consisting of a vertical hairline at the far side and a prism with a sight at the observer's side, which allows the object and the graduated scale to be viewed simultaneously. Readings taken with such a compass are true bearings from magnetic north.

Proboscidea. The order of mammals that includes the modern elephants and the extinct mammoths. Fossil proboscideans are known from the Oligocene. They were small creatures with long jaws, both upper and lower bearing tusks, and short trunks. Evolutionary modifications associated with the subsequent increase in size have occurred: solid limbs and flat feet support the great weight; the trunk has evolved into an efficient food-gathering organ; the teeth have lengthened, and the jaws have shortened, in modern forms accommodating only one large grinding tooth at a time, which is replaced through life. Formerly a widespread and diverse group, the Proboscidea are today confined to Africa and S Asia.

profile. The arrangement of soil *horizons found between the ground surface and the parent material. The normal depth of a profile in temperate latitudes is about a metre. Pedologists, notably Dokuchayev, have assigned letters to certain horizons. The surface horizon is known by the letter A and is usually rich in organic matter and plant nutrients. As material is often leached from this horizon down the profile to the subsoil B horizon, it is known as the *eluvial horizon*. The B horizon (*illuvial horizon*) contains less organic matter and more closely resembles the parent material owing to the lesser effect of the soil-forming processes. This horizon usually merges into the C horizon, which is the weathered parent material. Well-developed soils consist of more than these three horizons and subdivision occurs. Characteristics of certain horizons are symbolized by a suffix or prefix, e.g. Bh = humus-rich B horizon; Ap = ploughed A horizon. Superficial organic horizons are denoted by the letters L (litter), F (fermenting), and H (humus). Groups of soils having a similar suite of horizons are linked together in broad soil zones.

progressive wave. A wave that can be recognized by the progressive movement of the wave form at the sea surface. For example, such a wave would be propagated along a channel of infinite length, having been generated at one or other end of it by a wave paddle. In progressive waves, the speed of propagation of the wave form will largely depend upon the depth of water, one example being a tide wave that may be very long in relation to the water depth. As with wind-generated waves, the speed of wave propagation far exceeds the speed at which the water particles themselves advance. The wave-induced currents associated with progressive waves are at their maximum at the highest point of the wave crest and the lowest point of the wave trough, though the direction of the current as between crest and trough is reversed.

projection (in cartography). The method of obtaining a two-dimensional representation of the earth's surface, giving the least error for any particular task. Lines of latitude and longitude are drawn according to different mathematical formulae, depending on the area to be mapped. Some projections give the property of equal area (homolographic), others true bearings (azimuthal), and others achieve a compromise.

Proterozoic. A division of *Precambrian time on the basis of its unmetamorphosed sedimentary rocks (occasionally only the more recently deposited of these (see Eozoic, Archaeozoic)). It was formerly thought that Proterozoic rocks in all parts of the world were stratigraphically higher than the igneous and metamorphic *Archaean rocks; it now seems unlikely that they represent consistent time divisions. Sometimes the Proterozoic is used as a synonym for Precambrian.

Protista. A kingdom, separate from the plants and animals, proposed to contain the single-celled organisms. These include the *bacteria, the *Protozoa, unicellular *Algae, and others of more dubious affinities.

Proto Atlantic Ocean. An ocean that existed between the late Precambrian and early Devonian times. Within this ocean, which reached its maximum extent during the Ordovician, a series of sediments were deposited on an ocean floor of pillow lavas. When the two continents on either side of the ocean closed, these sediments were subjected to orogenic processes that resulted in the formation of the Caledonian mountains of Norway and Scotland, and the Appalachian mountains of North America. Evidence for the closure of this ocean can be found in Anglesey, where typical rocks associated with a destructive plate margin are present in fairly close association with pillow lavas.

Protozoa. Small, usually microscopic, animals whose bodies are not divided into cells (*compare* Metazoa). They are sometimes included with single-celled plants and other unicellular organisms in a kingdom distinct from the plants and animals, the Protista. Protozoa of the orders *Foraminifera and *Radiolaria possess skeletons, either secreted or of agglutinated material, which may be fossilized. They are present in large numbers in marine plankton, and some Forminifera are benthonic. Fossils are known from the Cambrian Period onwards, perhaps even the Precambrian; they are important in micropalaeontology, and in stratigraphic correlation, especially of rocks from borehole cores. Under certain conditions their remains accumulate in sufficient numbers to contribute to rock formation.

provenance. The source area from which the particles composing sediments are derived.

province (faunal province). A large region characterized by a particular assemblage of animal species, which differs from contemporaneous assemblages in similar environments elsewhere. The differences between faunal provinces have arisen because the communities have been geographically isolated from each other over long periods of time and have evolved in different ways. The detection of ancient faunal provinces is valuable in reconstructing palaeogeography.

psammite. A metamorphosed *arenaceous rock. *Compare* pelite, psephitic rock.

psephitic rock. A metamorphosed *rudaceous rock. *Compare* pelite, psammite.

pseudo-bedding. *See* unloading.

pseudo-karren. *Karren (grooves) found on the surfaces of rock types not normally associated with the process of solution. —

pseudomorph. 1. A mineral that has assumed the external form of another earlier mineral. Pseudomorphs may be produced as a result of:
a. Replacement or alteration of one mineral by another. In certain cases the pseudomorph may be a *polymorph of the original mineral, e.g. calcite after aragonite. Other common examples of pseudomorphism include gypsum after anhydrite, iddingsite after olivine, and kaolinite after feldspar.
b. Encrustation or investment when a mineral is deposited as a crust on crystals of another, e.g. quartz on fluorite. Sometimes the first mineral is removed leaving a negative pseudomorph.
c. Infiltration by a different mineral or substance of a cavity or mould previously occupied by a soluble crystal, e.g. clay pseudomorphs after halite.
2. A fossil in which the original skeletal substance of the organism has been replaced by a secondary material in the course of fossilization, which preserves its shape. *See also* cast, mould.

pseudotachylite. A glassy material produced by the fusion of crushed rock by frictional heating, and found as narrow veinlets and streaks in mylonite zones.

Pteridophyta. A division of plants that includes the horsetails and ferns. They are predominantly terrestrial and have a vascular system, leaves, stems, and roots. The Pteridophyta were especially abundant in the late Palaeozoic but declined during the Mesozoic. They formed much of the coal-measure forests in the Carboniferous Period, when many grew to the size of modern trees.

pterodactyls. A colloquial term for the *Pterosauria, taken from the name of one of the genera of this order (*Pterodactylus*).

pteropod ooze. A calcareous deep-sea ooze deposit (*see* pelagic ooze) containing over 30% organisms. It comprises the shells of pelagic molluscs and may also include the dead bodies of tiny swimming snails and marine butterflies, especially in the vicinity of the equator. It is limited to a depth range of 1500 to 3000 metres, i.e. it lies in generally shallower water than *globigerina ooze, being particularly common in the vicinity of coral islands and on submarine elevations that lie well offshore. Viewed on a global scale, it is very limited in extent, occupying a fairly small north-south strip in the centre of the S Atlantic and several deep-water sites off Brazil and in the N Atlantic. Collectively, these areas amount to only 1% of the total ocean floor.

Pterosauria. An order of extinct flying reptiles (subclass *Archosauria), prominent in the Mesozoic. The body was small in relation to the size of the wings, which were formed of a thin membrane of skin supported by an elongation of the fourth finger. This arrangement differs from that found in the birds (*see* Aves). The early Jurassic species were suited to flapping flight, but by the late Cretaceous pterosaurs were characteristically adapted for gliding, and were among the most efficient gliders known. They ranged from sparrow-sized creatures to the enormous *Pteranodon*, which had a wing span of up to 9 metres. Some had teeth; others were toothless.

pulaskite. *See* syenite.

pumice. Highly vesicular, usually acid, volcanic rock. *See* pyroclastic rock.

pumpellyite. A hydrous calcium-bearing mineral found in low-grade regionally metamorphosed rocks.

push moraine. A ridge of material accumulated by the bulldozing action of an advancing glacier or ice sheet. They tend to be more convex in profile than *terminal moraines and can easily be differentiated by considering the internal structures, which show signs of faulting and thrusting. If really distinct faults occur in the material, then it was almost certainly frozen when incorporated into the push moraine.

P waves. *See* primary waves.

pyralspite. A chemical series of *garnet minerals.

pyramidal peak (horn, horn peak). An individual steep-sided mountain peak formed in a similar way to an *arête but in this case involving three or more converging *cirque headwalls, thereby isolating a single residual rock mass rather than a linear divide.

pyranometer. Any instrument for measuring scattered and global radiation on a horizontal surface. Instruments that measure global (direct and diffuse) radiation are also known as *solarimeters.*

pyrheliometer. A radiation instrument for measuring direct solar radiation only. Diffuse radiation is excluded by having a 5° aperture continuously facing the sun. It requires sophisticated equipment to maintain the aperture in this position and is therefore only used at a few special sites.

pyriboles. *Pyroxenes plus *amphiboles.

pyrite (iron pyrites). A pale brass-yellow mineral, FeS_2, commonly occurring as cubes and octahedra. It is the most widespread and abundant sulphide mineral, found as an accessory in igneous rocks, in hydrothermal and replacement deposits, in contact metamorphic rocks, and in sediments laid down under reducing conditions.

pyroclastic rocks. Rocks formed by the accumulation of fragmental materials thrown out by volcanic explosions (literally, fire-broken). Such material is known as *tephra* or *ejectamenta* and may be expelled as solid fragments or in the molten state, chilling in the air and producing vitreous material. All volcanic eruptions are the result of the release of gas that has been confined under pressure. This gas may be derived from the magma or from the transformation to steam of water from the sea or a crater lake coming into contact with magma. Phreatic eruptions are caused by steam produced when lava flows comes into contact with groundwater.

The main kinds of pyroclastic materials and rocks are as follows:

Bombs and *blocks.* Bombs are large fragments with a rounded to subangular shape and erupted in a plastic condition. During flight, aerodynamically modified shapes are produced, the most common being a spindle form. Blocks are large angular fragments ejected in a solid condition. Accumulations of blocks and bombs, known as *agglomerate,* occur near volcanic vents. Showers of hot blebs of magma that flatten and weld on impact with the ground are called *spatter* or *agglutinate.*

Lapilli. Round to angular fragments of diameter between 64 and 2 mm. Most of the irregular vesicular fragments known as cinders or *scoriae* are of lapilli size. A special form of lapilli, known as *Pele's tears,* are droplets of lava that solidified in the air to pear-shaped pieces of glass. The droplets trail behind them threads of liquid that solidify to glass filaments, known as *Pele's hair.*

Ash. Tephra fragments less than 2 mm in diameter. Consolidated ash is known as *tuff.* The most common variety, vitric ash, is formed by the disruption of magma by expanding gas. The gas causes a frothing of the magma, which becomes torn apart. Some highly vesicular masses survive as pumice. Most is completely disintegrated to *shards.* These small glass septa, which separated individual bubbles, have characteristically curved and forked shapes. Ash may be carried a great distance from the volcanic source by the prevailing winds and is deposited in layers, often graded, draping over the underlying topography. Consolidated ash with a high proportion of larger fragments is sometimes called *lapilli tuff. Crystal tuff* contains a high proportion of broken crystals, which represent the *phenocrysts present in the magma before eruption.

Ignimbrites (welded tuffs). Fragmental flows having some of the characteristics of lava and some of air-fall pyroclastic material. Ignimbrites typically have a streaky or banded appearance known as eutaxitic structure. The glossy streaks, usually darker in colour than the surrounding matrix, are laterally discontinuous, unlike flow banding. Individual streaks called *fiamme* are arcuate or elliptical in plan and are thought to represent pumice fragments or lava blebs flattened by the weight of the ignimbrite and welded together as the flow deflates. The shards that compose the matrix are also flattened and drawn out.

The flows producing these deposits are called *ash flows* and the rocks produced are ignimbrites, ash-flow tuffs, or welded tuffs. Not all ash flows become welded and in many flows welded eutaxitic material passes up into unwelded material.

Ash flows are mostly of acid composition and are the result of deposition from *nuées ardentes, incandescent clouds of gas and ash produced by the explosive vesiculation of magma.

pyrope. See garnet.

pyroxenes. A group of ferromagnesian rock-forming minerals. Pyroxenes are orthorhombic or monoclinic and have a continuous chain structure of SiO_4 tetrahedra linked by sharing two of the four corners. Cations link the chains laterally. The general formula is $X_{1-p}Y_{1+p}Z_2O_6$, where X = Ca, Na; Y = Mg, Fe^{2+}, Mn, Li, Al, Fe^{3+}, Ti, and Z = Si, Al. In the *orthopyroxenes* (orthorhombic pyroxenes), p = 1 and the content of trivalent ions is small. In *clinopyroxenes* (monoclinic pyroxenes), p varies from 0 as in diopside ($CaMgSi_2O_6$) to 1 as in spodumene ($LiAlSi_2O_6$).

Orthorhombic pyroxenes.
The orthopyroxenes have a composition $(Mg,Fe^{2+})_2Si_2O_6$ and are a series from *enstatite* ($MgSiO_3$) to *orthoferrosilite* ($FeSiO_3$) formed by the replacement $Mg \rightleftharpoons Fe^{2+}$. Intermediate compositions in the series include *bronzite* and *hypersthene*. Orthopyroxenes are found in

basic and ultrabasic igneous rocks and high-grade metamorphic rocks.
Monoclinic pyroxenes.
Most clinopyroxenes can be considered to be members of the four-component system, $CaMgSi_2O_6-CaFeSi_2O_6-MgSiO_3-FeSiO_3$. Within the system, three series are recognized:
1. diopside—salite—hedenbergite $Ca(Mg,Fe)Si_2O_6$
2. augite—ferroaugite $(Ca,Na,Mg,Fe^{2+},MnFe^{3+}Al,Ti)_2(Si,Al)_2O_6$
3. pigeonite—$(Mg,Fe^{2+},Ca)(Mg,Fe^{2+})Si_2O_6$.
The pigeonite series are calcium-poor clinopyroxenes. The diopside series have higher Ca/Mg + Fe ratios than the augites. Clinopyroxenes rich in titanium are called *titanaugites*.
Pigeonite is found in basic lavas but under the slow cooling conditions associated with plutonic crystallization, pigeonite expels calcium-rich ions as lamellae of augite and inverts to an orthorhombic structure.
Diopside and hedenbergite are found in calcium-rich and iron-rich thermally metamorphosed sediments respectively. Hedenbergite also occurs in intermediate and acid igneous rocks. Pyroxenes of the augite-ferroaugite series are found in basic igneous rocks. *Omphacite*, a high-pressure pyroxene resembling augite but with some CaMg replaced by NaAl, is found in *eclogites.
Sodic pyroxenes may be considered to be members of the system $CaMgSi_2O_6-CaFeSi_2O_6-NaFe^{3+}Si_2O_6$, in which the replacements $Ca(Mg,Fe^{2+}) \rightleftharpoons NaFe^{3+}$ occur. The sodic end-member is aegirine (or acmite), $NaFe^{3+}Si_2O_6$, and as the name implies, aegirine-augite, $(Na,Ca)(Fe^{3+},Fe^{2+},Mg)Si_2O_6$ is of intermediate composition. Sodic pyroxenes are found in intermediate and acid alkaline igneous rocks and glaucophane schists.
Other pyroxenes include *spodumene* ($LiAlSi_2O_6$), found in lithium-rich pegmatites, and jadeite ($NaAlSi_2O_6$), found in high-pressure metamorphic rocks. *Compare* amphiboles.

pyroxenite. An ultramafic rock consisting wholly of *pyroxenes. Pyroxenites may be monomineralic or bimineralic.

Q

quaquaversal. See pericline.

quartile. If a data series is arranged in order of magnitude, a quartile indicates a quarter of the values. It is more frequently quoted as upper and lower quartile, the former separating the highest quarter of the values and the latter the lowest quarter. It can therefore be used as a measure of the dispersion or range of the data.

quartz. See silica minerals.

quartzarenite (orthoquartzite). An *arenaceous rock having a composition including more than 95% quartz.

quartzite. A tough massive rock consisting almost wholly of *quartz and usually having a pale colour. A quartzite is the product of the metamorphism of a pure sandstone during which process the quartz grains recrystallize and become interlocking. See also psammite.

quasi-geostrophic motion. Atmospheric motion that approximates to the *geostrophic wind. It is one of the assumptions used in the preparation of numerical weather forecasts. Since it is not quite geostrophic flow, it cannot be used for deriving other quantities based on the geostrophic wind.

Quaternary. The period of geological time following the *Tertiary Period (recent recommendations suggest it be considered as a sub-era and the term be restricted to informal usage). In either scheme it is formed of two epochs, the *Pleistocene and *Holocene, and extends from 1.8 million years ago until the present. During this time parts of Europe were subjected to four major advances of the ice sheets, which were separated by warmer interglacial episodes, and most British Pleistocene rocks consist of glacial and associated fluvial deposits. Fossil animals and plants were essentially modern. The land fauna alternated between forms adapted to cold conditions, such as the mammoth and woolly rhinoceros, and species now restricted to the tropics. Pollen and the remains of beetles have proved valuable in monitoring climatic change. The Quaternary is the time when man became the dominant terrestrial species.

R

radar meteorology. The investigation or determination of aspects and properties of the atmosphere by radar. Using suitable wavelengths, radar offers great possibilities of investigating the areal distribution of many meteorological elements, which otherwise would be unobserved. By scanning in the horizontal field (*Plan Position Indicator*), radar can measure the distribution and intensity of surface precipitation and distinguish particularly intense storms such as tornadoes, hurricanes, thunderstorms, and hailstorms. Scanning about the vertical (*Range-Height Indicator*) enables the height and structure of precipitating clouds to be obtained as well as the altitude of the melting level, if present. Operation over a period of time clarifies the evolution of many of these atmospheric systems and it is at the sub-synoptic scale that most advances in radar meteorology have occurred.

radial drainage. A drainage pattern that develops when structural control is in the form of a volcanic dome or cone, or some other sort of dome. Slope will cause streams to radiate out from their common centre at the crest of the dome like the spokes of a wheel, e.g. in the English Lake District.

radial dyke. A dyke that radiates from a central-vent volcano. This radial fracture pattern is the result of the volcano's superstructure swelling prior to an eruption as pressure builds up.

radiation. 1. (in meteorology). The portion of the *electromagnetic radiation spectrum that is emitted by the earth and sun. In terms of wavelength, this is radiation between 0.1 μm and 70 μm, encompassing part of the ultraviolet, all the visible, and part of the infrared spectrum. This type of wave differs from most other waveforms in that it does not require an intervening medium for its propagation; it can travel through a vacuum.

The behaviour of electromagnetic radiation is described by certain physical laws. All substances above the *absolute zero of temperature ($-273\,°$C) emit radiation in amounts and wavelengths dependent on their temperature. Some bodies emit and absorb radiation in certain wavelengths only; this is particularly true of gases (see atmospheric window). The ideal radiating body is a *black body, which emits the maximum amount of radiation for its temperature, the amount being proportional to the fourth power of its temperature on the Kelvin scale. Absorption and emission take place at the same wavelengths for any substance. The hotter a body, the shorter will be the wavelengths at which the maximum amount of emission will take place. These laws determine the way in which bodies react to radiation and enable the utilization of solar energy by the earth and atmosphere to be explained.

The sun has an emission temperature of 6000 K giving an energy maximum in the visible light wavelength. This reaches the top of our atmosphere at the rate of about 2 calories per sq. cm per minute or 1.35 kW m^{-2}. On its passage through the atmosphere, some of this short-wave radiation is reflected back to space by clouds and dust, some is scattered by gas molecules and dust particles to give diffuse radiation, and some (about 18%) is absorbed by water vapour, carbon dioxide, and dust. The remainder reaches the ground surface where some is reflected and the rest is absorbed. On a global average, this amounts to approximately 47% of the radiation reaching the top of the atmosphere.

The earth's surface has a mean emission temperature of about 290 K as a result of solar heating. Thus terrestrial radiation is in the longer wavelengths with a maximum about 10 micrometres. The gases of the atmosphere have a very different response to this radiation and much of it is absorbed (see absorption). Certain wavelengths are unaffected, especially those between 8 and 12 μm (*radiation windows*). The atmosphere warms as a result of this absorption and atmospheric counter-radiation is returned to the surface and helps to maintain higher temperatures than would otherwise be expected.

2. A type of *plane tabling in which points of detail are fixed by ascertaining direction using an *alidade and distance by measuring on the ground with a tape. The method may be used over short distances, dispensing with the necessity to set up the plane table at two stations, as in *intersection methods.

radiation balance. The net effect of the difference between incoming and outgoing radiation at any point. These two factors rarely balance. Normally there is a surplus of radiation on the ground surface during the day, which helps to warm the surface and atmosphere, and a deficit at night when cooling takes place. The atmosphere has a negative radiation balance at all times. Taking the earth and atmosphere together, the areas equatorwards of 38° have a radiation surplus and polewards there is a radiation deficit.

radiation fog. Nocturnal cooling resulting from terrestrial radiation losses can lead to the air near the ground surface reaching the saturation point so that condensation takes place, causing radiation fog. It is most likely to occur during long, clear, and calm nights with a moist atmosphere. In industrial areas, the abundance of condensation and hygroscopic nuclei facilitates fog formation and it may even occur with relative humidities less than 100%. However, urban warmth frequently counteracts this factor and so city centres may be almost clear of fog whilst it is still quite dense in the cooler suburbs.

Radiolaria. An order of the phylum *Protozoa whose members have an internal skelton composed of silica. They are one of the constituents of marine plankton. In certain conditions their remains accumulate to form *radiolarian ooze, and analogous ancient radiolarian cherts are known. Fossils from rocks as old as the Precambrian have been attributed to this group.

radiolarian ooze. A siliceous ooze (*see* pelagic ooze) deposit containing over 30% organisms. It is reddish or brownish in colour and results from the deposition of minute siliceous skeletal remains of radiolarians. The deposits are very limited in extent when viewed on a global scale, being almost confined to a narrow tract of deep-sea floor in the Pacific Ocean, located just north of the equator.

radiolarite. A hard fine-grained siliceous rock formed predominantly from the skeletal material of *Radiolaria.

radiometric dating. A method of dating rocks by determining the relative proportions present of parent and daughter isotopes of a radioactive element. Since these decay reactions progress at a known rate the age of the rock is calculated from the ratio present.

radiosonde. An instrument for measuring pressure, winds, temperature, and humidity in the upper atmosphere. It consists of a small radio transmitter attached to a balloon. Values of temperature and humidity are obtained by electrical means from a bimetallic strip and a gold-beater's skin respectively and then transmitted to the receiver. The balloon is located by radar and from its position wind velocities can be calculated. Nine stations in the British

Isles release radiosondes every six hours to determine the structure of the atmosphere; they attain heights of about 20 000 m (60 000 ft.; 50 mb).

rain. *Precipitation in the form of liquid water drops ranging in size from about 0.5 mm to 5 mm in diameter.

rainbow. An optical phenomenon consisting of an arc of light across the sky broken up into the spectral colours. It results from the refraction and internal reflection of sunlight through falling water drops. The intensity of the rainbow depends upon the size of the drops, larger sizes producing more spectacular colours. Some of the light may be reflected twice within the raindrop to produce a double rainbow effect.

rain day. A climatological *day from 9 am GMT within which 0.2 mm or more of rainfall is recorded. See also wet day.

raindrop size spectrum. The range of raindrop sizes within or beneath a precipitating cloud. The range of sizes varies with the rate of rainfall. At low rates (0.1 mm hr^{-1}) most drops will have a diameter less than 0.75 mm and there will be very few above 1.25 mm. With heavier rain, the upper range of drop sizes increases and the density of drops rises markedly.

rainfall. The water equivalent of all forms of precipitation from the atmosphere, received in a rain gauge. This includes dew, hoar frost, and rime on the collecting area of the gauge, since on melting it is indistinguishable from the rest of the catch. It is now recorded in millimetres in most countries of the world. The value quoted represents the amount of water that has fallen on a horizontal surface assuming no runoff, percolation, or evaporation.
Rainfall has been classified into three types depending on its mode of formation: convective, cyclonic, or orographic.

rain gauge. An instrument for measuring rainfall. In its simplest form it is essentially a funnel and a collecting vessel placed vertically into the ground. To maintain standardization of records, the official British gauge has a funnel diameter of 5″ and is placed 12″ above the ground surface. This is to avoid splashing during heavy rain, to retain snow, and to reduce the effects of wind eddying around the gauge. It is widely accepted that a rain gauge does not catch the precise amount of rain falling on a surface, largely owing to the wind eddying effect, but as long as all sites are standardized there is comparability between records. The rainfall is measured by emptying the contents of the collecting vessel into a special cylindrical flask, which is graduated in relation to the diameter of the gauge. The rainfall can be read off directly from the water level in the flask.

rain pits. Sedimentary structures formed in subaerially exposed soft fine-grained sediments as a result of the impact of raindrops upon the sediment's surface.

rain shadow. An area on the leeward side of a range of hills where rainfall totals are less than would be expected from their latitudinal position. It is the result of a drying-out of the winds through precipitation on the upwind side of the hills.

rainsplash. The impact of raindrops on the soil. It influences slope evolution in two ways: firstly, as the drop hits the ground and rebounds, it brings up with it particles of soil, which tend to fall downslope; secondly, this process will, if continued, compact the soil surface, often breaking up soil structures, and reduce the infiltration capacity (ability to hold and store water) of the soil. This promotes surface flow, either as an *overland flow or as *rills, which then erode the surface.

rain wash. *See* overland flow.

raised bog. *See* organic soils.

rapakivi structure. An *orbicular structure exhibited by some granites in which large oval pink orthoclase crystals are mantled by white oligoclase.

rapids. A stretch of fast-flowing turbulent broken water at a break in the long profile of a river that is not a vertical drop. Rapids often mark *knickpoints, sometimes in the form of the remains of an eroded waterfall. If the fall in base level causing rejuvenation results in a retreat of the shoreline some distance offshore, because the coastal area is gently sloping, the knickpoint may be spread over a considerable horizontal distance and rapids will be created rather than a waterfall. Rapids can also occur where the river crosses a hard rock band, not yet graded to fit a smooth long profile. Rapids and waterfalls tend to be fairly quickly eliminated owing to the increased turbulence and erosion they themselves create.

raw soil. Soil with an (A)C profile, produced by incipient soil-forming processes on fresh rock.

Rayleigh waves. One of two types of surface wave produced either naturally by earthquakes or volcanic eruptions, or artifically by an explosion. In Rayleigh waves the motion of surface particles is in the vertical plane containing the direction of wave propagation. *See also* love waves.

reaction rim. A *corona structure consisting of a concentric shell (or shells) or a mineral often arranged in a radial or fibrous manner around a primary mineral. Such rims, in igneous rocks, may be the result of a reaction between an early-formed mafic mineral and the liquid with which it is no longer in equilibrium. Thus a later member of the *reaction series is produced, e.g. olivine may be mantled by pyroxene or amphibole. *Kelyphitic rims* are secondary coronas formed by late-stage or metasomatic fluids reacting with primary crystals, e.g. iddingsite rimming olivine.

reaction series. During magmatic crystallization, in order to maintain equilibrium between crystals and liquid, minerals interact chemically with the liquid. The reaction may be progressive so that a continuous series of homogeneous solid solutions is produced. In the plagioclase feldspars, the first-formed crystals are richest in calcium and as the temperature falls these react with the liquid to become progressively more sodic. The reaction series involving the ferromagnesian minerals is discontinuous, each reaction taking place only over discrete temperature intervals and corresponding to the transformation of one mineral to another of different crystal structure. At high temperatures, magnesium-rich olivine crystals are the first to appear in a basic magma but as cooling proceeds, olivine is no longer stable and magnesium-rich orthopyroxene crystallizes. Likewise orthopyroxene is stable over a limited temperature range and reacts to produce clinopyroxene. Ferromagnesian minerals have high- and low-temperature variants, those rich in magnesium preceding those rich in iron. The common rock-forming minerals have been arranged by N. L. Bowen in the order in which the reactions take place and constitute two series.

The early high-temperature members of both series generally crystallize together; hence gabbros contain magnesium-rich olivine and pyroxenes together with calcic plagioclases. The low-temperature minerals, alkali feldspar, mica, and quartz, are associated in granitic rocks. When the reaction between crystals and the liquid is unable to go to completion owing to too rapid cooling, early-formed members of the reaction series persist as relics in the final rock and zoned crystals (see crystal zoning) and *reaction rims are often observed.

realgar. An orange-red arsenic mineral, AsS, found in hydrothermal veins.

Recent. See Holocene.

recompilation. Once a map has been compiled, at a particular scale and according to certain specifications, any updating of the information can be by either revision or recompilation. The latter is necessary if the basic detail, i.e. relief, drainage, and planimetry, needs to be redrawn.

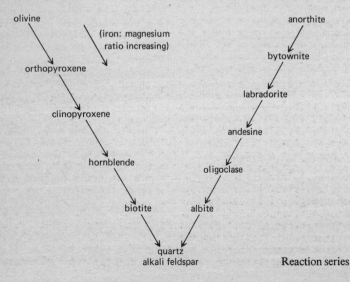

discontinuous reaction series

continuous reaction series

olivine

orthopyroxene

clinopyroxene

hornblende

biotite

(iron: magnesium ratio increasing)

anorthite

bytownite

labradorite

andesine

oligoclase

albite

quartz
alkali feldspar

Reaction series

Rectangular drainage

rectangular drainage. A drainage pattern that is characterized by streams flowing in two directions at right angles to each other. Neither direction is subordinate, both being equally developed. The most usual control is right-angled faulting in an area of little other structural guidance.

rectilinear slope. A slope or individual facet of a slope that is straight, i.e. has a single angle of slope.

recumbent fold. A fold type in which the axial plane is almost horizontal. See diagram at *fold*.

red (brown) clay. A pelagic deposit that covers large parts of the abyssal floor, actually about a quarter of the Atlantic and Indian Oceans respectively, and something approaching a half of the Pacific Ocean, or collectively some 28% (approximately 130 million sq. km) of the total ocean floor. The deposit is characterized by a low silica and carbonate content. The clay particles may be admixed in places with manganese nodules, whale bones, sharks' teeth, pumice, and other assorted materials.

red earth. *See* ferrallitic soils.

reduction. A chemical process that occurs in rocks and in the gleyed and leached parts of soil, whereby oxygen is removed from the weathering material. The continuous presence of water renders oxygen scarce, leading to its displacement, for example from ferric iron (Fe_2O_3) to give ferrous iron (FeO), in which state it is rendered more soluble and hence potentially more mobile. The characteristic red and yellow colours of *oxidation are absent, being replaced by greens and greys. Bacteria are important in this process.

reef. A ridge, island chain, or area of rocks that projects above the surface of the sea for all or part of the tide or may be permanently submerged. Reefs constitute distinct navigational hazards. A reef may be formed of solid rock or pebbles, but the term is more commonly applied to organic reefs (*bioherms). They are sometimes attached to the coast and act as groynes by collecting debris against them (*fringing reefs*), sometimes parallel to the coast and separated from it by a lagoon too deep for coral growth (*barrier reefs*), sometimes in tabular sheetlike masses (*apron reefs*), and sometimes in circular form (*atolls*). Coral, a hard calcareous material, dead or alive, may be predominant in all of these (corals are at present the commonest reef-building organisms). Coral reefs are common in the tropics. Other organic reefs include *oyster reefs and serpulid reefs (which result from the cementing action wrought by certain types of marine worms). The presence of a freshwater outflow from reefs locally inhibits organic growth, causing gaps through the reefs.

reflection profile. A seismic profile produced and recorded by equipment designed to reflect energy from layered rock bodies.

refolded folds. Folds that have been subjected to more than one period of folding. The folds produced in the first period of folding have further fold trends overprinted on them by subsequent periods of folding.

reg. A type of arid desert plain consisting of gravel, especially in the Sahara. *See also* erg, hammada.

regelation. A process of thawing and refreezing within a *glacier, which contributes towards the down-valley movement of ice. It is believed that pressure within the ice of a glacier causes the melting of some ice crystals. The resultant meltwater will move to locations at which pressure is less, i.e. normally downslope, and then refreeze. The process has been classed as the primary cause of ice motion but many authorities on the subject consider it to be only a secondary factor arising from flow.

regime. The total economy or habit of a natural system, e.g. fluvial regime, estuarine regime, coastal regime. *See also* equilibrium regime.

regolith (waste mantle). Unconsolidated weathered material between the ground surface and the bedrock, which may reach thicknesses of 60 metres in the tropics. It is formed either in situ, by the weathering of the underlying bedrock, or it is transported into the area by water, wind, or ice. The upper biochemically weathered portion of the regoli is the soil.

regosol. A thin azonal soil that may develop where one soil-forming factor delays the soil-forming processes. They are young in development and lack a B horizon, resulting in an AC profile with the A horizon, because of organic matter, being darker than the C. Regosols are typically developed in unconsolidated deposits such as loess, recent till, or sand dunes, and the parent material dominates the characteristics of the profile. They are classified in the *entisol order of the Seventh Approximation.

regression. The retreat of the sea from a land area.

rejuvenation. The revitalizing of streams by an increase in their erosive capacities resulting from a fall in *base level. This causes oversteeping of the lower reaches, and increased erosion cuts out a new long profile which will intersect the original long profile at a *knickpoint. Tributary valleys meeting the main

stream seaward of the knickpoint will also be rejuvenated and begin to cut down; if they do not keep pace with the incision of the master stream, there will be a marked break of slope at the junction, leaving them "perched". Below the knickpoint, the former valley floor will be left hanging above the stream as it cuts down to a new level, becoming a *river terrace. The knickpoint will advance upstream at a rate dependent on the lithology of the bed material and the nature of the flow over it; if it meets a hard rock band it may be halted, and so the effects of the rejuvenation will not be felt upstream. Valley-side slopes will also be rejuvenated, as the incision of streams will oversteepen their lower portions, and temporarily create a valley side facet adjacent to the stream.

rejuvenation head. *See* knickpoint.

relative humidity. The most frequently used index of atmospheric *humidity. It is the actual vapour pressure of the air expressed as a percentage of the saturation vapour pressure at the same temperature. It can be measured directly by changes in length of a hair or a skin in a hygrometer, or indirectly using wet- and dry-bulb temperatures. As the value of relative humidity changes inversely with temperature, even for the same moisture content of the atmosphere, it is not a very precise unit.

relative relief. The degree of dissection of a landscape, shown by the difference in height between the tops of drainage divides and the bottoms of adjacent valley floors. Cartographically it is approached by calculating the difference between the highest and lowest points in each grid square of the relief map, and then expressing the results as a series of isolines joining areas of equal relative relief. According to the normal *cycle of erosion, relative relief increases to a maximum in maturity and thereafter decreases. One geomorphologist has based a scheme for landscape attractiveness on relative relief, high relative relief producing high scenic appeal.

relic sediments (in oceanography). Marine deposits, usually those present on shelf areas, that are incompatible with contemporary marine environments. For example, much relic sediment on the continental shelf surrounding Britain was intially deposited there under glacial or interglacial conditions. Much of the material lying on the shelf off S California is relic, especially the sands that contain extinct shallow-water foraminifera, and which currently lie on outer parts of the shelf. Some sands off Long Beach, California, have been found to include Pleistocene fauna. Many relic shelf sediments are now undergoing sorting and transport, under the action of waves and tidal flow, gradually shifting to more compatible sedimentary environments. *Modern sediments* are those being derived under contemporaneous conditions.

relief. The variation in elevation or physical outline of a landscape, shown on maps by the use of contours, spot heights, hypsometric tinting, and hillshading. Relief is also used synonymously with *relative relief. Positive relief indicates land rising above the general level, i.e. hills.

remnant magnetism. The magnetism frozen into a mineral or rock as it cools through its Curie point.

rendzina. Soil developed on soft calcareous parent material with an AC profile (no illuvial B horizon). The A is usually dark brown or black, rich in carbonates and humus, with a good crumb or granular structure, and a pH value above neutral. There are no free sesquioxides as in the related *terra rossa soils, which also develop on calcareous material. It may be that the rendzinas are less mature than the terra rossa soils, or that the terra rossas develop on hard limestone, whilst rendzinas develop on soft. Rendzinas occur in humid to semiarid climates, under grass or grass-and-tree vegetation,

and are perhaps best known as the soils of chalk downland.

reniform. Denoting the massive kidney-shaped form in which some minerals occur. Reniform haematite is called kidney iron ore. *Compare* botryoidal.

representative fraction (R.F.). The ratio between distance on a map and distance on the ground, expressed as a fraction.

Reptilia. A class of cold-blooded terrestrial vertebrates whose young complete their development within a tough-shelled egg; they are therefore protected from desiccation and totally independent of an aquatic environment. Reptiles evolved from the *Amphibia in the Carboniferous period and their main radiation began at the end of the Permian. During the Jurassic and Cretaceous a great variety of reptiles came to dominate life on land. These ranged from the giant *dinosaurs to the flying *Pterosauria and the secondarily aquatic *Ichthyosauria and *Plesiosauria. All these groups became extinct at the beginning of the Cenozoic, when they were replaced by the mammals. Modern reptiles include crocodiles, lizards, and snakes.

reservoir. A rock that has a high porosity and good permeability and is able to store and transmit fluids or gases.

resorption. The remelting of crystals due to reaction with the magma from which they originally crystallized. Early-formed phenocrysts frequently fail to maintain equilibrium with the melt and are partially resorbed. Markedly anhedral crystal forms are produced and a *reaction rim of a new mineral may result.

resultant wind. A wind velocity may be divided into zonal (east) and meridional (north) components. To determine the resultant wind of a series of wind velocities, the individual components of the actual wind are summed, squared, added together, and the square root taken. That is:

$$\text{Resultant wind} = \sqrt{\left(\Sigma V_N\right)^2 + \left(\Sigma V_E\right)^2}$$

reverse fault. A type of fault in which the movement along the inclined fault plane has been up-dip. This results from a principal stress configuration in which the maximum principal stress is vertical, whilst the intermediate and minimum principal stress directions are horizontal. (See diagram at *fault*.)

Reynolds number (Re). The extent to which viscosity modifies a fluid flow pattern depends upon the speed of flow (*u*), the width of an obstacle placed across the flow or of the flow passage (*D*), and a value for the kinematic viscosity (*v*). The relationship, uD/v gives the Reynolds Number.

It is an important number in laboratory simulations of prototype flow conditions, since ideally the Reynolds number for scale hydraulic model flow should be the same as for the prototype, i.e. to maintain scale relationships, the small model size has to be compensated by increasing the flow rates in the model.

rheidity. Deformation of a substance by plastic flow as a result of an applied stress over a long period.

rhodocrosite. See carbonate minerals.

rhombochasm. A parallel-sided break in the earth's continental crust, the break being filled by oceanic crust. The fracture is thought to be the result of *sea-floor spreading.

rhumb line (loxodrome). A line of constant bearing, used in navigation, cutting all meridians at the same angle. *Compare* great circle.

rhyodacite. See rhyolite.

rhyolite. Rhyolites, rhyodacites, and dacites are the volcanic equivalents of *granites, adamellites, and granodiorites respectively. Rhyolites usually contain sanidine, the high-temperature form of potassium feldspar, both as phenocrysts and microlites in the groundmass. Phenocrysts of sodic plagioclase and quartz are also common, the latter often markedly anhedral owing to resorption. The dominant mafic mineral is biotite but hornblende and clinopyroxene also occur.

In dacites, sodic plagioclase is dominant over sanidine and, together with quartz, occurs as phenocrysts. With a decrease in the amount of quartz, rhyodacites and dacites pass into *latites and *andesites but the relative proportions of minerals are difficult to assess in fine-grained volcanic rocks and classification is often based upon chemical analyses. Rhyolitic and andesitic lavas constitute the calc-alkaline volcanic suite, which is characteristic of island arcs and orogenic regions.

Strongly alkaline rhyolites, rich in sodium and poor in aluminium, are found in continental areas, particularly those subjected to rift movements, and are the volcanic equivalents of alkali granites. These lavas contain anorthoclase feldspar and soda *pyriboles. An arbitrary division at 12.5% femic constituents separates pantellerites from the more leucocratic comendites. With a decrease in the amount of quartz, alkali rhyolites pass via quartz-trachytes into *trachytes.

Many lavas of rhyolitic composition occur in the glassy state, as do *obsidian* and *pitchstone*. Obsidian is a black natural glass with a conchoidal fracture but pitchstone has a dull appearance. Whereas obsidian contains very little water, pitchstone may contain up to 10% and owes its appearance to secondary hydration and devitrification. Most volcanic glasses contain crystallites; many contain spherulites and exhibit perlitic cracking.

Rhyolitic lavas are often flow-banded and it is sometimes difficult to distinguish such rocks from ignimbrites with parataxitic structure. *See* pyroclastic rocks.

ria. A *drowned valley eroded by subaerial (nonglacial) processes at a time when the sea level was lower than it now is. Like river valleys of the present, rias have a V-shaped cross section, which deepens seawards and narrows inland, possibly bifurcating. Former *monadnocks may remain as small islands. Rias are produced wherever a dissected area of hills and valleys, perpendicular to the coastline, has been submerged as a result of a postglacial rise in sea level. Erosion of the projecting interfluves eventually reduces the indentation of such coasts.

richterite. A monoclinic *amphibole.

Richter scale. A logarithmic scale devised by C. F. Richter in 1935 for comparing the magnitude of earthquakes. Although originally devised for Californian earthquakes, it has since been adopted for worldwide use. The upper limit of the scale at 9 is a function of the strength of crustal rocks.

ridge. 1. An extension of high pressure away from the main centre of an anticyclone, the area of higher pressure separating two depression systems. Weather in a ridge tends to be similar to that of a true anticyclone, but is less persistent.
2. See median ridge.

riebeckite. A monoclinic *amphibole.

rift valley (taphrogeosyncline). A structural and topographical feature formed within the earth's crust consisting of a steep-sided flat-bottomed valley, the rocks of the valley floor having subsided between two parallel faults or two parallel series of step faults. There are conflicting views as to the origin of rift valleys, the main ones favouring tension in the earth's crust, compression, or the cracking of a crustal dome along the crest. There is often associated volcanic activity along the sides of the valley floor. Famous rift valleys include the East African system, extending over 4000 kilometres from Syria to the Zambesi and the Rhine rift valley between Mainz and Basle. See also graben.

rigidity modulus. The ratio of stress to strain when the stress is a shear. This is calculated by dividing the tangential force per unit area by the angular deformation.

rill marks. Small channels found on beaches, aligned more or less up and down the beach. They develop because of the seaward flow of water that has percolated into the upper parts of the foreshore during the period around mid- to high-water or just after, or during the action of *storm waves with powerful swash action between low- to mid-water. As the tide retreats, or as the waves subside, the infiltrated water may flow out on to the beach face and cut the rills. Once developed, the rills tend to channel this flow seawards and possibly enlarge themselves. The seawater may be reinforced by freshwater seepages from landward, for instance where springs issue from a rock platform beneath the beach.

rills. Minute ephemeral channels at the head of drainage systems, forming at the point where unconfined sheet wash becomes concentrated into definite channels. This usually occurs on the lower concave portions of slopes, as there the volume of sheet flow has built up to a sufficient amount for channelling to occur. Rills are said to be responsible for shaping the concavity of the basal part of the slope. Downslope they run into more permanent gullies, which constitute the smallest tributaries of drainage systems. Rills only carry water in storms. See also gully erosion, overland flow.

rime. A deposit of white ice crystals formed by the freezing of supercooled water droplets onto surfaces below $0°C$. It grows on the windward side of the surface, especially on sharp edges, by impaction as the droplets drift past in the wind. Rime is not uncommon in upland areas of Britain where supercooled fogs are frequent, but it is rare in lowland sites.

ring complex. A circular igneous intrusive body of rock including both concentric dykes and cone sheets.

ring dyke. *See* concentric dyke.

rip. A turbulent area of water where tidal currents meet head-on, where waves meet a current flowing in the opposite direction, where a tidal current suddenly enters shallow water, or in a *rip current.

rip current. A strong well-defined current that flows away from the shore. Such currents are wave-induced, providing the mechanism whereby water piled up at the coast because of mass transport, and possibly wind, is returned seawards. The current speeds are usually fairly high. They are usually manifested by a fairly narrow zone of agitated water and by an accentuated amount of sandy material in suspension. They consist of *feeder currents* that flow inshore of the breakers and more or less parallel to the shore as longshore currents, the *neck*, where the current is concentrated into a *rip and flows seawards through the breaker zone, and the expanding *rip-head* where the rip loses impetus within or beyond the breaker zone. They account for many drownings.

ripple bedding. Small-scale cross bedding resulting from the rapid deposition of sand in the form of ripples.

ripple marks. The most common minor beach morphological form, consisting of fairly regular and generally small ridges formed in sediment (usually sand, but possibly shell and fine gravel) on a river bed, in the inter-tidal zone, or on the seabed seaward of low-water mark. Fossil ripples or ripples formed by the wind may occur above high-water mark. Ripples are caused by water or wind flow, and are aligned more or less perpendicularly to the flow direction. They can be used, therefore, to indicate the existence of and something of the nature of wind and water currents. Ripples tend to be larger in more exposed areas and in deeper water offshore. Very large ripples are usually termed mega-ripples or *sand waves. Dune areas above high-water mark may display numerous ripple features.

rise. A broad elevated area of the sea floor, similar to a *mid-ocean ridge but lacking a median rift valley.

river capture. The diversion of the headstreams of a river into an adjacent river with more powerful headward erosion. It cuts back its valley into that of the weaker river, thus enlarging its drainage basin at the expense of the other. Rivers whose headstreams have been captured often flow as *misfits in valleys that are too large to have been eroded by the present capacity of the river. The *elbow of capture* is the bend at which the captured headstreams are diverted.

river terrace. A benchlike landform bordering many rivers, elevated above the current streams and ending in scarps suspended on the valley side. These constitute all that remains today of past abandoned valley floors formed when the river was flowing at a higher level than today. Most commonly they are paired on either side of the valley, the product of *rejuvenation of the river or climatic changes (via their influence on stream discharge, base level, and sediment load). They consist of a rock-cut bench, with or without a thin veneer of alluvium.
Some rivers, such as the Thames, Avon, Severn, and Trent, have staircases of terraces rising above the current stream, produced in the climatic fluctuations of the Pleistocene.

Roaring Forties. The region between 40°S and 50°S where the westerlies blow with great regularity across the open ocean. The frequent depressions and strong winds produce a stormy climate unfavourable to shipping.

Roche moutonnée

roche moutonnée. A glacial erosion
form found in areas of low relief and
consisting of a resistant rock mass,
eroded to comprise a gently sloping up-
valley face and a steep down-valley
face. The up-valley face is smoothed,
polished, and striated, the effects of
glacial abrasion, whilst the down-valley
face has a broken shattered appearance
as a result of freeze-thaw processes,
which are assisted by increased pressure-melting induced by the presence of
the rock mass.

The term is extremely old and is widely
used for similar landforms of greatly
contrasting size. As a more suitable
alternative, the term *stoss and lee topography* has been suggested.

rock crystal. A colourless variety of
quartz. *See* silica minerals.

rockfall. A type of landslide involving
purely dry materials. Basal sapping or
some other type of trigger mechanism
will institute an instantaneous downslope movement, leaving a pock-marked
slope at the source and a confused pile
of talus at the foot. The nature of this
talus or colluvium depends on the
height of fall and the nature of the
weathering, lower falls and less rigorous
weathering leaving larger blocks. *See
also* mass movement.

rollers. Large waves rolling in onto
exposed coasts, often following a storm,
increasing their height before breaking
in a rather destructive manner. The
waves make up a series of long-crested
forms. They characterize such coasts as
the South Atlantic, the South Indian

Ocean, and the West Indian islands. A
hydrographic chart of, for example, the
E coast of North Island, New Zealand,
would indicate the presence of rollers
on its more exposed beaches.

roof pendant. A small downward projection of country rock into an underlying igneous body. *See also* cupola.

Rossby wave. *See* long wave.

roughness length. A measure used in
micrometeorological studies as an indicator of degree of roughness of a surface
to airflow. It is determined by ex-
trapolating the observed relationship
between wind speed and height to the
point where the wind speed becomes
zero. Its value is about one tenth that of
the true height of the roughness elements, i.e. for a lawn of thickness 1 cm
it is about 0.1 cm.

ruby. *See* corundum.

rudaceous. Denoting a *clastic sedimentary deposit or rock in which the
constituent fragments are of relatively
large size. It is formed of *gravel, i.e.
the clasts are greater than 2 mm in
diameter.

runnel. A depression extending along a
beach perpendicular to the direction of
wave approach. Runnels separate and
lie parallel with *beach ridges.

running means. A statistical method of
smoothing the variations in a time
series. It is calculated by determining
the mean of a set of numbers (frequently
five or ten year periods), then omitting
the first value and taking the next
succeeding value, the mean is again
calculated. A series of running means is
thus obtained for a specified time
period, and helps to illustrate the
overall trend by reducing the influence
of individual extreme years.

runoff. That part of total precipitation
left to flow into rivers after evaporation
and transpiration by plants has taken
place. It has several components: rain
falling into the channel of the river,
surface runoff, rainfall that soaks into

the soil moving laterally towards the river to reach it as "interflow", and water that percolates through the soil to the water table, feeding steadily all the year round to the stream as groundwater. Over the world as a whole, around one fifth of rainfall becomes runoff, but regional variations are very great, dependent on climate, the nature of vegetation and soil, whether the rain comes in severe storms or widespread gentle showers, etc. In any one region it varies over time according to climatic cycles and the seasons.

rutile. A brown, violet, or black tetragonal mineral. It is the commonest polymorph of TiO_2 and is widespread as an accessory mineral in igneous and metamorphic rocks. It also occurs in high-temperature veins with quartz and apatite and as an alteration product of sphene and ilmenite. It is an important ore of titanium.

S

saccharoidal. Denoting a fine- to medium-grained granular rock resembling sugar.

saddle. A broad shallow depresion in a mountain ridge forming a pass.

salic. Denoting the silicon- and aluminium-rich minerals of the CIPW normative classification. *Compare* femic.

salinity. The extent to which water contains dissolved salts. Together with temperature and oxygen content, it is one of the fundamental properties of sea water. A wide range of salinity occurs in the various seas of the world: normal sea water has a salinity of approximately 34.33 grams per thousand grams (3.433%) although it may be as high as 4.0% (in the Red Sea and Persian Gulf) or less than 3.3% (at high latitudes). The differences arise largely as a result of variations in the rate of evaporation. Increased salinity raises the relative density, lowers the freezing point, and greatly influences marine ecosystems to

the extent that fauna and flora have to adapt to saline conditions. A knowledge of salinity is also important in understanding the circulation of ocean water.

salite. A monoclinic *pyroxene.

Saltation

saltation. A mechanism of sediment transport, whereby individual grains move by bouncing off the surface. It is the most common form of transport by wind. It is much less significant in rivers owing to the viscosity of water as compared with air; the "stickiness" of water slows down the rise of the grain and cushions its fall, so the height of saltation is but a few grain diameters as compared with several thousand grain diameters in air. The initial rise of the grain is near vertical, followed by a gentle downward flight in the direction of wind or stream flow, terminated by impact again with the surface at an angle of 10–16°. In air, this impact may cause the grain itself to rebound, or dislodge another grain on the surface, which will then saltate. In water, the lifting force is eddy turbulence, which temporarily overcomes the weight of the grain, imparting an upward movement.

salt-earth podzol. *See* solod.

salt flat. A level salt surface constituting the bed of a former salt lake.

salt lake. A highly saline lake formed in an *inland basin.

sand. According to the British Standard Code of Practice, particles of rock with

a size range of 0.06-2.00 mm in diameter (i.e. between silt and gravel):
0.6-2.0 mm coarse sand.
0.2-0.6 mm medium sand.
0.06-0.2 mm fine sand. Rocks formed from sediment in this range are known as sandstones.

According to Bagnold (1941), sand is that material lying above a lower limit of material capable of carriage by suspension (mostly dust) and below an upper limit of material incapable of movement either by direct wind force or by the impact of falling grains. Wind-blown sands are said to be mostly 0.3 to 0.15 mm.

Most sands are predominantly made of quartz, other material being too easily eroded to survive for long. The quartz is derived from the weathering of quartz-bearing rocks, subsequently reduced in size by water or ice abrasion. Desert sands are more rounded than fluvial or marine types.

sand banks. Banks of sand and other sediments that occur in estuaries and along the open coast where the tidal streams tend to flow in a rectilinear fashion and where transportable sediments are fairly abundant. The form of the bank and the pattern of a group of banks often reflect the nature of tidal flow. The surrounding or included channels may be of the ebb or the flood type, depending on the relative dominance of one or other tidal stream. The banks tend either to be linear or parabolic in shape.

sand (or mud) volcano. A sedimentary structure produced in poorly consolidated sands and clays that have a high water content. As a result of shaking, a lower layer of sediment will be injected up and through the overlying bed. When this process is completed the lower bed builds up as a small cone above the upper bed. Where the process does not reach completion or the overlying bed is very thick, *flame structures are produced.

sand ribbons. Submarine morphological forms of linear shape that, like sand waves, occur where tidal streams are suitable for their formation and where transportable sediment is sufficiently abundant. They occur within certain estuaries and along parts of the open coast, seaward of low-water mark. They are often only a few centimetres thick, and, in the Bristol Channel for instance, may be up to 100 metres wide and nearly 2.5 kilometres long. The general trend of sand ribbons off the S coasts of Britain is parallel to both the coast and the directions of the strongest tidal steams. Where surface streams are less than 1 knot, the boundaries of the ribbons tend to be somewhat obscure; in contrast, where surface tidal streams attain more than 1 knot, the boundaries become more strongly defined. Such morphological information is clear from high-precision echo sounding.

sand shadow. See aeolian forms.

sand sheet. See aeolian forms.

sandstone. A lithified *arenaceous deposit. It is a *clastic sedimentary rock composed of grains between 1/16 mm and 2 mm in diameter. The particles may be bound by a secondary cement such as *calcite or various iron minerals, or be welded together by pressure. A great variety of sandstones are known, and they can be classified by both mineralogical and textural characteristics.

sand stream. A broad tract of moving sediment (largely of sand grade) seaward of low-water mark, possibly tens of kilometres in width. Sand streams tend to extend over considerable distances, roughly parallel to the coast. The streams are evident from various field data, including morphological forms such as *sand ribbons, *sand banks, and *sand waves, information relating to sediment grain-size distribution, and a knowledge of waves and tidal streams. Sand streams may occur anywhere on shelf areas, but are especially developed near to coasts when the tidal currents flow in rectilinear fashion. One such stream moves northwards out of the southern bight of the North Sea, towards Holland and Germany. Others move northwards and southwards respectively from the region of N Norfolk. Yet another stream trends westwards through the English Channel. Such streams tend either to converge or to diverge.

sandur. *See* outwash plain.

sand wave (mega-ripple). A morphological form that resembles a desert dune and has been called an underwater dune. The sediment is usually of sand grade. They are created by tidal flow, and, if large, may have many smaller sand waves superimposed upon them. They often occur on the surface of *sand ribbons. They tend to be orientated perpendicular to the main tidal flow direction. Most display a measure of asymmetry, which enables the net direction of sediment transport to be determined, the steepest face indicating the direction of travel. A small difference, perhaps only 0.1 knot, in the flood and ebb peak velocities, is sufficient to cause asymmetry of form and to make the sand waves migrate in one or other direction. The crests of sand waves may be straight or sinuous; their height, as in the case of the southern North Sea, may be as much as 15 metres. In contrast, off Florida, many of the sand waves are less than 1 m in height. Some sand waves are formed in the relatively deep water near the shelf edge, for example off SW England, where their heights vary between 8 and 12 m, and their average length is some 850 m.

sanidine. A potassic alkali *feldspar.

Sanson-Flamsteed projection. A modified *conical projection and a special case of Bonne's projection. Both the central meridian and the equator (standard parallel) are straight lines that are truly divided and at right angles to each other. All other parallels are horizontal straight lines, equally divided and equal distances apart. This is a sinusoidal map projection as the meridians are sine curves drawn through predetermined points on the parallels. Though the shapes are distorted away from the centre of the projection, it is an equal-area projection and therefore commonly used in atlases for areas astride the equator, e.g. Africa.

sapphire. *See* corundum.

saprolite. The part of the weathering profile that, though weathered, remains in situ and retains such original structures of the parent rock as jointing, banding, and veining.

satellites. Since 1957, numerous satellites have been placed in earth orbit. Some of these have had specific meteorological purposes and tremendous amounts of new information have appeared as a result of these instruments. Continuous records are now received of cloud patterns and infrared photographs and experiments have shown that it is possible to obtain vertical temperature profiles. A recent technique has been the development of geostationary satellites, which are orbiting at the same rate as the earth and are therefore providing a continuous record of the same portion of the atmosphere and surface. As a result, they can determine the wind field at cloud level from the varying *cloud patterns, in addition to the other facilities offered by the normal satellite.

saturated adiabatic lapse rate. The rate of cooling of a parcel of saturated air as it rises. Because the amount of latent heat released depends upon air temperature, the lapse rate is not a constant. At high temperatures the rate is slow as much latent heat is released on condensation, whereas when it is very cold little heat is released and its value approaches the *dry adiabatic lapse rate. *See also* environmental lapse rate.

saturated rocks. Igneous rocks that contain neither quartz nor feldspathoids. *See* silica saturation.

temp./°C

Saturation vapour pressure curve

saturation. 1. The condition in which a sample of moist air is in equilibrium with an open water surface at the same temperature and pressure. In this state there is a balance between the number of molecules leaving the water surface and the number returning from air to water. The point of saturation can be reached by adding moisture to a system or cooling it. The capacity of air to hold water is largely determined by temperature as shown in the diagram of the saturation vapour pressure curve.
2. *See* silica saturation.

Saurischia. An order of dinosaurs distinguished from the ornithischians by having a pelvis constructed on the typical reptilian plan. They were primarily carnivorous and some grew to a very large size: *Tyrannosaurus,* nearly 7 metres high, was the largest carnivorous land animal known and the herbivorous species were even larger, *Diplodocus,* for example, reaching a length of nearly 28 metres. Like other dinosaurs the group became extinct at the end of the Cretaceous period. *Compare* Ornithischia.

saussuritization. The alteration of plagioclase to a fine-grained assemblage of albite, epidote, calcite, and sericite during low-grade metamorphism and hydrothermal processes.

savanna climate. A tropical climate with a seasonal rainfall regime. It has similar properties to the monsoon climate, the rain being associated with the *intertropical convergence zone, though the seasonal reversal of winds is not necessarily as well developed. The name is derived from savanna vegetation characterized by tall grasses.

scapolites. Minerals that vary in composition between $Na_4(Al_3Si_9O_{24})Cl$ to $Ca_4(Al_6Si_6O_{24})CO_3$, mainly by the substitution $NaSi \rightleftharpoons CaAl$. They are found in a wide variety of metamorphic rocks.

scarp (escarpment). A steep clifflike slope often of considerable size, which rises above the surrounding land surface. Such structures result from faulting (*fault scarps*) or the differential erosion of gently inclined strata (*see* cuesta).

scattering. The electromagnetic radiation from the sun is affected by air, dust, and water vapour molecules in the atmosphere, which break up or scatter its unidirectional beam to give diffuse radiation. This scattering is selective in that blue wavelengths are scattered more easily than the longer red wavelengths and so diffuse radiation from the sky appears blue. The reduction of blue light from the direct beam results in the sun's disc appearing red or yellow.
Larger dust particles scatter light without any wavelength dependence. Hazy conditions with high dust con-

centrations therefore give a whitish hue to the sky.

schiller. A striking play of colours exhibited by some minerals, particularly feldspars and pyroxenes, in hand specimen. This is due to very small inclusions of iron ore, orientated along certain cleavages or partings, which reflect the light when the crystal is rotated. See diallage.

schist. A strongly foliated coarse-grained rock in which mica minerals are abundant and their sub-parallel orientation produces a marked *schistosity. The schistosity is accentuated by the segregation of minerals into thin layers alternately rich in micaceous minerals and quartz/feldspar. Schists in general are the product of regional metamorphism.

schistosity. A variety of slaty *cleavage that is well developed in *schists and to a lesser extent in *gneisses. Platy minerals such as micas, amphiboles, and chlorites recrystallize or crystallize perpendicular to the direction of maximum stress. All traces of the original bedding are destroyed and the rock readily splits along schistosity planes. See also foliation.

schlieren. Streaked-out patches found in igneous rocks, representing softened xenolithic material drawn out along the direction of flow.

schorl. A black variety of *tourmaline.

sclrocco. See sirocco.

scolecite. See zeolites.

scoriae. See pyroclastic rocks.

Scotch mist. A mixture of thick cloud and heavy drizzle, which derives its name from frequent occurrences in the hillier parts of Scotland. It is formed in maritime tropical air when uplift over the hills produces large amounts of condensation and cloud droplets, some of which are large enough to give drizzle. It can occur anywhere that the conditions of weak uplift of almost saturated but stable air are fulfilled.

scour. Localized erosion, for example tidal scour in estuaries, removing sediment periodically and depositing it again at another stage; in rivers periodic bed scour occurs during periods of high flow, compensated at low flow by infill of depressions, a process sometimes called scour-and-fill. In connection with glacial erosion, scour refers to the etching and polishing of solid rocks by rock material incorporated in the ice.

screw dislocation. A type of defect in a crystal lattice that results from the twisting of one part of the lattice relative to the other.

SCUBA. Self-contained underwater breathing apparatus. Diving with SCUBA to conduct scientific investigations of the sea floor and the overlying waters is a relatively new technique. It enables marine geologists, ecologists, and others to make first-hand observations and measurements of various phenomena in the marine environment. For example, with SCUBA it has been possible to carry out underwater mapping and to correlate this information with sounding, sampling, and submarine geological data. It enables scientists and technologists to assess the performance of their equipment, and enables many manual tasks such as oil-well connections to be performed on the spot without many of the problems of remote control.

scud. See fractostratus cloud.

Scyphozoa. The class of the phylum *Coelenterata that includes the jellyfish. As they possess no hard parts they are rare as fossils, though remains attributable to them have been found in rocks as old as the Precambrian.

sea breeze. A local wind resulting from differential surface heating between land and sea. It only blows during the day when land areas heat up relative to the sea to produce a weak thermal pressure gradient from sea to land.

Initially the wind blows down the pressure gradient force at right angles to the coast, but as the system continues the Coriolis force comes into play causing a veering of the wind until eventually the breeze may be almost parallel to the coast. It can extend up to 50 miles or even more inland and is separated from the warmer air by a sea-breeze front, rather like a cold front. Above the surface sea breeze is a returning circulation from land to sea maintaining continuity. *See also* land breeze.

sea-floor spreading. A concept formulated in the 1960s by which a satisfactory mechanism for *continental drift was found. This theory showed that the ocean floor is one of the youngest and most active parts of the earth's surface. Magma rising from the earth's mantle reaches the surface along the *mid-ocean ridges. The magma cools and becomes part of the earth's crust. Repeated rifting of the area accompanied by the addition of further magma causes the older material to be displaced sideways. As the earth is not expanding in diameter, the generation of new sea floor is compensated by its destruction and reabsorption into the mantle at destructive plate margins. As the oceans spread the continents are moved across the surface of the earth as part of a large *plate. The ocean continues to expand until the movement of other plates causes its rate of destruction to exceed its rate of construction. At that time the ocean begins to close. Examples of spreading oceans are the Red Sea and Atlantic Ocean; an example of a closing ocean is the Mediterranean Sea. Spreading rates are quite low, being in the order of 4 cm per year but varying from place to place along a mid-ocean ridge, and from ocean to ocean.

sea fog. Any fog over the sea, whatever its origin. It is most frequent over cold sea surfaces where contact cooling can lead to saturation of the overlying moist air. An exception to this is *Arctic sea smoke, which is an evaporational fog.

sea level. The average level of the sea surface at a given time and in relation to a chosen datum (*see* mean sea level). In Britain, this datum is usually taken as *Ordnance Datum. Because of the numerous irregularities and slopes present on the sea surface, an accurate measure of sea level is rather difficult. Apart from day-to-day variations, sea level has changed with time, sometimes showing a net upward trend, at other times showing the reverse. This has happened for many different reasons; among these are isostatic readjustment, geosynclinal sinking, local tectonic instability, geodetic changes, and glacio-eustatism. Hence, superimposed on the short-term fluctuations of sea level due to tides, winds, etc., are longer-term fluctuations. *See also* base level.

seamount. A submerged and isolated elevation on the deep-sea floor. Seamounts stand over 500 fathoms (some 1000 m) above the surrounding sea floor. Their slopes are comparatively steep and they display relatively small circular or elliptic summit areas. On a global scale, seamounts are very numerous and widespread, being especially numerous in the Pacific Ocean. Their summits lie in depths of between 200 m and 2500 m, though the majority of them lie between 1000 and 2000 m. Many stand on the *continental rise. Though some seamounts are found clustered in roughly linear groups, many others rise from the sea floor quite independently of their immediate neighbours, the floor between them often being relatively flat. Three or more seamounts in a line comprise a *seamount chain*, three or more not in a line make up a *seamount group*, and three or more sited on a rise or ridge comprise a *seamount range*.

season. A sub-division of the year consisting of a period of supposedly uniform or similar climatic characteristics. The length and properties of the seasons vary across the globe. In tropical areas, temperatures are fairly uniform throughout the year and distinction is made between the wet and dry seasons only. In Britain, the seasons are based on the equinoxes and solstices, but for climatological purposes the divisions are on a monthly basis: spring—March, April, May; summer—June, July, August; autumn—September, October, November; winter—December, January, February. These periods do have some average significance, but individual days may have weather conditions appropriate to any season. In polar regions, the changeover from winter to summer and vice versa is very sudden and there is thus a two-season year as in the tropics.

sea valley. An elongated depression cut in the sea floor and having a valley-like form. They display a variety of forms: *submarine canyons are deeply incised and possess steep walls, while many others have a broad cross-sectional valley form, with relatively gently sloping sides that contrast markedly with the steep canyon walls. Some valleys have a troughlike form, like that off the Mississippi Delta or that off the Ganges Delta. Their floors are broad and flat. Some resemble land valleys by having levée features along one or both flanks (see levéed channels). Some are merely short gullies, sometimes arranged in a sub-parallel series. Eroded submarine valleys have been grouped into shelf channels and submarine canyons. The former group may be further subdivided into glacial troughs, tidal scour channels, and drowned river valleys.

sea waves. Waves in the generating area, i.e. the area in which waves are being actively formed. As the waves travel beyond this area they become longer-crested and more regular, being known as *swell. Because there may be present at any one time waves of quite different lengths (perhaps ranging from a few centimetres to several hundred metres) and different heights, superimposed one upon the other, the sea's surface may present a very confused picture. The size of sea waves depends largely on three variables: the speed of the wind, wind duration, and available fetch. See also wave.

secondary depression. A depression that forms along a front within the general circulation of a primary depression. Initially it is less intense than the parent low, but on many occasions it intensifies and eventually incorporates the original depression. Secondary lows often give Britain its worst weather as they tend to be in their most active phase nearer Britain than the earlier depression.

secondary enrichment. The concentration of valuable metals in the lower part of a vein as a result of the weathering of the upper part. Dissolved metals seep downwards and react with the lower-grade compounds, enriching them with metal content.

secondary minerals. Minerals present in a rock as a result of the chemical alteration or breakdown of the original minerals.

secondary reflection. A signal received at a receiver such as a geophone (hydrophone) from a particular reflecting rock horizon after it has been reversed in its direction of propagation at least twice by other reflecting horizons, and therefore arrives considerably later than a primary reflection from that horizon which has had a direct path of propagation.

secondary waves (S waves, shear waves). A type of seismic wave that travels through the solid body of the earth. It is propagated by the oscillation of the particles at right angles to its direction of propagation. This type of wave cannot be transmitted by liquids. See also primary waves.

secular trend. A climatic variation that can be observed during the period of instrumental records and indicates a persistent tendency for the mean value to increase or decrease. It is most easily determined by smoothing the data series by *running means.

secular variation. Changes in the properties of the earth's magnetic field over a long period of time.

sediment. Particulate material that has been deposited in a fluid medium. The fluid concerned is mostly water, but aeolian sediments are not uncommon. Sedimentary rocks consist of lithified sediment. *Clastic sedimentary rocks are formed from the erosion and redeposition of fragments of pre-existing rocks. Organic sedimentary rocks include *coal, many *limestones, and others derived from plants and animals. Chemical sedimentary rocks are those formed by chemical processes, and include the *evaporites and some ironstones.

sedimentary structures. Structures formed within sedimentary rocks during their deposition (*primary structures*) or after deposition (*secondary structures*). Such structures include *cross bedding, *flute casts, *bioturbation, and *rain pits.

sedimentation. The process of sediment deposition. Sedimentation of any particular particle size takes place when the velocity of flow in the transporting medium falls below its terminal, or settling, velocity.

sedimentology. The study of sediments and sedimentary rocks.

sediment trap. A natural or man-made device that serves to trap part of the sediments moving across or above the sea floor. Man-made traps have been successfully used for experimental purposes in certain limited situations, for example in some Alpine lakes, and in scale hydraulic model experiments. In nature, certain types of seaweed, mangrove, spartina, marram grass, and so on perform similar functions. Soft algae, which in temperate seas may attain lengths of up to 10 metres, not only break the force of waves but may reduce the orbital velocity beneath waves to the extent that sediments being carried in suspension may settle out on the seabed. Off S France, poseidonia beds in depths of between 5 and 50 m have led to deposition rates of up to 1 m per century. Synthetic seaweed, which is made of a special plastic material, is now being used in experiments to test its effectiveness in building up beaches. Spartina traps marsh muds, marram grass traps dune sands, and mangroves collect estuarine and tidal lagoon muds.

seiche. A fluctuation in water level sometimes occurring in the open sea, in semienclosed bays, harbours, lakes, and other water bodies. The period of oscillation generally ranges from a few minutes to several hours. Small seiches may be a permanent characteristic of many harbour basins. The period of oscillation is determined by the resonance characteristics of the water body in question, usually being a function of the actual dimensions and shape of the water body. The more severe seiches often result from rapid changes in wind fields and barometric pressure. Harbour basin seiches may result from wave penetration.

seif dune (longitudinal dune). A sand dune occurring as a long chain running parallel to the prevailing wind direction. They tend to form in areas where the wind regime is two-directional, with a gentle prevailing wind that supplies the sand and short-term cross winds, often of greater strength, that help build the dune, producing curved faces. They can originate ab initio, or from *barchans when the wind regime changes. Their characteristic form is of lines of ridges, running parallel over long distances, rising to summits periodically. The dunes grow downwind of the prevailing wind, with little lateral movement. Individual chains reach 100 kms in length, but several distinct chains can continue one line for much greater distances. Heights up to 210 m have been recorded, whilst the distance between successive lines varies from a maximum of 500 m to a minimum of 20 m.

seismic array. A series of seismometers laid out in an L- or T-shaped pattern.

seismic event. A short-lived event that acts as a source of energy for the formation of seismic waves, e.g. an earthquake or explosion.

seismic noise. See microseisms.

seismic reflection. The technique of determining the structure of a rock body by measuring the time taken for a pulse from a source at the surface to travel to that body, be reflected from a seismic discontinuity within that rock body, and return to the surface.

seismic refraction. The technique of determining the velocity and attitude of a subsurface rock body by measuring the shortest-time travel path from a source to a set of receivers distributed around the rock body.

seismic waves. Waves generated by an explosion or earthquake within the earth or on its surface. There are four main types of seismic wave: *primary waves, *secondary waves, *Rayleigh waves, and *love waves.

seismic zones (earthquake zones). Narrow well-defined belts in which the majority of earthquakes occur. These zones usually coincide with the junctions between lithospheric plates, especially in association with island arcs, mid-oceanic ridges, major fracture zones, and young orogenic belts. There are two main continental seismic zones, one bordering the Pacific and the other corresponding to the Alpine-Himalayan chain. There are larger areas which experience virtually no seismicity.

seismogram. A record of the frequency and magnitude of the oscillations produced during an earthquake, recorded on a time-correlating device.

seismometers. An electronic or mechanical device that detects, amplifies, filters, and records the motions of the earth in a particular direction. A seismic set is a series of three se-ismometers orientated at right angles to each other.

selenite. See gypsum.

sericite. Secondary muscovite occurring as fine-grained flaky aggregates formed from the alteration of *feldspars.

series. A division of rock in the Stratomeric scheme of stratigraphic nomenclature (see chronostratigraphy). It indicates the body of rock that has formed during one *epoch. A series consists of several *stages grouped together and several series may be combined to form a *system. In the past the term has been applied loosely to bodies of rock characterized on the basis of gross lithology and contained fossils, but a continuation of this informal practice is not generally recommended.

serozem. See sierozem.

serpentine. One of a group of minerals having the general composition $Mg_3Si_2O_5(OH)_4$ and a layered structure. They are monoclinic, typically green or white, and occur in two main forms: *chrysotile* and *antigorite*. Chrysotile is fibrous and is used in the manufacture of asbestos, whereas antigorite has a platy habit. Serpentines are found in altered basic and ultrabasic rocks where they have formed from the breakdown of olivines and pyroxenes.

serpentinite. A rock consisting largely of *serpentine, formed by the hydrothermal alteration of ultramafic rocks such as dunite and peridotite in which olivine and pyroxene have been converted to serpentine.

Seventh Approximation (New American Comprehensive Soil Classification). The current U.S. soil classification system, published in 1960. Its name comes from the fact that it represented the seventh attempt by its authors to find an "ideal" classification. Unlike earlier classifications based on pedogenesis, the emphasis is placed on properties of soils and diagnostic horizons that affect pedogenesis or result from it. As a result the ten orders of soils have some unusual groupings; for example, there is no separate group for gleys, and podzols occur in more than one order. Although the nomenclature is somewhat obtuse, and laboratory analysis to measure certain properties is necessary prior to definite classification, there is the great advantage that the major levels are as tightly defined as the field mapping units, so that there is no awkward gap between mapping and broad classification, as so typically happened with many older systems. To some extent, the Seventh Approximation is now being used at a world level, and the F.A.O. have published a world soil map based on it. See aridisol, entisol, oxisol, mollisol, spodosal, ultisol, vertisol, alfisol, inceptisol, histosol.

shadow zone. An area on the earth's surface whose *epicentral angle is greater than 103° and less than 143° from an earthquake focus. Within this area seismic waves are received only after they have been reflected at the earth's surface.

shale. A well-laminated *argillaceous sedimentary rock that is fissile, and splits easily along bedding planes (compare mudstone). The fissility is related to the disposition of clay minerals within the rock.

shallow inland seas. See epeiric seas.

shard. See pyroclastic rocks.

shear joint. A shear fracture, constituting a site of possible future shearing.

shear (shearing stress). A force tending to deform a rock mass through the movement of one part of it relative to another, as for example at a fault or thrust plane. See also differential shear.

shear waves. See secondary waves.

sheet erosion. See overland flow.

sheeting. See unloading.

shelf edge (shelf break). The break of slope between the *continental shelf and the *continental slope, where a marked slope increase occurs. The shelf-edge depth varies considerably from place to place, ranging between about 100 and 350 metres, but the norm is taken as roughly 200 m.

shells. The hard casings of certain marine organisms. On the death of the organisms the shells are deposited on beaches or on the sea floor. Many remain virtually intact for long periods, especially in environments devoid of marked wave and tidal action. Others rapidly become pulverized into minute particles or broken into several fragments. In tropical areas, beaches often consist of shell sands, perhaps admixed with bryozoa, foraminifera, and echinoid fragments. Outside tropical areas, shell beaches are much less common. They are usually of rather coarse material and therefore tend to be steep. Shelly material may figure prominently in reef-building, for instance in the case of *oyster reefs.

shield. A very large rigid area of the earth's crust made up of Precambrian rocks, which have been unaffected by later orogenic episodes. Shields represent areas of the earth's earliest formed continental crust. Examples include the Baltic and Canadian Shields.

shonkinite. See syenite.

shoreface. The narrow zone that lies to seaward of low-water mark and which is, therefore, always covered by water but which is shallow enough to permit active movement of sea-floor sediments under the influence of waves. Some authorities use the term to mean that part of the beach that is periodically covered then uncovered by the tide, i.e. the *foreshore zone.

shoreline. The line that is produced by the intersection of a sea or lake surface with the sloping beach-face or shoreface. With regard to U.S. Coast and Geodetic Survey marine charts and surveys, the shoreline approximates to the average line of high tides. However, the term is often used loosely to indicate coastline.

sial. The earth's *continental crust, which is composed of granitic rock types that are rich in silica (Si) and aluminium (Al).

siallitic soil. A soil with a medium to high silica to aluminium ratio. Such soils are typical of the temperate zone, as tropical weathering removes silica and lowers the ratio, producing a soil in which the aluminium content is high.

Siberian anticyclone. A large area of high pressure that dominates the mean pressure field over the USSR in winter. It is emphasized by extensive radiational cooling of the Eurasian landmass.

siderite. See carbonate minerals.

siderophile. See lithophile.

sierozem or **serozem (grey desert soil).** A soil occurring in semidesert areas in more arid zones than the *chestnut soils, and characterized by low organic matter contents, a lack of leaching, and accumulations of lime at the top of the C horizon or lower B, typically within a foot of the surface, and possibly reaching up to the surface. Vegetation cover is scanty: short grass and scattered brush. These soils are now included in the aridisol order of the *Seventh Approximation classification.

significant wave. A wave that has the average period and height of the highest 33.3% of the waves in the *wave spectrum. Calculation of significant wave characteristics requires careful wave measurement at sea and subsequent analysis of this information, or the use of a wave analyser in a scale model that involves wave action.

silica minerals. *Quartz, tridymite,* and *cristobalite* are the three commonly occurring polymorphs of silica (SiO_2). Tridymite and cristobalite are stable at intermediate and high temperatures respectively but neither form persists at high pressures and both are absent from plutonic rocks. The polymorphs have distinct crystal structures built from SiO_4 tetrahedra but the pattern of linking is different in each case. In addition, each polymorph has a low- and high-temperature modification, the transitions taking place rapidly at the particular inversion temperature involved. Changes from one polymorphic form to another are very sluggish and tridymite and cristobalite both exist metastably at ordinary temperatures.

Coesite and stishovite are high-pressure high-density forms of silica found near meteorite impact craters. *Chalcedony* is the cryptocrystalline form of silica containing minute crystals of quartz with submicroscopic pores. *Opal* is a hydrous cryptocrystalline or amorphous form of silica. *Lechatelierite* is a rare metastable silica glass.

Quartz.

Quartz is stable over a wide range of physical conditions and because silica is the most abundant oxide in the earth's crust, it is a very common mineral. The different coloured varieties are: colourless—*rock crystal,* yellow—*citrine,* grey-brown to black—*smoky quartz,* pink—*rose quartz,* and violet—*amethyst.* Quartz is trigonal and the absence of cleavage is characteristic. On Mohs' scale it is the standard mineral of hardness 7.

Quartz is an essential constituent of silica-rich igneous rocks, such as granites, rhyolites, and pegmatites, and is found in oversaturated, intermediate, and basic rocks. Quartz often occurs intergrown with alkali feldspar in graphic granite. Vein-quartz, precipitated from hydrothermal solutions, is often associated with ore minerals. Because of its hardness and resistance to chemical weathering, quartz is the most abundant detrital mineral and is concentrated to give rise to sands and gravels of various types, which, on lithification, constitute the arenaceous rocks. Authigenic quartz is often deposited around detrital grains, cementing them together.

During metamorphism, the quartz of sediments and igneous rocks recrystallizes to a coarser grain size. Quartz is also produced by the released silica during the metamorphic breakdown of pre-existing minerals. At high grades, segregation and mobilization take place giving rise to quartz veins and pegmatites.

Tridymite and cristobalite.
These minerals are typically found in cavities in acid volcanic rocks, such as rhyolites and andesites, and may be produced as a result of the passage of hot gases.

Chalcedony.
There are numerous varieties of chalcedony. *Carnelian* is red. The banded variety, *agate*, is formed by intermittent deposition in cavities. *Jasper* is a red-brown colour. *Chert* and *flint* are opaque, dull-coloured, or black varieties, the former being the massive or stratified form and the latter being found as nodules in chalk. Chalcedony is found in hydrothermal veins, amygdales, and sediments.

Opal.
Opal occurs in many colours, the precious variety being iridescent. It is deposited at low temperatures from silica-bearing waters and is found around geysers and hot springs. *Diatomite* is a rock made up almost entirely of the accumulated opaline skeletons of diatoms. Radiolarian and diatomaceous deposits may recrystallize to form chert.

silica saturation. The extent to which a rock contains silica, this measure constituting a convenient method of classifying igneous rocks into three groups:
1. oversaturated—rocks containing free silica as quartz.
2. saturated—rocks in which all the silica is combined and in sufficient quantity to exclude feldspathoids.
3. undersaturated—rocks containing feldspathoids.

silicates. A group of minerals constituting about one third of all minerals and approximately 90% of the earth's crust, in which feldspar (60%) and quartz (12%) are the most abundant. The basic structural unit common to all silicates is the SiO_4 tetrahedron. Silicates are classified on a structural basis according to how the tetrahedra are linked together. The six classes are nesosilicates (olivine), sorosilicates (hemimorphite, melilite), cyclosilicates (beryl, axinite), inosilicates (amphiboles and pyroxenes), phyllosilicates (micas and clay minerals), and tektosilicates (quartz, zeolites, feldspars).

sill. A near-horizontal tabular intrusive body of igneous rock, usually dolerite, of roughly uniform thickness but thin relative to its areal extent. It is concordant with the planar structures of the rock types into which it intrudes. *See also* dyke.

sillimanite. *See* aluminium silicates.

silt. A fine-grained deposit that ranges in sediment particle size from 0.06 mm to 0.002 mm, and is therefore significantly finer than sand. Like clays, silts may include clay minerals, and also hydroxides and oxides of iron, silica dioxide, and numerous other fine material particles. Clay and silt together form the *argillaceous division of sediments. Silts result not only from decomposition of certain in-situ rocks and rock particles but also from gradual abrasion processes (impact, grinding, and rubbing). Fine silty material tends to collect in sheltered quiescent marine environments and can be a serious threat to navigation. It is sometimes difficult to dredge, often returns rapidly from spoil-grounds to the dredged areas, and can inundate seaweed beds where fish and other marine organisms normally abound.

Silurian. The last period in the Lower *Palaeozoic, beginning about 445 million years ago, at the end of the *Ordovician Period, and lasting about 30 million years, until the start of the *Devonian. The Silurian System is divided into three series: the Llandovery, Wenlock, and Ludlow. The environments suggested by the Silurian rocks in Britain are similar to those inferred for the Ordovician: shallow shelf seas with sandstones and limestones and deeper regions with shales and mudstones. This similarity is reflected in the fauna, which seems to be a continuation of the Ordovician fauna. Trilobites and graptolites became less common; the latter were almost extinct by the end of the period. Brachiopods were very varied and crinoids and corals increased in importance. Ostracoderm fish became more abundant and the first gnathostomes (jawed vertebrates) appeared. The first evidence of land plants also comes from Silurian rocks. Towards the end of the period the Caledonian orogenic episode came to a climax, producing new land areas and a shallowing of the adjacent seas.

sima. The earth's *oceanic crust, which is composed of basaltic rock types that are rich in both silica (Si) and magnesium (Mg). The term was formerly used for that portion of the continental crust below the *Conrad Discontinuity but this was inaccurate and led to confusion with the oceanic crust.

singularity. The annual recurrence of particular types of weather at certain times of year as illustrated by the *Buchan spells. Unfortunately their reliability is low except in a very general sense.

sinistral fault. A fault at which movement is to the left relative to the side of the fault plane on which the observer is standing. Compare dextral fault.

sink hole (sink, pot-hole). A saucer-like hollow, typical of limestone areas, varying from 1 to 1000 metres in diameter and from a few centimetres to 300 metres in depth, produced by solution (see limestone solution) or by rock collapse. The ratio of diameter to depth is usually about 3:1. They are usually formed on flat or gently sloping surfaces, since here water can accumulate and stand, thereby causing solution. Sink holes may also be simply enlarged vertical joints, but whatever their shapes

they often act as channels down which surface water seeps to underground drainage systems. See also swallow hole.

sinusoidal projection. See Sanson-Flamsteed projection.

sirocco (scirocco). A wind of similar origin to the Egyptian *khamsin occurring further west between Algeria and Libya. It is a hot dry southerly wind on the North African coast, but on crossing the Mediterranean it can pick up much moisture and bring extensive low stratus cloud to the Italian coast.

SI units (Système International d'Unités). A system of units used, by international agreement, for all scientific purposes. It is based on the metre-kilogram-second (MKS) system and replaces both the centimetre-gram-second (cgs) and Imperial (fps — foot, pound, second) systems. It consists of seven base units and two supplementary units (see Table 1). Measurements of all other physical quantities are made in derived units, which consist of combinations of two or more base units. Fifteen of these derived units have special names (see Table 2). Base units and derived units with special names have agreed symbols, which are used without a full stop.

Decimal multiples of both base and derived units are expressed using a set of standard prefixes with standard abbreviations (see Table 3). Where possible a prefix representing 10 raised to a power that is a multiple of three should be used (e.g. mm is preferred to cm).

skarn. A calc-silicate mineral assemblage produced during the *contact metamorphism and metasomatism of highly calcareous rocks.

skill score. A method of determining whether the results of medium- and long-range forecasts are better than if random forecasts had been made.

Table 1. Base and Supplementary SI Units

physical quantity	name of SI unit	symbol for unit
length	metre	m
mass	kilogram(me)	kg
time	second	s
electric current	ampere	A
thermodynamic temperature	kelvin	K
luminous intensity	candela	cd
amount of substance	mole	mol
*plane angle	radian	rad
*solid angle	steradian	sr

*supplementary units

Table 2. Derived SI Units with Special Names

physical quantity	name of SI unit	symbol for SI unit
frequency	hertz	Hz
energy	joule	J
force	newton	N
power	watt	W
pressure	pascal	Pa
electric charge	coulomb	C
electric potential difference	volt	V
electric resistance	ohm	Ω
electric conductance	siemens	S
electric capacitance	farad	F
magnetic flux	weber	Wb
inductance	henry	H
magnetic flux density (magnetic induction)	tesla	T
luminous flux	lumen	lm
illuminance (illumination)	lux	lx

Table 3. Decimal Multiples and Submultiples to be used with SI Units

submultiple	prefix	symbol	multiple	prefix	symbol
10^{-1}	deci	d	10^{1}	deca	da
10^{-2}	centi	c	10^{2}	hecto	h
10^{-3}	milli	m	10^{3}	kilo	k
10^{-6}	micro	μ	10^{6}	mega	M
10^{-9}	nano	n	10^{9}	giga	G
10^{-12}	pico	p	10^{12}	tera	T
10^{-15}	femto	f			
10^{-18}	atto	a			

slack tide (slack water). The period or state of the tide in which there is negligible horizontal flow of water or when the tidal currents are at virtually zero velocity. This period occurs, in the case of a rectilinear tidal stream, when the currents are reversing their direction. Some authorities consider the period covers that time when flood and ebb velocities are less than 0.1 knot.

slate. A fine-grained rock in which the parallel orientation of platy crystals of mica and chlorite results in the production of a perfect slaty cleavage. The individual constituent minerals cannot be resolved by the naked eye but some slates contain porphyroblasts or are spotted, the spots representing embryonic porphyroblasts. Slates are formed during the low-grade regional metamorphism of mudstones, siltstones, and other fine-grained argillaceous sediments.

slaty cleavage. A parallel alignment of platy minerals in fine-grained rocks, at right angles to the direction of compression. Slaty cleavage is usually also a form of *axial plane cleavage.

sleet. Precipitation comprising melting snow or a mixture of rain and snow. In America, sleet is used to indicate ice pellets.

slickensides. Small parallel grooves or striations formed on the surface of fault or joint surfaces as a result of the movement of rocks against one another. Small platy minerals are developed on them, from which the relative sense of movement of the rocks can be determined. The surface of the slickenside is smooth in the direction of movement, but rough in the opposite direction.

Section through a meander bend

slip-off slope. The gentle slope on the inside of a *meander bend opposite the undercut slope that occurs on the outside of a meander bend owing to erosion.

The deposition of *point bars and creation of slip-off slopes is mostly attributable to the *helical flow in meandering reaches, which constantly transfers sediment from eroding areas on the outside of bends to the depositing areas on the inside.

slip sheet. A gravity collapse structure developed in the beds on the limb of an anticline. If the beds at the base of the limb fracture, the overlying beds will slip downwards under the influence of gravity and then spill out onto the adjacent strata.

slope. An inclined surface whose length is determined by the horizontal distance from crest to foot and whose angle is determined by the inclination of the slope from the horizontal. Usually a slope is said to have one angle in broad terms, but most slopes are composed of a number of different parts, called facets if straight and elements if rounded, each having its own slope angle. *See also* slope concavity, slope convexity, slope decline, slope evolution.

slope concavity. The bottom parts of hill slopes are typically concave, except in certain areas where this basal concavity has been buried by aggradation. Analogies have been drawn between the profile of a concave slope and the long profile of a river; this similarity of form has also provoked claims of a similarity of origin, the concavity being essentially a product of running water action, especially rill and gully action. This type of slope form is pronounced on lower slopes because there is a greater catchment area for running water than on upper slopes, there is increased weathering of debris downslope, producing smaller particles that can move on a more gentle slope, and there is increasing impermeability as debris becomes finer downslope, leading to increased running water action. For running water action, an impermeable surface is a prerequisite and consequently concave slopes are best developed on the finer rocks, e.g. clays, shales, and argillites, and less well developed on the permeable rocks, e.g. sandstone, chalk, and limestone. Plentiful rainfall is also important and, other things being equal, the concave parts of slope profiles tend to become more pronounced with increasing age, as weathering of debris advances, making it finer and less permeable, and hence more able to support running water. *See also* slope convexity, slope evolution.

slope convexity. The upper parts of hill slopes are characteristically convex in shape, and a good deal of discussion in the literature on slope evolution is directed at suggesting causes for this shape. Early workers included Gilbert, who said convexity was a product of *creep; as the soil mantle moves from upslope, the volume passing a given point increases downslope, so an increasingly steep slope is needed to transmit the debris, hence a convex slope. Today, this idea is still widely accepted, even though creep is now thought to operate as a slide rather than a flow, so that the thickness of the debris does not increase downslope. W. Penck said convex slopes were a product of uplift acting faster than downcutting; Fenneman (1908) thought it might be due to the action of wash; S. Schumm has found that creep does produce a convex profile, but since it only operates on clay lithologies, convex profiles tend to form only in clayey materials. It may be also that since the upper part of a hill is attacked by weathering on all sides, the tendency is to weather out a convex slope. In reality a number of factors may be responsible.

slope correction. The reduction of distances measured on a slope in the field to their correct horizontal value for presentation on a map. The corrected figure is obtained by multiplying the measured length by the cosine of the slope angle.

slope decline. The original *cycle of erosion, as formulated by W. M. Davis, was based on a progressive lowering of slope angles (slope decline) as contrasted to the later schemes of W. Penck and L. King, emphasizing *parallel retreat of slopes. Slopes will decline when more material is eroded upslope than is removed from the foot of the slope, leading to a differential rate of evolution, the upper part retreating faster and hence lowering the overall slope. For material to accumulate at the foot of a slope there must be no effective *basal sapping, e.g. in a sea cliff cut off from the sea by the growth of a shingle bank or sand spit, protecting it from wave action, it has been seen that parallel retreat gives way to slope decline. Others have found that lithologies of certain types favour slope decline, e.g. S. Schumm found decline was a feature of slope evolution in clays. Originally, this type of slope evolution was seen as characteristic of the normal cycle in humid temperate areas, i.e. as a climatically controlled process. Today it is known that slopes in the same climate can undergo very different evolutions and slopes in different climates take the same course. Whether or not a slope undergoes decline depends on process and lithology as well as climate.

slope evolution. Studies of slope evolution are concerned with the relation between slope form and the processes operating on that slope, the lithology of the rock, and the stage of evolution. It is intimately linked to studies of the general tendencies of landscape form, i.e. whether they tend to retreat parallel to themselves (*see* parallel retreat) leaving *inselbergs and *pediments or whether they tend to decline (*see* slope decline), ultimately producing a *peneplain.

Many different techniques and ideas have resulted from these studies. Some have studied the current evolution of small-scale slopes of different rock types to see the influence of lithology; others have studied the role of climate, through its control of geomorphic process, by comparing slopes in different latitudes, or on the shady and sunny sides of valleys; others have related slope form to tectonic action, or studied the role of base-level changes in producing polycyclic slopes. Early workers inferred a series of sequential stages through which any slope might evolve with time, whilst some modern workers have successfully identified actual time series in the form, for example, of a growing spit at a cliff foot progressively cutting that cliff off from wave action and hence inducing a change of process. Finally, some have employed a statistical approach, measuring the angles of slopes and finding those values around which angles tend to bunch (characteristic angles). Despite all these efforts, slope evolution is still a highly complex topic, although many general models have been produced. In any particular slope, its shape is determined by the balance of losses of rock by erosion and gains by deposition, but since the geomorphic processes operating may have changed through time, there is no reason why current slope forms should have any strong relation to the current processes operating on them.

smectite. *See* clay minerals.

smog. Smoke fog. Less frequent than formerly, it results from the admixture of fog and smoke. If the smoke is unable to escape because of a persistent *inversion, the concentration of toxic chemicals may build up to harmful levels as occurred in London in 1952. Smoke control can prevent the worst smogs, but invisible gases may still be contained within the fog, such as ozone, nitrous oxides, or carbon monoxide. They do not thicken the fog as does smoke.

Snell's law. A law stating that the angle of refraction R is related to the angle of incidence I by the equation: $\sin I/\sin R = \mu$, where μ is a constant called the refractive index of the material.

snout. The down-valley margin of a glacier.

snow. Solid precipitation composed of ice crystals or snowflakes. The former occurs when temperatures are well below freezing and moisture content of the atmosphere is not high. As temperatures approach $0°C$, snowflakes are found and these increasingly aggregate into larger flakes at about freezing point. Snow is very difficult to measure accurately. It tends to block rain gauges or be blown out. It is normally recorded by inserting a graduated ruler into a flat surface of undrifted snow. The water equivalent of 1 foot of snow is approximately equal to 25 mm (1") of rainfall.

snow-line. The altitude of the lower limit of permanent snow. In tropical areas the snow-line is about 5000 to 7000 metres, but gradually decreases polewards, until it reaches sea level in the Arctic Seas, Greenland, and Antarctica. In general terms, its altitude is determined by mean summer temperatures, but local climate conditions such as aspect or shelter from snow-bearing winds can produce variations.

snow patch erosion. *See* nivation.

soapstone (steatite). A rock composed largely of *talc.

sodalite. *See* feldspathoids.

soil. The natural accumulation of unconsolidated mineral particles (derived from weathered rocks) and organic matter (humus) that covers much of the earth's surface and forms the supporting medium for plant growth.
The exact classification of soils is difficult because soil occurs as a graded continuum, breaks in this continuum being chosen subjectively for classification. In the past classification was based on the *profile, but in the new *Seventh Approximation classification the unit is the *pedon and rather than being based purely on factors of soil formation (as formerly) it is concerned with morphology, *horizon arrangement, and

255

Fig. 1. Soil Structure Types

type	characteristics
platy	thin leafy flaky layers
prismatic	prismlike units with flat tops; mainly subsoil
columnar	prismatic units having rounded tops
blocky	rectangular blocks; common in humid zones
subangular blocky	blocky with rounded edges
granular	rounded and porous; mainly surface soil
crumb	soft, rounded, and very porous; mainly surface soil

Fig. 2. Soil Texture Classes

name	composition
sand	$< 85\%$ sand percentage of silt plus 1.5 times the percentage of clay is not more than 15%
loam	$7-27\%$ clay $28-50\%$ silt $< 52\%$ sand
silt	80% or more silt $< 12\%$ clay
clay	$< 40\%$ clay with $< 45\%$ sand and $< 40\%$ silt

other properties. A *soil phase* is the lowest unit in the hierarchy of soil classification, and it reflects the erosional state of the soil, e.g. its depth, stoniness, and degree of erosion. A *soil association* is a collection of soils grouped on the basis of geographic proximity even though they may differ greatly in profile characteristics (this grouping is usually used in the generalization of a detailed map in order to reduce it to a smaller scale). A *soil series* is a collection of soils similar in all respects except for the texture of the surface horizon and its erosional state. Series are the basic soil mapping units. A *soil type* is a subdivision of a soil

series on the basis of the texture of the A horizon, these textural variations usually being related to slight changes of slope. A *soil group* is a group of soils sharing a similar type and sequence of horizons, occurring over wide areas with similar temperature and moisture regimes (differences in surface horizon due to agriculture are discounted). A *soil order* is the highest level of generalization in soil classification (the Seventh Approximation has ten orders) and is based on the type and development of horizons present.

Soil structure denotes the mode of binding together of individual soil particles into secondary units (*aggregates* or *peds*), mostly by organic matter. There are seven main structure types (see table) and the grade of structure can be classified into structureless, weak, moderate, or strong, depending on the observable degree of aggregation. Structure is important to soil fertility, as it influences *porosity (and hence air and water supply), bulk density, heat transfer, etc. Cultivation tends to break down structures by removing organic matter, the major binding agent.

Soil texture denotes the proportion of the various *particle sizes in a soil. There are four main texture classes (see table) and many intermediate grades. Texture can be determined accurately by laboratory analysis and allocated to a specific class by a *texture triangle*, or more approximately in the field by rubbing a wet sample between the fingers and estimating the proportion of sand (gritty feel), silt (silky feel), and clay (plastic). Loams are generally the best agricultural soils as they contain a good mixture of all particle sizes.

Soil consistency denotes the degree of cohesion and adhesion in a soil, hence its ability to resist deformation or rupture. It is described by the following terms: wet, sticky, plastic, nonplastic, moist, loose, friable, firm, dry, and hard, with a number of intermediate grades.

Soil colour as defined by the Munsell Color System is composed of three variables: hue, value, and chroma. Hue is determined by the wavelength of the light reflected from it, chroma is the purity or strength of the colour, and value is the relative lightness or intensity of the colour. Using a colour code, a soil sample is allocated to a particular class that is composed of varying degrees of these three variables. Colour is an important factor in the recognition and description of soils, particularly as it often reflects formation, e.g. blue-grey colours typify gleying, red the concentration of ferric oxide, and grey or greyish brown often shows the accumulation of calcium carbonate.

Soil moisture is fundamental to plant growth and whether it becomes available to plants depends to a large extent on the size and distribution of the soil pores (*see* porosity) within which the water is held. In general the finer the texture of the soil the greater its capacity to store water. Water is held by the soil with varying degrees of tenacity; the less the moisture content the more firmly it is held.

Each soil horizon is determined by the original parent material and subsequent additions, losses, and transformations of materials within it. Especially important in the processes accomplishing horizon differentiation are those that transfer material from one horizon to another, as these differentiate the eluvial A horizon from the illuvial B. *See also* humification, eluviation, leaching, illuviation, lessivage, podzolization, laterization, gleying, cheluviation, decalcification, soil formation, conservation of soils, erosion, abnormal erosion.

soil formation (pedogenesis). The early Russians, particularly Dokuchayev, stated that soil forms as a result of five factors: local climate, *parent material, plant and animal organisms, relief and elevation, and the age of the land surface. More recently the American Jenny has tried to formulate the Russian work in a mathematical equation, $s = f(cl, o, r, p, t ....)$, where s = soil, cl = climate, o = organisms (including man), r = relief, p = parent material,

and t = time. However, all the factors are interrelated and the equation would be very difficult to solve in the field, but in certain cases it is possible to evaluate the effect of one of the factors against the background of the others where these are constant.

Climatic factor. This is thought to be the most important factor in soil formation. It is very complex as it can considerably influence the effect of the other factors. Parameters of fundamental importance are rainfall (regime and intensity), temperature (maximum and minimum, soil temperatures, and duration of sunshine), and evapotranspiration. The effects of these single components can be measured, e.g. the depth to which calcium carbonate is leached can be broadly correlated with the amount of rainfall. The combined influence of temperature and precipitation is well illustrated in Russia, where the sequence of soil zones changes from north to south in relation to an increase in temperature and a decrease in precipitation. This relationship between soils and climatic zones forms the basis of the zonal classification of soils.

Organic factor. Organisms are responsible for the breakdown of plant tissue resulting in the accumulation of organic matter, the recycling of nutrients, structural stability, and profile mixing in the soil. Vegetation itself, by binding the soil together, prevents erosion. Man through his farming practices such as cropping, burning, and irrigation is playing an increasing role in soil formation. Organisms are often dependent on climate but they may act as independent variables. For example, certain major soil types are associated with particular vegetation types and when the vegetation type changes in the same climatic region a change in soil type may result.

Time factor. The time a soil takes to develop is measured from when fresh rock is first exposed at the surface, e.g. when the Pleistocene glaciation left the British Isles some 10 000 years ago. Soil develops gradually (the rate is partly dependent on parent rocks, e.g. soils on till will develop in less than 1000 years whereas those on resistant quartzite will take much longer), probably through an (A)C, AC, A(B)C, ABC horizon sequence, and eventually a stage is reached in which the soil is in equilibrium with the environment and can be called mature. However, since the system is dynamic and any environmental change will affect the soil, it is better to use absolute or relative datings than terms such as young, mature, and old.

Topographic factor. Topography affects soil moisture. Drier shallower soils occur at the top of a slope, where drainage is more rapid. Soils at the slope foot tend to be deeper because of an increase in subsurface weathering due to the presence of more moisture and the accumulation of material eroded upslope. As a result of aspect, soils on south-facing slopes tend to be drier than those facing north. Since vegetation type is closely related to soil moisture, through vegetation topography also has an indirect influence on soil development. *See also* catena.

soil temperature. The temperature recorded at any level within the soil (standard depths being 30 cm and 100 cm) with a soil thermometer, which consists of a mercury thermometer that has a horizontal section as usual, but is then bent through 90° to a predetermined length where the bulb is located. The diurnal temperature wave decreases very rapidly with depth and below 10 m there is usually little sign of an annual wave.

solar constant. The intensity of *radiation received from the sun on a unit area of a horizontal surface at right angles to the solar beam above the atmosphere, at the earth's mean distance from the sun. Its value is 2.00 calories cm^{-2} $min.^{-1}$ or 1.35 kW m^{-2}. There has been considerable debate as to whether this value is a constant or not. Prior to the use of satellites it had to be measured from high-altitude observatories where atmospheric interference

could be reduced but not eliminated. It now appears that the value is almost constant except in the shortest part of the spectrum where the amount of energy received is small.

sole marks. Sedimentary structures formed at the base of sandstone and siltstone beds that overlie softer sediments.

solid geology. The geology of rocks underlying glacial and other superficial deposits. *See also* drift.

solifluction. A process of mass movement on slopes, usually restricted in its application to areas of *periglaciation. The major process of solifluction concerns the presence of *permafrost. In spring, melting takes place in the top layer of the soil, but the water produced cannot drain away since beneath this active layer the ground remains frozen and hence impermeable. Consequently, the upper soil becomes highly saturated, and its cohesion may be reduced to such an extent that flowage can take place and material be moved downslope, often creating characteristic terrace forms and burying former vegetation layers, though the presence of well-developed vegetation usually hinders the process.

Solifluction sometimes also embraces the effects of *needle ice and *congeliturbation.

solitary wave. A wave consisting of only one elevation which, once formed, may travel practically unchanged as a single hump for a considerable distance. The actual water particles move forward a short distance as the wave passes by, i.e. the passage of a solitary wave causes a net shift of the water particles beneath the solitary wave in the direction of wave propagation. The solitary wave is neither preceded nor followed by other waves, unless these are generated quite independently. *Tsunami waves, which may be of very limited height at sea, possess some of the characteristics of solitary waves.

sol lessivé. A soil that corresponds to the grey-brown podzolic soil of America. The profile is characterized by a thin surface accumulation of moder humus. Below this the A and Eb horizons have been depleted of clay, which has been eluviated down the profile to form a textural Bt horizon (a process not present in a true brown earth). This is clear from a study of the structure of the soil as the Bt horizon has a prismatic or blocky structure whereas the surface horizon often has a weak crumb/blocky structure. These soils are common in the humid climate of NW Europe on freely drained fine-textured parent materials. They fall into the alfisol order of the *Seventh Approximation.

solod (salt-earth podzol). A soil resulting from the leaching of a *solonetz soil, forming a white-grey A horizon from the upper B horizon of the solonetz. This bleached A horizon, as in true *podzols, is deficient in iron and aluminium, has a sandy texture and an acid reaction. The B horizon is gleyed, with mottlings and a columnar and prismatic structure developed in a compact clay. These soils represent the leached end of the development continuum from *solonchak through *solonetz to solod in which salts are progressively removed through leaching, either naturally, sometimes owing to a falling base level, or artifically through leaching by irrigation water.

solonchak (white alkali soil). Saline soil in which sodium chloride and sodium sulphate form more than 0.3% of the total soil. During drought the salts dry out at the surface giving a white colour. Saline groundwater exists within two metres of the surface, and this supplies the salts for upward rise by *capillarity to the surface soil; it also imparts gley features to the soil, usually just the lower part of the profile but possibly the whole profile if the water table is near the surface. These soils are characterized by a pH value of more than 8 (more than 15% of exchangeable cations are sodium), a flocculated structure, no illuvial B horizon, and one or two salt layers; they are friable and soft in a moist state, crusty when dry. They are fairly common in arid, semiarid, and subhumid regions, where they may occur naturally in depressions or as a result of secondary salinization of the zonal soils, or they may be artificial due to excessive irrigation or irrigation with water dominated by sodium salts. In the Seventh Approximation they are classified in the *aridisol order.

solonetz (black alkali soil). Soil dominated by sodium carbonate. Solonetz develops from *solonchak by the leaching of some of the sodium, due to increased rainfall, improved drainage, or irrigation, which deflocculates the soil mass. As a result the structure is single-grain when wet, but on drying the illuvial horizon develops a massive columnar structure. It is this structure difference that originally divided the solonetz from the solonchak. Whereas the solonchak has an AC profile, increased leaching in the solonetz produces a dark grey or brown B_1 horizon enriched with colloids, and lighter grey B_2. The C horizon is enriched with carbonates and salts, whilst at the surface alkaline solutions of humic material accumulate in wet periods which on drying produce black crusts. They may be partly zonal soils, being concentrated at climatic transition zones at 15° and 40°N, but traditionally they are considered as intrazonal. In the *Seventh Approximation they are classified partly as aridisols, partly as mollisols.

solstice. The time of maximum or minimum declination of the sun. The summer solstice in the N hemisphere occurs on 22 June when the sun is overhead at the Tropic of Cancer, its farthest north. The winter solstice is about 22 December when the sun reaches 23.5°S, the Tropic of Capricorn. At the summer solstice is the year's longest day and at the winter solstice, the shortest.

solum. The surface soil and the subsoil, excluding the parent material.

solution. A basic form of chemical weathering in which solid materials are dissolved by water. Rates of solution vary considerably from one substance to another; silica is fairly insoluble and its removal rate increases with temperature, whilst the most soluble rock minerals are calcium, sodium, magnesium, and potassium. Salt and gypsum are very soluble, subsequent recrystallization sometimes causing mechanical breakdown of rocks (*see* granular disintegration, flaking). The efficiency of the solution process depends largely on the volume of water flowing, but the presence of weak acids within the water may cause increased solution. *See also* limestone solution.

sonic log. A subsurface logging technique run in a bore hole, which measures the time taken for a compressional sound wave to travel through one foot of the adjacent formation. In this way a continuous record of the properties of the rocks against depth is recorded.

sonoprobe. A continuously recording acoustic reflection instrument, which has already made an important contribution to the study of the continental terrace and some deeper areas. Their use provides data on the approximate thickness, distribution, and character of marine sediments and the surface morphology and internal structure of exposed or buried rock areas. Various sound sources are employed to give varying degrees of penetration of the seabed. There are many applications of the sonoprobe technique to offshore mineral exploration and engineering surveys, for example in the laying of submarine pipes and cables and in the siting of oil rigs.

sorting. The process by which materials forming a particular sediment are graded according to size by natural processes. If the size range is confined within narrow limits, so that most of the material is silt size (as in aeolian brickearth) or fine sand size (as in many beach sands), the deposit is well sorted. If the deposit has many size ranges (as in a slump deposit, for example) it is poorly sorted.

Sorting is best in sediments subject to a long distance of transport, with repeated re-working, as happens to beach sands being washed along a coast by wave action. In slump deposits, transport is sharp and short with no time for any sorting.

The basis of sorting concerns the settling velocity of a particle; each size and density of grain has a minimum level of energy necessary to overcome its weight and keep it in suspension. If the energy environment falls below that critical level, the grain settles out. Hence on a coast, where wave energy shows a gradient from high on headlands to low in bays, there is a corresponding sorting of sediment, the coarsest fractions in the high-energy areas, the finer fractions in the low-energy areas.

sound. 1. A waterway somewhat wider than a *strait linking two bodies of water, or a passage between an island and the mainland.
2. A relatively long sea arm or inlet.

sounding. A measure of the depth of water. Before the advent of modern echo-sounding techniques, a sounding-lead was used, but this often gave very inaccurate readings because of the effect on the sounding-line of wave and current action. Almost all soundings are now obtained using echo-sounders. These devices are usually set to record at speeds of some 800 fathoms (1600 metres) a second. Modern sounding techniques largely stem from the use of acoustic equipment in submarine warfare during World War II.

sparite. Coarse calcite of a grain size in excess of 0.01 mm in diameter, which may infill cavities within and around *allochems in *limestone. The terminology used in the petrographic description and classification of limestones is based on the presence of sparite, *micrite, and allochems.

species. The basic group in the taxonomic classification of organisms, which is usually defined as a collection of similar individuals that are capable of interbreeding to produce fertile offspring. In classifying fossil species this criterion is impossible to satisfy, and these species are usually defined on the basis of structural similarities (which in practice are also used in classifying modern species). This type of species, defined solely on morphological characteristics, is known as a *morphological species*. Difficulties in defining fossil species arise because of the absence of soft parts, whose structural characteristics provide an important means of classifying modern species. In addition the boundaries between the successive fossil species of a continuously evolving line must be arbitrary, since the species tend to grade into each other. Some fossil species do not show obvious affinities with any organisms alive today. Examples of such species are members of the Conodontophorida (conodonts): different skeletal elements belonging to this group are given different specific names, although in life they may have formed part of a single individual.

A species is defined with reference to a *type specimen, which is selected as a standard and formally described. The name of a species is always italicized and preceded by the name of the *genus to which it belongs. For example, the species that includes modern man is *Homo sapiens*, or *H. sapiens*. A species name is often followed by the name (in abbreviated form) of the author who first formally described the species.

specular iron ore. *See* haematite.

spessartite. *See* garnet.

sphalerite (zinc blende). Zinc sulphide (ZnS) found in hydrothermal veins and metasomatic replacements.

sphene (titanite). A monoclinic mineral of composition $CaTiSiO_5$ but with some replacement of O by OH and F. Sphene is a common *accessory mineral in igneous rocks. It is also found in metamorphosed calc-silicate rocks.

sphenochasm. A triangular block of oceanic crust between two continental areas.

spheroid. A figure resembling a sphere, used as a reference surface for geodetic surveys. Depending on the area of the world in which the survey is being carried out, different spheroids are used as a reference datum, e.g. in the British Isles Airey's spheroid is used, whereas in much of Africa Clark's spheroid (1880) is used.

spheroidal weathering. A form of *exfoliation that takes place on boulders below ground level. Initially angular joint blocks are gradually rounded owing to preferential weathering on the corners, a resultant block consisting of a solid rounded core surrounded by spheroidal shells. The term is sometimes restricted to exfoliation involving no change in volume (any weathering products are removed in groundwater), in contrast to *flaking. The layering within spheroidal blocks is due to the chemical migration of elements within the rock, creating zones of enrichment and depletion. Any totally rounded blocks found above ground level have probably been exhumed.

spherulitic. Denoting a texture commonly found in glassy or cryptocrystalline acid rocks in which acicular crystals of quartz and alkali feldspar are radially arranged to form a sphere. Spherulitic growth is the result of *devitrification of glassy material or rapid crystallization of viscous magma. *See* variolitic texture.

spilites. Basaltic lavas containing albitic plagioclase and in which the primary mafic minerals have been altered to chlorite and epidote. Altered acid rocks associated with spilites are called *keratophyres* and may contain phenocrysts of albite and hornblende in a groundmass of albite, chlorite, epidote, and quartz. Spilitic rocks occur as *pillow lavas interbedded with marine sediments. They appear to be basalts and rhyolites of the ocean floor, which have suffered postmagmatic soda metasomatism due to interaction with sea water. *See also* ophiolites, Steinmann trinity.

spinel. One of a group of oxide minerals with cubic symmetry, often occurring as octahedral crystals. The general formula is $R^{2+}R_2^{3+}O_4$ where R^{2+} = Mg, Fe, Zn, Mn, or Ni and R^{3+} = Al, Fe, or Cr. Most spinels fall into one of three series dependent upon the nature of the trivalent cation: *spinel* (Al), *magnetite* (Fe^{3+}), and *chromite* (Cr). *Ulvöspinel* also has a spinel structure.
There is a continuous chemical series between *hercynite* (Fe^{2+}Al$_2$O$_4$) and true spinel (MgAl$_2$O$_4$) because of the replacement Fe^{2+} $\rightleftharpoons$ Mg. Minerals of the spinel series are a wide variety of colours including red, brown, blue, green, and black.
Magnetite (Fe^{2+}Fe$_2^{3+}$O$_4$) is black and forms a continuous series with ulvöspinel (Fe$_2^{2+}$TiO$_4$).
Chromite is Fe^{2+}Cr$_2$O$_4$ but with some replacement Mg $\rightleftharpoons$ Fe^{2+}. There is a complete chemical series between chromite and hercynite due to the replacement Cr $\rightleftharpoons$ Al. The brown variety, *picotite*, is a chromium-rich hercynite.
Spinels occur in high-temperature metamorphosed rocks, especially limestones. Hercynite is found in metamorphosed pelites and in basic and ultrabasic rocks. Magnetite is ubiquitous in metamorphic and igneous rocks and is an important iron ore. Chromite is the chief chrome ore and, like magnetite, often occurs in monomineralic bands in layered basic igneous bodies.

spirit level structure. *See* geopetal cavity.

spit. An elongated accumulation of sand or shingle (or both) attached to the coast at one end and extending out to sea. It occurs most frequently where the coastline changes direction abruptly. The longshore movement of beach material is an essential factor in the formation of spits. The material is moved along one straight section of the coastline and, rather than rounding a sharp headland, accumulates seawards in the original direction of movement. Spits sometimes form across estuary mouths, whilst two may approach each other from two facing headlands (a *double spit*). A common feature is a seaward end that curves towards the land (e.g. Spurn Head on the Humber). This may be produced by wave refraction or two different sets of waves may be in action, one causing accumulation and the other the rounding of the end.

spodosol. One of the ten soil orders of the *Seventh Approximation classification including ashen or podzolized soils, characterized by a spodic B horizon containing humus and silicate clays with aluminium or iron that has been moved down the profile from the bleached A horizon above. This includes the true *podzols, plus the *podzolic soils and groundwater podzols. Spodosols develop mostly in humid cool temperate climates or on acidic parent materials.

spodumene. A lithium-bearing clinopyroxene. *See* pyroxene.

sponges. *See* Porifera.

spontaneous potential (S.P.) log. A subsurface logging technique that continuously records the spontaneous potential present at different depths. This results from electrochemical reactions between the drilling mud and formation fluids, and small electromotive forces resulting from the penetration of drilling fluids into the formation.

spot height. A height above the vertical datum, represented on a map by a dot locator with the elevation printed beside the dot. Unlike bench marks or trigonometrical points, spot heights are not identifiable on the ground.

spreading rate. The rate at which new ocean floor is added to the oceanic plates at constructive *plate margins. It is therefore directly related to the rate at which new ocean floor is produced.

spring tide. A *tide that has a relatively large range, rises and falls to the greatest extent from mean tide level, and occurs at or near the times of full and new moon. A period of spring tides allows waves to break further up or down the beach, and at those times when strong onshore winds coincide with the time of high water, this may lead to flooding of the land behind the beach. A wider tract of beach is intermittently uncovered compared with a period of *neap tides. Also, tidal currents tend to be stronger during spring tides than during neap tides.

squall. A sudden increase of wind speed lasting for several minutes before dying away quickly. To be classed as a squall, the wind should rise by at least 8 m s⁻¹ (16 knots) and reach at least 11 m s⁻¹ (22 knots). A squall is often, though not necessarily, accompanied by heavy rain or a thunderstorm.

stability. The state of the atmosphere where vertical air movement is limited owing to the slow rate of cooling of the environmental lapse rate. If the environmental lapse rate is less than the saturated adiabatic lapse rate then the state is known as *absolute stability*, as no rising thermal can cool at a slower rate and so will quickly become colder than the environment and sink back. These conditions are typical of summer anticyclones.

stabilized dune. A coastal dune in which the cutting off of direct wind action by the growth of another dune line in front, and the development of a virtually continuous vegetation cover, has ended sand movement by the wind. These dunes generally have a very subdued topography, unlike the *mobile dune, and a species-rich vegetation.

stage. 1. The point to which a landscape has evolved in a *cycle of erosion, which determines its appearance. Landscapes used to be labelled youthful, mature, or senile, but this labelling is now being dropped because most landscapes are *polycyclic, so one cannot attribute their appearance purely to the stage of evolution in the current cycle, and because evidence is increasingly being produced that landforms do not adjust steadily with time through equally long stages: they evolve very rapidly at first and then achieve a steady state of little further change. **2.** A division of rock in the Standard Stratomeric scheme of stratigraphic classification (see chronostratigraphy). It indicates the body of rock that has formed during one *age. A number of stages grouped together constitute a *series and the stages themselves are formed of several *chronozones. Stages are often spoken of in exclusively biostratigraphic terms but they may be calibrated and defined by methods not involving fossils. They are usually named after geographical localities and have the ending -ian, as in the Oxfordian, a stage of the Jurassic System.

stagnant ice. An ice mass that no longer receives an adequate supply of ice in the accumulation zone to maintain movement. The ice melts downwards from the surface, meltwater frequently forming lakes marginal to the ice, which may subsequently be evidenced by deltaically-bedded terrace deposits. Debris-covered ice will melt more slowly than that exposed, and in this way large masses can be isolated, resulting in *kettle hole formation at a later stage. The large amounts of meltwater present are responsible for the characteristic ice-stagnation features, namely *kames and *eskers.

stalactites and stalagmites. Stalactites are tapering pendants projecting from the rocks of limestone caverns. They are formed from drips of water containing dissolved calcium carbonate, which on evaporation deposit a small trace of solid material. Stalactites take many thousands of years to form and are usually associated with stalagmites, which develop on the cave floor in a similar way. Stalagmites tend to be much broader at their bases than stalactites, and in time they extend upwards. Eventually stalagmite and stalactite may join to form a complete pillar.

standard atmosphere. The idealized atmospheric structure in terms of temperature and pressure for all heights. It is used for the calibration of altimeters, etc. Surface characteristics are taken as 15°C and 1013.25 mb for temperature and pressure with a lapse rate of 6.5°C/km up to 11 km at the tropopause.

standard parallel. The line of latitude selected in the construction of a map projection that is projected at its true length.

standing wave (stationary wave). A type of wave in which there is a surface oscillation that does not travel along the sea's surface. The surface oscillates up and down between fixed points (*nodes*). A crest at one moment becomes a trough at the next, and so on. Water particles have maximum horizontal travel at the nodes and maximum vertical travel at the *antinodes* (or loops). The height of a standing wave is approximately twice that of the initial incident waves. Such a situation is best observed when waves approach a vertical barrier such as a cliff or seawall and are reflected so as to meet the incoming waves. The depth of water must be sufficient to prevent the incoming waves from breaking. Standing waves may also be produced at sea, for instance when similar *progressive wave trains meet from opposite directions.

staurolite. A mineral with an approximate composition $Fe^{2+}Al_4Si_2O_{10}(OH)_2$. It shows orthorhombic symmetry and is brown to yellow. It has a structure of alternating layers of kyanite and a

composition $Fe^{2+}(OH)_2$ but with some replacement $Mg \rightleftharpoons Fe^{2+}$. Staurolite is found in medium-grade regionally metamorphosed argillaceous rocks, often in association with kyanite and almandine.

steatite (soapstone). A rock composed largely of *talc.

steering. The control of the direction and speed of movement of pressure systems by some atmospheric factor. Thermal steering, or movement in the direction of the thermal wind, works quite well for nonintensifying depressions, but in developing lows and anticyclones it is less reliable.

Steinmann trinity. The common association within geosynclinal sediments of *spilites, *chert, and *serpentinites (and other ultramafic rocks). See also ophiolites.

Stevenson screen. The standard housing for meteorological instruments. It consists of a wooden box on legs, the base of the box being 1 metre above the ground, in which thermometers are placed. Ventilation is provided by louvred sides, which in normal conditions allow adequate air movement but prevent solar radiation reaching the thermometer bulbs. Access is provided by the north-facing side of the screen being hinged; this again prevents sunlight affecting the temperature records when records are being taken.

stibnite. A lead-grey metallic antimony mineral (Sb_2S_3) found in hydrothermal veins and replacement deposits.

stilbite. See zeolites.

stishovite. See silica minerals.

stock. A discordant igneous intrusion, usually of coarse-grained granitic rock, resembling a batholith but having a surface exposure of less than 50 square kilometres. Compare boss.

stone polygons or circles. A form of periglacial *patterned ground found in flat areas. The polygons or circles consist of fine-grained material, which is usually saturated with water and frequently domed upwards, surrounded by slightly raised walls of coarser stones, which project into the soil for several centimetres. The diameter of these features, which may occur either in large groups or in total isolation, varies considerably: the larger forms are several metres across and are found in areas of long-continued freezing and extensive summer thaw, whilst smaller examples reflect more frequent freeze-thaw cycles. Their method of formation is still not totally clear, but is probably concerned with pressures set up by repeated freezing and thawing, which move the coarser fragments both upwards and outwards.

stone stripes. A type of periglacial *patterned ground that forms in a similar way to *stone polygons when the processes responsible are acting under the influence of gravity on a slope. The result is a series of alternating coarse and fine parallel downslope stripes of stone. The coarse lines can vary from a few centimetres to about two metres wide, whilst the finer stripes between them are often at least twice this width. Stone polygons developed on flat ground may become elongated towards a slope and then grade into stripes as the slope angle increases.

stony iron. See meteorite.

storm beach. An accumulation of coarse beach material found at the very highest levels of a beach profile, far above the highest points reached by high spring tides. These boulders and shingle blocks attain such a height as a result of the extreme power of very infrequent storm waves. Though their overall effect on a beach is destructive, the *swash of these waves can throw some material to great heights and rapid percolation of water prevents its subsequent removal by the *backwash.

storm surge (storm tide). The rapid rising of water level during a storm as a result of wind stresses acting on the sea's surface, or a *progressive wave resulting from certain meteorological circumstances. If this situation occurs at the time of high *spring tides, the tidal levels may significantly exceed predicted values and serious flooding and damage may result. This occurred with disastrous results at Galveston, Texas, in 1850 and in 1953 a similar˙ situation developed in the southern North Sea, causing widespread havoc and considerable loss of life.

strain. The deformation of a body of rock as a result of stress. It may be a change in shape, volume, or both. See homogeneous strain, heterogeneous strain.

strain hardening. The increasing strength of a rock as it deforms plastically.

strain rate. The rate at which a material deforms. This is usually expressed as a percentage by which the original length is altered per second.

strain-slip cleavage (crenulation cleavage). A type of cleavage superimposed upon slaty cleavage. It is typified by tabular bodies of rock between regularly spaced cleavage planes.

strait. A comparatively narrow waterway that links two sea areas or other large bodies of water. Some authorities, however, restrict the term to gaps in isthmian links or island chains.

stratification. The condition shown by sedimentary rocks of being disposed in horizontal layers or *beds, known as strata. The term is also occasionally applied to igneous bodies that display analogous parallel textures.

stratigraphy. The branch of geology concerned with the description and classification of bodies of rock and their *correlation with one another. Various aspects of this are dealt with in *lithostratigraphy, *biostratigraphy, and stratomeric and chronomeric *chronostratigraphy. This separation of the various concepts involved in stratigraphy is necessary if different levels of inference are to be distinguished.

stratocumulus cloud. A layer cloud within which weak convection is taking place. It often forms extensive sheets, which have dark areas separated either by small areas of clear sky or by thinner cloud. It occurs most frequently in winter anticyclones or over cool ocean areas where anticyclones are dominant.

stratomere (in stratigraphy). Any segment of a sequence of rock. Stratomeres are not of standard uniform size nor need they have been formed during equal intervals of geological time.

stratopause. The boundary between the stratosphere and mesosphere. It is found at a height of about 50 km and represents the temperature maximum of about 0°C resulting from energy release in the ozone layer.

stratosphere. That layer of the atmosphere above the troposphere extending to a height of about 50 km. The lower stratosphere is almost isothermal but temperatures increase gradually to their secondary maximum of about 0°C at the stratopause. Winds in the stratosphere can be quite strong, especially the *polar night jet.

strato-volcano. *See* composite volcano.

stratum. *See* bed.

stratus. A layer cloud with a fairly uniform base found at lower levels in the atmosphere or actually at the ground surface in the form of hill fog. It may give drizzle or Scotch mist.

stream frequency. *See* drainage density.

streamline. A line that is parallel to the instantaneous direction of the wind field at all points along it, showing overall air movement. The term is used particularly in tropical areas where isobars are of little use in indicating the wind

Stream order in a hypothetical drainage pattern

field because of the breakdown of the geostrophic relationship.

stream order. The classification of a stream in an integrated drainage pattern that is broken down into stream segments and the segments then ranked in a hierarchy according to their allotted order.

At the head of the basin, the first small tributaries are first order; two or more first-order tributaries unite to give a second-order tributary; two or more second-order tributaries unite to produce a third-order tributary, etc., up to the major stream of the basin, whose order defines the order of the basin. Quantitative comparisons can then be made between basins, and studies made of the relationships between orders. Studies of this kind have produced apparent laws of drainage basin development. *See also* bifurcation ratio.

stress. An applied force per unit area, causing rocks to undergo *strain. Stress can take the form of tension, compression, or shear.

striations. Lines that have been cut or scratched into rock surfaces over which a glacier has passed. They are usually short, but sometimes exceed one metre, and are best seen on gently sloping faces of fine-grained hard rock, up and over which the ice moved. Ice itself cannot cause such abrasions; the projections of rock debris, held rigidly in the basal ice, act as the cutting tools. Each striation can indicate two diametrically opposed directions of ice movement, and they have often been used to discover movements of former ice masses.

strike. The direction along a rock stratum at right angles to the true dip.

strike line (structure contour). A line joining points of equal elevation above or below a selected stratigraphic datum.

stromatolites. Laminated concentric structures formed of calcium carbonate and occurring in some Precambrian sediments. They were probably formed by algae similar to those that produced analogous bioherms in the Palaeozoic.

stromatoporoids. Extinct organisms that built laminated reef structures in the Palaeozoic. They were particularly common during the Silurian Period. Their taxonomic affinities are obscure but they may belong to the Hydrozoa, a class of the phylum *Coelenterata. They and the tabulate corals (*see* Anthozoa), which were also important reef-builders in this era, seem to have preferred different conditions, for they are rarely found in association.

strontianite. *See* carbonate minerals.

structural high. A geological structure of positive relief, such as a dome or anticline.

structural low. A geological structure of negative relief, such as a syncline or basin.

structure contour. *See* strike line.

subcrop. The disposition of a bed of rock beneath the surface and its contact with the undersurface of younger beds. The term is used by the petroleum industry in the reconstruction of the palaeogeography of an area.

subduction zones (destructive plate margins). Areas on the earth's surface where ocean floor is destroyed by one lithospheric plate overriding another.

The overriding plate may be of oceanic or continental material. The oceanic plate that is overridden is pushed down into the mantle, its position being marked by a series of earthquake foci. Such zones are marked by oceanic trenches.

subhedral. Denoting crystals with partially developed crystal forms. *Compare* anhedral, euhedral.

sublimation. The process by which ice is converted to vapour and water vapour into ice with no intervening liquid state. Chemically, the term is only used for the first process.

submarine bar. An offshore accumulation of sand, more or less parallel with the coastline, that never becomes exposed by the tide. Submarine bars occur in areas in which the tidal range is extremely small and usually form in groups of two or three. They are formed at the point at which steep storm waves break. Seawards of this point material is moved towards the land, whilst after the wave has broken movement is seawards. Thus sand accumulates from two directions, though an optimum size is reached eventually, beyond which no further increase in height is possible, owing to the effect of the bar on waves passing it. The outermost bar, in deepest water, is infrequently fully developed and is formed by the rare strong storm waves; it is unaffected by the smaller storm waves responsible for the bars nearer the shore. The innermost bar tends to move its position as wave heights vary; movement is seawards with increasing wave height and landwards with decreasing height.

submarine canyon. A deep steep-sided valley or trench cut into the continental shelf or continental or insular slope. Many are deeply incised into the solid rock of the sea floor, with V-shaped cross profiles, while some form deep winding gorges. Well-known submarine canyons include those off the mouth of the River Congo (Zaïre), the Hudson River, and Cape Breton in S France.

Canyons may have tributary incisions and and these sometimes display a dendritic pattern; others occur singly or as part of a system of sub-parallel incisions. These features are thought to have originated through erosion by submarine *turbidity currents. See also sea valley.

submarine fan. A fan-shaped mass of sediment normally found at the lower end of a *submarine canyon. Much of this material may have been deposited under the action of submarine slides and turbidity flows. For example, a very large fan exists at the lower end of the Congo Canyon, where slides or turbidity flows occur about 50 times annually. The Mississippi Delta is flanked on its western side by a trough valley that leads, at a depth of some 1800 metres, into a large submarine fan. In both cases, very substantial amounts of muddy sediments are carried to the coast by the rivers.

submarine valley. See sea valley.

subsequent stream. A stream that has developed on a weak substructure, such as a clay vale, or in regional joint or fault patterns, at right angles to streams consequent to the dip of the slope. Subsequent streams owe their development to the accelerated rate of headward erosion they are able to perform in these weaker areas, rapidly extending themselves and often coming to integrate and dominate the drainage pattern. See also consequent stream; obsequent stream.

subsidence. The widespread downward movement of air associated with surface *divergence. The rate of descent is usually fairly slow, of the order of a few metres per hour, but this results in adiabatic warming and a low relative humidity. Near the ground, mixing takes place so that extreme values of relative humidity are unusual. The weather associated with large-scale subsidence is always dry though cloud layers may result from mixing with moister air near the ground.

subsoil. See profile.

subsurface eluviation. The process by which water falling on the soil and sinking in eventually moves downslope as a subsurface flow; as it does so it dissolves or transports soil and rock material with it. This process has tended in the past to be overlooked in studies of slope evolution. However, evidence has shown that in places it can be very effective.

subtropical high. One of the anticyclones in the belt of semipermanent high pressure in the subtropics.

succession. The vertical sequence of rock units in a particular place. A number of local successions may be combined to produce an idealized succession demonstrating the sequential order of strata over a larger region.

sugar loaf. An *inselberg, especially in the S coastal area of Brazil.

sulphur. A native element (S) of characteristic yellow colour found around volcanic vents and hot springs.

sulphur oxidation. A process in soil science analogous to nitrification, in this case the bacterium Thiobacillus converting inorganic sulphur compounds into the sulphate form. This may occur solely by chemical means but most appears to be biochemical in nature.

sun cracks. See desiccation cracks.

sunshine. Direct radiation received from the sun. It is one of the climatological elements recorded at most observing stations. In Britain annual totals of sunshine range from about 1850 hours on the Channel coast to about 1200 in N Scotland.

sunshine recorder. Sunshine is normally measured by the Campbell-Stokes recorder, which consists of a glass sphere that focuses the sun's rays onto a card, burning a trace on the card whenever bright sunshine occurs. The length of the trace indicates sunshine duration. Allowance is made for the seasonal variation in declination of the sun. As it only records bright sunshine many hours are not recorded, especially in early morning or late evening, or in conditions of severe haze. No distinction is made between the different heating capacities of winter and summer sunshine.

supercooling. The cooling of a liquid to a temperature below its normal freezing point. This is a very common phenomenon in the atmosphere as ice does not form in cloud droplets at 0°C because of the sparsity of suitable *condensation nuclei. Supercooling is essential to the *Bergeron-Findeisen theory of precipitation formation.

superficial deposits. Material of Recent and Pleistocene age that lies on top of the solid geology, being extraneous material transported and deposited by various geomorphological processes. They include glacial drifts, terrace gravels, alluvium of rivers, raised beach deposits, windblown sand and loess, solifluction deposits, etc. Often such deposits as clay-with-flints and various relic weathering horizons are included in this term, but this is not strictly correct as these materials are related to the rocks beneath (and in the case of clay-with-flints, those that formerly lay above).

supergroup. The largest division in the hierarchy of the lithostratigraphical classification of bodies of rock (see stratigraphy, lithostratigraphy). A supergroup is formed of two or more associated and adjacent *groups.

superimposition. The most common process by which a drainage pattern becomes discordant. Drainage originates on a land surface and develops a conformable pattern with the structures in that surface; as dissection proceeds this surface is eroded away, and the drainage is let down onto the newly exposed rocks below. These have different structures and lithologies from the original surface, and so the drainage pattern no longer conforms to the structure over which it flows. Hence it has been superimposed from a former cover onto the one it currently occupies.

Once superimposition has occurred, the drainage may adjust to the structures of its new surface, and mask its true origin. On Dartmoor, the E-W and N-S rectangular pattern superimposed from the former Eocene and Cretaceous cover has been supplemented by a NW-SE and NE-SW pattern following the joint pattern of the granite. Current drainage is therefore a mixture of accordant and discordant streams. A great deal of the British drainage pattern is superimposed.

superposition. The principle, propounded by William Smith, that if one set of strata occurs on top of another in a succession the upper unit was formed later (except in the case of strata that have been overturned tectonically). This principle provides the basis of understanding the sequence of events in time as shown by a particular succession of rocks.

supersaturation. The state of air that contains more water vapour than the amount required to saturate it. However, the abundance of condensation nuclei usually prevent this situation arising in the atmosphere.

superstructure. The higher levels within an orogenic belt, which have deformed in a brittle manner as a result of their near-surface position. These levels have suffered only minor metamorphism. Compare infrastructure.

supplementary contour. In areas of detailed or irregular relief patterns it is sometimes necessary to show supplementary contours as well as those at the standard interval for the area. For example, in an area where the land is generally level but there are several isolated small hills a contour interval of 200' may not show up the hills. (See diagram.)

supratenuous folding. A form of folding that results from differential compac-

100 ft. contour interval with
supplementary contours to show a small
hill

tion. Sediments are bent around more
competent materials such as concretions
or coral reefs.

surf. Broken water resulting from turbulent wave activity between the outer
limit of the *breaker (or surf) zone and
the swash-backwash zone on the beach.
The surf zone is highly dynamic and
may, if the wave crests are angled to the
shoreline, experience wave-induced
currents along the shore. The width of
the surf zone fluctuates with constantly
changing wave conditions; also, it is
usually relatively wide in the case of
sand beaches and narrower in the case
of shingle or boulder beaches.

surf beat. A type of long wave activity
that is evident at the coast by irregular
oscillations of water level in the surf
zone. These oscillations have periods of
several minutes. For example, typical
periods of surf beat for beaches in N
Cornwall range between 1 and 5
minutes. A possible cause is the arrival
of groups of higher-than-average waves,
which have the effect of piling up water
in the nearshore zone and causing a
reflection of long-wave energy. The
presence of surf beat has been demonstrated by precision wave recorders set
up in the offshore zone.

surf zone. *See* breaker zone.

surveying. The construction of maps
and plans by accurately recording the
relative positions and heights of features

on the earth's surface, and plotting them
to some suitable scale. This is achieved
by measuring distances, directions, and
heights, the major surveying methods
being: *triangulation, *traversing,
*chaining, *plane tabling, *tacheometry,
and *levelling. *See also* geodetic surveying.

suspended load. The sediment carried in
suspension within a body of water,
beneath waves or in current flow, as
opposed to the sediment that moves
wholly or intermittently in contact with
the bottom (bed load and saltating
load). Shoreward of wave break-point, a
great deal of fine material may be
carried in suspension beneath waves.
(This also occurs in deeper water
offshore provided that the material is
sufficiently fine-grained.) Experiment
has shown that at the break-point of
waves and in the swash zone, sandy
material held in suspension is fairly
evenly distributed from the sea surface
down to its bed. Suspended load transport is of great importance in the dispersal of pollutants in the sea.

swale. *See* full.

swallow hole. A *sink hole that is
usually the site at which a stream
disappears underground. See diagram.

swash. The movement of a fairly thin
layer of turbulent water up a beach,
following the breaking of a wave. This
water can move material, the extent of
the movement depending on the nature
of the waves and of the beach. Most
landward movement is achieved by flat
waves, within which the oscillation of
water particles tends to be elliptical.
The oscillation in steeper waves is more
circular, and the breaking water strikes
the beach material from directly above,
giving equal opportunity for up and
down beach movements.
Some of the swash water infiltrates into
the beach material and the rest returns
to the breaker zone as *backwash. The
edge of swash action is frequently
obvious from such signs as the wetted
area of beach and the line of seaweed,

driftwood, mica flakes, etc., left at the upper limit of swash flow. Swash action on a falling tide may lead to the formation of swash channels, as water tends to become channelled on its return flow down the beach.

S waves. *See* secondary waves.

swell. 1. Waves that, having developed under wind stress in the generating area, have sufficient energy to travel beyond the wind field or to survive after the wind has dropped. They may travel into an area in which the winds are far weaker or absent or they may ultimately travel into another wind field. Such swell waves are usually fairly regular in form, with somewhat rounded crests. Their energy may enable them to travel considerable distances. In general, swell decreases in height and increases in length as it travels away from a wind field. Swells from several directions may be superimposed and swell may also carry relatively short and sharp-crested waves, which are generated by local winds.
2. A dome or anticline, esp. one that rises from the sea floor without reaching the surface.

surface stream

stream disappears underground at a swallow hole, usually conical and occurring where stream meets permeable rock

stream reappears usually at the base of permeable layer of rock and continues as surface stream

Swallow hole

syenite. A coarse-grained intermediate igneous rock in which the proportions of alkali feldspar or feldspathoids are dominant over sodic plagioclase; in fact many syenites contain no plagioclase. The intermediate plutonic igneous rocks and their volcanic equivalents are divided as follows:

Intermediate Plutonic Rocks with Volcanic Equivalents

plutonic *(sodic plagioclase)*	*volcanic* *(andesine/oligoclase)*
syenite	trachyte, phonolite
(dominant alkali feldspar/feldspathoid)	
syenodiorite	trachyandesite
(monzonite)	(latite)
(alkali feldspar = plagioclase feldspar)	
diorite	andesite
(dominant plagioclase feldspar)	

Syenites range from oversaturated quartz-bearing types through saturated types containing neither quartz nor feldspathoid to undersaturated strongly alkaline varieties containing little or no feldspar. Division may also be made according to the composition of the feldspar into potassic (orthoclase, microcline), sodipotassic (perthites), and sodic (albite, oligoclase) types. The mafic minerals are usually hornblende and biotite but the more alkaline varieties contain sodic pyriboles. Common accessory minerals include magnetite, apatite, and sphene.
Nordmarkite is an oversaturated sodipotassic syenite containing microperthite, quartz, aegirine, and riebeckite. With an increase in the amount of quartz to over 10%, nordmarkite passes into alkali granite. *Perthosite* and *pulaskite* are sodipotassic leucocratic syenites. In the former, the feldspar is perthite and in the latter, antiperthite. *Larvikite* is a distinctive variety containing dark blue feldspars displaying strong *schiller. The feldspars are antiperthitic oligoclase and orthoclase and, in addition, the rock contains

aggregates of mafic minerals, titanaugite, olivine, and biotite. *Shonkinite* is a saturated potassic melasyenite containing orthoclase feldspar and mafic minerals. Nepheline is the commonest feldspathoid present in undersaturated syenites but other varieties contain sodalite, analcime, and leucite. Some of the many different kinds of alkali syenite are:

Borolanite, containing orthoclase and nepheline-orthoclase intergrowths termed pseudo-leucite, thought to have been formed from the breakdown of leucite; *malignite,* containing potassic feldspar and nepheline; *foyaite,* containing a perthitic feldspar and nepheline; *litchfieldite,* containing potassic feldspar, albite, and nepheline. Syenites containing nepheline and albite are called *monmouthite* or *mariupolite;* in the former nepheline predominates, in the latter, albite. The feldspar-free types constitute the *ijolite series.

Microsyenites are the medium-grained equivalents and the plutonic rock names apply with the prefix micro-. Most are porphyritic and contain phenocrysts of orthoclase. The volcanic equivalents of syenites and alkali syenites are trachytes and phonolites.

Syenitic rocks are found in intrusive complexes often associated with continental rifting, in eroded volcanic islands of alkaline affinity, and within differentiated dykes and sills. *See also* diorite, syenodiorite.

syenodiorite (monzonite). A coarse-grained acid and intermediate rock that lies chemically and mineralogically between syenites and diorites. Syenodiorites are characterized by approximately equal amounts of alkali feldspar and plagioclase of oligoclase-andesine composition. The mafic minerals are usually either hornblende or biotite or both but in some varieties augite occurs, often rimmed by hornblende. Syenodorites containing accessory quartz are called quartz-monzonites and with an increase in the amount of quartz pass into adamellites. With a change to plagioclase of more calcic composition and an increase in the amount of mafic minerals, syenodiorites pass into syenogabbros.

Syenodiorites usually occur in small volumes associated with granite masses. The medium-grained varieties are termed *micromonzonites* or *microsyenodiorites* and the volcanic equivalents are the *trachyandesites* or *latites.* The alkali feldspar in trachyandesites is usually sanidine, occurring as microlites in a pilotaxitic or trachytic groundmass set with plagioclase phenocrysts. Trachyandesites occur in association with andesites in calc-alkaline orogenic volcanic suites. *Compare* syenite, diorite.

syenogabbro. *See* alkali gabbro.

symmetry. *See* crystal symmetry.

symplectite. An intergrowth of two minerals, one mineral being riddled with complex wormlike inclusions of the other, as in *myrmekite.

syncline. A basin-shaped fold in which the beds dip towards each other. See diagram at *fold.*

synclinorium. A syncline of regional extent, which is composed of a series of minor folds.

synform. A synclinal structure composed of sediments whose precise stratigraphic relationships are not known. See diagram at *fold.*

synkinematic. Denoting minerals formed during a period of deformation.

synoptic indices. Methods of assessing the sequences of pressure systems in a quantitative manner. Instead of isolated wind readings the overall direction of system movement is taken into account, then aggregated to give 10-day or monthly totals. A recent scheme is the PSCM index (Progression, Southerly, Cyclonicity, and Meridionality). Progression is an index of the frequency of westerly systems crossing the British Isles; a day with this type would have a score of $+2$, an anticyclone centred on Britain -2, with intermediate states valued accordingly. Its main use comes in climatic change and long-range forecasting.

synoptic meteorology. The section of meteorology concerned with the description and analysis of the *synoptic chart*. This is built up from surface weather observations of such elements as wind velocity, air temperature, cloud amount, dew point temperature, and pressure tendency. Isobars are constructed from pressure observations and fronts inserted where appropriate. It is most directly concerned with day-to-day weather forecasting.

syntexis. *See* assimilation.

system. A division of rock in the Standard Stratomeric scale of stratigraphic classification (*see* chronostratigraphy). It indicates the body of rock that has formed during one *period. System and period generally have the same name; for example, the Triassic System is the body of rock formed during the Triassic Period. A system, which does not have a standard uniform thickness, is formed of a number of *series grouped together.

T

tacheometry (tachymetry). A surveying method for finding the location and height of points using a theodolite (set up at a point of known height and position) and a levelling staff (placed at the unknown points). The directions of the unknown points are obtained by measuring horizontal angles from a known direction, whilst the distance from the theodolite position is calculated using a formula involving the difference in staff readings for two cross-hairs on the diaphragm of the theodolite, and the angle of elevation or depression, derived from the vertical circle reading. Another formula, using the staff reading of the central hair and the angle of elevation, permits the height of the point to be calculated. The height of the theodolite must always be

taken into account whenever this method is being used.

tachylite. A dark basic glass formed by the rapid chilling of *basalt and found particularly at the margins of dykes.

talc. A white or pale green mineral with a mica-like layered structure and composition $Mg_3(Si_4O_{10})(OH)_2$. Talc is greasy to the touch and very soft, having a hardness of only 1 on the Mohs' scale. It is formed during the hydrothermal alteration of ultrabasic and basic rocks and during low-grade thermal metamorphism of siliceous dolomites. Rocks known as soapstone or steatite consist almost wholly of talc.

talus. *See* colluvium.

tangential folding. A type of folding produced in homogeneous rocks, analogous to the bending of a block of rubber with circles drawn on it; the circles become distorted but there is no sliding movement of any kind present.

tangential stress. *See* shear.

taphonomy. The study of the processes affecting an organism from its death to its possible fossilization. Taphonomy elucidates the many differences that exist between a fossil assemblage and the community (or communities) of living plants or animals from which it came (*see* thanatocoenosis). It is a necessary preliminary to investigations in *palaeoecology. *See also* actuopalaeontology.

taphrogeosyncline. *See* rift valley.

taxonomy. The study and practice of naming organisms and classifying them into a hierarchy of groups based on the similarities between them. It is implied that this also represents their evolutionary relationships. Thus the members of a lower group show more similarities and are therefore more closely related than those of a higher group. The group at the base of the hierarchy is the *species. The groups above the level of species, in ascending order, are *genus, *family, *order, *class, *phylum (animals) or *division (plants), and *kingdom. Any of these groups may be subdivided into smaller ones; for example a class may contain several subclasses.

tear fault (wrench fault, transcurrent fault). A fault in which the movement is horizontal, i.e. along the strike of the fault. This results from a stress configuration in which the maximum and minimum principal stresses are horizontal, whereas the intermediate principal stress is vertical. See diagram at *fault*.

tectogene. A buckling of the earth's crust that results in the down-buckling of granitic rocks deep into the earth's crust to form the roots of mountains. It also results in the upward-buckling of the shallower levels in the crust to form orogenic mountain belts.

tectonics. The study of the earth's deformational movements and their effect on sedimentation and geomorphology.

tektite. *See* meteorite.

Teleostei. The group of bony fish dominant since the Cretaceous, occurring in both freshwater and marine environments. The body covering is usually reduced to thin scales of bone. Teleosts show great morphological variation and many fossil species are known.

telluric currents. Naturally occurring electrical currents at or near the earth's surface.

tellurometer. A modern surveying instrument for precise distance measurement. Like the *geodimeter it is indirect in its measurements. The time required for radio microwaves to travel from one point to another is determined and corrections applied for the meteorological conditions to convert this time to that in a vacuum. The distance is then calculated from the known velocity of the waves, and further corrections applied for slope and altitude. The best results are obtainable along a line with few obstacles, in moderate sunshine, with a light breeze and low relative humidity.

temperate glacier. A glacier containing considerable amounts of water above, within, and beneath the glacier ice. Water at the ice-rock boundary promotes easy sliding and consequently such glaciers flow faster than other types. This movement produces erosion of the abrasive type, whilst the presence of water allows freezing and thawing at the ice margins, an important factor in *glacial plucking.

temperature. An index of the heat content of a substance, which determines the flow of heat between one substance and another. Because the specific heat capacity of different substances varies appreciably, temperature cannot be equated directly with heat. A variety of scales are in use. In most parts of the world the Celsius (centigrade) scale is used, though Fahrenheit is still retained in the U.S. For scientific work, the *absolute temperature was formerly used but temperature is now measured in *kelvins. *See also* maximum temperature, minimum temperature, soil temperature.

tension cracks (gashes, fissures, or fractures). Cracks that develop in competent beds as they are deformed. The rock is put under tension and fractures. This usually happens at several sites and sets of tension cracks develop en echelon. These fractures are usually infilled by secondary minerals such as calcite.

tension joints. Joints produced as a result of tension, usually developed parallel to the fold axis of an anticline.

tephra (ejectamenta). Fragmental materials thrown out by a volcano, including bombs, ash, cinders, pumice, and lapilli. *See* pyroclastic rocks.

tephrite. *See* alkali basalt.

terminal moraine. An accumulation of *till material that develops against the front of a glacier. They are best formed when the front is slowly advancing or is stationary, since in these circumstances the front will be high and fairly steep. Such forms will finally be deposited on retreat of the glacier, thereby marking its farthest limit from the source.

termites. Ants that are abundant in tropical soils, their activity being conspicuous in the form of termite mounds, which generally are about one metre high. Their main benefit appears to be in improving the structure of the soil

terra fusca. A soil that, like *terra rossa, develops on limestone in a warm subcontinental climate. Terra fusca are brown clay loam soils, neutral or slightly alkaline in reaction, occurring under cork oak or maquis vegetation. Beneath the brown A horizon is a relic red B horizon, suggesting that they may be degraded terra rossas.

terra rossa. Red soil that develops on hard limestone in warm subcontinental climates. These soils typify the karst areas adjacent to the Mediterranean, and also occur in S Australia, Texas, central Spain, and Israel. They typically have a clay-loam texture, with some free sesquioxides, a variable depth, and low base status; they pass directly and abruptly to the parent material below, with perhaps a humus surface horizon. Their origin is uncertain: they were formerly thought to represent a weathering residue. They may develop from *terra fusca on deforestation, as they only occur under garrigue vegetation. They are related in some way to *rendzinas, which seem to occur more typically on soft limestone (e.g. chalk); also it may be that the terra rossa soils are more mature, as their lower base status and content of free sesquioxides shows more intense weathering.

terra roxa. A Brazilian red earth (*see* ferrallitic soils) with a high percentage of titanium and manganese oxides and a low aluminium oxide:iron oxide ratio, developed on a parent material of basic igneous rocks. *Compare* terra rossa.

Tertiary. A period of the *Cenozoic Era that follows the *Cretaceous, about 65 million years ago, and lasts some 63 million years until the beginning of the *Quaternary. The Tertiary was formerly regarded as an era, but because of its short length it is now classified as a period. The divisions of the Tertiary, which previously formed periods, are now regarded as epochs. They are the *Palaeocene, *Eocene, *Oligocene, *Miocene, and *Pliocene. Some authorities have recently suggested that the Tertiary should be regarded as a sub-era, which would consist of two periods: the *Palaeogene and the *Neogene.
Only the lower part of the Tertiary System is represented to any large extent in Britain. The rocks reflect a marine regression, consisting mainly of shallow marine sandstones and clays giving way later to freshwater deposits. Volcanic activity occurred in Scotland and Ireland. The Alpine episode of orogenic movements extended through this period, and was at its most active in the Miocene. The period saw the evolution and gradual increase in abundance of modern invertebrates and mammals, with a corresponding reduction of primitive groups. The modern angiosperms became the dominant plants.

teschenite. *See* alkali gabbro.

Tethyan Ocean. Prior to the northward movement of Africa relative to Europe, a large ocean existed, of which the Mediterranean Sea is the surviving remnant. Within this ocean, which existed for a long period of time, the sediments of the Alps and Himalayan mountains were deposited. As the ocean closed as a result of *sea-floor spreading this wedge of sediments was compressed into the present-day mountain chains and associated orogenic features.

tetragonal. *See* crystal system.

texture. The small-scale structures recognized in hand specimens and *thin sections of rocks, originating from the geometrical relationships of the minerals that constitute the rocks. Some of the textural terms in common use are:

1. Terms describing grain size: coarse-, medium-, and fine-grained, *aphanitic, *hyaline.

2. Terms describing the degree of crystallinity: *holocrystalline, *hyalocrystalline, *hyaline.

3. Terms describing grain shape: *euhedral, *subhedral, *anhedral, *idiomorphic, *allotriomorphic, *hypidiomorphic.

4. Terms describing the relationships between grains: *equigranular, *intergranular, *ophitic, *poikilitic, *porphyritic, *aphyric, *poikiloblastic, *pilotaxitic, *spherulitic, interstitial.

thanatocoenosis (death assemblage). An assemblage of fossils composed of the remains of animals that have been accumulated by various agencies after their death and thus may not have lived together in life. They may have become affected by scavengers and by mechanical breakage in the process. Most fossil occurrences are thanatocoenoses. *Compare* biocoenosis.

theodolite. An accurate surveying instrument used for the measurement of horizontal and vertical angles, consisting of a telescope that can be rotated in both the horizontal and vertical planes. The instrument stands on a tripod and must be levelled before use by adjusting the footscrews. Objects are viewed through the telescope and the angles read off graduated circles seen through a second eyepiece. A diaphragm within the telescope has engraved crosshairs, which can be used in conjunction with a levelling staff for fixing and heighting points of detail by *tacheometry. Theodolites in general use are those reading to 20 seconds of arc, and more accurate ones that allow angular measurement down to the nearest one second.

theralite. *See* alkali gabbro.

thermal. A volume of air that possesses buoyancy relative to its cooler surroundings. Thermals tend to arise as a result of strong insolational heating at the ground or a steep environmental lapse rate. Some will reach the condensation level producing cumulus clouds, others may lose their buoyancy earlier. The thermal rises by slowly mixing with its cooler surroundings at its upward margin and by entrainment in its wake. The admixture with environmental air means that strictly the thermal is not cooling adiabatically but in practical terms the difference is rarely significant.

thermal depression. An area of low pressure produced by intense solar heating of the ground surface. The heating reduces the density of the air, which often results in rising air and a fall in surface pressure. The best examples of thermal depression are the monsoon lows, such as those over the Thar Desert. These do not give rise to rain as they are capped by strong anticyclones, which prevents all thermals reaching condensation level.

thermal efficiency. A concept devised by Thornthwaite (*see* Thornthwaite classification) for use in his climate classification scheme. It is a measure of the amount of heat given to a specific area expressed in terms of the potential evapotranspiration that would result.

thermal equator. The line of highest mean surface air temperature. As land areas tend to absorb heat more than oceanic areas, the thermal equator has a mean position in the N hemisphere. In July, it reaches about 20°N over the continents and in December is located at about the actual equator except in E South America where it does extend further south over Amazonia.

thermal high (low). A closed centre of high (low) values of *thickness on a thickness chart. It represents a high (low) temperature averaged through the isobaric layer covered by the chart.

thermal metamorphism. *See* contact metamorphism.

vector of upper wind
28 knots 280°

Thermal wind

thermal wind. A theoretical wind used to indicate the horizontal temperature field in a layer of air. Actual winds change in the vertical as a result of variations in the thermal field at higher levels. The thermal wind is a measure of the difference between the wind at the top and at the base of the layer. It is obtained by subtracting the geostrophic wind vector at the base of the layer from that at the top. *See* diagram.

thermistor. An instrument for measuring temperature based on the property of substances that their electrical resistance varies with temperature.

thermocline. A subsurface layer of water within the ocean in which there is a marked decrease in water temperature as the depth increases. The water layer above the thermocline is essentially homogeneous or isothermal: the differences in temperature and salinity in the vertical column are minimal. This uppermost layer seldom exceeds 100 metres in thickness. Hence, the thermocline is located at the bottom of the surface water masses. The maximum vertical temperature gradient is generally found at depths between 100 and 200 m. Some distance beneath the thermocline, in depths greater than 200 to 300 m, the water masses are surprisingly constant in their characteristics, the temperature gradient rapidly decreasing as one descends to the ocean floor.

thermodynamic diagram. A diagram on which the properties of a parcel of air may be indicated in terms of its pressure, temperature, and humidity. Adiabatic lapse rates are also frequently included on the diagram from which it is possible to make assessments of atmospheric stability and cloud base.

thermograph. A self-recording thermometer, which consists of a temperature-sensing mechanism and a system of time portrayal. A continuous record of temperature can be obtained from it.

thermohaline circulation. The circulation of sea water within the oceans that arises from differences of salinity and temperature, which cause differences in density. Ocean water circulation tends to be controlled by two principal factors: the wind stresses that affect the sea's surface and the distribution of density within the water masses. These two factors are closely related and influence one another. Thermohaline convection, largely due to the cooling of surface waters at high latitudes, gives rise to pronounced currents operating in the oceans.

thermometer. An instrument for measuring temperature by recording a change in a heat-dependent property of a substance. The property chosen will depend on such factors as the accuracy required and the range of temperatures to be measured. The most common method relies on noting the length of a column of mercury (or alcohol where low temperatures are involved) enclosed in a sealed glass capillary rising from a small bulb. The length of the column varies as the mercury expands and contracts with changing temperature. Other properties used include electrical resistance (*resistance thermometer*), the variation in the pressure of a gas kept at constant volume (*gas thermometer*), and the magnitude of the EMF produced by a bimetallic junction (thermocouple). A *dry- and wet-bulb thermometer* consists of two thermometers side by side, one of which has its bulb enclosed in a wet muslin bag. The difference in readings between the two thermometers enables the relative humidity of the atmosphere to be calculated from standard tables (the wet-bulb thermometer will have a lower temperature due to the cooling effect as the liquid evaporates).

thermosphere. The layer of the earth's atmosphere above the mesosphere, in which the temperature increases with height. The pressure ranges from about 0.01 mb to 10^{-8} mb. The thermosphere falls within the *ionosphere.

thickness. The vertical thickness of air between any two specified pressure levels. The most common layer is the 1000 mb–500 mb, but others could be used. The thickness of the layer is directly proportional to its mean temperature, warm temperatures being associated with a thick atmosphere.

thin section. A thin slice of rock, cut and ground to a uniform standard thickness (usually 0.33 mm) and mounted on a glass slide for petrographical study under a microscope.

tholeiite. *See* basalt.

thomsonite. *See* zeolites.

Thornthwaite classifications. A system of classifications based on climatic efficiency, or the capacity of a climate to support the growth of plant communities. It is based on available moisture, the annual variation of temperature, and the degree of association between the temperature and precipitation regimes. The climate of an area is described by a four-digit label from which it can be identified and its characteristics in terms of rainfall, temperature, moisture index, and concentration of thermal efficiency understood. Because of its complexity and difficulties, it has not become widely used in the 30-year period since its final version appeared.

throw. The vertical change in level of a previously continuous bed of rock as a result of faulting.

thrust. A low-angle reverse fault (see diagram at *fault*) that extends over a large distance. In thrusting large rock bodies can be displaced over one another, with the overriding block moving upwards as it passes over the lower block. It results from a principal stress configuration in which the maximum and intermediate stresses are horizontal, while the minimum stress is vertical. The Moine Thrust of NW Scotland, which is 150 km long, carries Precambrian rocks far over Cambrian and other Precambrian rocks. These large displacements are often facilitated by gravity and the presence of fluids in the pores of the rocks undergoing deformation.

thulite. *See* epidote.

thunder. The noise heard accompanying a lightning flash resulting from the sudden heating and expansion of air as the flash passes through the ionized atmosphere. As the speed of sound is far less than that of light, thunder is always heard after the flash. An approximate measure of distance from the storm is 1 mile for every five seconds between flash and thunder.

tidal current. 1. The periodic horizontal flow that occurs in response to the rise and fall of the tide. Such a current, like the vertical oscillation of the tide, arises from the gravitational attraction between the earth, the sun, and the moon. Near the coast, tidal currents tend to be rectilinear and reversing. Further offshore, they tend to flow in a more rotary manner. Tidal currents are responsible for the transport across shelf areas of large quantities of sediment, partly along the sea floor, partly in suspension above it. Because they are reversing currents near the coast, the residual flow in one or other direction often determines the net direction of sediment transport. Tidal currents, which in limited situations attain speeds even in excess of 9 or 10 knots, tend to flow most rapidly at the sea surface, but rather more slowly near the seabed. Bottom friction accounts for this difference. Tidal currents create several distinctive morphological features, including tidal banks and channels, and depressions eroded out of soft rocks.

2. The movement of water between two places differentially affected by the rise and fall of the tides. Two tidal regions may operate in close proximity, such that the water level at one point is, at any particular time, higher than at a neighbouring point. A tidal current will be produced causing water to move from the high to the low area. Though moving with some velocity tidal currents are not noted as erosive agents, but may be important in the transport of material thrown into suspension by waves. The most notable tidal currents operate within straits where high tide at each end occurs at different times.

tidal hypothesis. A theory of the origin of the solar system, which suggested that a star approached close to the sun, and that the tidal attraction coupled with the sun's unstable nature caused some of the sun's mass to be torn off, later to cool as the planets.

tidal prism. The quantity of sea water that floods into or ebbs out of a harbour, estuary, or other sea inlet as a result of tidal flow (not taking into account the freshwater discharge from streams, rivers, or canals). It is usually measured in cubic metres. The stability of tidal inlets is largely determined by the relationships that exist between the tidal prism and littoral drift: the ebb flow, reinforced by freshwater discharge, tends to evacuate sediments from inlets whereas the flood flow, reinforced by the littoral drift, tends to infill inlets with sediments. Dredging is often necessary to maintain the desired balance as most inlets tend towards progressive siltation.

tidal range. The difference in height between the water level at high and low tide. This range is never a fixed value since wherever tides occur there is always variation between great ranges, associated with the especially high and particularly low tides of spring type, and small ranges associated with the neap tides. Whenever a single value for tidal range is quoted for a place, it is a mean value. A major geomorphological importance of the tidal range is that it controls how much of a beach profile will come under the influence of wave action, and therefore the nature of the coastal features.

tidal stream. A movement of water into and out of bays, estuaries, and other restricted coastal openings, associated with the rise and fall of the tides. These streams may move comparatively rapidly and can cause considerable erosion both in flood and ebb. In the fine sediments of estuaries different streams are utilized by the rising and falling tide, and the results of their erosion are complex patterns of interdigitating channels, termed flood and ebb channels according to their mode of formation. *See also* tidal current.

tidal wave. *See* tsunami.

tide. The regular rising and falling of water level resulting from the gravitational attraction that exists between the earth, the sun, and the moon. Depending on their relative positions, either spring tides or *neap tides result. Tidal predictions can be made, although other influences such as local meteorological conditions make very accurate predictions difficult. With the rise and fall of the tide, the horizontal movement of water gives rise to *tidal currents. The response of the oceans to tide-producing forces is based on a series of amphidromic points (*see* amphidromic system), around which the tide oscillates in the manner of a *progressive wave. Diurnal tides are those with one low water and one high water during the tidal day; semidiurnal tides have two low waters and two high waters during the tidal day.

tie. See chaining.

tight fold. A type of fold with parallel or slightly diverging limbs, with an inter-limb angle of less than 30°. See diagram at fold.

till (boulder clay). The unstratified material deposited by glaciers and ice sheets. Characteristically unsorted, it contains angular material ranging from clay-sized particles to huge boulders. These may exhibit *striations and can be derived from a wide variety of rock types. See also ablation till, lodgement till.

till fabric. The general pattern of orientation of elongate stones within *till material. Analysis of the positioning of pebbles has shown that in many cases a large proportion are located with their long axes parallel with the direction of former ice flow, and with a low angle of dip downstream. Frequently another minor concentration exists, consisting of stones whose long axes are perpendicular to the direction of movement. It is believed that the former were moved by sliding and the latter by rotation about their long axes. Tills of different ages have been distinguished on the evidence of their different stone orientations.

time series. A set of data arranged in order of occurrence with equal time intervals between each value. Such series are common in climatology as standard records are taken at equal intervals and extend over many years. A time series can be for individual values or for averaged values such as annual mean temperature. Time series can be analysed by a variety of statistical techniques such as spectrum or harmonic analysis.

tinguaite. See phonolite.

TIROS. A series of ten satellites put into orbit between 1 April 1960 and 2 July 1965. They represented the first attempts at space photography and provided much new and valuable information on weather systems and cloud patterns.

titanaugite. A titanium-rich variety of *augite. See pyroxene.

titanite. See sphene.

tombolo. A form of coastal *spit, composed of sand or shingle, that links an offshore island to the mainland. Two tombolos (double tombolos) may link one island to different parts of the coast, enclosing a lagoon between them. The usual existence of comparatively shallow water in the straits between island and coast assists in the reduction of wave energy in this area, thereby promoting deposition of material. Tideless areas seem especially suited to tombolo formation, the Mediterranean containing many fine examples. Where the coastal outline is suitable, normal longshore movements of beach material may produce a spit, which eventually extends to reach an island.

tonalite. A quartz-diorite. See diorite.

topaz. A variably coloured orthorhombic mineral of composition $Al_2(SiO_4)$-$(OH,F)_2$ found in acid igneous rocks, such as granites and pegmatites.

topoclimatology. The study of the interaction between topography and climate at the local scale. Stress is placed on the varying slope conditions (as they affect radiation receipt), the local water balance, raindrop trajectories, the geostrophic wind flow, and gravitational winds. These modifications of the heat and water balances produce a distinctive topoclimate, which may be widely different from the macroclimate as recorded in a Stevenson screen on a horizontal surface.

topography. The relief, drainage, roads, vegetation, and cultural features of the earth's surface.

topography or terrain correction. The correction of gravity measurements for the effects of local topography, since hills and valleys cause variations in the strength of the earth's gravitational field.

topset beds. *See* delta deposits.

tor. A small hill projecting abruptly from a gently undulating land surface. Tors usually consist of stacks of joint blocks, which remain in situ and attached to bedrock at depth, together with many collapsed blocks. The most favoured explanation of tor formation postulates two cycles: the first involves initial differential *deep weathering, the least jointed rocks being the least weathered; the subsequent period of *exhumation exposes the former undulating *weathering front and leaves the unweathered blocks as tors. Many tors display *unloading sheets, which must have developed as exhumation proceeded.

tornado. A violently rotating column of air characterized by a funnel-shaped cloud, which may reach to the ground surface, accompanied by a roaring noise. On a local scale the tornado represents the greatest wind intensity of all surface weather conditions. Most anemometers and even barographs are damaged if a tornado passes overhead, but falls of up to 200 mb and wind speeds of up to 200 knots are believed to be experienced. The tornado moves across country with the wind flow and direction of the wind at a higher level, leaving a swath of destruction wherever the funnel cloud has reached the ground. The precise origins are not fully understood, but in their severest form the following environmental conditions are required: warm moist air at low levels, an *inversion at about 2000 m, a tongue of dry air between 850 and 700 mb, and a triggering mechanism to initiate the individual storm. These factors occur most frequently in the mid-West of the U.S., where tornadoes are a great problem. However, tornadoes of lower intensity occur in many countries; even in temperate Britain about one is recorded every other year.

torrid zone. The tropical areas between 23.5°N and 23.5°S.

tourmaline. The tourmaline minerals have a general formula $NaR_3^{2+}Al_6B_3Si_6O_{27}(OH,F)_4$ where R = Fe^{2+}, Mg, or (Al + Li). They have trigonal symmetry and are variably coloured although black varieties are common. Tourmaline is found in veins and pegmatites associated with granites.

The pneumatolytic alterations of granitic minerals caused by the introduction of boron is called *tourmalinization*. The rock luxullianite is a tourmalinized granite in which the biotite and much of the alkali feldspar has been replaced by radiating aggregates of acicular tourmaline. Quartz is the only mineral to survive tourmalinization and the end product is a tourmaline-quartz assemblage known as *shorl* rock. *See* pneumatolysis.

tourmalinization. *See* pneumatolysis, tourmaline.

trace fossil. A fossilized remnant of the effects of an organism in the past, rather than the remains of the organism itself. Trace fossils may be the fossilized faeces of an organism or structures produced by it that have been preserved in the sediment, such as tracks and burrows. *Actuopalaeontology is used in relating these fossils to the species that produced them. Trace fossils are classified in a taxonomic system analogous to that applied to the organisms themselves, characteristic trace fossils being described as *ichnospecies*. They are often used in elucidating the *palaeoecology of a species.

trachyandesite. *See* syenodiorite.

trachybasalt. The fine-grained equivalent of *syenogabbro, displaying mineralogical and chemical features intermediate between *trachytes and *alkali basalts. *Hawaiite* and *mugearite* are members of the alkali basalt volcanic suite containing andesine and oligoclase feldspar respectively together with basaltic mafic minerals. These lavas are distinguished from andesites largely on chemical grounds and fiel· associations. *Benmoreite* is chemic·

intermediate between mugearite and soda trachyte.

trachyte. The volcanic equivalent of syenite, ranging from oversaturated to undersaturated in composition. Some varieties contain sanidine and oligoclase feldspars, others contain a single anorthoclase feldspar. Feldspars occur both as phenocrysts and as close-packed microlites in the groundmass. The microlites usually have a sub-parallel flow orientation and swirl around the phenocrysts imparting a characteristic trachytic texture. Mafic minerals include biotite, clinopyroxene, and hornblende. In the sodic varieties, soda pyriboles and fayalite are common. Trachytes may contain up to 10% accessory quartz. Oversaturated sodic varieties are termed pantelleritic trachytes, which, with an increase in the amount of quartz, pass into pantellerites (alkali rhyolites). Varieties containing accessory nepheline are termed phonolitic trachytes. When the nepheline content reaches 10%, phonolitic trachytes pass into phonolites. Kenytes are a variety of sodic phonolitic trachyte containing distinctive rhombic phenocrysts of anorthoclase.

Trachytes are the intermediate members of the alkaline basalt volcanic suite and are found mainly in ocean islands and areas of continental rifting and vulcanism.

trade winds. The predominantly easterly winds that blow steadily over the ocean areas and less steadily over continental interiors in the tropics, converging towards the equator. They play a very important role in the *general circulation of the atmosphere by evaporating moisture in large quantities from the tropical seas, which helps to maintain the global heat balance by removing surplus heat from these areas. On the eastern side of the tropical oceans, the trade winds are very steady in direction and speed and have a very strong low-level inversion preventing the vertical development of cloud. These areas, such as the Canary Islands or the Galapagos

Islands, tend to have low rainfall. Crossing the oceans increases the depth of the moist layer near the surface, the inversion becomes less intense, and disturbances more frequent, so that on the western sides of the oceans the trade winds provide an adequate rainfall in most areas.

trajectory (in meteorology). A line drawn to indicate the actual movement of a particle of air over a certain time interval. Ideally the path should be three-dimensional, but as little is normally known in detail about the vertical component, the horizontal projection of the path is portrayed. The term is also used for the downward motion of a precipitation particle as far as it can be assessed from upper air information.

transcurrent fault. *See* tear fault.

transform fault (conservative plate margin). A fault present within the earth's oceanic crust (see diagram at *fault*). They have strike-slip displacement and are orientated at right angles to the mid-ocean ridges (constructive plate margins), which they offset for several tens or even hundreds of kilometres. These faults lie parallel to small circles the axis of which is the axis of rotation for the relative motion of the plates on either side.

transgression. Flooding of land area by a positive movement of *base level, resulting in onshore migration of the high-water mark. A transgression results in the shortening of rivers by the drowning of former valleys, leading to the creation of fiords, rias, and estuaries: these features are shortlived as rapid aggradation soon fills them up with silt. Past transgressions at a particular point can be identified by studying the deposits left, e.g. in the Fenland area transgressions are seen from the interdigitation of silt (marine or brackish deposit) and peat (land deposit). Fossil remains may also show changes from freshwater to marine types. In the postglacial period there have been two major transgressions, the first one in the

Boreal period (7600-5500 B.C.) being the most important, which have elevated sea level to its current extent after the low stand of the last glacial period. Marine transgression can be local or worldwide.

transport. The link in the geomorphological system between sites of erosion and sites of deposition. The media of running water, wind, and currents transport material in varying proportions by bed creep, saltation, and suspension. In rivers bed creep is dominant; in air saltation is most important. Solution can also be important in rivers. Waves transport by beach drift of pebbles and sand in the surf zone, and the setting up of *longshore currents. Ice transports as a solid medium, by shunting material in front, incorporating material in its base, and carrying slope-eroded material on its top. Gravity is inherent in most transport; on slopes it is directly responsible for downslope movements and it provides energy for flowing water.

transverse Mercator projection. A map projection constructed in the same way as the Mercator projection but having the cylinder tangential to a meridian rather than to the equator. It is used mainly for small areas with a north-south orientation, and for all British Ordnance Survey maps. Rhumb lines on this projection are curved.

trap. A geological structure in which hydrocarbons accumulate. Hydrocarbons migrate away from their source rock under pressure and accumulate where an effective barrier to their further migration exists. Traps can occur in a variety of ways. Since hydrocarbons, both oil and gas, are less dense than water, they tend to accumulate in the highest points of the trap, displacing most of the water previously present in the rock pores. The barriers to further migration can result from tectonic activity, as in the case of fault, unconformity, and anticlinal traps, and from lateral changes in the properties of the rock body, as in the case of facies change traps and reef traps. When more than one type of trap exists in the same place it is termed a *composite trap.*

traversing. A surveying method for finding position by measurement of direction and distance, using either a prismatic compass and tape (*compass traverse*), or a theodolite and levelling staff (*tacheometric traverse*). If the starting and finishing points are of known position, whether a single or two distinct stations, then the traverse is *closed.* If only one station, at one end of a traverse line, is of known position the traverse is *open* or *unclosed.* The former type is better since it allows easier correction if errors are made. Unlike a compass traverse, a tacheometric traverse will not only fix position but also height. To obtain heights for points fixed by compass and tape, a levelling traverse must be run, starting and finishing at a point of known height. *See* tacheometry.

travertine. Deposits of calcium carbonate formed by precipitation from hot springs.

Trellis drainage

trellis drainage. A drainage pattern that develops where two sets of structural controls of a different type occur at right angles. If a steep regional slope is crossed by varying hard and soft lithologies, short stream segments will follow the slopes, while the soft lithologies will rapidly develop long subsequent streams that will come to

Fig. 1: Unconformity trap

Fig. 2: Facies change

Fig. 3: Fault trap

Fig. 4: Anticlinal trap

Fig. 5: Salt dome trap

Types of trap

dominate the pattern. One example is in the Jura Mountains of France; another is the Ridge and Valley province in the Appalachian mountains of the eastern U.S.

A similar pattern can also arise if glaciation of an area of former consequent streams proceeds at right angles to the initial drainage. Subsequents will develop following the grain of the glacial advance, as expressed in fluted ground moraine or drumlins, and come to dominate the system.

tremolite. A monoclinic mineral of the *amphibole group.

trench (foredeep). A long narrow deep furrow in the earth's crust, generally developed at the margin of a continent where an oceanic plate is being subducted (see subduction zones), and often bordered by an *island arc. They can also develop where one oceanic plate overrides another. They mark the site of a destructive *plate margin and the surface expression of a *Benioff zone. Most trenches have steep V-shaped walls and are often terraced, with a flat floor that is formed by a sediment infill. They are the deepest parts of the oceans: the greatest known depth (5933 fathoms or 10 850 metres) was recorded in the Mariana Trench, and similar depths occur in the Tonga and Kuril Trenches.

trend. General alignment, direction, or bearing. See diagram at *fold.

triangulation. The accurate location of a number of points by dividing the area containing them into a series of triangles for which the values of internal angles and the lengths of sides are ascertained. Only one side of one triangle need be measured physically, since once all the angles are known, the side lengths can be computed using trigonometrical ratios. After a *base line has been measured very accurately, the angles are measured using a *theodolite, usually a one-second instrument, which is set up in turn at all the stations to be fixed. Triangulation schemes are the basis of all surveying since they provide the locations of the few initial control points, from which subsequent detail mapping may take place using other methods.

Triassic (Trias). The first period of the *Mesozoic Era, beginning about 240 million years ago, at the end of the *Permian, and lasting for some 40 million years until the beginning of the *Jurassic. The Triassic System has three main divisions. The Lower Triassic

Trench

consists of the Induan and Olenekian Stages; the Middle Triassic comprises the Anisian and Ladinian Stages; and the Karnian, Norian, and Rhaetian Stages form the Upper Triassic. In Britain rocks of the Triassic System are of a continental facies, consisting of desert sandstones and shales similar to those of the preceding Permian (*see* Permo-Trias). Triassic faunas, following the Late Palaeozoic extinctions, show a typically Mesozoic character. Modern corals appeared, ammonites developed, and bivalves replaced the declining brachiopods. The evolution of the Reptilia produced such diverse types as the dinosaurs and the marine ichthyosaurs and plesiosaurs.

triclinic. *See* crystal system.

tridymite. *See* silica minerals.

trigonal. *See* crystal system.

Trilobita. An extinct class of the phylum *Arthropoda whose members are common and widely distributed as fossils. Trilobites had an oval flattened segmented body divided longitudinally into three lobes and transversely into three regions: an anterior *cephalon*, a *thorax*, and a posterior *pygidium*. They possessed a large number of appendages, including one pair of antennae. Most trilobites were about 50 mm in length though a few reached over 500

mm. The first fossils are found in lower Cambrian rocks; the group declined from the Ordovician Period onwards and by the end of the Palaeozoic it was extinct. The trilobites formed a widespread, diverse, and rapidly evolving group and their fossils are of great value in the calibration and correlation of Lower Palaeozoic rocks.

triple junction. A point at which three lithospheric plate margins meet.

trochoidal wave. *See* cycloidal wave.

troctolite. A *gabbro consisting of olivine and plagioclase feldspar of labradorite composition.

trondhjemite. *See* granite.

tropical black soil. A black heavy-textured soil characteristic of tropical lowland areas, either plainlands or the downslope ends of *catenas, which are subject to seasonal drying and cracking due to the shrinking and swelling of the dominant montmorillonitic clay during dry and wet periods respectively, caused by the ability of the clay to take up water in its lattice. During the wet swelling periods, soil is pushed up to form swells (*gilgai*) and in the dry phases cracks develop, which infill themselves from the surface, thereby maintaining a kind of cycle, which makes the soils self-mulching or inverting. There are possibly 40 or so different names for these soils, including vertisol, mbuga, tir, black cotton soil, grumusol, morgatitic, black earth, black turf, and regur, each of which denotes a regional variant differing in some small way. As a group, they are similar to *chernozems, but have less organic matter and differences in the surface horizons, due mainly to the higher temperature and greater evaporation of their environment. Tropical black soils have indistinct horizons due to their self-mulching nature, often with calcareous or gypseous concretions; silt and clay content is high (possibly 85%+), pH is neutral or alkaline, and parent materials typically basic, e.g. marine alluvium, limestone, or basalt.

tropical cyclone. A low pressure system of tropical latitudes accompanied by strong winds. It is a general term used to describe a cyclonic storm of any intensity, distinctions of wind strength being made by other terms such as tropical depression, tropical storm, and hurricane. The diagram shows the distribution of tropical cyclones, which are clearly restricted to certain areas. They only develop in oceanic areas where the sea temperature is above 27°C and at least 5° of latitude away from the equator. It appears that the warm sea surface must provide energy through evaporation, 27°C representing its lower limit, and as the *Coriolis force is zero at the equator, the storm must be at least 5° away before rotational components of airflow can develop. The precise origins of tropical cyclones are debatable, but some form of initial disturbance in the airflow seems to be a prerequisite.

tropical easterlies. See trade winds.

tropical (groundwater or geant) podzol. A soil developed in low-lying tropical areas, often adjacent to riverine, marine, or deltaic areas, subject to a fluctuating water table. They are characterized by their striking colours and overdeveloped

Areas with sea-surface temperature of the warmest month above 27°C

Distribution of tropical cyclones

A_2 horizon, which can be two metres deep. They develop by the leaching of sesquioxides and organic material to the B horizon, with precipitation taking place at the level of the water table.

tropopause. The boundary between the troposphere and the stratosphere. It represents the point at which temperatures stop falling prior to the isothermal conditions of the lower stratosphere. On occasion, there may be more than one tropopause. The height of the tropopause varies, being higher above warm air than cold. Consequently its mean height is greatest over tropical latitudes at above 16 km but only about 8 km over polar latitudes. It also changes because of different weather conditions. The tropopause is not a continuous surface between the tropics and poles, but is broken at the latitude of the subtropical jet stream and is suddenly lower on the poleward side. These breaks enable mixing to take place between tropospheric and stratospheric air, which would otherwise not occur because the isothermal layer of the stratosphere acts as a stable inversion.

troposphere. The lowest layer of the atmosphere, where almost all weather phenomena develop. It takes its name from the Greek word tropos meaning a turn: it is the atmospheric layer where turning and convective mixing is dominant.

trough. A pressure system on a weather chart distinguished by an isobaric pattern of low pressure having much greater length than width and a concave curvature of the isobars towards the main depression centre. All fronts occupy troughs of low pressure, but not all troughs are frontal. They are normally associated with precipitation and cloud.

trowal. Trough of warm air aloft. This indicates the presence of a layer of warmer air in the upper atmosphere, which is not in contact with the ground surface. This type of situation occurs in an occlusion.

tsunami. A seismic sea wave generated in the ocean by submarine earthquakes, explosive volcanic eruptions, or mass slides underwater. Although fairly rare, they can have catastrophic effects when they do occur. Perhaps of limited height (about a metre) in the open ocean, they may travel hundreds or even thousands of kilometres, and they attain considerable heights (up to tens of metres) in shallow coastal water and at breakpoint. Their length at sea may be 150 km or more, and they usually travel at high speeds, probably between 300 and 500 knots. They have caused immense havoc and destruction and heavy loss of life, especially along low-lying coasts. Tsunamis are sometimes incorrectly called *tidal waves.*

tufa. Deposits of calcium carbonate formed by precipitation from water and including stalagmites, stalactites, flowstone, and travertine.

tuff. *See* pyroclastic rocks.

turbidite. A sediment deposited in water by *turbidity currents. Because the speed of a turbidity current is proportional to the square root of effective density, its lower part will be more heavily charged with sediment and will move faster than the less heavily charged upper part. For this reason the particle size of the sediment transported decreases from the base of the flow upwards, a consequence being that a form of sediment grading, or graded bedding, occurs in the deposit ultimately laid down. A typical sequence in such a deposit is for coarse material at the base to give way to finer material above, and possibly be covered in turn by lutite. If a series of turbidity flows occur in the same area, a rhythmic pattern of sedimentation arises, with superimposed layer upon layer of graded turbidite material. Many sandy turbidites contain a significant amount of silt and clay.

turbidity. 1. (In meteorology). The property of the clear atmosphere that leads to a reduction of solar radiation, usually due to particles of dust and smoke, which lead to attenuation rather than molecular scattering. It is therefore a measure of natural and man-made atmospheric pollution. **2.** (In oceanography). The stirring up of sediment by water.

turbidity current. A flow of dense sediment and water. These currents develop with the stirring of sediment, resulting in the formation of a layer that is denser than the surrounding water. Such a situation occurs if strong wave action, a submarine slide, or an earthquake disturbance affects the sea floor in an area in which sediments, especially the finer-grained ones, are reasonably abundant. In the case of a flat seabed and in the absence of currents, the suspended material would tend to settle out again, but where the seabed slopes (e.g. on *continental slopes) the suspended material usually begins to flow, most rapidly when the slope is steep, and thereby initiates a turbidity current. Turbidity currents can be very dense and may possibly attain speeds of 80 kilometres per hour or more. They have been powerful enough to break submarine cables and to erode channels in the deep-sea floor. They lead to sediment deposits in characteristic morphological forms.

turbulent flow. The usual type of movement characteristic of air and water in nature, in which the net forward movement of the fluid has superimposed upon it a chaotic pattern of secondary eddies, carrying molecules from one layer in the flow to either higher or lower layers. This constant exchange of molecules speeds up slower layers and slows down faster ones; the eddies are principally responsible for creating hydrodynamic lift, so important in sediment transport. *Laminar flow becomes turbulent when the viscosity of the water falls as temperature increases, releasing the liquid from the confines of flowing purely as laminar layers. Alternatively, increased velocity, increased bed roughness, or a decrease in water depth can all promote turbulent flow. In waterfalls and rapids the greatly increased velocity and lowering of the water surface promotes a special type of turbulence, "shooting" flow, which accelerates erosion and leads to rapid lowering of the falls or regrading of the rapids.

The scale of turbulence in the atmosphere is wide, ranging from small eddies rising above a strongly heated ground surface to mid-latitude depressions, which represent large-scale turbulence in the westerlies. It is important in the atmosphere as an effective mechanism of dispersal.

type locality. 1. (In palaeontology). The place from which a fossil that is the *type specimen of a species comes. **2.** (In stratigraphy). The site of the outcrop of rock used to define a particular stratigraphical division. See type section, formation, stratigraphy, lithostratigraphy.

type section. The particular outcrop of rock that has been selected as the standard section for the definition of the limits of a lithostratigraphical unit because it clearly demonstrates the characteristic lithological features of the unit. The place in which it occurs is known as the *type locality*. See also formation, lithostratigraphy, stratigraphy.

type species. The species regarded as typifying the *genus to which it belongs. The type species is often the species whose characteristics were used in defining the genus.

type specimen. A specimen of an organism that was orginally selected and preserved to define the morphological characteristics of a *species. It may not necessarily be typical of the species as a whole.

typhoon. A tropical cyclone or hurricane with winds above Force 12 on the

*Beaufort Scale. It is used for such storms in the W and N Pacific Ocean and comes from a Chinese word meaning great wind.

U

ugrandite. A chemical series of *garnet minerals.

ultisol. One of the ten soil orders from the *Seventh Approximation classification, denoting highly weathered soil formed in subtropical to tropical climates, which has a surface horizon containing residual iron oxides and an illuvial horizon beneath rich in clay. Base status and fertility is low. It is so named because it contains soils at the ultimate stage of weathering and includes the red-yellow podzolics, redbrown lateritics, and associated hydromorphic variants.

ultrabasic rocks. Igneous rocks containing less than 45% silica (by weight). Most ultramafic rocks (consisting largely of ferromagnesian minerals) are ultrabasic but some pyroxenites may have more than 45% silica and are basic rather than ultrabasic in composition. Current usage has tended to equate the two but strictly, ultrabasic and ultramafic are chemical and mineralogical terms respectively. See ultramafic rocks, acid rocks.

ultramafic rocks. Igneous rocks consisting largely of *ferromagnesian minerals. They may be divided into three groups:
1. Peridotites, in which olivine is dominant and feldspar absent (dunite, harzburgite, lhersolite, wehrlite).
2. Pyroxenites, consisting wholly of orthopyroxenes and clinopyroxenes (bronzitite, websterite).
3. Picrites, which contain accessory feldspar (oceanite, ankaramite).
With an increase in the amount of plagioclase, picrites grade into gabbros. Most ultramafic rocks are plutonic and occur in layered intrusions, ophiolite complexes, zoned ultrabasic bodies, and as nodules in basaltic lavas.

ulvöspinel. See spinel.

uncompahgrite. See ijolite series.

unconformable. See discordant (def. 2).

unconformity. A surface representing a period of nondeposition or erosion separating rocks of different ages. Some unconformites show a marked angularity, the beds above and below the unconformity surface having different dips and strikes, whereas other unconformities can only be detected by palaeontological means. Compare disconformity.

underground drainage. In limestone areas solution can take place to such an extent that joints, bedding planes, and other fissures become progressively enlarged, forming hollows (*sink holes *uvalas, or *poljes) on the surface, and cavern systems underground. Linked cave systems can lead the water of a stream from a sink hole at one point to a spring some considerable distance away, thereby eliminating surface drainage for that stretch.

undersaturated rocks. Igneous rocks that are deficient in silica and therefore contain *feldspathoids. Undersaturated rocks include ijolites, nephelinites, and alkali basalts. See silica saturation.

underthrust. A low-angled fault resulting in the movement of the foot wall relative to the hanging wall.

undertow. A seaward flow of water beneath, or in the vicinity of, breaking waves. Some authorites claim that the backwash of waves constitutes a periodic sheet-flow seawards, describing this as an undertow. The term has also been used (erroneously) to mean the *rip current flows that occur within fairly confined zones.

uniformitarianism (actualism). The theory, now generally accepted, that all geological changes have occurred by the gradual effect of processes that have been operating over a long period of time and are still going on today. *Compare* catastrophism.

units. For general scientific purposes, *SI units are now widely used throughout the world. However, in some disciplines older systems of units still persist. For example, in meteorology and climatology many elements are still measured in Imperial units in the U.S. and knots continue to be used for wind velocity and ocean currents in most countries. Although the SI unit of pressure is the pascal, it has been agreed that the millibar will continue to be used in meteorology.

unloading (sheeting, pseudo-bedding, pressure release). A weathering process resulting in the division of rock masses into sheets separated by fractures. These sheets tend to increase in frequency and decrease in thickness towards the top of an exposure; they are concentric, and essentially follow the topographic outline of the ground surface. The usual explanation is that the fractures are due to the expansion of the rock on reduction of the confining pressure, achieved by the removal of overlying materials by erosion. These features occur most frequently in granites.

unmixing. *See* exsolution.

upslope fog. A form of advection fog resulting from the cooling of moist air to saturation point as it is forced to rise up the windward slope of uplands. It has the appearance of stratus cloud from below.

upwarp. The uplifting or uparching of a large area of the earth's crust, usually in response to isostacy. The area of Scandinavia has gradually been rising after having been depressed by the weight of the ice during the last ice age.

upwelling. An ascending water current, not necessarily from the bottom of the sea, which transports colder water up into the surface layers of the sea. Such currents occur particularly in tropical and subtropical seas, and in the water

flanking the Antarctic, especially in those regions where surface currents diverge (*divergence zones). Upwellings also occur in some inland or marginal sea areas, including the Caspian Sea and Black Sea. They may stem from strong offshore winds that tend to drag the surface water layer seawards so to be replaced by colder water from beneath. Upwellings occur off the coasts of California, Peru, and Ghana. They tend to operate seasonally and to form cold zones within otherwise warm sea areas. They are of primary importance in bringing to the surface waters that are rich in nutrients; these in turn may support thriving fisheries. Shifts in the zones of upwellings have proved disastrous to the fishing industry.

uralitization. The late-stage or *metasomatic alterations of primary igneous pyroxenes to fibrous pale green amphiboles.

uraninite. A black radioactive uranium mineral, UO_2, found as an accessory in acid igneous rocks and in hydrothermal veins. *See also* pitchblende.

urban climate. The distinctive modification of the macroclimate produced by extensive urban areas. The marked difference in the nature of the surface in rural and urban areas alters the local heat balance to such an extent that, even in an area of uniform topography, the city evolves its own climate. This has become the subject of much research in recent years and to distinguish it from the macroclimate determined from Stevenson screens at standard exposures, it is called the urban climate. *See also* heat island.

urtite. *See* ijolite.

U-shaped valley. A well-developed glacial valley with a characteristic U-shaped cross profile, as opposed to the V-shape of fluvially developed valleys. Such development can take place by simple widening of pre-glacial valleys, or by a combination of widening and deepening, the latter process depending upon the glacier's ability to cut into the bed-rock. The typical steep sides of glacial valleys reflect the fact that whereas rivers only occupy the bottoms of their valleys, a glacier tends to fill much of it, erosion taking place wherever there is an ice-rock contact. The extent to which a valley can be deepened depends greatly upon the amount of weathering active in the valley before the appearance of the glacier, since *glacial plucking is the major process of rock removal.

uvala. A large depression found in limestone areas, resulting from solution (see limestone solution). They may be several kilometres in diameter, and frequently result from the coalescence of a number of adjacent *dolines. In such a case the uvala may have a scalloped margin. See also polje.

uvarovite. See garnet.

V

vadose water. Groundwater above the water table in permeable rock, e.g. limestone. Underground streams in this zone flow with free air surfaces. Compare phreatic water.

valley breeze. The daytime equivalent of the *mountain wind. It is formed by greater solar heating on the inclined mountain slopes relative to the air at the same level over the valley. As wind speeds tend to be higher during the day as a result of general turbulence and convection, the valley breeze is more easily masked than the mountain wind.

valley glacier. An accumulation of ice moving down a pre-existing valley and restricted in width by the valley walls. They may develop as a result of the merging of a number of *cirque glaciers in valley-head locations at times of deteriorating climate, in which case they are known as the Alpine type, or they may be developed at the very edge of an *ice cap or *ice sheet, when they are known as the outlet type. If the supply of ice to the source areas is sufficient, valley glaciers can extend down-valley to comparatively low altitudes.

vapour pressure. The pressure exerted by the molecules of a liquid or solid that escape from the surface. In meteorology it is that part of the total atmospheric pressure exerted by water vapour. It is measured indirectly from dry- and wet-bulb *temperatures using tables or a humidity slide rule to obtain the precise value.

variolitic. Denoting a texture occurring in basaltic glasses similar to *spherulitic texture in acid glassy rocks. Variolites usually consist of radial or sheaflike aggregates of plagioclase crystals.

Variscan. The period of mountain-building in late Palaeozoic time that affected Europe and includes both the Armorican and Hercynian phases.

varve. A thin bed of sediment in glacial lakes that represents a seasonal increment. Spring and summer glacial melting produces a sudden influx of coarse sediment upon which finer materials settle during the remainder of the year. These annual rhythms can be used in dating events within the *Pleistocene.

vent (conduit). The subterranean passage from the underlying magma chamber through which volcanic products, i.e. lava, ashes, and vapour, are discharged at the earth's surface. Where a volcano has only one such hole, debris accumulates around it as a roughly symmetrical cone: this is termed a central-vent volcano. Where there is more than one eruptive site, usually along a large fracture in the crust, this is termed a fissure volcano.

ventifact. A pebble or stone worn and polished by the action of wind and sand, and found in the gravel-strewn parts of the deserts. If a ventifact becomes worn in such a way that a roughly triangular cross section evolves, it is known as a Dreikanter (German = three sides).

vermiculite. See clay minerals.

Vertebrata. The subphylum of the Chordata to which *fish, *Amphibia, *Reptilia, *Aves (birds), and *Mammalia belong. They possess an internal skeleton of cartilage or bone, including a jointed backbone formed of vertebrae. Vertebrates are active animals and consequently are usually bilaterally symmetrical. The sense organs and feeding apparatus are grouped anteriorly, where they and the brain are protected by a skull. Vertebrates have a dorsal hollow nerve cord and, in most higher groups, two pairs of limbs. Fossil evidence indicates that vertebrates appeared in the Ordovician (see Ostracodermi), since when they have evolved to occupy a great variety of environmental niches.

vertisol. One of the ten soil orders of the *Seventh Approximation classification, denoting mixed and inverting soils of the *tropical black soil group. Vertisols are split into uderts, which crack open for less than three months in a year, and usterts, which open and close more than once a year.

vesicles. Small rounded cavities within lavas formed by bubbles of gas coming out of solution during the solidification of the lava. The concentration of vesicles at the top surfaces of lava flows serve as a way-up criterion. Elongate hollow tubes formed by the escape of steam through lavas flowing over wet ground are called pipe vesicles. Highly vesicular lava fragments are termed pumice. See also amygdale, pyroclastic rocks.

vesuvianite. See idocrase.

viscous flow. Flowage that occurred in once molten rocks, for example lavas, or imperfect fluids, such as asphalt. This results in highly complex fold patterns, each fold being distinct from and related to its neighbours.

visibility (in meteorology). The greatest distance that the eye can see. If there is a marked variation with direction then the lowest visibility is recorded, because visibility is mostly used for aviation purposes and therefore the minimum value is important. Reports at night are based on distances to unfocused lights of moderate or known intensity.

vitrophyre. A *porphyritic lava in which the groundmass is wholly glassy.

volatile (fugitive). A substance, normally gaseous, that is dissolved under pressure in a magma. The main volatile constituents of magmas are water and carbon dioxide, together with smaller quantities of chlorine, hydrochloric acid, fluorine, hydrofluoric acid, hydrogen sulphide, sulphur, and boron compounds.

The solubility of volatile substances increases with pressure so that during the ascent of magma and the attendant lowering of pressure, the magma is unable to retain these constituents in solution. Volatiles concentrate at the top of the magma chamber in a residual fluid from which pegmatites, hydrothermal veins, and mineral deposits may originate. During escape, volatiles effect mineralogical changes on the early-formed crystals (*pneumatolysis).

Volcanic eruptions are accompanied by the release of large quantities of steam and carbon dioxide. The explosive release of these gases produces pyroclastic rocks. Water and gases are also released at minor vents, geysers, hot springs, fumaroles, and solfataras.

volcanic bomb. See pyroclastic rocks.

volcano. A fissure or vent on the earth's surface connected by a conduit to the earth's interior, from which lava, gas, and pyroclastic material are erupted. Each volcano has its own characteristics, but they can be classified generally as:

1. *Hawaiian.* Fairly quiet eruptions in which fluid lava is erupted from fissures or pits, with gas being liberated freely. When the eruption is accompanied by spurting gases, incandescent spray is thrown into the air.

2. *Strombolian.* More violent than the

Hawaiian type, the eruption taking place more spasmodically as trapped gas escapes from a more viscous lava confined in a crater. Eruptions may be every few minutes. During violent activity bombs are ejected, which may be accompanied by lava flows.

3. *Vulcanian.* Characterized by viscous lava whose surface rapidly solidifies. Beneath this crust gas accumulates and builds up pressure until the crust shatters. This results in large quantities of pyroclastic deposits ranging from large bombs to fine ash.

4. *Vesuvian.* Similar to 2 and 3 but with gas-charged lava being shot violently up into the air, emptying the lava column to considerable depth.

5. *Plinian.* A culmination of type 4 in which a violent blast of gas rises to a height of several kilometres. The gas and vapour on reaching this height spreads into a large cloud. The fallout of ash is low, being confined to material removed from the conduit.

6. *Pelean.* Very violent eruptions accompanied by nuées ardentes and hot avalanches of incoherent constantly expanding self-explosive lava, lubricated by hot gases and vapours. Such eruptions are characteristic of highly viscous lava, whose gas content cannot readily escape.

vorticity. The three-dimensional rotation of a fluid about an axis, measured as a vector of twice the local rate of rotation of an individual fluid element. As rotation occurs in most aspects of atmospheric motion, vorticity is very important. Even if air is still relative to the earth, it will still be rotating in space because of the earth's rotation. To distinguish these two types, *relative vorticity* is taken as rotation relative to the earth's surface; it is positive if cyclonic, i.e. rotating in the same direction as the earth and negative if anticyclonic. *Absolute vorticity* is the relative vorticity plus the component of the earth's rotation about its axis; this is zero at the equator and a maximum at the poles.

V-shaped valley. Traditionally, fluvial valleys of youthful and mature rivers are said to have a V cross profile, with steep walls and narrow bottoms, whilst by senility, the broadening floodplain produces more of a U-shape. Irrespective of age, most valleys display a V-shape near their source, with some trend towards a broadening bottom near their mouth. Streams with sandy and gravelly banks tend to have a V-shape as the material slumps on erosion of the foot slope to its angle of rest, and rainfall landing on the valley sinks in and does not run off and sculpture the gentle side walls; conversely, valleys in cohesive silty or clayey material tend to maintain their walls as the river cuts sideways, leaving a flat bottom, with steep side walls and hence a U-shape. Climate can also be important: shady (north- and west-facing) valley sides have a different microclimate from sunny (south- and east-facing) walls and this can influence the rate and type of processes acting, hence lowering the two side walls at different rates to produce an irregular valley shape. If precipitation is high, the valley walls become clothed in dense vegetation, which slows down erosion, maintaining a V-shape, whilst in arid zones where there is no vegetation U-shapes often result from increased erosion of valley walls.

vugh (vug). A cavity within a volcanic rock lined with deuteric or *secondary minerals. *Compare* amygdale, miarolitic cavity.

W

wadi. A normally dry valley in a desert or semidesert environment. In such locations rain falls very infrequently but when it does so it is often in the form of violent downpours of limited duration. As normal fluvial activity does not exist, large amounts of weathering debris accumulate in situ. Channel flow following a desert cloudburst can have a considerable erosional effect, cutting these narrow valleys with nearly vertical walls into the weathered rocks. Wadis may be relics from times of wetter climate.

wake. The trail of eddies or vorticities that develop on the leeward side of an obstruction to wind flow. Large vertical velocities may be induced in essentially horizontal flow by this method as on the lee side of hills, buildings, or wind breaks.

waning slope. The gentle concave footslope lying beneath the *free face. The waning slope is equivalent to the pediment, by which name it is more commonly referred to. It comprises the gentle slope of the valley floor, terminating in a drainage line or floodplain. Waning slopes are said to become more widespread at the latter part of the cycle of erosion, as the dominant process becomes retreat of hillsides (backcutting), rather than downcutting of valleys. See also waxing slope.

warm front. A strong thermal gradient in the atmosphere in which, from its direction of movement, warm air is replacing cold air. The slope of a warm frontal surface is about 1 in 150, and so weather phenomena associated with it precede the surface front by many kilometres. The first indication is the spreading of cirrus clouds across the sky, followed by cirrostratus, altostratus, then nimbostratus as the rain starts falling. Temperatures rise, relative humidity increases, and the wind veers as the front passes. Warm fronts are a major contributor to annual rainfall totals in coastal locations of temperate latitudes. Compare cold front.

warm rain. Rain falling from clouds that are entirely warmer than freezing and which therefore must have developed by the *coalescence process alone.

warm sector. The region of warmer air existing in a *depression between the warm and cold fronts. It eventually disappears from the surface during the evolution of the depression as the cold

front catches up the warm front (see occlusion). Weather in the warm sector is usually noticeably milder than the preceding and following air streams. Precipitation is very variable, varying from none if there is a strong ridge of high pressure to heavy, especially over mountain areas, if the warm sector is potentially or conditionally unstable.

wash. See overland flow.

washout. A filled-in river channel that cuts into pre-existing sediments. It is usually developed on deltas and other areas of slow-flowing rivers. The channels are usually infilled with sands, which often contain fragments of the eroded bed. They are very common in the Coal Measures and deltaic Jurassic beds. The sand body infilling the channel is sometimes known as a *horse*.

wash slope (alluvial toe-slope). That part of a hill slope lying at the foot of the *constant slope, formed by the washing out of fines from the scree in the constant slope. This fine material, often lying in the river valley, has a lesser angle of rest than the coarser constant slope debris, and so there is a gentle break of slope between the two components.

waste mantle. See regolith.

water balance (in meteorology). The movement of water between and within the atmosphere and ground surface on a global scale. It involves the balance between precipitation, evaporation, advection of moisture in the air, ocean current circulations, and river runoff on land. There is a long-term balance, so that no area of the earth is continuously losing or gaining moisture. The values of the components of the water balance are often known only very approximately, especially over the ocean areas.

waterfall. A vertical fall of water at a steep break in the long profile of a stream. This may be the product of base-level fall producing a large *knickpoint, local displacement due to an earthquake, or irregularities in the long profile produced by hard bands of rock through which the river has been unable to grade a smooth profile owing to lack of erosive power or insufficient time. In areas of horizontal strata, breaks through individual rock beds will often result in a steep fall. Once created the falls immediately begin to retreat upstream and become less pronounced owing to lowering of their height through the concentration of erosion on the lip. Deposition below the falls also obscures the break and tends to restore a smooth long profile.

watershed. See divide.

waterspout. The oceanic equivalent of a *tornado. It occurs over seas or large lakes when a funnel-shaped cloud descends from a cumulonimbus cloud to produce violent agitation of the sea surface and a very local intense rotation of wind. They are never as severe or long-lasting as the variety of tornado found in the mid-West of the U.S.

watertable. See groundwater.

water vapour. The distribution of water vapour in the atmosphere varies greatly, with largest amounts in the humid tropics and least in polar regions and to a lesser extent the desert areas. As well as being necessary for precipitation, water vapour has another important meteorological role in absorbing long-wave or terrestrial radiation. With carbon dioxide, it acts as a very effective mechanism for preventing the loss of radiation that would otherwise occur. The mean temperature of the earth is therefore partly a response to the presence of water vapour; without it, it would be appreciably lower. Water vapour also represents the highest energy state of water and so it can act as an energy store. When condensation to liquid or sublimation to solid takes place, energy is released, which may give rise to an increase of temperature.

wave. A water wave is an undulation or deformation of a water surface. The period of water waves ranges from a

second or so to several hours. The size of waves ranges from tiny capillary waves (a few centimetres long) to the large storm waves, tidal waves, and long waves over 150 km in length. Many types of waves are wind-induced, directly or indirectly; others arise because of submarine earthquake disturbances or submarine sediment slides. See also ocean waves, sea waves, constructive wave, destructive wave.

wave base. The lowest limit of orbital motion beneath waves. Below the sea surface in deep water, the orbits of water particles remain, as with surface particles, almost circular, but the diameter of the orbits decreases with depth. For every 1/9th of the wavelength in depth, the size of the water particle orbits are roughly halved. At a depth that is equivalent to the wavelength, the orbit size is 1/535th of the orbit size at the surface. Where orbital motion becomes almost negligible, wave base is reached. The concept of wave base assumes importance in problems of sediment transport beneath waves, since bed movements due to waves are influenced by the wave-induced oscillatory currents experienced close to the seabed.

wave-cut platform. An irregular gently sloping bare rock platform extending out to sea and usually backed by cliffs. The mechanism of platform erosion is still not totally understood: it is not clear whether the waves are themselves responsible for the rock breakdown or merely for the removal of debris weathered by subaerial processes. Whichever processes are active, however, it is the wearing back of the cliffs that causes the enlargement of the platform. As these forms will not develop where there is a covering of beach material, the most favourable sites are headlands.

wave cyclone. A low-pressure system developing as a wave along a front. Most mid-latitude depressions form in this way.

wave diffraction (in oceanography). The transfer of the energy of wave crests as they negotiate a structure, such as a breakwater or sharp promontory. Diffraction usually leads to a marked reduction in wave height. The various diffraction patterns that result from, for example, the passage of sea waves through a restricted harbour entrance, can be calculated mathematically provided the characteristics of the waves and the receiving basin are known. Diffraction may allow some of the energy of incident waves to affect the water area in the lee of a breakwater.

wave forecasting. The prediction of future wave conditions using empirical observations of wave conditions that have already occurred or theoretical calculations. Such calculations take into account predicted meteorological conditions and such factors as *fetch distance. Of the various methods of wave forecasting that have been devised, two main types have emerged: those that take account of the significant height and period of the predicted waves (*see* significant wave), and those that take account of the total *wave spectrum. Wave forecasting is of great importance to navigation and to studies of expected coastal changes.

wave hindcasting. A consideration of wave conditions that may have applied at an earlier period and in a particular area. The method employed usually involves synoptic wind charts and other wind data for the period in question, and (if available) hydrographic charts covering that same period. The method is useful if coastal changes have been carefully documented and have to be accounted for.

wave ray. *See* orthogonal.

wave refraction (in oceanography). The turning of wave crests so that they become more parallel to the coastline as they approach it. The process is due to the effects of the shallowing of water: as the depth of water decreases so the wave velocity decreases; consequently,

a wave crest approaching the land obliquely will be slowed initially at the end nearest the shore, whilst the other end will continue moving faster until the crest has become almost parallel to the coastline. Wave energy can be represented diagrammatically by lines drawn perpendicular to the crests. As refraction takes place on an indented coast more energy becomes concentrated on the headlands than the bays, thereby favouring coastal straightening.

wave spectrum. 1. The complete array of waves present on a water surface in a particular place at a particular time. Careful measurements at sea or in a scale model enable graphic wave records to be produced, which show such an array of waves. A typical wave spectrum in the open sea will nearly always consist of waves of many different heights and periods superimposed one upon the other. The measured wave records enable their size and frequency distributions to be determined.
2. A graphic classification of waves, varying from capillary waves with a period of less than 0.1 second to the trans-tidal waves with periods of 24 hours or more. Most of the energy of such a spectrum would lie in two of the period ranges: the ordinary tides and the ordinary gravity waves.

Waxing slope

waxing slope. The convex slope at the upper part of a hill slope profile. According to King, the waxing slopes are most prominent at the early stages of the cycle of erosion, when the main processes are the incision, rather than widening, of valleys. These slopes are said to be dominated by *creep. See also slope convexity, waning slope.

way-up structures. Sedimentary structures that can be used to determine the way up of a series of unfossiliferous beds. Typical way-up structures are cross bedding, mud cracks, ripple marks, graded bedding, included fragments of older beds, convolute bedding, burrows, roots, and geopetal cavities.

weather. The state of atmospheric conditions at any one place and time. The total synthesis of these individual weather states is *climate. The state of the weather has been classified into a code form for use in synoptic meteorology. In this way, current and past weather can quickly be identified, though greatest stress is placed on precipitation or other weather factors likely to be considered important in forecasting or in their impact on man.
Efforts have been made to modify the weather, but without much success. The most publicized work has been on *cloud seeding, but hurricane steering and fog clearance have been attempted. Because of the vast amounts of energy involved in the weather and the large area affected, the prospects for large-scale modifications are not hopeful. Unintentional modifications are far more numerous, such as the effects of towns on weather (see urban climate), or the effect of irrigating arid lands.

weathering. The process of breakdown and alteration of rock on the earth's surface in response to the changes in environmental conditions since the time of their formation. During formation many rocks were subjected to great pressures or high temperatures, away from the effects of atmospheric air and water. Under present-day conditions these rocks are at comparatively low temperatures and pressures and will naturally be influenced by the presence of air and water. The resulting products of weathering are materials more nearly in equilibrium with their environment

than those from which they were derived. See also mechanical weathering, chemical weathering, organic weathering, deep weathering, differential weathering.

weathering front. The junction between sound and weathered rock within a weathering profile. Certain rocks, especially dense types with well-developed jointing, such as granite and basalt, display extremely sharp transitions, whereas in porous or fissile rocks the junction is frequently so unclear that there is no real weathering front.

websterite. An ultramafic rock consisting of hypersthene and diopside.

wehrlite. An ultramafic rock consisting largely of olivine with accessory augite.

welded tuff. See pyroclastic rock.

westerlies. The main winds blowing between 40° and 70° latitude. It is in the westerly circulation that depressions form and maintain the vital meridional heat exchange, and in this zone the strongest undisturbed wind flows are found.

West Wind Drift. A circumpolar current that constitutes one of the earth's large and significant permanent ocean currents. In the S part of the Pacific Ocean, it occupies a wide tract of water and generally flows in an easterly direction to the south of the subtropical convergence zone. At about latitude 55°S, the Antarctic Convergence cuts across the West Wind Drift. In the S Atlantic Ocean, the West Wind Drift occupies the wide tract of water that lies approximately between latitudes 35°S and 63°S. It moves with surprising constancy, and is often characterized by very large sea waves and swell.

wet-bulb depression. The temperature difference between the dry- and wet-bulb *thermometers in a Stevenson screen. It is a measure of the amount of cooling resulting from evaporation of water on the wet-bulb thermometer.

Relative humidity of the air can be calculated from this value using tables.

wet day. A period of 24 hours commencing 9 a.m. GMT in which 1.0 mm or more of rainfall is recorded. The concept has its limitations as 1 mm could fall from a single heavy shower or be the result of prolonged drizzle throughout the day. See also rain day.

wetting-and-drying weathering. The mechanical breakdown of fine-grained rocks through alternate wetting and drying, causing surface *flaking or major splitting of blocks into two or more large pieces. A possible explanation involves the fact that water is a polar liquid, with positive charge on the hydrogen atoms and negative charge on the oxygen atom. Lines of mutually attracted water molecules may develop within the rocks on wetting and drying and these may subsequently exert the expansive forces that cause fracture.

whirlwind. A small revolving vertical eddy of air, which whirls around a local low-pressure area. Stronger whirlwinds may be heard, but they are more frequently noticed because they pick up small pieces of litter or debris. They are formed during periods of local heating and instability, appearing as small-scale tornadoes.

white alkali soil. See solonchak.

white-out. Drifting snow or blizzard conditions on a pre-existing snow surface in polar regions. The horizon disappears and everything then becomes white with no shadows or identifiable landmarks.

wind. The horizontal movement of air relative to the earth's surface. Air movement results from thermal differences, which produce pressure variations, or by dynamic factors such as divergence of the air flow itself. Wind is one of the basic elements of weather. It is measured in knots and its direction is that from which it blows. Wind speeds at the ground surface can be very variable

from absolute calm during anticyclones up to 200 knots in a tornado.

wind-break. Any barrier having the deliberate effect of reducing surface wind speeds. It can be artificial or natural, though the latter is more frequently called a shelter-belt. The degree of shelter that a barrier offers depends upon its height, its degree of permeability, and distance. For a dense barrier, wind speeds fall dramatically immediately to the leeward, but soon recover to the prevailing wind speed. With a barrier that offers about 50% permeability, the effect reaches a maximum in terms of overall reduction of wind speed and distance affected downwind. Even by a distance of forty times the height of the barrier there is still some reduction.

wind-chill index. An index of the effects upon living creatures of cold winds. The stronger a cold wind is blowing the more rapid will be the rate of heat removal from a mammal. Consequently, cold but calm conditions are more physiologically acceptable than warmer temperatures in a strong wind. The wind-chill index was devised for the U.S. army to determine clothing requirements under different climatic conditions; it is measured as a cooling effect in kilocalories per square metre of exposed flesh.

wind drift current. A current that results from wind stresses on the sea's surface, part of the wind energy producing surface waves and part generating these currents. Indirectly, the wind is responsible for most of the currents in the surface and near-surface waters. Because of the earth's rotation and the resulting Coriolis force, the wind-induced currents in the open ocean have a mean direction approximately 45° to the wind direction (somewhat less than this near the surface, and greater than this at depth). The currents flow to the right of the wind in the N hemisphere and to the left of the wind in the S hemisphere. A wind blowing fairly hard for a long period may produce a thick homogeneous layer of isothermal water, for example, under the influence of the steady trade winds. In the shallower water near the coast, onshore winds tend to drag the surface water shorewards, while offshore winds cause the reverse to happen; in both cases, the related currents near to the seabed may be flowing in the reverse direction to the surface wind-induced current.

window (fenster). An outcrop of rock lying beneath a recumbent fold or thrust. These rocks are exposed as an enclosed outcrop, as a result of erosional processes cutting down through the overlying rock mass to the younger rock beneath.

wind rose. A diagram for illustrating the frequency of wind directions over a specified time period. It is normally split into eight or sixteen points of the compass and can also give an indication of the frequency of wind speeds within specified ranges by direction as shown in the diagram.

wind set-down. The lowering of the still-water level on the down-wind flank of a body of water because of wind stresses acting on the water surface, or the difference in levels between the up-wind and down-wind flanks resulting from wind stress. Like *wind set-up the term is usually applied to the phenomenon as it affects reservoirs, lakes, estuaries, and other bodies of water that are relatively

Wind rose

0 – 3 knots
4 – 10 knots
11 – 21 knots
22 – 23 knots

0   5   10   15 %

% of total wind flow

limited in size. One example is the River Plate estuary of Argentina: here winds blowing up (or down) the estuary cause set-up (or set-down) and also change the current patterns. Statistical analyses of wind data show that for some 220 days per year, tidal levels differ by up to a half a metre or more from the predicted values.

wind set-up. The raising of the still-water level on the down-wind flank of a body of water because of wind stresses acting on the water surface, or the difference in levels between the up-wind and down-wind flanks resulting from wind stress.

wind shear. The local rate of change of wind velocity, usually at right angles to the horizontal air flow. Vertical shear may also be considered.

witherite. See carbonate minerals.

wolframite. A tungsten ore mineral, $(Fe,Mn)WO_4$ found in pneumatolytic and hydrothermal veins.

wollastonite. A white triclinic mineral of composition $CaSiO_3$. It is found in metamorphosed limestones and in some alkaline igneous rocks, such as nepheline-*syenites.

worm casts. See earthworms.

wrench fault. See tear fault.

WWW. Abbrev. for World Weather Watch. A programme planned by the World Meteorological Organization to provide a worldwide coverage of surface and upper atmospheric data. This will then be used to provide an initial detailed data set for numerical models of the atmosphere.

X

xanthophyllite. See micas.

xenoblastic. Denoting crystals in metamorphic rocks that are anhedral, exhibiting no crystal faces.

xenocryst. A crystal superficially resembling a *phenocryst, which is not in equilibrium with the other minerals in an igneous rock. It is commonly anhedral, having suffered resorption due to reaction with the magma.

xenolith. An inclusion within an igneous rock body. The inclusion may be a block of country rock that has been caught up in the intrusion, but has not been completely assimilated. It may alternatively be a block of the igneous body itself that solidified at an earlier period and therefore has a slightly different composition.

Y

yield point. The point at which a rock ceases to deform elastically to an applied force, and beyond which further force will cause it to fracture.

Young's modulus. A stretch modulus (Y), equal to the ratio of the stress on a cross-sectional area of a rod of material to the longitudinal strain.

Z

zenith. The point in the sky that is vertically above an observer. It is frequently used in radiation geometry for calculating solar radiation input.

zenithal projection. See azimuthal projection.

zeolites. A large group of minerals with a general formula (Na_2,K_2,Ca,Ba,Sr) $((Al,Si)O_2)_n.xH_2O$. Zeolites have a structure similar to feldspars and feldspathoids and consist of a very open framework of linked $(Si,Al)O_4$ tetrahedra, with the metal cations filling the large cavities in the structure, which also contains loosely held water molecules. The compositions of some of the more commonly occurring zeolites are as follows:
natrolite $Na_2(Al_2Si_3O_{10}).2H_2O$
mesolite $Na_2Ca_2(Al_2Si_3O_{10})_3.8H_2O$
scolecite $Ca(Al_2Si_3O_{10}).3H_2O$

thomsonite $NaCa_2(Al_5Si_5O_{20}).6H_2O$
heulandite $(CaNa_2)(Al_2Si_7O_{18}).6H_2O$
phillipsite $(1/2Ca,Na,K)_3(Al_3Si_5O_{16}).$
$6H_2O$
harmatome $Ba(Al_2Si_6O_{16}).6H_2O$
stilbite $(Ca,Na_2,K_2)(Al_2Si_7O_{18}).7H_2O$
chabazite $Ca(Al_2Si_4O_{12}).6H_2O$
laumontite $Ca(Al_2Si_4O_{12}).4H_2O$
Most zeolites are colourless or white and are relatively soft, varying in hardness from 3.5–5 on Mohs' scale. Natrolite, mesolite, scolecite, and thomsonite have fibrous habits.
Zeolites are commonly found as late-stage minerals in *amygdales in basic lavas. They also occur as alteration products after feldspars and feldspathoids. The occurrence of zeolites on a regional scale in volcanic rocks and sediments is considered to indicate a very low-grade metamorphism termed the zeolite facies.

zinc blende. See sphalerite.

zinnwaldite. See micas.

zircon. A mineral of composition $ZrSiO_4$ found as an accessory mineral in intermediate and acid igneous rocks. Being very hard and resistant to weathering, it is a common detrital mineral in sediments.

zoisite. See epidote.

zonal circulation. Wind circulation with a dominant west-east directional component. The main zonal circulations are the *westerlies of middle latitudes and the *easterlies of the tropical oceans. Easterly winds are normally defined as being negative. Compare meridional circulation.

zonal index. A measure of the strength of the zonal circulation in a specified area and time period. The index most commonly used is that for the N Atlantic Ocean between latitudes 35°N and 55°N based on the differences in mean pressure along these lines across the ocean.

zonal soils. Soils occurring over wide areas owing to the dominance of the

bioclimatic factor in soil formation, which determines soil-forming processes. Where the bioclimatic influence is locally replaced by relief and drainage, *intrazonal soils occur. The zonal concept stems from the Russian Sibertzev at the turn of the century, who conceived soil as a climatic succession running from the tundra soils to laterite. This simplification still underlies much thinking on soils but is increasingly regarded as outmoded owing to the location of many soils outside their zone through the local influence of some other factor (e.g. podzols on sandy parent materials in the brown earth zone) and the climatic change of the recent past, which has varied zonal boundaries.

zone. 1. (In metamorphism). A spatial division in an area that has undergone *metamorphism, based on the first appearance of successive index minerals within the metamorphosed rocks in the progression towards rocks of the highest metamorphic *grade. The progressive nature of metamorphism was developed by Barrow working in the Scottish Highlands, where he identified a number of zones in pelitic rocks. The index minerals occurring in *pelites in order of increasing grade are: chlorite, biotite, almandine garnet, staurolite, kyanite, sillimanite. A line drawn on a map representing the first appearance of a particular index mineral is termed an *isograd*. These are lines of equal grade and link rocks originating under similar physical conditions of metamorphism. The almandine zone, for instance, is that occurring between the almandine and staurolite isograds. However, in rocks of other compositions, an index mineral may appear at a higher or lower grade than that corresponding to its first appearance in pelitic rocks. Different mineral zones have been correlated with different rock types and this correlation is embodied in the concept of metamorphic *facies.
Sequences of metamorphic zones other than those proposed by Barrow have been identified in other areas. In NE

Scotland, the Buchan zones are defined by the index minerals staurolite, cordierite, andalusite, and sillimanite. The Buchan zones represent a different metamorphic gradient involving relatively lower pressures than those represented by the Barrow zones.

2. (In stratigraphy). The fundamental division used in biostratigraphical methods of calibrating and correlating rock successions. A zone is demarcated by the fossils it contains and is usually named after a *zone fossil; when applied to a zone the name of the fossil should be italicized. Examples of various types of zone are as follows. An *assemblage zone* is characterized by the occurrence of a particular assemblage of fossils; an *acme zone* is characterized by the particular abundance of a single species or fossil group; a *total-range zone* comprises the entire thickness of rocks in which a fossil occurs; a *concurrent-range zone* consists of the strata in which the ranges of particular fossil species or groups overlap. In some situations a zone in biostratigraphy may correspond to a *chronozone in the chronostratigraphic scale, but the concepts they represent should be kept separate.

3. See seismic zones.

4. See crystal zoning.

5. See morphogenetic zone.

zone fossil (index fossil). A fossil species that is used in *biostratigraphy to delimit a *zone. Ideally a zone fossil should have a limited vertical range in the succession and should in life have been rapidly and widely distributed to permit correlation over a large area. Several species, forming a whole zonal assemblage, may be used in the definition of a biostratigraphical division.

zooplankton. Small, often microscopic, animals that float passively in the sea or other bodies of water (see plankton).

Appendix

Earth measurements

Dimensions	km
Mean radius	6371.0
Equatorial radius	6378.3
Polar radius	6356.9
Equatorial circumference	40 067.3
Meridional circumference	39 999.7

Area	millions of km²
Total surface area	510
Land area	149
Ocean area	361

Mass, density, volume	
Mass	5.976×10^{24} kg
Density	5.517×10^{3} kg m^{-3}
Volume	1.083×10^{21} m³

Gravity	
Acceleration of freefall	9.812 m s^{-2}

Relief	metres
Average height	875 above sea level
Greatest height (Mt. Everest)	8840 above sea level
Lowest point of Earth's land surface (shores of the Dead Sea)	396.2 below sea level
Average depth	3794 below sea level
Greatest depth (Marianas trench)	10 430 below sea level

Table of elements

element	symbol	atomic number	atomic weight	element	symbol	atomic number	atomic weight
Actinium	Ac	89	[227]	Francium	Fr	87	[223]
Aluminium	Al	13	26.98	Gadolinium	Gd	64	157.25
Americium	Am	95	[243]	Gallium	Ga	31	69.72
Antimony	Sb	51	121.75	Germanium	Ge	32	72.59
Argon	Ar	18	39.95	Gold	Au	79	196.97
Arsenic	As	33	74.92	Hafnium	Hf	72	178.49
Astatine	At	85	[210]	Helium	He	2	4.003
Barium	Ba	56	137.34	Holmium	Ho	67	164.93
Berkelium	Bk	97	[247]	Hydrogen	H	1	1.008
Beryllium	Be	4	9.01	Indium	In	49	114.82
Bismuth	Bi	83	208.98	Iodine	I	53	126.90
Boron	B	5	10.81	Iridium	Ir	77	192.2
Bromine	Br	35	79.90	Iron	Fe	26	55.85
Cadmium	Cd	48	112.40	Krypton	Kr	36	83.80
Caesium	Cs	55	132.91	Lanthanum	La	57	138.91
Calcium	Ca	20	40.08	Lawrencium	Lr	103	[257]
Californium	Cf	98	[251]	Lead	Pb	82	207.19
Carbon	C	6	12.01	Lithium	Li	3	6.939
Cerium	Ce	58	140.12	Lutetium	Lu	71	174.97
Chlorine	Cl	17	35.45	Magnesium	Mg	12	24.31
Chromium	Cr	24	51.99	Manganese	Mn	25	54.94
Cobalt	Co	27	58.93	Mendelevium	Md	101	[258]
Copper	Cu	29	63.55	Mercury	Hg	80	200.59
Curium	Cm	96	[247]	Molybdenum	Mo	42	95.94
Dysprosium	Dy	66	162.50	Neodymium	Nd	60	144.24
Einsteinium	Es	99	[254]	Neon	Ne	10	20.18
Erbium	Er	68	167.26	Neptunium	Np	93	[237]
Europium	Eu	62	151.96	Nickel	Ni	28	58.71
Fermium	Fm	100	[257]	Niobium	Nb	41	92.91
Fluorine	F	9	18.998	Nitrogen	N	7	14.01

(continued)

Table of elements (continued)

element	symbol	atomic number	atomic weight	element	symbol	atomic number	atomic weight
Nobelium	No	102	[255]	Silver	Ag	47	107.87
Osmium	Os	76	190.2	Sodium	Na	11	22.99
Oxygen	O	8	15.99	Strontium	Sr	38	87.62
Palladium	Pd	46	106.4	Sulphur	S	16	32.06
Phosphorus	P	15	30.97	Tantalum	Ta	73	180.95
Platinum	Pt	78	195.09	Technetium	Tc	43	[97]
Plutonium	Pu	94	[244]	Tellurium	Te	52	127.60
Polonium	Po	84	[209]	Terbium	Tb	65	158.92
Potassium	K	19	39.10	Thallium	Tl	81	204.37
Praseodymium	Pr	59	140.91	Thorium	Th	90	232.04
Promethium	Pm	61	[145]	Thulium	Tm	69	168.93
Protactinium	Pa	91	[231]	Tin	Sn	50	118.69
Radium	Ra	88	[226]	Titanium	Ti	22	47.90
Radon	Rn	86	[222]	Tungsten	W	74	183.85
Rhenium	Re	75	186.20	Uranium	U	92	238.03
Rhodium	Rh	45	102.91	Vanadium	V	23	50.94
Rubidium	Rb	37	85.47	Wolfram (Tungsten)	W	74	183.85
Ruthenium	Ru	44	101.07	Xenon	Xe	54	131.30
Samarium	Sm	62	150.35	Ytterbium	Yb	70	173.04
Scandium	Sc	21	44.96	Yttrium	Y	39	88.91
Selenium	Se	34	78.96	Zinc	Zn	30	65.37
Silicon	Si	14	28.09	Zirconium	Zr	40	91.22

Atomic weight figures given in brackets denote the mass number of the most stable isotope.

Composition of sea water; elements in solution (parts per million)

elements, etc	concentration	elements, etc	concentration
Cl	18 980	P (organic)	0–0.016
Na	10 561	Zn	0.005–0.014
Mg	1272	Cu	0.001–0.09
S	884	Mn	0.001–0.01
Ca	400	Pb	0.004–0.005
K	380	Se	0.004
Br	65	Sn	0.003
C (inorganic)	28	Cs	0.002
Sr	13	U	0.00015–0.0016
SiO_2	0.01–7.0	Mo	0.0003–0.002
B	4.6	Ga	0.0005
Si	0.02–4.0	Ni	0.0001–0.0005
C (organic)	1.2–3.0	Th	<0.0005
Al	0.16–1.9	Ce	0.0004
F	1.4	V	0.0003
N (nitrate)	0.001–0.7	La	0.0003
N (organic)	0.03–0.2	Y	0.0003
Rb	0.2	Hg	0.0003
Li	0.1	Ag	0.00015–0.0003
P (phosphate)	>0.001–0.10	Bi	0.0002
Ba	0.05	Co	0.0001
I	0.05	Sc	0.000 04
N (nitrite)	0.0001–0.05	Au	0.000 004–0.000 008
N (ammonia)	>0.005–0.5	Fe (in solution)	$<10^{-9}$
As (arsenite)	0.003–0.024	Ra	2.10^{-11}–3.10^{-10}
Fe	0.002–0.02		

Composition of the atmosphere (dry)

Gas	Molecular fraction
Nitrogen	78.09
Oxygen	20.95
Argon	0.93
Carbon dioxide	0.03
Neon	1.8×10^{-3}
Helium	5.24×10^{-4}
Krypton	1.0×10^{-4}
Hydrogen	5.0×10^{-5}
Xenon	8.0×10^{-6}
Ozone	1.0×10^{-6}
Radon	6.0×10^{-8}

Elements present in the earth's crust (parts per million)

O	466 000	F	300	Nb	24	Dy	4.5	Tm	0.2
Si	277 200	Sr	300	Co	23	U	4	Cd	0.15
Al	81 300	Ba	250	La	18	B	3	Ag	0.1
Fe	50 000	Zr	220	Pb	16	Yb	2.7	In	0.1
Ca	36 300	Cr	200	Ga	15	Er	2.5	Se	0.09
Na	28 300	V	150	Mo	15	Ta	2.1	Ar	0.04
K	25 900	Zn	132	Th	12	Br	1.6	Pd	0.01
Mg	20 900	Ni	80	Cs	7	Ho	1.2	Pt	0.005
Ti	4400	Cu	70	Ge	7	Eu	1.1	Au	0.005
H	1400	W	69	Sm	6.5	Sb	1 ?	He	0.003
P	1180	Li	65	Gd	6.4	Tb	0.9	Te	0.002 ?
Mn	1000	N	46	Be	6	Lu	0.8	Rh	0.001
S	520	Ce	46	Pr	5.5	Tl	0.6	Re	0.001
C	320	Sn	40	Sc	5	Hg	0.5	Ir	0.001
Cl	314	Y	28	As	5	I	0.3	Os	0.001 ?
Rb	310	Nd	24	Hf	4.5	Bi	0.2	Ru	0.001 ?

Composition of rocks (percent of an average rock)

substance	sediment	igneous rock	sandstone	limestone	shale
SiO_2	57.95	59.14	78.33	5.19	58.10
TiO_2	0.57	1.05	0.25	0.06	0.65
Al_2O_3	13.39	15.34	4.77	0.81	15.40
Fe_2O_3	3.47	3.08	1.07	0.54	4.02
FeO	2.08	3.80	0.30	—	2.45
MgO	2.65	3.49	1.16	7.89	2.44
CaO	5.89	5.08	5.50	42.57	3.11
Na_2O	1.13	3.84	0.45	0.05	1.30
K_2O	2.86	3.13	1.31	0.33	3.24
H_2O	3.23	1.15	1.63	0.77	5.00
P_2O_5	0.13	0.30	0.08	0.04	0.17
CO_2	5.38	0.10	5.03	41.54	2.63
SO_3	0.54	—	0.07	0.05	0.64
BaO	—	0.06	0.05	—	0.05
C	0.66	—	—	—	0.80

Table of Meteorological symbols

symbol	weather condition	symbol	weather condition
•	rain	~	glaze
	freezing rain	≡	fog
	drizzle	⇌	icy fog
	freezing drizzle	=	mist
▽	showers		spray
✳	snow	∞	haze
✲	snow pellets	S	dust haze
△	snow grains		smoke
	drifting or blowing snow	$	drifting or blowing sand or dust
	drifting snow		drifting sand or dust
	blowing snow		blowing sand or dust
▲	hail		sandstorm or duststorm
△	ice pellets		wall of sand or dust
—	ice prisms		sand or dust whirl
⌒	dew		thunderstorm
⊔	hoar-frost	T	thunder
∨	rime	⟨	lightning

Auxiliary symbols

These symbols provide information on the intensity of the weather conditions and the time and location of their occurrence.

symbol	information
▽	shower slight
▼	shower moderate or heavy
IX	condition (denoted X) has increased during the preceding hour
XI	condition has decreased during the preceding hour
X]	condition has occurred during the preceding hour but not at present
(X)	condition occurring less than 5 km from the weather station
)X(	condition occurring within sight but at a distance greater than 5 km

Cloud forms

symbol	type
⌒ or ∪	cumulus
⌂	large cumulus
⊟	cumulonimbus
—	stratus
∠	altostratus
⦜	nimbostratus
∪	stratocumulus
)	cirrus
2	cirrostratus
ω	cirrocumulus

Cloud conditions

symbol	code number	cover
○	0	Nil
◔	1	1/8
◔	2	2/8
◑	3	3/8
◑	4	4/8
◕	5	5/8
◕	6	6/8
◕	7	7/8
●	8	8/8
⊗	9	unknown

Table of glacial periods of the pleistocene

	Estimated duration (thousand years)	Britain	Northern Germany/ Poland	Alps	North America
LAST GLACIAL	100	Newer drift	Weichsel	Würm	Wisconsin
Interglacial	65		Eemian	Riss/Würm	Sangamon
GLACIAL	60	Gipping Till	Saale	Riss	Illinoian
Interglacial	190	Hoxnian	Needian	Mindel/Riss	Yarmouth
GLACIAL	50	Lowestoft Till	Elster	Mindel	Kansan
Interglacial	65	Cromerian		Günz/Mindel	Aftonian
GLACIAL	50	Weybourne Crag		Günz	Nebraskan
Interglacial	?	Norwich Crag		Donau/Günz	
GLACIAL	?	Pre-crag		Donau	Pre-Nebraskan